Edges of Care

Edges of Care

Living and Dying in No Man's Land

NOAM LESHEM

The University of Chicago Press
Chicago and London

The University of Chicago Press, Chicago 60637
The University of Chicago Press, Ltd., London
© 2025 by Noam Leshem
Published 2025
Printed in the United States of America

34 33 32 31 30 29 28 27 26 25   1 2 3 4 5

ISBN-13: 978-0-226-83595-2 (cloth)
ISBN-13: 978-0-226-83597-6 (paper)
ISBN-13: 978-0-226-83596-9 (e-book)
DOI: https://doi.org/10.7208/chicago/9780226835969.001.0001

Library of Congress Cataloging-in-Publication Data

Names: Leshem, Noam, author.
Title: Edges of care : living and dying in no man's land / Noam Leshem.
Description: Chicago : The University of Chicago Press, 2025. |
    Includes bibliographical references and index.
Identifiers: LCCN 2024017781 | ISBN 9780226835952 (cloth) |
    ISBN 9780226835976 (paperback) | ISBN 9780226835969 (ebook)
Subjects: LCSH: Terrain vague. | Vacant lands. | Terrain vague—Middle East. |
    Vacant lands—Middle East. | Middle East—Description and travel.
Classification: LCC NA9050 .L47 2025 | DDC 909.83—dc23/eng/20240515
LC record available at https://lccn.loc.gov/2024017781

♾ This paper meets the requirements of ANSI/NISO Z39.48-1992 (Permanence of Paper).

The worst sin towards our fellow creatures is not to hate them but to be indifferent towards them, that's the essence of inhumanity.

GEORGE BERNARD SHAW, *The Devil's Disciple*

Contents

Introduction: States of Uncaring 1

PART I Entry Points 21

1 Ruined Land with Barbed Wire 25

2 Contours 43

PART II Abandoned Lands 59

3 Gestures of Uncaring 63

4 Rock Bottom 74

PART III Beyond Care 91

5 Exposures 93

6 Left to Die 103

7 Disorders 113

8 Man's Land? 127

PART IV Wild Country 147

9 *Terra Fantastica* 151

10 Kings of No Man's Land 162

11 States of Nature 186

Epilogue: Care Returns 201

Acknowledgments 211
Notes 215
Bibliography 251
Index 275

Plates follow page 96

States of Uncaring

"Welcome to the end of the world," Hammed said with half a smile.

The passenger door of the small, beat-up Peugeot 205 needed some nudging, and by the time I got out, he was already a few steps away, pointing at the view.[1] It was a spectacular scene of hills that rolled from Jerusalem toward the Dead Sea and the desert just east of the city. That time of year, in late February, thin green grass still covered the nearby slopes, but it gradually gave way to barren, rocky terrain that continued into the hazy horizon. To the south, the outskirts of Bethlehem densely clustered on the ridge and half a dozen villages dotted the landscape to the east of us. We were standing on a small patch of gravel and weeds that opened up once the asphalt of the narrow road we had taken to get there abruptly ended. Hammed's tires would puncture in no time if we drove any further, but even on foot we would struggle to go very far. Steep slopes dropped to the bottom of Wadi Nar, which ran north and east of us, and even more steeply into the valley at the south.

Driving to this particular end of the world doesn't take long, and it's hard to get lost on the way there. There is only one road that snakes through the small Palestinian neighborhood of Sheikh Sa'ad, and making your way up it will inevitably lead to that single dead end where we were standing that morning in the winter of 2004. The clunker I owned at the time would have probably made it up the hill, but I had to park it just outside the neighborhood, at the bottom of the only road that links Sheikh Sa'ad to the rest of Jerusalem. A year earlier, the Israeli army placed three concrete blocks across the entrance road, meaning that no one could drive into the neighborhood. During my first visits in the early 2000s, residents were fighting to alter the route of the Israeli separation wall, which threatened to cut them off from the city. The barrier, they argued in court cases and several legal appeals, would block the single access road providing the daily lifeline of the neighborhood—school buses and garbage trucks, ambulances and vans bringing groceries to the local store, all depended on this road. Blocking the road, they said, would choke Sheikh Sa'ad.

Soon after the concrete cubes were put in place, the upheaval that residents were fearing began to materialize. Overnight, traffic into the neighborhood was brought to a halt. The cubes also stranded several dozen cars inside. Hammed, who showed me around, owned one of those. Unable to leave the neighborhood, his car and several like it became Sheikh Sa'ad's only means of transportation, and a new improvised economy emerged. In the absence of any alternative, these cars were used for anything, from delivery of goods and transportation of students, to the removal of garbage. In emergencies, they also became ad hoc ambulances that brought the elderly and the sick to the entrance, where an official ambulance could pick them up. In every other direction, sharp slopes made regular vehicle access impossible. In the years that followed, more than two dozen men joined Sheikh Sa'ad's new taxi collective. After Israel significantly curtailed the number of work permits issued to Palestinians, most of them were stranded in the neighborhood like the cars they were driving. And like these young men who no longer had papers that would grant them formal access into the city, the cars they were driving were almost never licensed or insured. "Who's going to give me a ticket?" one of the guys asked sarcastically. "Israeli police never come in for these things, and the Palestinian police isn't here either."[2]

I tried going back to Sheikh Sa'ad a decade later. All legal appeals against the route of the Israeli barrier were exhausted in 2010, when the Israeli Supreme Court approved the original plans drawn by the Defense Ministry.[3] Within a couple of years, the cubes had morphed into a permanent fence, and then into the nearly thirty-foot concrete slabs that have become the hallmark of the wall. The access road into the neighborhood was blocked by a fully built checkpoint, but only pedestrians could get through it. Cars were not even allowed into the vicinity, so visitors parked on the garbage-strewn verges of the road nearby and then continued by foot. It was early afternoon, and very few people were around. I walked up to an armed Israeli Border Police guard who stood by the gate.

"No entry," he said, easily recognizing I wasn't a local.

I asked if Sheikh Sa'ad was now a closed military zone.

"No," he replied, "it's open, but not from here. You can get in from the other side."

I tried to explain that there was no real "other side," that it was impossible to drive up the steep slopes that surround the neighborhood elsewhere, that the bridge down in the valley was flooded with sewage, and that the potholes in the alternative road made it impassable.

"I don't care," he answered.

Far from flippant, this simple and unapologetic statement of uncaring needed to be taken seriously. What did it mean that care ended right there, at that perimeter? If it stopped there, what was beyond it? What was this space that was trapped between the blatant absence of care and the "end of the world" that Hammed had pointed to a decade earlier?

In the years since, this systematic uncaring kept reappearing in radically different iterations: In records of the killing fields between the trenches of World War I; in a small Colombian village, where an unexploded bomb dropped from a plane in the early 2000s is proudly on display and sarcastically referred to as "the last government visit"; in an outdoor bar in Cyprus, where the barbed wire and barricades marking Nicosia's "dead zone" were made nearly invisible, turned into just another prop in a moody setting. Each had its particular political contexts and histories while also bearing the deep mark of abandonment, a systematic and deliberate abdication of care.

These weren't the geographies of abandonment that mark the aftermath of neoliberal reordering. There was no private contractor swooping in to fill the voids left by a callous state for a profit. Nor were these simply the familiar sites of late modern colonial violence, with their architectures of enclosure and the harms it inflicts on lands and lives. If anything, such regimes cared too much. They turn care into invasive control that is violently policed, or better, self-imposed by individuals as it gradually percolates into the intimate fabric of life.

What emerged between the "end of the world" and the blatant absence of care was no man's land. It was more than a geographical designation of a space trapped between militarized enclosures and topographical obstacles. It certainly wasn't a metaphor. Dead ends and the abdication of care were political contours that harbored a specific relation between the sovereign and those subjected to it. Beyond the perimeters, other orders of violence came to the fore, as did the tactics of life that emerged in their wake.

Tracing uncaring, its multiple iterations and the available vocabularies to express it, was one challenge. Doing so without foreclosing the vitality of life that remained, even at the "end of the world," was another. This is, after all, one of the persistent clichés of no man's land: an empty ruined space, devoid of life, unowned and uninhabited. Under the weight of these clichés, historical specificities and political nuances collapsed, turning no man's land into a convenient metaphor, easily interchangeable with wasteland or terra nullius. The empty signifier of no man's land left little room for all that inhabited these spaces of sovereign uncaring, for action and contestation, endurance, intimacy, and humor.

As a critical stance, refusing the cliché opens the possibility that these spaces are not solely sites of violent conflict, populated by its most obvious protagonists—soldiers and generals, politicians and diplomats. Instead, "dead zone" can be a home and a refuge. It can be a place for coca farmers and gold miners, for anarchists and fantasists with elaborate plots and dreams. Yes, there are bomb craters and piles of debris, but there are also trees and sewer pipes, colonies of rabbits and rumors of aliens. Life in the dead zone is messy and dynamic exactly because it is deemed beyond the pale, situated in a space from which conventional forms of state care have been withdrawn. Violence, loss, fear, and injury are omnipresent, though not all consuming. A young Palestinian with a beat-up Peugeot could still navigate this space that verged on "the end of the world" and just about make a living doing so.

Few places capture so vividly the calamitous combination of topography and segregative enclosure as Sheikh Sa'ad, but the underlying logic of uncaring that governs Sheikh Sa'ad is not unique. As Maria Margaroni points out, an ever-growing number of women and men today—refugees, immigrants, people caught in trafficking networks, and others—are forced to survive in a "pure relation of abandonment," exposed daily to a "banal" death that is not the product of sovereign decision.[4] But this abandonment happens somewhere; it has, in other words, a geography. No man's land is that place that emerges beyond sovereign care, abandoned not as punishment or for monetary profit, but explicitly because of an intentional withdrawal of care.

From this starting point, a landscape comes into view, dotted not only with instances of exposure to harm and "banal" deaths. Uncaring doesn't just result in inescapable catastrophe. Look long enough, and you will stumble upon the richness, nuance, and contingencies of "banal" life that persists, sometimes even thrives, in the absence of sovereign care. Tracing the logic of uncaring, its genealogies and spatialities, is the challenge of this book. Tracing the lives that are lived in the shadow of the dead zone is its hope.

Uncaring

The Hebrew term for no man's land, *shetach hefker* (שטח הפקר), literally translates to "space of abandonment." Absent from the Bible, abandonment (*hefker*) first appears in the literature of the second century at a particular moment of political crisis, potentially signaling one of the first moments that no man's land emerges as a distinct space of uncaring. After the destruction of the Jewish temple in AD 70, organized sacrifice was no longer available as an expression of religious dedication. It is at this point that acts of individual, deliberate abandonment—of land, property, or goods—begin to appear. In the absence of Jewish political sovereignty, owners willfully relinquished claims to their property and designated it, instead, as divine possession. This endemic renunciation became a radical act that redrew the boundary between terrestrial and divine space. The anarchic dimension of this form of abandonment was not lost on the Jewish and Roman elites. Both understood how it could potentially evade religious hierarchies and subvert legal frameworks of ownership, tenure, and therefore taxation.[5] After all, no one can place levies on land that is abandoned to a divine power.

Ancient agricultural plots may not be the spaces we associate intuitively with no man's land today, but the dynamic of abandonment found there resonates in such spaces well into the twenty-first century. Two elements in particular stand out. First, the abdication that takes place here is a deliberate, active form of abandonment, as opposed to passive forms like neglect or oversight. Renunciation happens not incidentally, but as a result of intention and premeditation. Second, abandonment infuses these spaces with a political charge that exceeds their economic value and utility. Dedicating a plot of land to divine possession may not enhance crop yields, but it nevertheless unravels, in an utterly grounded sense, the very foundations of political order.

Acts of land abandonment dating back nearly two millennia are hardly the most obvious starting point for the study of abandonment and its spatialities in the past hundred or so years. After all, critical theories of politics, law, and theology have been deeply concerned with abandonment—its acts, consequences, and underlying logics. Two elements in particular—the dereliction of protections and exposure to harm—cut across this vast scholarly corpus.[6] In political-economic critique, abandonment is a central structural component of the neoliberal state that sees the dismantling of protections and defenses against the rigors, vagaries, demands, and inequities of the market and the powers of capital. The changing relationships between economy, society, and the state to the greater advantage of capital in its global and local forms, increasingly produces a disenfranchised citizenry and even more precarious noncitizens.[7]

But care remains at the heart of this critical corpus. Neoliberal restructuring of state functions and provisions does not abandon care, but instead redesignates the responsibility for its delivery to the market or assigns the individuals to care for themselves. This reassignment of care is driven by a calculation of value and potential returns, what Elizabeth Povinelli calls the "modalities of expenditure and abandonment." Deciding whether this or that sacrifice is worth it relies on different calculations in "various domains of

social life—politics, market and civil society."[8] Yet fundamentally, these economic valuations and political calculations are deeply steeped with care, even
though care is always conditional: "In neoliberalism," she concludes, "to care
for others is to refuse to preserve life if it lies outside market value."[9] Conversely, as I trace throughout this book, our challenge—the challenge facing
anyone concerned with the fraying relation between the state and those subjected to it—is to consider radical conditions of abandonment-without-care,
political realities that fall outside such measurements of worth and calculations of value.

Abandonment is also central to the work of political theorists trying to
account for calculated withdrawal of protections and the exposure of lives to
the unrestrained force of law.[10] The initial focus on the abandonment of life
under genocidal totalitarian regimes and the production of entire populations
reduced to bare life has expanded in late modernity to a hallmark of sovereign power.[11] This corpus importantly interrogates the ways abandonment, as
a form of deadly exposure, is increasingly being normalized into ever-wider
practices and technologies of biopolitical governance.[12] Rather than merely an
abstract condition, there is an entire geography to the political logic, an archipelago of camps, plantations, and colonies where the incarcerated and the
enslaved are stripped of human agency and reduced to bare life. In all these
spaces, Achille Mbembe writes, "domination is exerted by modulating the
thresholds of catastrophe. If specific forms of control pass via confinement
and strangulation, others proceed via indifference and abandonment, pure
and simple."[13]

But what is this abandonment? When we examine this question not solely
as a philosophical proposition, but also as historically specific realities that
biopolitical abandonment generates, it is impossible to divorce abandonment
from care. In its most obvious spaces—the camp or the plantation—all aspects of life are measured against their ability to maximize value: labor out-
puts, caloric intakes, susceptibility to disease, and efficiency of movement are
all constantly monitored, analyzed, and adjusted. Death itself is the subject
of meticulous calculative efforts: to maximize productive extraction, efforts
are invested to prevent death, although in some cases, as in the Nazi death
camps, the ultimate goal was the perfection of killing as a rational, sanitized
industrial process.[14] The history of biopolitical governance has proved that
even medical care has been weaponized to probe, injure, and degrade life
(*bios*) to its pure biological components (*zoē*).[15] Biopolitical abandonment is
constituted by care and is governed by it, even when care takes on an intrusive, violent, and even genocidal form.

Uncaring, as I develop it throughout this book, constitutes a different relation between the sovereign and those subjected to it. It designates extreme conditions under which any pretense of sovereign care is severed, under which care itself is abandoned. To understand how this condition emerges and unfolds, it is helpful to return to the ways care constitutes one of the most archetypal political figures, that of the sovereign shepherd.[16] Much of the discussion in Foucault's 1977–1978 lecture series, *Security, Territory, Population*, is dedicated to the figure of the shepherd, a beneficent figure whose "only *raison d'être* is doing good."[17] Although "pastoral power is the power of care," Foucault recognizes that such care can easily be harnessed by bad shepherds, "who have squandered and dispersed the flock, who have been unable to feed it and take it back to its land."[18] Among his citations is a biblical reference to Ezekiel 34:2–4, where the prophet delivers a sharp denunciation of corrupt rulers—bad shepherds—and the harms they inflict on their flock: "Ah, shepherds of Israel who have been feeding yourselves! Should not shepherds feed the sheep? You eat the fat, you clothe yourselves with the wool, you slaughter the fat ones, but you do not feed the sheep. The weak you have not strengthened, the sick you have not healed, the injured you have not bound up, the strayed you have not brought back, the lost you have not sought, and with force and harshness you have ruled them."[19]

Yet one phrase that appears only two verses later is omitted from Foucault's citation. Cruelty leads to the scattering of the flock, but the sharpest accusation lies in what follows: "and none did search or seek after them."[20] Cruelties and harms are not the end point in the erosion of political relations of care. There is, as the biblical text points out, something beyond that, a condition of uncaring in which the shepherd disavows responsibility and severs fundamental obligations toward its flock. That, to my mind, is what lies behind the soldier's comment "I don't care."

This is a critical moment. It forces us to contend with the possibility that the sovereign abdicates not to punish, to inflict harm as a corrective measure. Neither is this abdication intended to force individuals to care for themselves, a process that emerges from Foucault's corpus on governmentality and later critiques of the bad shepherd as a quintessential figure in the governance of neoliberal life. Nor is this the murderous form of violent, necropolitical care that governs the camp, the plantation, or the colony. All of these, as I have detailed, are fundamentally forms of care, even when it is care wielded in a callous, punitive, and genocidal manner.

Uncaring is different from caring in both intent and consequence. It is a form of abandonment that, in its extreme form, no longer holds any pretense of care nor can simply be explained as an unintentional error or oversight. The complete abdication that is pointed to in the biblical text is a condition in which uncaring is crystallized into its own category of political relations, where the abdication of care is systematized into a logic of governance. Yet fundamentally, uncaring is a condition of life—it happens to someone, somewhere. This is the critical concern of this book.

Edge of Care

No man's land is located where care ends. It emerges out of uncaring and is ruled by it. Interrogating such spaces therefore brings into sharp relief a different kind of abandonment, set apart from the condition of exposure to harms that has been so central to studies of the fraying relations between the sovereign state and its subjects. Uncaring as I document it in this book is characterized by particular political logics and produces its own orders of violence. Throughout this book, these are recorded and interrogated in greater detail, but four important elements are worth briefly pointing out.

First, we should clarify what constitutes the care that is being withdrawn from no man's land. My focus here is specifically on care as a political relation between state and subjects rather than its more general application as an individual sentiment or state of mind. Extensive parts of this book are dedicated to fleshing out this relation and its precise abdications, but in its most fundamental sense of a governing logic, care is that "which sees to *living*."[21] This phrase was used by Foucault in his discussion of the police in the seventeenth and early eighteenth century, which he considered not "an institution or mechanism functioning within the state, but a *governmental technology* peculiar to the state; domains, techniques, targets where the state intervenes."[22] Instead of confining care solely to the familiar administration of guardianship or the provision of health, I situate it more broadly as a fundamental relation in every domain of individuals' lives that simultaneously underscores and buttresses the strength of the state. I follow John Hamilton's important observation that the basic sovereign promise of security is a promise of care.[23] At its heart is the assumption that the subject can lead a life without worry or concern because care is now administered by an external power.[24] Etymologically, Hamilton shows, the Latin *cura* (care) forms the root of security, *securitas*, which translates into modern English as the state of being removed from care, the state of being care-free.[25] Considering care as part of this more extensive assemblage—inherent to the "art of government," as well as to the symbolic promise of the sovereign relation—also explains the acute consequences of its abdication: what is being vacated is not a single service or "good," but a fundamental relation of governance; that is, the withdrawal of essential functions that underpin the sovereign-subject relation.

Second, uncaring does not equal disinterest. The state is a vital actor in the formation of no man's lands and the dynamics of life within them. Even when state care is withdrawn, sovereign interest remains in its pure, naked form. Often, the state scales back its presence to such an extent that its interests appear to have been disavowed altogether.[26] In practice, though, sovereign interest in the space of uncaring is focused on the management of exclusion: delimitation and enclosure, surveillance and monitoring, as well as more invasive use of violence. But above all, the state's efforts are directed at keeping at bay all that takes place in no man's land and ensuring that it remains outside the realm of normative sovereign care.

Third, the sequence of harms in the biblical text foregrounds the utterly sober realities of abandonment. Reading through these injuries dispels the risk of conflating the absence of care with a simple anarchic freedom from governance, although fantasies of escape, refuge, and riches densely populate the history of no man's land. Spaces of uncaring are not isolated from punitive acts of injury and loss that are perpetrated by the bad shepherd. Instead, the abdication of care brings about a set of evils that range from seemingly passive forms of apathy and indifference to more direct acts of exploitation, extortion, greed, and cruelty.[27] Perpetrators of these harms may be acting on behalf of the abdicator, but they are not seeking to reassert the care that was previously withdrawn. This violence is almost always inflicted with the intention of keeping an assumed threat at bay and ensuring it remains within the confines of a no man's land. At the same time that the sovereign abdication of care removes its obligations and duty to protect, it generates the conditions for others to fill its place. Efforts to take advantage of a perceived vacuum of power are often constituted through violence, as new forces seek to establish their dominance within the space of uncaring. Yet for as long as the no man's land exists, conventional forms of sovereign care—whether in their beneficent or malevolent guise—remain absent.

Moreover, the calculated abdication of care produces a particular topology of violence. Withdrawal, abdication, and abandonment are the first step. But if the space of uncaring and the lives it contains have any value—and they certainly do—other forms and agents of care may seek to replace it. Distance must therefore be maintained through a system of enclosures: technologies of demarcations that establish the no man's land as a legible, set-apart space, even though the demarcations may be highly dynamic; physical fortifications that hold the line; elaborate infrastructures for supply and support; and an administrative structure to oversee the daily functions of this confining endeavor.[28] Establishing uncaring as the ruling logic of no man's land doesn't mean that care disappears. Rather, it is displaced to the perimeter. This is not a suspension of the law in what Giorgio Agamben describes as spaces of exception, a withdrawal of protections from targeted populations that exposes them to the deadly force of the law.[29] Instead, what emerges here is a redistribution of sovereign care that intensifies it along a perimeter and condenses its often-violent effects along these thick lines while diminishing its presence beyond.

Fourth, and finally, it is important to note that uncaring rarely appears in pure form. The biblical text situates the final abdication of care—"and none did search or seek after them"—at the end of a long spectrum of harms, some punitive in nature, others exploitative, and still others emerging from indifferent negligence. In quite the same way, no space is completely devoid of care. Sovereign abandonment often clears the way for other forms of relational action and investment rooted in what feminist scholars have defined as an ethics of care.[30] But the spaces at the heart of this book have all seen the erosion of conventional sovereign duties to the point at which the abdication of care, or a state of uncaring, crystallizes as a governing logic. Instead of insisting on absolute forms of presence and absence, the critical challenge lies in understanding uncaring as the extreme end of a spectrum of care. This includes, of course, the possibility that uncaring may be reversed, that the shepherd-sovereign may again impose its care over the flock or, as is the case here, over the space from which that care was previously withdrawn.

Invoking no man's land as "the edge of care" takes seriously both components of this phrase. Care and its abdication point to the conceptual limits of a sovereign relation that is still dominated by pastoral duty. It interrogates, in other words, the potential of thinking conditions of life and power that are defined by the abdication of care rather than its provision or imposition. Yet it is equally concerned with the constitution of an edge as a concrete spatiality, with the material and symbolic production of marginality. In no man's land, care is withdrawn not only from the bodies of subjects (the flock). Instead, no man's land reveals the distinct geographies that are marked out by uncaring, spaces where the abdication of sovereign care is actualized and set apart.[31] Edge geographies are intuitively associated with borderlands, with frontier spaces situated at the physical edge of the sovereign territory. Some of the edges I write about are indeed approximate to borderlands, but others are situated at the geographical heart of the state's territory. Instead of its topology, the edge is defined by the care extended to it or, more precisely, by sovereign abdication of that care. There, the terrain of abandonment begins to emerge, a granular space that is ordinary, cruddy, and chronic rather than solely catastrophic, crisis-laden, and sublime.

Attending to sites where uncaring crystallizes into an organizing political logic tempts a return to a familiar vocabulary of border geographies, of frontiers and putative peripheries, to camps, plantations, and penal colonies. But collapsing no man's land into these vocabularies reduces it once again to an empty signifier that can stand in for any space of violence and enclosure. More importantly, doing so misses the qualitative relation of uncaring that produces no man's land in the first place, that enables the proliferation of its harms, and that partly fuels its lasting allure. Put simply, sovereign care is never abdicated from the border, the camp to the colony. In all, care may appear in variegated forms and be applied with greater or lesser intensity. Those administering care may be operating directly in an official capacity of a state apparatus or caring on the state's behalf for either monetary gains (private contractors) or ideological rewards (vigilante groups). Yet care constitutes these spaces, determines their function, and is all too often harnessed to justify the harms they produce.[32]

No man's land, this book argues, forces us to step out to the edges of care, to confront the consequences of abdication and the actual, living spaces that emerge in its wake.

Unlearning No Man's Land

"This is not no man's land." The objection came from the back of the room at an academic conference where I was presenting early work on this project. The objector was an older attendee who was adamant that a more stringent definition was needed to address such spaces. What he probably had in mind was a familiar mental image that seared itself into Western cultural memory in the aftermath of World War I, an image that forged a tight association of no man's land to the killing fields between the trenches of the Western Front. Rummaging through the archive offers one kind of answer that may satisfy this skeptic. We can recall, for example, that despite its familiar association with modern geopolitical front lines, no man's land has a much longer history. Originally denoting a piece of unowned land or wasteland, the term *none man's land* appeared as early as 1086 in the *Domesday Book*, the comprehensive record of land value and ownership in England. According to the *Oxford English Dictionary*, No Man's Land was the name of a plot outside the north wall of London, that was used as a place of burial during the Black Death in the fourteenth century. Before its conversion into a mass grave, the site had been used for executions. This bleak history seems like a fitting pre-cursor to what this space would come to denote in the early twentieth cen-tury and will likely go some way to placate the historically minded critic.

What, though, will the same skeptic make of a rather less spectacular dis-pute between two English monasteries that left a large piece of land beyond their official jurisdiction—aptly named No Man's Land Common—and which, in the seventeenth century, became a place of refuge for cattle rustlers and a legendary highwaywoman? Or the more recent emergence of no man's land at the northern outskirts of Chicago, not as an abstracted metaphor to its re-moteness or liminality but, at least until the mid-twentieth century, as a semiformal designation in city documents and maps that partly indicated entrenched racism and segregation. How does this kind of no man's land—minor, subtle, and still highly consequential—allow us to write more than just histories of border wars, watchtowers, and flagpoles? How do we also account for more ordinary practices of endurance and utterly mundane infrastruc-tures that populate these spaces? A different sensibility and other archives are needed. Eula Biss, for example, does this with subtlety and empathy in *Notes from No Man's Land*, where she documents life in 1990s Rogers Park on Chi-cago's Far North Side: "The Chicago trains end here, and the tracks turn back in a giant loop around the gravel yard where idle trains are docked. Seven blocks to the east of the train station is the shore of Lake Michigan, which rolls and crashes past the horizon, reminding us, with its winds and spray, that we are on the edge of something vast."[33] This portrait of a place defies conven-tional imaginations of what no man's land is. Even the edge here is marked by water rather than barbed wire.

"Esta no es tierra de nadie." It was several years after the first objection, but this time, the objector, Óscar, was not interested in policing definitions for the sake of historical precision. His concern was rather more personal and urgent. He was in his late twenties and came to a talk I gave in La Macarena, a town in the western Colombian Amazon. Along with four other municipali-ties, with a total population of 150,000 people, La Macarena was abandoned by the Colombian state to the control of the Fuerzas Armadas Revoluciona-rias de Colombia (FARC) guerrilla group in 1998.[34] Although he was just a young boy when all this happened, the label *tierra de nadie* still carries pain-ful memories of a state that made him and his community disposable. "This is our home, not just a war zone," he said. "The state likes to paint us all as *guerrilleros* only to justify the fact that it abandoned us." Óscar's unease about the political erasure that no man's land performs was well founded and had an even longer history. In an address to the Royal Geographical Society in May 1864, the Scottish geologist Roderick Impey Murchison described the areas surrounding the Nile south of Khartoum as "a sort of No-man's-land, in which numerous warring small tribes are kept in an excited and barbarous state by an extensive importation of firearms."[35] The reduction of a land to a subhuman, "barbarous state" points to the ease with which no man's land can be appropriated into the toxic vocabulary of imperial conquest and colonial expansion. That old trick: when its inhabitants are denied humanity, a land can easily be declared "no man's."

"The ideal way to start interesting research," Benedict Anderson advised in his memoir, "is to depart from a problem or question to which you do not know the answer."[36] Yet the starting point to this book was perhaps not as ideal as Anderson would have liked. When it first came up, the question "What is no man's land?" invoked not the great unknown, but the seemingly familiar. It has become an empty signifier that is intuitively familiar but otherwise carries little analytical precision or intellectual significance. Óscar's suspicion was therefore an invitation to unlearn what no man's land is—as a concept and a space—and to ask what might be revealed if it were to be learned again. Following Ariella Azoulay, I think about unlearning as a series of practices that involve "different types of *de-*,' such as decompressing and decoding; '*re-*,' such as reversing and rewinding; and '*un-*,' such as unlearning and undoing."[37] What emerges from this is an ethos as much as a method.

In its most conventional sense, as it emerges from largely European traditions of empire and cataclysmic wars, no man's land opens up a very narrow aperture. No wonder its obvious protagonists are soldiers and state officials, almost all men. The richness of life that exists in these spaces, the historical contingencies of their formation and nuanced political dynamics that govern them, have all flattened into three clichés. First, in the cliché of emptiness, the portrayal of no man's land is almost entirely devoid of human presence, primarily because it is too dangerous or too damaged for life to flourish within them. Closely related, a cliché of dispossession voids any form of ownership and tenure and effectively excludes no man's land from the orders of capitalist accumulation.[38] Finally, the common assumption that no man's land is solely a border phenomenon is the result of the cliché of remoteness, which relegates these spaces to the geopolitical edge of the sovereign territory. Seeking to debunk these clichéd understandings of no man's land was at the heart of this study from its inception, and much of this book is similarly concerned with that challenge.

Like all clichés, those that plague no man's land are worth interrogating, exactly because they reveal the conditions of possibility for political logics and cultural representations. But the fact that no man's land is largely understood through these generalizing and superficial prisms is indicative of a deeper crisis in what the term actually denotes. Despite its militaristic and Eurocentric association, World War I at the least made no man's land a clearly identifiable space. For the generation that witnessed the cataclysm of the campaign, there was no confusion about the meaning of no man's land. In the second half of the twentieth century, such clarity was largely lost. The gradual blurring of the site specificity and historical concreteness that typified scholarly and popular references to no man's land in the 1920s and 1930s can likely be traced back to World War II, a campaign that saw death transplanted from the open killing fields between the trenches to the enclosed spaces of the camp, or carried out remotely through aerial killing. As a result, deeper reflections on the term's critical import have largely dissipated. It turned into a convenient figure of speech, but one that has largely lost its spatial or intellectual specificity. If no man's land can be applied to anywhere—from offshore tax havens to inner-city ganglands—it has little use either as a geographical signifier or as a meaningful analytical concept.

As a starting point, unlearning no man's land is not a simple rejection of its more familiar historical chapters, but an effort to understand the lesser-known prehistories of these spaces, the deeper political logics they reveal, and the long shadow they continue to cast. It does entail, however, a refusal to confine the analysis to Anglo-European history and thought. Only by expanding its scope, the geographies it is concerned with, and the vocabularies through which it is articulated can this study speak to the realities that govern such spaces in most of the world. Rather than collapse a multiplicity of case studies into a preexisting mold or set out a rigid comparative framework, this endeavor is committed to an inductive ethos, to gathering fragments into a messy assemblage from which a new set of concerns and agendas may emerge, specifically regarding life under extreme conditions of sovereign uncaring. "What is no man's land?" was a question I learned to ask often and with genuine curiosity, partly because it recognized the inadequacy of existing answers and partly because it opened a space for critical reflection. It is also an invitation to speak no man's land differently, to articulate it in Arabic, Hebrew, or Spanish, thus avoiding well-trodden genealogies and the inescapable gendered form that the English term carries.[39] "In Nahuatl there is no phrase for 'no man's land,'" the Mexican artist Fernando Palma Rodríguez once told me when I asked whether it had any meaning in the Aztec language. After some further thought, he speculated that structures of Aztec property ownership meant "you couldn't just declare land as belonging to no-one."[40] It was this kind of open curiosity that enabled no man's land to reemerge as an object that merits serious discussion and critique.

Unlearning no man's land also involves a vital reorientation toward those whose lives have been caught in its gravitational force. Accounting for a wider set of voices was one step in this regard: I learned more about the life of no man's land from fishers and farmers, from artists and activists, than I did from generals and diplomats. But this was as much about recalibrating expectations, unlearning what people cared about in these spaces of uncaring. During an early visit to Cyprus, a conversation with two women leading an educational nongovernmental organization quickly turned from the importance of bicommunal peace education to bafflement over who empties the rubbish bins from the Nicosia Buffer Zone; in Jerusalem, a man who, as a child, used to play with friends in the no man's land between Israel and Jordan, spent much of our walk together describing the stench of sewage that flowed from that space. Of the many tales I have gathered about no man's land, almost none resembles the catastrophic space of mechanized war. Instead, many of the stories I heard were concerned with the intricacies of everyday life, and they conveyed a great deal of intimacy and even humor. In doing so, they also redefined the no man's land in which they were situated.

Although sovereign care has been systemically withdrawn from the space they inhabit, the individuals whose lives are woven throughout this book shared their accounts with immense care. In 2018, I went back to the Colombian village of Yarumales—just over a dozen wooden houses set along a single dirt road in the western Amazon basin—as part of a documentary I was making on the history of the region. When it was time to leave, my team and I packed the truck and started the long journey back to Bogotá. Only half a mile later, as we were slowing to cross a small creek, we saw six of our close collaborators flanking the narrow path, saluting us as the truck passed between them. There were wide smiles and some tears on their faces. These were tough campesinos, not prone to sentimentality, but we were carrying with us their stories, a valuable and fragile cargo. The camera and audio-recording cases were marked with Handle with Care stickers, and for a good reason. Each story was a fragment of life, and together, the stories carefully assembled and decoded the space of uncaring: a shuttered schoolhouse; a bridge that was bombed and its replacement that was washed away; the skeleton of a burnt SUV in the middle of a desiccated coca field. I hope that this book reciprocates this care by seriously thinking with these stories, by considering, following Michael Taussig, "muted and even defective storytelling as a form of analysis."[41] In the context of endemic state effort to dismiss these accounts—to disavow the stories, the storytellers, and the space these stories inhabit—this is far from taken for granted.

It is hard to unlearn from afar. Staying outside, or even observing from the margins of zones governed by uncaring, often reveals only their most obvious markers: the militarized enclosures that surround them. In themselves, these are not assemblages of uncaring. The barbed-wire coils, the checkpoints and the watchtowers, are ironically merely condensed performances of care, only they express a particular extreme of care-as-control. Observing no man's land from a distance is a position that not only reaffirms the assumed foreignness of what happens "on the other side," but also sees like the state, the same power that designated what lies beyond it as beyond the realm of care. This is not to say that attention to the contours of no man's land is pointless. It is an illuminating threshold that reveals a great deal about intensities of care and the diverse practices through which it is manifest. But there are nuances that are easily overshadowed. To better understand the logic of uncaring and its consequences, this threshold needs to be situated against and in relation to the space it demarcates.

Wherever possible, therefore, I try to offer a closer, more intimate account of a space that is rich and nuanced and subtle, even if the state determined that the space exists beyond its care. There have been excellent scholarly accounts of some of the places that feature in the book, like the Colombian Clearance Zone (Zona de Despeje) or the Cypriot Buffer Zone.[42] Others are more often written about from a safe distance—or not written about at all. There were other routes into these spaces, most notably though archives, reports, and journalistic accounts. Yet even these often proved frustratingly scarce and limited. Yes, it is possible to write about Bir Tawil, an unclaimed territory on the Egypt-Sudan border through historical records; one of the largest archives documenting Sudan in nineteenth and early twentieth century is, after all, conveniently held by my own university. But the colonial records have nothing to say about the dreams of miners flocking into Bir Tawil in recent years as part of the gold rush sweeping the vast desert between Egypt and Sudan. Spending time in an abandoned train station five hundred miles north of Khartoum, which these days serves as a refueling and restocking station for miners, was a different way to account for the cruddy, mundane, yet utterly consequential life of no man's land. To be clear, the granularity of experience and nuance of observation are not the sole property of the ethnographer in the field. But the willingness to travel long distances, to spend protracted periods asking and listening, carried specific ethical weight precisely because those inhabiting these spaces are too often unheard, disregarded, and dismissed.

This was not always possible. During the years I was working on this project, there was no way, for example, to physically reach Rukban, a camp on the

Syria-Jordan border where more than ten thousand people have been trapped for years. Access from either side was severely restricted in the first years of its existence and then blocked altogether. Journalists, aid workers, and scholars have all been barred from entering. "It's a real black hole," one foreign policy researcher who worked for a Western government told me. Thinking through the layered enclosures that surround Rukban and many places like it reveals the assemblage of uncaring, its formation as both a physical-material system and a political logic.[43] The record I was able to assemble, however, remains incomplete, despite my best efforts to find work-arounds: phone messages were one way to reach out to people in Rukban and generate some channels of communication. Remote sensing, primarily the use of satellite images, was another. Both raise important questions about the economy of knowledge and information that surrounds these spaces, dimensions that have become integral to the emergence and governance of no man's land in the twenty-first century. Neither, however, overcomes the enforced distance and isolation that play a fundamental role in maintaining places like Rukban beyond the realm of sovereign care. Unless we take on the impossible task of Borges's fabled cartographers and try to draw the world in its entirety, we are always bound to offer only partial accounts; nevertheless, I recognize that some of these distant portrayals are even more limited than I would have preferred.

Finally, unlearning assumes, I hope, a greater degree of humility with regard to the subject of its inquiry. In stating that "there are no new ideas," Audre Lorde was right to temper our desire for novelty, and her alternative is perhaps more inspiring than the mere pursuit of innovation: "There are only new ways of making them felt—of examining what those ideas feel like being lived on Sunday morning at 7 a.m., after brunch, during wild love, making war, giving birth, mourning our dead."[44] This book has much to say about modalities of governance, violence, political logics and practices of endurance. All these constitute the space of uncaring and situate it at critical intellectual junctures. By all accounts, these are more-than-sufficient reasons to write this book. But unlearning no man's land, for me at least, is a challenge worth confronting because uncaring is a lived reality for many, and many more than I was able to account for here. The harms it inflicts, the promises it harbors, the prospects it opens, and the horizons it forecloses, all mean that uncaring, to follow Lorde, is acutely felt. Those whose lives have been tied to the space of uncaring—some who inhabit it, others who reside on its perimeters, and others still who observe it from a distance of space and time—have all been companions in the unlearning of no man's land.[45] Their stakes are more obvious and immediate, but unlearning no man's land with these companions may also infuse the space of uncaring, or at least its study, with a shared ethics of care.

Writing on the Edge

This book can be read as a journey, bringing nearer those spaces often assumed to be too distant or too perilous to visit. Much like my own research process, some places are revisited at different moments throughout the book because they cannot be reduced to a single issue or facet. Overall, the book progresses from the general and historical to more particular and contemporary realities of no man's land. It moves from the outside in, asking how uncaring takes place, how it is experienced and what it leaves behind.

Part 1 offers two familiar points of entry into no man's land. It begins with the photographic archive that shaped Western cultural imagination of these spaces. Intuitively, the term *no man's land* invokes an utterly familiar image that is easily reduced to its most rudimentary components, a composition of ruined landscape with barbed wire. Yet behind the visual cliché, with its endless variations, lies a longer history of photography, of war and lesser-known experimentations with a space of modern catastrophe. There are, of course, more physical encounters with no man's land, although it is easy to stop at the most brute features that surround these spaces—concrete walls, barbed wire, military positions, and warning signs. I don't dismiss the significance of such material elements, but the analysis offers a subtler approach to the contours of no man's land, retracing lines that were drawn in ink, blood, and bodies. Even from the outside, it is still possible to discern the intricate dynamic of forces that simultaneously pull back and violently enclose: When care is withdrawn, it does not simply disappear. Instead, it intensifies and hardens along a perimeter, a thick line that marks the end of care.

Part 2, "Abandoned Lands," asks how uncaring actually takes place. Rather than a philosophical inquiry or a historical chronicle, I begin by documenting four gestures of abandonment, each offering an intimate glimpse into the banality of uncaring. Read together, the gestures are indicative of a deeper political logic that leads to the abdication of lives and lands, not through a genocidal plan of elimination, but simply through a set of minor acts—individual, nearly imperceptible—that embody the absence of care. Minor acts can, of course, lead to catastrophic outcomes. Rukban reveals the naked abdication of care in the twenty-first century. Following the geopolitical forces that led to the creation of an encampment housing thousands trapped for years in a barren desert berm, the analysis seeks to understand uncaring against the more familiar realities of siege warfare and develop a grounded approach to its study. Rather than a metaphysical condition or an instrument in the tool kit of catastrophic states, the analysis sheds light on uncaring as a lived reality, one that is endured and constantly negotiated.

Part 3, "Beyond Care," focuses on the realities that unfold once sovereign uncaring becomes a system of rule. It documents the exposure of populations and natural environments to harm, but it avoids a simplistic reduction of exposure to mere vulnerability. Put differently, those who are relegated into the space of uncaring are not helpless victims, even when they face severe harms and violence. In fact, exposure is also a condition of radical openness and possibility. I trace these potentialities and less expected moments of political action that take advantage of the void left once the state turns its back on no man's land. Recognizing the granular effects of exposure also foregrounds its deeply uneven impacts. Rather than a flat terrain where all bodies are reduced to bare life, what emerges from this analysis is a deeply racialized and gendered experience of those most likely to find themselves in the space of uncaring. Violent structures of race and gender often endure, even once sovereign care is withdrawn.

Part 4, "Wild Country," moves through the fantasies and imaginations that are projected onto no man's land and what they reveal about contemporary hopes and anxieties. The part begins with a question: If the Leviathan is the quintessential monster of the sovereign state, what happens in the spaces the state renounces? What, in other words, are the monsters that populate the space of uncaring? For many, fantastical monsters that populate no man's land convey stories and capture histories that are often too frightening or too heartbreaking to recall otherwise. For others, though, the space of uncaring is a canvas on which contemporary fantasies of Whiteness and masculinity, of environmental dystopia and Edenic utopias, can all play out. Contending with the imaginary and fantastical is not an escapist exercise, but a glimpse into a potential political future in which uncaring becomes a daily reality for a greater number of people around the world.

The book ends with the return of sovereign care, an often-violent reappearance that raises important questions about the contemporary relation between the state and those subjected to it. Revisiting some of the places that run through the book, and the fate of individuals whose lives are at its heart, the epilogue suggests that in spaces of uncaring, the return of care is often merely rhetorical. Rather than reversed, uncaring is increasingly normalized. When sovereign care returns, the reappearance of the state is often ruthless, ushering the full force of a punitive sovereign. Rather than wait for the state to care again, we should perhaps reimagine, through all the stories gathered in this book, other ways of being in abandon, registers of life and relation that persist even at the edges of care.

PART I

Entry Points

Millions of images documented no man's land during World War I, yet an eerie silence surrounds the space. The sonic archive of no man's land is nearly nonexistent. Until very late in the war, sound documentation technology was unable to provide "actuality" recordings, namely, recordings documenting a real location and event beyond the performative space of the studio, imprinted with the audible material trace of an actual moment in space and time. Thousands of gramophone records were released between 1914 and 1918, constituting a vast and heterogeneous repertoire of military bands, spoken word, political speeches, humor, celebrity testimonials, and patriotic and operatic numbers. This corpus had immense impact on both communication and commemoration of the war, but it comprised almost entirely studio recordings. The battle space itself left no audible trace.

The only seeming exception to the archival silence was a recording made by William Gaisberg, the head of the London Studio of the Gramophone Company, on October 9, 1918. Commissioned to produce a propaganda piece for the British Government's War Savings Committee, Gaisberg was able to transport recording equipment to the Western Front to capture the sound of British artillery shelling German lines with mustard gas. The *Gas Shell Bombardment* record—a twelve-inch His Master's Voice–label shellac disc, just over two minutes long—was released two months later, just as the war came to an end. The sound of shells being loaded and fired is accompanied by a series of shouted commands. For decades after its release, the record was assumed to be the sole recording from the front lines of the Great War, even though its authenticity was repeatedly questioned. Analysis of the recording itself, and a recent discovery of an alternative take containing only the shelling sounds and devoid of the gunnery commands, proved the skeptics right:

the record was likely produced using at least two rudimentary overdubs. Put simply, the record mixed distinct sound layers to form a compelling soundscape of war.

It is not the authenticity of Gas Shell Bombardment that stands out to me, but its utter predictability: It reduces no man's land to a sonic image of militarized violence, a space that is defined solely by exploding metal and poisonous gas. What, though, is lost when more subtle sounds of no man's land are drowned out by the overwhelming "force of destructive torrents and explosions"?[1]

Without doubt, shelling was inherent to the modern soundscape of no man's land, but even during World War I, the sonic landscape of this space was richer and more nuanced. First, because sound offered the ultimate compensation for the radical impairment of sight. For most on the front line, the war was largely invisible. Eric Leed noted that the invisibility of the enemy, and the retirement of troops underground, destroyed any notion that war was a spectacle of opposing forces clashing in broad daylight. Instead, the general inability to clearly see the enemy, or most of the battle space for that matter, "put a premium upon auditory signals."[2] The French artist Fernand Léger, who served as a sapper and then as a stretcher bearer during the war, provided a painter's sense of this radical visual disorientation: "The war was grey and camouflaged. All light, color and even tone were banned on pain of death. A blind existence in which anything the eye could register and perceive had to hide or disappear. Nobody saw the war hidden, concealed, crouched on all fours, earth coloured; the useless eye could not see anything. Everyone 'heard' the war. It was an enormous symphony that no musician or composer has yet been able to equal."[3]

Listening to no man's land meant detecting much fainter sounds that did not fit neatly with the cacophony of bombardment. Much like the auscultating physician, who listens in to the acoustic world of the body for diagnostic purposes, soldiers carefully tuned in to the sonic world around them.[4] Developing "diagnostic listening" was a critical skill that could help them to stay alive. Ernst Jünger recalled how soldiers would carefully listen for the sound of pickaxes used by sappers who were digging across the no man's land and planting explosives underneath the enemy's trenches. It was not the sound of digging that soldiers were worried about so much as the silence that followed it: Silence indicated that the digging was done and explosives were being prepared for detonation. Silence spelled an impending doom. Numerous accounts from the front capture this heightened sonic awareness, a form of "seeing by listening" that transformed trench life into what Dorothee Brantz calls "a synesthetic experience."[5]

Chronicles of war rightly draw attention to this wider sonic array. However, while those chronicles succeed in capturing the militarized mobilization of sound, either as a tactical component of modern warfare or as part of the personal experience of war, they remain firmly within a familiar spectrum. Put simply, these important historiographies largely confine the sonic world of no man's land to the soundscape of war. However, in researching this book, those who shared their stories of no man's land repeatedly asked me to unlearn its obvious association with the military history of World War I. A FARC combatant in Colombia described how he learned to discern the rustle of leaves disturbed by animal movement from the sound made by human footsteps. In Jerusalem, an elderly woman remembered neighbors placing old corrugated metal sheets in backyards that bordered the city's no man's land as a rudimentary alarm system that would sound whenever anyone tried crossing over from the east. What other histories and critical pursuits might emerge if we were to deliberately seek out such muted and mundane sensory experiences?

There are entirely different archives of no man's land, repositories that expand the sensual scope through which these spaces are understood and experienced. From these archives, other protagonists and other registers of harm come to the fore. This was, for example, the impetus behind Mishka Henner's project *No Man's Land* (2011–2013), in which the artist traced images on Google Street View that documented seemingly innocuous spaces at the edges of southern European cities, places where sex workers often spent their days waiting for potential customers. I return to this work later in the book specifically because it challenges the conventional perceptions of no man's land as almost always masculine and militarized. But one component of the project offers a radical new sense of the soundscape of no man's land. Though far less auspicious than the thunder of bombardment, it captures what uncaring sounds like in the political present. Henner stumbled on an online platform popular among amateur sound recordists documenting sounds from around the world, geotagging the files, and jointly compiling a repository to store the recordings. As he puts it: "Just out of interest I searched that database for the areas the women were working in and weirdly found a lot of birdsong recorded in various regions of Italy and Spain. And when I started putting them together I found them to be quite beautiful but also, on a literal level, it's a kind of landscape that the women listen to. There's a kind of wildness to it; there are the mating calls."[6]

Birdsong is not the intuitive soundtrack of no man's land, but this is only because Western cultural imagination has bounded the space to a rather narrow sensorial experience of warfare. Henner's soundtrack is a sonic prompt to unlearn no man's land, to imagine other spaces where uncaring crystallizes into a dominant political logic, where harms proliferate while the sovereign turns its back. It reveals subtle entanglements with a natural world that is not simply reduced to an object of violent destruction but is a witness to it. And it invites us to look beyond the figure of the soldier that has dominated no man's land, that figure who sought its heroic conquest and often fell victim to its violence.

These avenues of unlearning are the starting points for this book, opening new directions of inquiry and new companions for conducting it. Revisiting the sensorial landscape of uncaring, this part begins with the most obvious representation of no man's land: its photographs. Images shaped cultural imaginations of this space but also turned it into a visual cliché. My return to this repository is partly in search of other histories where critical uncertainty and experimentation prevail. Those who documented uncaring through their camera lens were not interested in uncaring as abstract political logic; instead, their jittery photographs are haptic documents that are acutely attentive to the movements and habits of bodies, both in front of the camera and behind it. Such gestures are my main concern in chapter 2.

War may be a starting point to this inquiry, but to truly grasp the condition of uncaring and the spaces that are dominated by it, any analysis must move beyond spectacular catastrophes. Many of the experiences and political realities in this book appear elusively tranquil. They sound like birdsong. They are unremarkable almost to the point where they are no longer recognizable as uncaring at all. That is perhaps their most piercing power.

1

Ruined Land with Barbed Wire

If you are fortunate enough, you've probably never set foot in no man's land. You have been spared the experience of waking up one morning to the realization that the state left and left you behind. You do not have to worry about whether the checkpoints that suddenly surround you are too dangerous to cross, whether basic services will come through, or who you can rely on for your safety and security. Police and soldiers and tax collectors are all gone, but so is the violence and corruption that government officials routinely practice. If you are lucky, all this seems like a faraway reality, a nightmare that happens somewhere else to someone else.

Even so, there is a good chance that if you close your eyes, you can conjure an image of no man's land. Here's what likely comes to mind: a space of desolation, emptiness, ruination; ashen remains and the smoldering wreckage of past violence, or the anticipation of violence yet to come. It is an image that often lacks historical and geographical specificity, fusing real places from past calamities with the apocalyptic landscapes of science fiction films, natural disasters and cataclysms that are entirely human creations.[1]

Too easily, uncaring is relegated to a "place in the middle of nowhere," as the Swedish photographer Torbjörn Larsson described it to me when we discussed one of his photographs, taken in 2009 on the border of Syria and Iraq. At first sight, the photograph seems to be composed of predictably familiar components. The vast barren land and wide empty sky, the absence of human presence made more pronounced by the garbage strewn on the roadside and the concrete barrier that stretches into the distance.

When Larsson first entered this seven-kilometer-wide strip between the American military base on the Iraqi side and the Syrian border post, he was accompanying Swedish immigration officers heading to the al-Tanf refugee camp. At the time it housed Palestinians fleeing violence in Iraq. A few years later, after the conflict in Syria escalated, seventy thousand Syrians sought shelter only a few miles away, in Rukban, a camp I extensively write about later in this book. Larsson admitted that on the four-hour drive from Damascus he repeatedly asked himself, "Is this what things look like in the no man's land?" Later in our conversation, he added, "In a way, I think this was what I thought it was supposed to look like."[2]

That phrase, "supposed to look like," implies an expectation and some prior knowledge. What is assumed here is an existing literacy in the visual vocabulary of no man's land. This is not a recent phenomenon: By 1917, this familiarity was already well in place. In his records from the Western Front, the Irish artist William Orpen recalled a conversation with a military officer. "Paint the Somme?" the officer asked, "I could do it from memory—just a flat horizon-line and mud-holes and water, with the stumps of a few battered trees."[3] After three years of relentless devastation of the frontlines, these visual tropes were simply a matter of fact.

A century after World War I, the same visual tropes have become a cliché. Reflecting on the constant reproduction of this genre of images in contemporary photography, the artist Mishka Henner noted the ease of making this kind of images: "I got very disillusioned with that style because it's very common. It's not that challenging for the photographer. It offers the opportunity to make nice compositions in un-testing environments."[4]

Henner's disillusionment was not about aesthetics per se. Instead, it was a concern with the ease with which this familiar aesthetic erases any trace of the photographic event, the conditions that facilitate an encounter between photographer, camera, and photographed subject: "What I found really frustrating as a photographer working in landscapes like that was that it didn't really convey any of the technological stuff that was at the heart of the whole process. You're working with these cameras, which have a certain optic, there's a process involved which is really removed from the finished piece. You just end up with these very clean beautiful pictures. But there are no glitches, there's no trace of the process, of the technology in a sense. The whole thing is about hiding it all."[5]

Technologies of visualization are not the only thing vacated here. The aesthetic concealment that Henner refers to is a critical instrument in erasing the political logics that produce these spaces in the first place. How have images of violence, enclosure, and systemic political abdication crystallized into such a seemingly sanitized pictorial imagination? And at what cost? What has been lost over a century of perpetual reproduction during which violent experiences have been turned into clichés? Were there critical junctures that could have pointed toward potential alternatives, or is this imagination really just a matter of fact—variations on a theme of ruined land with barbed wire?

Uncaring is coded into images of no man's land. Logics of abdication, exposure to harm, and fantasies of refuge have all left their mark on the photographic archive of this space. But more often than not, they appear through faint traces rather than blunt markers. Instead of resorting to "clean beautiful pictures" of devastation and desolation that only affirm the most conventional cultural imaginaries, the visual corpus I return to—some of it familiar, some perhaps less so—draws attention to facets of uncaring that are not as evident but are just as significant. First, that visual corpus foregrounds the technological apparatus on which photography relies. Technological advancements in the years preceding World War I made the camera portable enough and simple enough to operate, which meant it could be just as easy to mount it on a reconnaissance plane as it was to tuck it into one's vest pocket. Consequently, photography registers the space of uncaring as the object of unprecedented military surveillance and tactical documentation while at the same time documenting the most intimate, embodied, and deeply personal experiences.

But photography does more than document uncaring. From its very early days, it was an instrument in turning no man's land into a cliché. The common association of no man's land with a remote, depopulated death zone that is removed from any organizing governing logic is a direct by-product of an elaborate photographic corpus. More than any other medium, photography made possible the transformation of no man's land into a widely circulating cultural trope, even when its existence as a prominent tactical space waned dramatically after World War I. Yet the popularity of this conventional image eroded its critical import: the easier it was to see no man's land as merely a generic visual trope, the harder it was to trace the political logic of uncaring that produced such spaces in the first place or to account for the real effects they have on lands and lives. Rather than document uncaring, photography is complicit in its disappearance from view.

Still, early photographs of no man's land are worth returning to. This is not a search for an uncorrupted "original," a photographic relic that somehow reveals hidden truths. Instead, early visual archives of no man's land retain a quality of uncertainty and experimentation that was lost once this space was reduced to a conventional visual trope. This chapter is therefore structured around three visual practices: the individual photograph, the composite print, and the montage. Each enabled practitioners and viewers to grapple with the space of uncaring, with the utter disposability of human life and destruction of unimaginable proportions. Together, they illuminate a critical search for legibility that cuts through this book: a simultaneous effort to make sense of fragmented images and to come to terms with the broken world they depict.

"Images Wrenched from the Chaos"

When Raoul Hausmann wrote, in 1931, about the effort to formulate an artistic response to the horrors of mechanized war, he noted how the cataclysm of modern violent conflict was "as new to the eye as is was to the mind."[6] War, he noted, retrained the eye. It brought about new ways of seeing, novel technologies of visualizing the world and making sense of it. Visibility and legibility went hand in hand. But such training took time. Before it so effectively rendered fragmented landscapes into comprehensible tactical data or aesthetic form, did the camera also record chaos, confusion, or simple curiosity? Is there, in other words, a photographic corpus that predates the visual cliché?

The first images that explicitly sought to capture no man's land were taken during World War I by individuals newly able to carry portable personal cameras to the front lines. One of the earliest traceable photographs was taken by Mairi Chisholm, who, together with Elsie Knocker, gained iconic public stature for setting up an emergency dressing station in the autumn of 1914 not far from the Belgian trenches near Pervyse. Equipped with cameras, both women photographed each other, as well as the landscape around them. One of Chisholm's photographs, titled *No Man's Land*, depicts a barren winter landscape that seems to blur into a sky of a similar shade (fig. 1). Although the dating is uncertain, the photo is likely to be from December 1914, once the warring sides dug into trenches that formed the in-between strip of land. The austerity of the landscape is juxtaposed to a densely jumbled entanglement of wood, metal, and barbed wire that cuts horizontally across the photograph, an assemblage that in the following years would become a quintessential reflection of the material composition of the war.

Chisholm's photograph is surely not the first visual documentation of no man's land during World War I. By that point, there would have already been thousands like it. During the very first months of the war, despite restrictions on photography in the battlefield by military censors, commanding officers authorized individual servicemen to use their cameras to create a semiofficial record on behalf of their unit. This enabled a detailed photographic documentation of the retreat from Mons, early fighting in the Ypres Salient, the evolution of trench warfare on the Western Front, and the Gallipoli Campaign. No man's land would have also featured in those early repositories.

But even in the nascent photographic corpus, Chisholm's image stands out, first and foremost because it "fails" to perform the most obvious tasks

FIGURE 1. Fortifications in the Western Front, near Pervyse. Likely December 1914. Photographer: Mairi Chisholm. © Imperial War Museum (Q 105859).

of war photography—to spy, to provoke, to commemorate, and to persuade. Bodo von Dewitz identifies these unconventional images as a particular genre of battlefield photography, one that often depicts blurred and out-of-focus landscapes.[7] Their poor visual quality, in fact, suggests that the person behind the lens was in close proximity to the enemy. Often appearing without captions, the photographs convey little intuitive information to the viewer. However, their imperfect composition, slanted angles, and obstructed views offer a sharp alternative to the fantasy of linearity, legibility, and tactical utility that other genres of frontline visualizations were supposed to deliver. Perhaps most notably, early images of no man's land diverge from the strict functionality of tactical war visualization. The scale and complexity of the modern battlefield forced military planners in World War I to rely more than ever before on the abstracting capacities of the map and, later, on the documentary promise of the aerial photograph and the detailed reliefs of stereoscopic images.[8] For these purposes, photographs like the one taken by Chisholm are completely useless.

There was more in these images than a defiance of utilitarian functions.

The austere visual corpus also seems at odds with the aesthetic conventions that have become central to depictions of violent conflict from the Crimean War to contemporary battlefields. Susan Moeller pointed out that most photographs in World War I fell into one of two aesthetic categories. The first reflected "the stylized set photography of the nineteenth century that emphasized—what seems now to modern eyes—incongruous backdrops and awkward props." Contemporary art photography was the second corpus, which "emphasized unconventional vantage point, complex spatial geometry, and syncopated rhythms denoting time and motion."[9] Early no man's land imagery fits neither of these conventions. It comprises instead a misfitting corpus that frustrates any easy compartmentalization into logics of tactical functionality, on the one hand, or established genres of artistic expression, on the other.

Obviously, the early visual archive of no man's land does not emerge ex nihilo. Despite its historical relation to the Great War, the iconography that comes to be associated with the concept seems to predate the devastating events of Ypres and Gallipoli. Chisholm and others who pointed their portable cameras at the barren spaces between the trenches already had an aesthetic inspiration to draw on: Roger Fenton's iconic photograph *The Valley of the Shadow of Death* from 1855, which was shot during the Crimean War and depicts a curving road through a deserted landscape, empty but for numerous cannonballs scattered across it. Although debates have emerged around the photo's authenticity, there is another aspect worth noting.[10] Fenton introduced a stripped-down representation of war that diverged from romantic visualizations of the eventful, spectacular battlefield without resorting to the graphic form of photojournalism that emerged in the latter half of the nineteenth century. Instead, his iconic image of the war constitutes a new photographic object, what Simon Grant calls the "landscape of aftermath." Grant notes that this "aesthetic of reduction" would later inspire other artists to explore not emptiness per se, but rather "places where human remains had been blasted to merge with the mud."[11]

As the war progressed, spreading into new fronts, so did no man's land and its images. In one of these photographs, dated 1915, an unknown Australian photographer who took part in the Gallipoli Campaign photographed the no man's land in front of Lone Pine (fig. 2). The photograph depicts the barren, almost featureless landscape that recurs in many of these early images. A later photograph taken by Lieutenant T. P. Roger during the British effort to take Gaza in 1917 again conforms to a bare "aesthetic of the reduction" (fig. 3).

These are not just variations on a theme. For one, the images are an im-

FIGURE 2. No man's land in front of Lone Pine, ANZAC, 1915. Photographer unknown. Australian War Memorial.

FIGURE 3. No man's land, near Gaza, taken from the frontline trenches, 1917. Photographer: T. P. Roger. © Imperial War Museum (Q 13134).

portant reminder that the decimated state of the photographed landscape does not equate to mere emptiness. Specifically, visualizations of natural landscapes deconstructed by prolonged periods of mechanized warfare also placed much greater emphasis on the earth as an active pictorial element, often replacing the traditional focus on troops and war machinery. As Peter Paret notes, the churned earth of the battlefield "is man-made, but men are not present."[12] This absence of human figures from many of the images of the no man's land—a dominant characteristic to this day—drew the attention of critics early on. In the biographical sketch of Paul Nash by Jan Gordon, which introduced the volume of *British Artists at the Front* dedicated to his work in 1918, Nash's representation of landscapes largely devoid of human presence is understood as a metaphor for human suffering that was literally unspeakable: "It is not possible to paint truly how this war has swept man, because horror will not permit this truth to be told. It is possible to depict the devastation of Nature, because partly we cannot understand the full horror, and partly because through it we may come to a deeper realization of what the catastrophe may mean to man."[13]

At first sight, what was true for Nash's painting was also true for the numerous photographs taken of the no man's land. Even if they were not empty, all human presence had been swept away. But unlearning is an invitation to unwind and look again. The photographic event that constitutes each of these images—which includes not only the photograph as a physical object, but also the photographer, the camera, and the subject being photographed—reveals minute details that make each of these images more than just a generic reproduction of emptiness. Each tells small tales that can be easily missed. Roger's photograph from Gaza, for example, is speckled with white dots. Did sand grains or dust find their way into the camera and leave their mark on the film? Such faint traces on the surface of the image can direct attention to the landscape itself, to the desert environment that was so different from the waterlogged fields of northern France. Yes, no man's land repeatedly saw the devastation of nature, whether it be in Gaza or Verdun. But there is a risk in flattening the particular materiality of these spaces or their climate into a symbolic landscape of catastrophe. As this book documents at length, no man's land is often the site of devastation. But the surfaces on which that devastation leaves its marks—flesh, tree barks, photographic film—matter just as much.

Nor should we accept at face value the assumption that the human body is wholly absent from these images. In the photograph from Lone Pine, the camera appears to be tilted to the left. Did the photographer lack the time to steady the camera and compose the frame? Moreover, two objects at the bottom corners of the frame remain out of focus, obscuring the view between the photographer and the landscape. Are they sandbags? Was the photographer too afraid to raise their head above the parapet and mustered the courage only to lift the camera from within a trench for the second or two it took to take the photo? This photograph, seemingly of an empty landscape, documents so much more: a hunched body in the trench, the paralyzing fear of standing up, but also the revolution brought about by the miniaturization of the camera in the years preceding the war and the simplification of the technology, which democratized photography and enabled so many to use it.

Just over a decade after the war, Walter Benjamin noted how "people who returned from the front grew silent . . . not richer but poorer in communicable experience."[14] Increasingly, new vocabularies were sought, ones that could face the realities of shattered lives and landscapes. The redemptive promise of aesthetics, the promise of ordered compositions and mastery over the captured subject, seemed obsolete. In this search, the fragments of the battlefield caught in the blurry and hurried photographs of soldiers and frontline personnel began circulating and gaining hold: The austere visual representations of no man's land provided a visual language that brought the viewer into an almost intimate encounter with the catastrophically fragmented reality of war. Their claustrophobic narrowness and rudimentary composition frustrated any attempt to confidently situate them geographically or historically, making it nearly impossible to reconstruct location or temporal orientation. Their minimalism and granularity obscured the more intricate identifying details and left only the vary bare pictorial elements—variations on a theme of ruined landscape with barbed wire. These in turn, became the visual gestures of uncaring long into the twentieth century, appearing, for example, in a 1953 photograph taken by a soldier in I Company of the Forty-Fifth Infantry Battalion of the US Army during the Korean War, or overlooking the no man's land in Jerusalem from a sniper position on the Israeli front lines. Stripping the visual vocabulary of no man's land to its elemental features enabled it to travel easily through radically different contexts without losing its metaphorical power as a signifier of devastation, abandonment, and violent enclosure.

This malleability and transferability came with a price. The repetitive visual reproduction of no man's land to stand for any site of degradation and violence—from the nuclear catastrophe in Chernobyl to the deindustrialized landscapes of twenty-first-century Detroit—resulted in the gradual conventionalization of this aesthetic. Rather than a fragment of horror, the austere image of no man's land gradually assumed familiarity; its picturesque qualities of ruination largely devoid of any human presence offered a glimpse into spaces of extreme physical and material devastation, but from a safe distance. Although the cultural circulation of no man's land in the latter part of the twentieth century deserves a lengthier discussion, its proliferation through visual representation partly turned this concept into a floating signifier, an

easily appropriated visual trope, but one largely devoid of grounding specificities. The space of uncaring lost its tactile and visceral essence: Gone were
the hunched body in the trench, the trembling hand holding the camera, the
specks of sand or mud leaving minuscule marks on film.

Composite: Ruins Reconstructed

In his often-cited essay "The Storyteller," Walter Benjamin returns to the devastated landscapes of World War I as a pivotal turning point in the meaning
of experience and remembrance.[15] Benjamin notes how the integrated, nar-
ratively meaningful variety of experience known as *Erfahrung* is unraveled by
the war and its aftermath, leaving only the lived, fragmented experience or
Erlebnis. This distinction, which is developed throughout Benjamin's oeuvre,
is importantly grounded in a highly humanistic depiction of the decomposed
spaces of war: "A generation that had gone to school on a horse-drawn street-
car now stood under the open sky in a countryside in which nothing remained
unchanged but the clouds, and beneath those clouds, in a field of force of destructive torrents and explosions, was the tiny, fragile human body."[16]

Benjamin's concern was first and foremost with the condition of experience. But one element in Benjamin's description is imprecise: the sky above
the battlefield was, in fact, changing. Although much has been written about
the introduction of aerial and chemical warfare into the "battle-space environment" of World War I, the transformation of the sky was part of a more
fundamental change in the visual vocabulary of no man's land.[17]

One of the iconic images of World War I was taken by Frank Hurley on
October 12, 1917, the morning after the First Battle of Passchendaele (fig. 4).
It depicts wounded Australian infantrymen in the shelter of a blockhouse
near the site of Zonnebeke Railway Station. About half a dozen soldiers lie on
stretchers by a square concrete structure. Three other soldiers are standing
among them, one leaning down and extending his hand toward a wounded
man. The desolate landscape of the no man's land appears behind the figures,
dotted with the familiar stumps of trees, a ruined structure, and an expanse of
bombed-out soil that stretches into the horizon. The composition of the photograph uses the skyline to divide the image, with the upper third featuring
dramatic sun rays bursting through dark clouds, the light creating a bright
canopy that hovers over the scene of man-made devastation. This image was,
in fact, a composite print of two photographs: the lower section depicting
the aftermath of the battle while the skyscape was cropped from another image and later added when Hurley was preparing for his exhibition of Australian war pictures at the Grafton Galleries in London in 1918.[18] To make space

FIGURE 4. Morning at Passchendaele, 1917. Photographer: Frank Hurley. National Library of Australia.

for the addition of the skies, Hurley reoriented the image from landscape to portrait. When compared with the austere images of no man's land that were taken by soldiers at the front line, Hurley's composite is symbolically excessive and pathos laden. Contra Benjamin, nothing remained the same, especially not the clouds.

Through major international exhibitions and mass reproduction, Hurley's composite prints gained prominence in the pictorial canon of World War I. However, the use of composites also set Hurley on a collision course with Charles Bean, Australia's chief war correspondent and official war historian. In a diary entry from October 1, 1917, Hurley expressed his frustration with his superiors at the Australian Imperial Forces: "Our authorities here will not

permit me to pose any pictures, or indulge in any original means to secure
them. They will not allow composite printing of any description, even though
such be accurately titled, *nor will they permit clouds to be inserted in a picture.*
This absolutely takes all possibilities of producing pictures from me."[19]

The core argument between Hurley and his commanders surrounded
questions of authenticity and fidelity to conventions of historical representation. But as Martyn Jolly importantly notes, this debate in fact "took place
before the full development of the documentary genre in the 1920s and '30s
which established the technical slice of the shutter-blade, guillotining and en-
capsulating a contingent moment, as the only guarantor of truth."[20] In other
words, the composites Hurley produced emerged out of a moment in the history of photography when the clear distinctions between historical practice
and artistic license had yet to claim separate and often mutually exclusive
domains.

Rather than a distortion of historical records, Hurley saw composite as a
compensatory technique. He was not interested in creating a visual chronicle
of war, but he was eager to give viewers a more holistic access to the unprecedented magnitude and overwhelming force of the mechanized battlefield.
His diary entries record the death, injury, and destruction he witnessed while
at the same time conveying a deep sense of despair. On September 20, 1917,
during the Third Battle of Ypres, Hurley notes that the horror of war "almost
makes one doubt the very existence of a deity—that such things can go on
beneath the omnipotent eye."[21] The radical deformation of the battlefield not
only unraveled personal convictions but also exposed the limits of available
visual documentation. In his essay "War Photography," Hurley notes these
limits explicitly and hints at the technical solution he harnessed in response:

> None but those who have endeavoured can realise the insurmountable dif-
> ficulties of portraying a modern battle by camera. To include the event on a sin-
> gle negative, I have tried and tried, but the results are hopeless. Everything is
> on such a vast scale. Figures are scattered—the atmosphere is dense with haze
> and smoke—shells will not burst where required—yet the whole elements are
> there could they but be brought together and condensed. The battle is in full
> swing, the men are just going over the top—and I snap! A fleet of bombing
> planes is flying low, and a barrage burst all around. On developing my plate
> there is a disappointment! All I find is a record of a few figures advancing
> from the trenches—and a background of haze. Nothing could be more unlike
> a battle. It might be a rehearsal in a paddock. Now if negatives are taken of all
> the separate incidents in the action and combined, some idea may be gained
> of what a modern battle looks like.[22]

Thousands attended the Australian war photographs exhibition in London in June 1918. Hurley's photographs were popular partly because he was so adept at utilizing aesthetic conventions that would have been unmistakable to his audiences—sublime skies framing the picturesque ruins carefully arranged according to a pictorialist rule of thirds.[23] Through these familiar tropes, his composites provide the viewer with a visual path into no man's land, using the photographic medium to compensate for what is otherwise physically inaccessible and existentially incomprehensible.

Composite representations of no man's land articulate in visual-technical terms a desperate effort to reconstruct fragments into a unified whole and reassert order where chaos reigns. It harnesses the power of photographic technology to re-create what Allen Feldman described—in a very different context—as a "sensory prosthetic," "a cultural form of story telling and fact setting."[24] In practice and essence, it functions as a reconstructive representational form that responds to and seeks to compensate for the destruction of the corporeal body and the physical environment. Even more so, it tries to rebuild the deteriorated visual field of war, where "those visual markers that allow an observer to direct [their] attention to what comes first and what later" have been catastrophically removed.[25] Hurley reconstructs the visual field not to reestablish a lost chronology—the before and after of the event, and the markers of its transformations—but to re-create a compressed simultaneity of objects, figures, scales, and relations. By its essential ability to bring together elements that may otherwise be only tangentially linked spatially or temporally, the composite offers viewers a reorganized aesthetic structure that visually makes whole what has been smashed.

Rather than acknowledge the violent fragmentation of physical forms and modes of thought that cannot be simply stitched back together, the composite seeks to compensate, reconstruct, and reassert a degree of certainty and solace. It is easy to see the allure of these images: rather than an austere space that embodies stasis and distance, the no man's land reemerges from Hurley's composites as a cinematic landscape that catastrophically fuses bodies, machines, and soil while easily fitting a new visual economy of commodification, mass circulation, and consumption. This reconstructive effort to compensate for the deterioration and fragmentation of the visual field is, at its core, an effort to reassert legibility over a world that is otherwise seen as chaotic beyond comprehension. In this respect, Hurley's photographs relate directly to the history of composite technology and its effort to reconstruct orders of knowledge at moments of social and cultural anxiety.[26] In quite the same way, Hurley's composite photographs—first from his work with Shackleton's polar expedition and later from the war—share an effort to harness the photographic medium to sublimate and reorganize a violently disorienting and unintelligible world.

The aesthetic vocabulary used to formulate no man's land in the composites of the Great War is dense, spectacular, and sensational. Printed in very large formats for internationally touring exhibitions that attracted tens of thousands of visitors, they had great appeal to audiences in the postwar period that sought pictorial legibility in the face of bewildering carnage. With their mass exposure and popular resonance, it is hard to overstate the impact that composites of the Western Front had on the visual genealogy of no man's land and the crystallization of its visual imagination.

Yet the aesthetic conventions of these composites mark a radical deviation from the austere images of no man's land taken through the curious eye of a nurse or the shaking hands of a soldier in a trench. What is perhaps even more surprising in these photographic spectacles is the absence of the state. The grandiosity of the composites functions as the ultimate distraction, rendering largely invisible the sovereign logic of abdication that fundamentally governs the space and turning its catastrophic consequences into aesthetic extravaganza. The soft rays of sublime melancholy effectively replaced the harsh light of uncaring.

Destruction Montage

There is nothing special about the three small cardboard boxes containing World War I photographs at the archives of the Warburg Institute in London. Their ubiquity and resemblance to so many similar boxes containing old photographs in attics and cupboards is partly what makes them significant. Few people, after all, will ever encounter such images in the ordered environment of an archive where chronologies, captions, and contextual appendixes determine meaning and significance. Most will likely open a dusty old box, pull out a stack of photographs, and begin to flick through them, staring for a while and turning them over to see whether a caption or date was added, or setting several side by side to see whether an order can be surmised or meaning made. What does it mean to encounter no man's land in this way, not as a stand-alone image but as part of a visual assemblage?

The three boxes are easily overlooked in the vast collection of books, documents and images that constitute the lifework of the German-Jewish cultural scholar Aby Warburg. From 1914 to 1918, his Bibliothek für Kulturwissenschaft began amassing a diverse collection of more than five thousand visual documents, including press photographs, images bought for use by the German army, postcards, and postage stamps. Much of the collection was lost, probably during the rushed relocation of the library from Hamburg to London in 1933. But the three boxes survived, containing 1,505 war related items that make for a highly eclectic collection—surveillance photographs, images documenting weaponry, damage to infrastructure and military machinery, portraiture, social events attended by military personnel, everyday life of soldiers in the front, and folkloric scenes from Turkey, the Levant, and Eastern Europe. One of the unmistakable features of this collection is the incessant documentation of modes and technologies of mobility. A whole world is captured on the move: motorized vehicles, naval vessels, heavily loaded convoys of all sorts— donkeys, mules, and camels; carts, airplanes, and zeppelins—as well as an endless assortment of mobility infrastructure: roads, bridges, ports, and docks.

The destruction unleashed by the war sparked what Paul Valéry called "the crisis of the mind," an acute awareness of the increasing fragility of the very foundations of culture and knowledge. It was not surprising, then, that during the years of conflict, Europe was engulfed by what Georges Didi-Huberman calls a "paper storm," an archive fever to gather and document the war's enormous visual and textual output in the face of an impending cataclysm.[27] Some saw this as a private endeavor—a collection of images that captured the personal experiences of war and could be shared with loved ones in its aftermath.[28] For others, like Warburg, this was part of a broader intellectual challenge of coming to terms with an unfolding catastrophe. The events of the war profoundly fractured his belief in the power of the Enlightenment and forced a dramatic reconsideration of cultural practice and methods.[29] Gathering photographs was one way to try to hold on to a world tearing itself to pieces.

In many respects, the images Warburg collected during the war are utterly unspectacular. There are numerous photographs in countless collections around the world that are almost identical to these. On their own, the images don't offer new or obviously valuable knowledge. Individually, they don't make sense. That is the inherent limitation of the stand-alone photograph. However, observing the images together, as they create sequences and assemblages, opens a different view of the space of uncaring, its violence and its meaning.

Take, for example, the actual modes of visual production—the mechanics of photography and printing, as well as the wider technological apparatus that makes it possible—that are often left outside the frame. In most photographs, these elements are obscured from view or taken for granted. However, Warburg's image archive invites the viewer to draw critical links between technologies of visualization and technologies of physical violence.

The devastated landscapes of no man's land are the consequence of the simultaneous operation of the two. One aerial photograph depicts a bombed
wooded landscape. The trees have all been stripped of any foliage revealing
a devastated terrain strewn with large waterlogged craters. The photograph
preceding it depicts a German dirigible hovering over a landscape quite similar to the one later seen in utter devastation. The sequence turns the viewer's
attention to the technical infrastructure on which the production of images
relies, although much of it remains conventionally outside the frame. Writing
about one photograph in the collection that depicts German soldiers photo-
graphing the front from within a shallow trench, Didi-Huberman observes:
"Everywhere the stigmata of the *Urkatastrophe*, but everywhere, equally, we
find signs of the devastation's technological management, as in documents
where the military demands that the war be reproducible in photographic or
cinematographic images."[30] The visual-industrial complex that emerged so
prominently during World War I produced at once new ways of seeing and
new ways of killing.

But the photo boxes do more than highlight the emergence of visual conventions and their complicity in mechanics of violence: they begin to set out a
different relation to the act of viewing. When images of no man's land appear,
sporadically, in the stack of images, they offer little interpretative information. Instead, they demand active engagement. They require the viewer to ask
the question that animates this book more broadly—What is this space captured in these photographs? It is an analytical exercise that requires willingness to make sense of images rather than passively assume their meaning. This
was an important feature of Warburg's monumental *Mnemosyne Bilderatlas*
project, in which, during the latter part of the 1920s, he sought to illuminate
the pictorial afterlife of gestures and motifs from antiquity into the modern
age. Through the *Bilderatlas*, Warburg experimented with the production of
"knowledge through montages," a broad search for nonstandard structures of
knowledge that was practiced and theorized in the same period by his con-
temporaries, notably Walter Benjamin in his *Arcades Project* and Georges Bataille in his journal *Documents*.[31] Yet a decade before he started the work on
the *Bilderatlas*, Warburg had already begun his search for ways to critically
mobilize the massive visual corpus of World War I.

Warburg started putting together his war collection as a desperate recuperative effort that was never fully realized. For him, this was not a detached,
forensic intellectual exercise, but a project with deep personal stakes. Like
Walter Benjamin's *Arcades*, Warburg's project during World War I was halted
by depression and mental breakdown; the magnitude of destruction and violence was too much to bear. In a 1923 letter to his family, Warburg notes his

long search for knowledge, enlightenment, and cultural historical development. Quoting his favorite Latin idiom, he admits defeat: "*Per mo[n]stra ad astra*: the gods have placed the monster in the path to the idea. The 1914–1918 War had confronted me with the devastating truth that unchained, elemental man is this world's unconquerable ruler."[32] What we are left with is an image-assemblage of a world in pieces, a world that cannot be stitched back together.

Approaching the images of the no man's land as a constellation rather than fragments or even elements in a chronological sequence potentially helps us situate uncaring in a living realm of experience, reflection, and feeling. Warburg's boxes of war photographs are an invitation to think through affinities between and disjunctures in multiple images. Experimental reenactments of this sort harbor the potential to further illuminate the historical, affective, and conceptual import of no man's land. In this way, the return to the visual archive of no man's land attains a new experimental quality that identifies a critical horizon in what is often a discombobulating experience: "Provisionality and impermanence coupled with synchronic array, contingency of relations coupled with significant associations, and a mnemonic function that suggests the ever-present possibility of interpretation."[33]

For anyone seeking a grand visual theory sovereign abandonment, this must be a disappointing conclusion. It seems speculative at best and hardly relevant to the vast majority who will never make it to the archive itself. But the first step in pushing against the clichés that have hollowed no man's land of its critical significance is to revisit its most obvious forms. If one is at all to encounter images of the sort that I trace here, a variation of the theme of ruined landscape with barbed wire, it is likely to be in the company of other images. In some cases, this multiplicity and the critical potential it opens can be found in a family album or a box of old photographs. In other cases, they make their way to the stacks of public libraries or stalls in a flea market. Each repository will likely plot a different path through the ensemble of uncaring. The critical task is to make those connections where they are hard to make, reintroducing human presence and meaning into a space that that all too often seems inhumane and senseless.

Image Afterlife

Early photography reveals the entanglements of no man's land with histories of violence, technology, and cultural crises, but staring at old photographs can easily turn into a rather solitary, navel-gazing exercise. Occasionally, though, stories emerge from the chance encounters that surround the image rather than directly through the photograph itself. During one of the days I spent in the close quarters of the Warburg Institute archive, the archivist, Eckart Marchand, shared his own experience of no man's land. The boxes of war photographs were open on my desk, and some images were set side by side across it. While I was trying to make connections, he was making his own. At first, he appeared with a 1938 newspaper clipping that he remembered having come across in another file; it was about a Jewish man stranded between Czechoslovakian and Polish border posts for several weeks.[34] Our conversation, however, quickly turned to another, directly personal experience of no man's land. Having lived in West Berlin during the late 1980s, he had crossed the border to East Germany and no man's land on a number of occasions. "It had been part of normal life. Of course, one knew that people had risked their lives to cross it, but for us crossing it, it was mostly an inconvenience." Yet the direct encounter with this space after the collapse of East Germany in 1989 was deeply unnerving: "Driving, however slowly, through the border installations, crossing points and no man's land, still full of mines, after the fall of the wall suddenly showed the arbitrariness of it all, that this was something installed by people against people. In German I would say it was 'like a dead grimace' [*eine erstarrte Grimasse*], [that is,] an empty mask staring at you, deeply unsettling. And, of course, everybody who had been involved in it a month earlier was still around, but now the border guards were waving us through."

I often return to Ariella Azoulay's work on the photograph as a political forum, where meaning is always made with others.[35] No individual, she argues, possesses sole authority over the photograph or in the process of its interpretation. Political meaning is derived not from the content of the photograph per se, but from the potential encounters and interactions that are inspired by it. It is a profound proposition that signals the potential emergence of new political communities and new histories, a critique that is deeply invested in photography but never venerates the visual medium.

Indeed, no single photograph fully captures no man's land. But the constellations of stories the swirl around it, as they unfold its prehistories and posthumous interpretations, may be as close as we—a potential polity of viewers—may ever get to the space of uncaring.

Contours

As the edge of care, no man's land has its own rough edges. From a distance, the perimeter is all we can see. But the boundary lines are important: that's where care goes once it is withdrawn. The lines indicate an intensification of care along an outer limit, only to signify its abdication elsewhere. Most often, these contours are marked by a blunt materiality of trenches and coils of barbed wire, watchtowers, and warning signs. Beyond them, a land of uncertain rules and certain perils. But the beginnings of no man's land also take place in more prosaic and unspectacular settings, where the grueling stasis of trench warfare is replaced with a swift movement of a pencil along a map. Points of origin are made into a starting line. Often such lines are drawn in haste, with false confidence that rarely foretells their murky future.

Lines are not abstract. The graphic gesture of line drawing is not oblivious to the physical entanglement of bodies, soils, and machines that amasses on the brink of no man's land. So often in history these lines are a testament to a failure of pushing forward and reaching farther, a forced paralysis. At other times, though, the line becomes predictive, preceding and catalyzing the zone that emerges in its wake. The very act of drawing in such cases deserves attention not only for the mess it will create—ruptured lives and broken lands—but also for the untidiness of its own creation. For most of history, the line involved a tactile pigment and its absorption into a surface. A blunted pencil tip, diluted ink that overflowed, or the uneven surface of a drawing board leave numerous reminders of the line's graphic physical tactility. The line, we are reminded in these cases, has its own uncertain edges. No man's land can start from there as well.

Yet all too often, the contours of no man's land are drawn with blood on the ground, making them hard to trace but also hard to wipe clean.

Bleeding

On August 10, 1945, during the final days of World War II, an all-night meeting was held in the Executive Office Building next to the White House. American policy makers were seeking a response to Japan's impending surrender and its wider effects in Asia. Around midnight, two young officers were sent to an adjoining room to determine the American occupation zone in the Korean Peninsula. The two worked "in haste and under great pressure," using a *National Geographic* map for reference.[1] Dean Rusk, who was one of the officers, and later secretary of state under presidents Kennedy and Johnson, admitted he had no expertise for the task and that no professional cartographers were consulted in the process.[2] In the absence of an obvious landmark that could guide them in dividing the Soviet and American zones of influence, they drew the line along the Thirty-Eighth Parallel.

Straight lines drawn in haste in the middle of the night by ill-prepared military officers is hardly a scenario likely to spell success. It took eight years and one war for the line to officially morph into a zone: during the three-year war in Korea, the convenience of a single cartographic parallel—a Cartesian fantasy of a neat, zero-width mark—was replaced by a constellation of entangled lines that trapped spaces in between them, designating strict exclusions as well as routes of access and crossing. It was not water that was poured over an inky line that caused it to seep and expand, but hubris and blood.

Lines dominated the ceasefire negotiations between the United Nations Command (UNC) and representatives of the Chinese and North Korean forces in the summer and autumn of 1951. Sixty-five meetings were held between July and November in an effort to agree on a Military Demarcation Line (MDL) between the sides; it would be followed by the establishment of a demilitarized zone to secure a longer-term cessation of hostilities. At the outset, positions diverged radically. The Chinese and North Korean negotiators, partly seeking to reverse recent military setbacks, insisted on a return to the Thirty-Eighth Parallel and a withdrawal of all foreign forces from the peninsula.[3] The UN Command dismissed outright a return to the Thirty-Eighth Parallel, proposing instead a line running well north of the military positions it held at the time.[4] Speaking at the Armistice Conference in Kaesong on July 27, the UNC's chief negotiator Admiral Charles Turner Joy not only rejected his counterparts' position but also posited a critical shift in the status of the line itself. "An imaginary geographical line such as a parallel of latitude has no validity whatsoever in developing a military armistice," he contended. The neat linear imagination was instead replaced by zonal perception: "In approaching the problem of a demilitarized zone, the United Nations Command delegation desires to call attention to certain military realities."[5] More-over, instead of a single zone, Joy distinguished the ground zone of the battle-field from naval and aerial zones. Because the UN side maintained aerial and naval superiority throughout most of the peninsula, he argued, it should be awarded additional territory on the ground.

The shift from lines to zones was not only taking place around the nego-tiation table. "The DMZ is drawn on the footprints of the past," the American columnist James Brady commented when he returned to Korea decades after having served there as a rifle platoon commander. Brady saw that past in the very landscape he was observing, noting how "the ridgelines and high ground blooded by the young men of half a century before."[6] The emergence of the zone was indeed a bloody affair. As talks stalled at the end of August, the UNC launched a series of military offensives that sought to gain better defensive terrain farther north of its front line. Two and a half months of fighting followed, concentrated around the "Punchbowl," a bowl-shaped, ex-tinct volcano ringed by the mountains of the Taebaek range. Describing its significance, the UNC commander in chief, General Matthew B. Ridgway, noted, "Much blood was spilled . . . to win control of this area. In the Eighth Army's possession, it would shorten the line, provide better observation, and lessen the chance of strong enemy surprise attacks in that quarter. Once we had seized it, we never gave it up."[7] In utterly utilitarian terms, Ridgway states the obvious: "shortening the line" and creating a zone required that blood be spilled.

And the lines bled. Before ground troops began their ascent up the ridges and toward the fortified North Korean positions, heavy artillery fire and aerial bombardment gradually eliminated any trace of vegetation from the ridge-line, turning it into "a brown landscape with skeletons of trees clawing at the air."[8] As one US Marine recalled, the rugged soil was reduced to "the con-sistency of powder. When you walked, you sank into the ground up to your ankles."[9] The devastation left "a naked mountain" but failed to completely de-stroy the North Korean bunkers.[10] Once the bombardment ceased, UN forces made the final push up the steep slopes, only to find themselves exposed to heavy gunfire and grenades. During the three weeks of what would be known as the Battle of Bloody Ridge, UNC forces suffered more than 2,700 casual-ties, and an estimated 15,000 North Korean soldiers were killed.[11]

The heavy toll did not distract James Van Fleet, the commander of the Eighth Army, from his determination to "tidy up" a "sag" in the line by taking the ridge just north of Bloody Ridge and another north of the Punchbowl.[12] The Battle of Heartbreak Ridge, as it was named by reporters covering the events, lasted over four weeks into mid-October 1951. In his memoir of the war, Bill Wilson notes the utter destruction of terrain: "There was no tree left standing or any piece of wood larger than a man's forearm remaining on the top half of the mountain or its ridges. The rocky ground had been pulverized as though it had been ploughed."[13] Even when UNC forces were able to overcome intense fire to ascend the ridgeline, they were often too exhausted to withstand the North Korean counterattack and were forced to withdraw. These seesaw battles up and down the ridgeline and over exposed routes resulted in thousands of casualties on both sides.[14] In the series of battles that took place from July to November, the UNC suffered 60,000 casualties and the communist forces approximately 234,000.[15] It was a heavy price to pay for a straighter line.

But blood is rarely inscribed on the maps. In search of the economization of resources and rationalization of tactical advantages, military strategists and diplomatic planners often rely on a geometrical logic that reduces a dynamic, organic, and haptically experienced space to a graphic mark. It is a familiar hierarchy that prioritizes the legibility of a graphic order—maps, tactical plans, platoon rosters, and ammunition inventories—over the messy corporeality and materiality of violent conflict.

Unsurprisingly, then, when Korean talks resumed in late October, lines once again topped the agenda. The parties first turned to fix the Military Demarcation Line and establish the Demilitarized Zone (DMZ).[16] Within a month an agreement was reached on the route of the line, with the understanding that each side would withdraw two kilometers from that line of contact to create the new zone. Again, a linear logic seemed to guide the parties' positions: The communist negotiators agreed to concede the Thirty-Eighth Parallel as their only acceptable ceasefire line; the UNC, meanwhile, was grappling with the effect of the proposed MDL on forces positioned on other tactical lines and the unlikely change in the frontline battle positions following the restriction on offensive UN actions.[17] Although the war would continue for another twenty months, the crushed earth and bloodied ridges had no place on the gridded surface that marked the new zone. It was conceived in blood but sanitized from it.

Yet there is perhaps more to the relation between lines and lives than merely an indifferent act of cartographic mastery. Rather than just an erasure of the lives and lands that were exposed so violently, we can think of the zone and the lines that constitute its neat perimeter as a more anxious effort to assert rational control, exactly in the face of the explosive violence that left behind naked mountains and shattered bodies. Another catastrophe, the Lisbon earthquake of 1755, was one critical moment that redefined Enlightenment Europe's relation to the uncontrolled materiality of the earth.[18] For Kant, a response to the destruction of Lisbon required "not only a new kind of subject, capable of taking charge of its own inclinations, but also a very different earth: a natural order made over so thoroughly by the collectivity of selfwilled agents that it would cease to pose a palpable threat to human existence."[19] More recently, the Chernobyl Zone of Exclusion marked the Soviet military's effort to "circumscribe the disaster," a delineation that at its core, sought to project stability and bureaucratic confidence onto a ruptured space plagued by prolonged uncertainty.[20] As a mark of catastrophe, the drawing of lines that give birth to no man's land is more than just a distantiated graphic abstraction. Instead, it signals an effort to keep violence at bay, to graphically contain a bleeding reality that threatens to spill beyond its neatly marked edges.

Nor should the line be understood as merely a graphic fiction, potent as ink marks on maps may be. The Military Demarcation Line that runs through the exact center of the Korean Demilitarized Zone was also marked by 1,392 small, yellow, metal signs placed at two-hundred-meter intervals, written in Chinese and Korean on one side, and in English and Korean on the other. Exposed to the elements, the signs themselves are rusting and require constant upkeep. North Korea is responsible for the maintenance of 696 of the signs, while the United Nations is responsible for the other 696. What emerges is the mundane materiality of the line, its tactile composition and decomposition, as well as the labor of its preservation. These are not secondary considerations. In 1969, the Central Intelligence Agency interpreted North Korea's disruption of routine maintenance work to replace worn markers as nothing less than part "of a deliberate attempt by Pyongyang to revive a high level of tension with the United States."[21] The future of the Korean no man's land was inseparable from the minutiae of tending to the rusting metal markers and their fading scripts.

Decades after the MDL was drawn, intercontinental nuclear fears seem to dwarf old attrition battles over barren ridges. As thick foliage covers the pulverized earth, it is all too easy to reduce the no man's land of the DMZ into a geopolitical oddity that attracts thrill-seeking tourists and offers an eye-catching background for journalistic reports or geopolitical theatrics. It is much harder to see, long after the fighting subsided, the catastrophic entanglement of bodies, inanimate objects, and graphic forms that make up the space of uncaring. Such attention entails a commitment to the granular lived realities that make possible these spaces. Formal dimensions of international law, military strategy, and political statecraft are not the prime concern here, despite their conventional prominence in the historiographies of no man's land to date. The critical challenge lies, instead, in the often-subtle entanglements that turn abstractions of law and politics into grounded, embodied, and often bloody affairs.

Smearing

After the bloodletting that brought about the emergence of the Korean DMZ, the 1945 line that was amateurishly drawn to divide the peninsula became little more than a footnote in the violent history of the war. Like so many other lines, it was a graphic fiction, though a fiction with deadly repercussions. More recent lines were drawn into the complex writing maze that made up the long imperial fantasy of a world mastered and made legible through diaries and diagrams, letters and laws. The ruler in such (carto)graphic endeavors, Tim Ingold reminds us, designates both the instrument for drawing straight lines and the figure who governs.[22] For good reasons, the very real violence that resulted from dispassionate geometric markings of lines generated critical suspicion of those who were so eager to exploit the privileges of Cartesian linear perspective, with its claim to embody a supposed "harmony between the mathematical regularities in optics and God's will."[23] Linear graphics were, at best, a dangerous abstraction that obfuscated the urgent actualities of violence, social fragmentation, and territorial dismemberment.

But lines are not just abstract figments. Even on the pristine surface of the page, lines never assume their mathematical status as zero-width, zero-depth graphic abstractions. Once drawn, the graphic line has its own materiality that is affected by and reacts to its strata and substrata.

In a particular way, the spaces at the heart of this book bring to the fore the materialities of the line itself, both its graphic tactility and the ways it takes physical form on the surface of the earth. The actualities of lines, the untidy acts of drawing them and even messier attempts to contend with their consequences, highlight the rough contours of no man's land as both constitutive and disruptive: lines enclose and distinguish inside from outside, designating the space of normative order and marking out the space of uncaring that falls beyond it. At the same time, the graphic life of lines—the mess of smears, errors, and imperfections—magnifies the excessive and unruly realities that come to inhabit no man's land.

The Jerusalem no man's land was one result of such linear mess. This strip of land, which separated Jordanian and Israeli forces in the city for nineteen years, highlighted the volatile life of the line, which at times seemed more significant than the space it was enclosing. One Israeli report from the early 1950s described the line that carved out the no man's land as "the most complicated and ridiculous line that could ever be imagined."[24] Unsurprisingly, perhaps, its inception was wholly accidental. In late November 1948, a meeting was held between Abdullah al-Tell, the commander of the Jordanian forces, and Moshe Dayan, who commanded the Israeli brigade that fought in the city. The two met in an abandoned house in the Musrara neighborhood, and using a 1:20,000 British survey map, they marked the location of their forces along the urban frontier. Dayan used a green chinagraph pencil and al-Tell, a red one. The lines they drew ran at an uneven distance from each other, in some parts creating only a white sliver between the red and green markings. In other parts, they carved out thick wedges that fell outside the control of either force. In between these lines, a no man's land emerged.

Meron Benvenisti, who served as deputy mayor of Jerusalem during the 1970s, describes the demarcation as a rather haphazard endeavor. Assuming that the lines were being drawn only for temporary purposes and would be replaced by more detailed maps during later negotiations, "no one had taken the trouble to have a flat surface beneath the map. As a result, the grease pencils skipped over some places. And the lines were also disjointed, zigzag, or sketchy due to uncertainty or error in their initial drawings."[25] The formal ceasefire agreement signed a few months later between Israel and Jordan in Rhodes included additional maps, but contradictions between the maps did little to resolve the ambiguity. In fact, the agreement determined that the finalized "armistice lines were identical with the lines set out in the agreement of November 30, 1948."[26] In other words, despite their rough and inaccurate nature, the markings on the map hastily drawn by the two generals became a reference point in an official UN-backed agreement.

Inaccuracies that plagued the initial ceasefire lines were not the only thing that would haunt the contours surrounding the no man's land. The materiality of the drawing itself became a highly significant part of the struggles that prevented any settled demarcation of this space and loomed over the lives of those who resided on its smeared edges. On a 1:20,000 map, the thickness and softness of the chinagraph resulted in lines that were, generally, three to four millimeters wide. On the ground, however, these lines covered areas that were sixty to eighty meters wide, running along streets, through entire neighborhoods, and over individual houses. Benvenisti rightly notes that this was more than just a historical anecdote or oddity. It was, he noted, "a cartographer's nightmare and a geographer's catastrophe."[27]

Yet most often, this "graphic monstrosity" resulted in human tragedy: a great deal of blood was shed as a result of the linear vagueness and ambiguity.[28] When a UN committee inspected one minuscule section of the no man's land, its members discovered that one house in the Musrara neighborhood

had its eastern side within the Jordanian area, its western side was in the Israeli zone, and its southern terrace in the no man's land. The absurdity was
often lethal: two Israeli soldiers were injured by Jordanian fire when walking
down a street that fell under the line. Israel considered the line part of its territory, but Jordan saw it as part of the no man's land, which made the two soldiers fair targets for Jordanian snipers. "It all depended on where they were—
NML or Israel," jotted an Israeli official in his notes from the Mixed Armistice
Commission meeting. Underneath he added, "the thickness of the line."[29] For
seven years Israeli and Jordanian teams argued over this that issue: did each
side possess the width of its respective line, or did the lines constitute part of
the no man's land itself? It was finally agreed that the sides would have control
of their respective lines, although even that was never formalized. The lines
remained blurred.

The smeared contours of no man's land bring to the fore elements that, if
considered solely through graphic conventions, would be considered flaws
that ought to be avoided or concealed: a jittery hand, an unsharpened pencil,
a bumpy surface. Yet when tracing the contours of no man's land, bodies, materialities, and space are explicitly what is at stake. For Justine Clark, smudges
and smears are residues of action and process directing our attention toward
"materiality and the body, at the work necessary for representation."[30] Retracing the body into the smeared line becomes an urgent concern when the blurry
edges of the line mark the uncertain perimeter of a killing zone. This critical
reorientation of focus helps us draw a clearer connection between graphic
technology and political logics: As lines drawn in the midst of war, the care-
lessness with which the initial contours were sketched was perhaps expected,
but it foretold the uncaring that would come to dominate the space that fell
between them.

In April 1949, Jordan and Israel reached an agreement to partition the
no man's land north and south of the city, with each party gaining control
over approximately an even share of the territory. Inside Jerusalem, however,
the Jordanians rejected a similar agreement, fearing that such a move would
be interpreted as a concession over their territorial claims in the city. The
blurred lines on the map resulted in porous spaces that confused the distinction between inside and out, between territory that fell squarely within the
sovereign realm and the space of uncaring beyond it. In a 1925 essay on the
city of Naples, Walter Benjamin and Asja Lacis use the concept of porosity to
capture blurred boundaries between public and private space, the blending
of daytime and nighttime activities and the mingling of diverse publics in the
city spaces they observe. In their formulation, porosity preserves in everything "the scope to become a theatre of unforeseen constellations"; it is where

"the stamp of the definitive is avoided."³¹ Porosity designates not simply movement between spaces, but a more profound "interruption of the opposition between the singular and the closed on the one hand and the completely open on the other."³² On the blurred perimeter of the no man's land, the potentiality of the indefinite and the unforeseen was simultaneously ominous and promising.

Everyday life on the smeared lines of Jerusalem's no man's land was a daily routine of exposure to sniper fire, to stretches of minefields and to the depressing sight of a space strewn with ruins and refuse. But in the absence of a contiguous fence that clearly enclosed it, the edges of no man's land also became a porous space where encounters, illicit activity, and even play could take place. At times, this was lethal: in 1950, Alberto Saving, a seventeen-year-old immigrant from West Jerusalem, was killed while collecting scrap metal in no man's land.³³ At other times, the porosity of no man's land allowed exactly that "theatre of unforeseen constellations." Rafi Marziano, who grew up in the Musrara neighborhood on the edge of no man's land, recalled how periodic inspections of the no man's land by Israeli, Jordanian, and UN officials would spark an "invasion" of children from both sides. Knowing that military forces held their fire during the visits, kids would run around until they were chased out by city workers and UN soldiers.³⁴ Raphael Hajbi, a petty criminal known as the "underwear robber," for once having carried out a gas-station heist without wearing trousers, took advantage of the porosity of the line to stash a gun beyond the reach of the Israeli police.³⁵

Exposure takes on a dual meaning through these fragments. On the one hand, it is the precarity of life in the sight of a sniper, of the depressing image of ruined land strewn with mangled debris, and of being subjected to the stench of sewer that flows openly in the abandoned space between the barbed wire. On the other hand, it is also exposure as encounter between Jewish and Arab children running through the field of ruins, where normative order is suspended. Playfulness can come in through the porous perimeters of no man's land, exposing in turn the potential for change and dynamism in the face of restrictive realities. This partly explains the allure of porosity as a critical concept and its ability to remake the exposure of life in no man's land from a deadly reality into a line of flight. A similar dynamic emerges time and again in the different histories of no man's land, but in this context, porosity is not simply a hopeful potentiality for transformation. Instead, vulnerability and the potentiality of harm are inextricably intertwined with a possibility of change and radical action.

Beyond bodies, materialities, and surfaces, tracing the smeared contours of no man's land exposes the frayed edges of the story itself. The initial account of the encounter between the Israeli and Jordanian commanders appeared in a memoir of an Israeli general, Uzi Narkis, but it lacks any clarity regarding its source. In their own memoirs, neither Dayan nor al-Tell provide any details about this event. There are even contradictory accounts regarding the color of the lines: some argue that the Israeli general used the green chinagraph and his counterpart a red one, whereas others argue that it was the other way around. And while a quick glance at the map would settle the issue, archives in Israel, Jordan, and at the United Nations have yet to make any of the original maps public. According to some sources, one map is held by the Israeli military archives but remains classified.[36] A true-to-size color photocopy of the map hangs in the office of director of the Ammunition Hill Memorial site in Jerusalem, but that's as close as I've ever gotten to the original.

These uncertainties, contradictions, and ambiguities are not incidental. Throughout this book, the stories of no man's land repeatedly draw on rumors and legends as much as they do on more conventionally verifiable sources. At times, the stories told about these spaces seem to be pure fabrications. Yet these are telling tales that reveal deeper anxieties and aspirations of those who inhabit these spaces or their immediate vicinity. In the smeared edges, where the storylines blur fact and fiction, one often finds some of no man's land's most powerful and enduring experiences.

Holding I

Sergeant Reeves stopped the Toyota Hilux at a Greek checkpoint on the southern outskirts of Nicosia. A bored-looking young soldier slung a rifle over his shoulder and opened the gate. Once the blue flag of the United Nations was secured to the back of the truck, we were soon driving through a small eucalyptus grove and into the Buffer Zone that divides the Greek Cypriot military from the Turkish forces that have occupied the north since the 1974 invasion. Reeves was part of the First Battalion of the Irish Guards, who were on deployment as part of the UN peacekeeping mission after a 2013 tour in Afghanistan.

It was late spring, and the open fields were already dry and yellowing. We drove north on a dirt track running through the Buffer Zone, with both Greek and Turkish military positions appearing at regular intervals, marking the edges of the Cypriot no man's land. According to their official mandate, UN peacekeeping forces were deployed in Cyprus in 1964 to prevent the escalation of intercommunal violence that had broken out the previous year. In the first half of the twentieth century, Greek- and Turkish-speaking communities in Cyprus increasingly coalesced around antagonistic national

FIGURE 5. The control tower at the Nicosia Airport, abandoned in 1974 and now headquarters of the UN peacekeeping force inside the Buffer Zone, 2015. Photographer: Elliot Graves.

identities and promoted diverging visions for the future of the island, the former seeking unification with Greece, and the latter, territorial partition along communal lines.[37] When Turkey invaded Cyprus in 1974 and established an occupying force in the northern part of the island, the UN forces turned their focus to preventing any additional unilateral actions that would jeopardize the fragile status quo. In practice, this meant ensuring that forces on either side remained static and that the fortified lines that marked the contour of the Buffer Zone were not breached.

But holding the line on a daily basis also means constant preoccupation with minute details of the material composition of the line itself. A classified intelligence folder held by UN forces documents each and every position in detailed color photographs. Only a week before our visit, Reeves was out taking photos to keep the folder up to date. "So, if the Turks or the Cypriots want to make any change, add another layer of sandbags, they have to put in a request. But even if they do something without letting us know, the guys are all over them." It would not be outlandish to assume that somewhere in the UN mission headquarters that occupies the old Nicosia Airport there is a cabinet with photos of the Buffer Zone dating back to the 1970s (fig. 5). These surveillance folders are a visual archive of lines, at once documenting the outer perimeters of no man's land and providing static reference point that holds it in place. "To hold," AbdouMaliq Simone noted in a very different context, "easily mutates into a form of capture."[38]

Folders of photographs that document the line are only one mnemonic form that takes part in holding the lines of no man's land. There is another kind of spatial literacy that is at play here, one that supplements the interpretation of visual cues with a tactile and embodied experience of the terrain. Before heading to Afghanistan, British troops underwent Ground Sign Awareness training to identify slight changes in the landscape as warning signs of hidden improvised explosive devices (IEDs).[39] "I can do it now as we're driving along," Reeves said. "I'd pick up stuff like that mast," pointing to a cell phone antenna. "I'd class that as a marker. The same with natural features on the ground and unnatural features. Bits that are dug in, and bits that aren't dug in. If something looks disturbed—for instance that color of dirt is different from the track—it sticks out to me." Such attentiveness to materiality has proved a transferable skill: it could prevent you from getting blown up in Afghanistan, and it makes you an effective peacekeeper in Cyprus.

Holding the line is done here through visceral knowledge that is imprinted on bodies and soils as much, if not more so, as it is part of more abstract practices of surveillance, planning, and logistics. I noted earlier how the linear mathematical abstraction is repeatedly called into question by the messy demarcations of no man's land: hands jitter, color smears, bodies are wounded, and lands are exposed. In his work on the natures of war, Derek Gregory proposes a shift away from the abstract cartographic imaginary, to a "corpography" that focuses on soldiers' lived experience of military violence.[40] Bodies, natures, objects, and machines are (often catastrophically) entangled in the making of no man's land, and the material enmeshment challenges any attempt to hold on to an abstract linear logic. The writer Mary Borden, who served as a nurse in World War I, opens her collection of sketches and short stories with a long, poetic description of the mud that dominated life in and around no man's land. "There is no frontier," she wrote, "just a bleeding edge."[41] The tactical literacy that Reeves brought from Afghanistan into the Cypriot Buffer Zone is one way of holding at bay what otherwise threatens to spill over.

But holding must not be confined to a form of military containment. This is partly a matter of who is doing the holding: historiographies of no man's land have almost exclusively focused on the soldier as the protagonist of this space. But even in spaces ravaged by violence and ruination, acts of holding take multiple and often nuanced forms. They are intended for more than aggressive enclosure and capture, and they are carried out by others who hold no official credentials or status. Holding the lines becomes as much an act of care as one of control.

Holding II

From their very inception, the lines marking Jerusalem's no man's land were vague, but the fortifications marking its edges were wholly unambiguous. Both Israel and Jordan barricaded buildings and streets along the no man's land. Within the width of the grease-pencil line, in the towers of the Old City's wall, on the roofs of monasteries and churches, in communication trenches and concrete pillboxes, Israeli units and Arab forces faced each other for nineteen years. The improvised positions left over from the days of the 1948 war were reinforced and improvements were made; concrete trenches were built, some of them subterranean. On both sides, the line became a stretch of barricades and fortification. In all, thirty-six Jordanian and nineteen Israeli fortified positions marked the edges of the no man's land over a seven-kilometer stretch.

Other architectures were harnessed to dispel any ambiguity of the Israeli Green Line. In the early 1960s Israel constructed a set of large tenement blocks that ran parallel to the edge of no man's land. The sides facing east toward the Jordanian part of the city were built with narrow windows that would be less susceptible to sniper fire. Along the roof-line, the architects designed firing slits. These housing blocks became emblematic of Israel's wider border architecture: they function as a mammoth physical obstacle, restricting views into the Jewish neighborhoods behind them and readily providing strategic vantage points for the Israeli forces. What Le Corbusier imagined as the ultimate architectural expression of the "living machine" was an architectural emblem of the war machine as it sought to command and control the violence of no man's land.

In other cases, holding the lines involved intrusions into the most personal spaces. The Baramki House is a villa originally designed in 1934 as a family home by the prominent Palestinian architect Andoni Baramki in the Sa'ad Said neighborhood, just north of the Old City walls. He called it *nour hayati*, Arabic for "light of my life." As the battles of the 1948 war intensified, the family was forced to flee and seek shelter outside the city. After the partition, the house was trapped on the Israeli side of no man's land while the family was in East Jerusalem, under Jordanian control. Exquisitely built and strategically positioned, the Baramki House's imposing three-story stone structure was taken over by the Israeli army only weeks after its Arab owners were forced to flee. In the days after the border was established, the Israeli military transformed the house into an army post. Weapons were placed behind the home's thick limestone walls and aimed across a mixture of mines and barbed wire that separated Israeli forces from those of the Jordanians only a few meters away. The doors were reinforced and the front entrance

sealed. The arched windows were filled in with concrete and made into tur-
rets so that only a thin aperture, narrow enough to accommodate a gun and
the gaze of a marksman, remained. The interior was cleared for the housing
of troops. The violence along the city's dividing lines and the hits absorbed by
the home-turned-fortress wore down the structure's ornamental exterior as
bullets and shrapnel scarred its face.

Unlike most Palestinians who were forced to leave their homes, the Baramkis lived close enough to be able to peer across the frontier at their home
throughout the years of the divided city. Gabi Baramki, the architect's son,
then a man in his thirties, remembers the overwhelming powerlessness he
felt: "By the mid 1960's it became clear to me that if we were ever going to
reclaim the property at all, it would not be in my father's time."[42] From the
heights of the YMCA building, he and his family could stand and see their
home only a hundred meters away, yet never within reach.

When Israel occupied East Jerusalem in 1967 the fortified barricades marking the no man's land were removed. The lines that were murky to begin with
appeared to have been removed altogether. But the Baramkis soon found that
new lines were created through law and bureaucracy that would prevent them
from reclaiming their home. In particular, the Israeli Absentee Property Law
(1950) expropriated Palestinian lands and homes and entrusted their administration to a specially created custodian. "You know," Gabi Baramki recalled
in an interview, "this question of being defined 'absent' or 'absentee' by the
Israeli Government is unbelievable. Imagine, my father at the time [1967], a
70-year-old person going to the Israelis and telling them that 'here I am now
and I want my property' and them telling him that you are an 'absentee.' And
he would tell them 'how am I absent? I am present!' "[43] Until his death in 1971,
Andoni Baramki was unable to set foot in his home.

The holding that emerges here is clearly distinct from the visceral surveillance performed by those policing it from within. Standing on the outside,
facing the brute markers of enclosure and forced displacement, holding takes
a dual form of affective projection: On the one hand, it is a form of holding on, an enduring longing and unyielding expression of care, while simultaneously remaining on hold, suspended through both physical means and
political structures that mark new lines of belonging, mobility, and agency.
Despite its immaterial form, this dual holding proved more enduring than
the militarized fortifications that sought to hold the contours of no man's
land in place. Removing the barbed wires and clearing the minefields did not
weaken Palestinian determination to hold on to the right of return. Nor did
it undo the political strictures that leave entire populations on hold, in a state
of perpetual suspense and endemic abandonment. But through these mul-

tiple holdings—embodied, visually consumed, and affectively political—the contours of no man's land mark the deeper entanglements that make up these spaces and what is at stake once we endeavor to look beyond their colloquial imaginations.

Beyond the Line

Too often, the view of no man's land seems obscured by the line. Trying to look in, it is easy to stop at the most obvious material features: concrete walls, barbed wire, military positions, and warning signs. Yet these are only meaningful in constituting a particular relation toward the space beyond them and the people whose lives are entangled with it. As Wendy Brown astutely observed, fortified lines are a condensed, spectacular performance of state power, but more often than not, they are markers of an anxious sovereign.[44] There is a similar anxiety in the walls and barricades I write about here, although it is not a fear of the encroachment of competing sovereign orders from across the territorial border. Instead, the barricaded perimeters that enclose no man's land are primarily driven by an effort to prevent the imagined unruliness of no man's land from spilling over and upending the sovereign order that state territories supposedly maintain within. As we stare at the fortifications, we are asked to believe that beyond them is a space of monstrous chaos. That space, we are told, is significant only in the sense that it ought to be subdued and kept at bay, prevented from disrupting the reassuring promise of state care here, on the "safe side" of the wall.

It is a powerful story and a false one. Many of the spaces documented in this book both dismantle the clichés that dominate how we think about no man's land and encourage a more rigorous engagement with the political forces that dominate it—first and foremost, the deliberate abdication of sovereign care and the endurance of life once it is withdrawn. Crossing the barricades to see and hear these realities of uncaring is the first step in refusing the clichés and beginning to recognize the significance of these spaces to our political present.

It is perhaps helpful, then, to see the contours of no man's land as an invitation. Their brutal appearance often conceals a more intricate composition, an amalgamation of material objects, animate bodies, graphic markings, and elusive visions. But to those willing to linger long enough, they also reveal threads that can be followed further. From the blurred edges we might begin to see what constitutes the space of uncaring: the violence and loss that are in full view but also the possible contours of a new horizon.

PART II

Abandoned Lands

No man's land is not a metaphor. Reducing such spaces to metaphor kills the ability to contend with specific historical conditions that produce them, the political logics that sustain them, and the lived realities that endure within them. Yet in one of the most influential discussions of abandonment as an endemic political condition, no man's land makes an appearance as a convenient literary trope. In *State of Exception*, Giorgio Agamben famously considered how abandonment becomes the primal act of the sovereign. Only the sovereign, he posits, can create a liminal condition that exposes its subjects to the unremitting force of law while simultaneously withdrawing from them. Agamben describes this particular geography of inclusive exclusion as a "no man's-land," although it is often interchangeable with "zone of undecidability" or "threshold of indeterminacy."[1] This semantic ambiguity reduces no man's land to a convenient trope, a signifier that is easily mobilized primarily because it has lost its actualizing traits. The problem is not so much the lack of precision in the use of terms, but the erosion of the actual realities that govern such places.

A rare reference in Agamben's corpus to a concrete articulation of no man's land is found in his short discussion of the Israeli expulsion of Palestinian political activists to the mountains of southern Lebanon in the winter of 1992. Agamben follows this brief reference with a far-reaching conclusion: "The no man's land in which they are refugees has already started from this very moment to act back onto the territory of the state of Israel by perforating it and altering it in such a way that the image of that snowy mountain has become more internal to it than any other region of *Eretz Israel* [the Land of Israel]."[2] Similar to other mentions of this space in Agamben's work, no man's land is mostly used metaphorically, a reference to a liminal condition and to forms

of violent exclusion. Perhaps inadvertently, Agamben points to the threat that
no man's land poses to the material and symbolic coherence of the nation-
state. It is as if no man's land retained a grip on the sovereign powers that
seek to wash their hands of it, finding ways to haunt the heartlands that are
supposed to be its diametrical opposites.

I note the 1992 expulsion primarily because it provides important insights
into more concrete temporalities and territorialities, dimensions that Agamben's theorization seems to largely ignore. The details of this event, which I
recount in greater length in the following chapter, enable us to shift attention
from abandonment as a concept in political theory to its granular realities.
Before the deportation, the deportees sat for fourteen hours blindfolded and
handcuffed in buses while Israel's Supreme Court debated the legality of the
order, which was eventually approved by a deeply divided court. Each detainee was provided with a blanket, a paper bag of food, and fifty dollars and
brought to the northern part of the "Security Strip," a zone Israel occupied in
southern Lebanon. When the deportees began walking toward the Lebanese
checkpoints, Lebanon responded by ordering its military to block access routes
and prevent the deportees from leaving the border region. Stranded just next
to the town of Marj al-Zuhur, they were, indeed, in no man's land.

It would be easy to see this as the abandonment of life to an extreme space
of utter vulnerability. But contrary to the passivity often associated with one of
Agamben's quintessential spaces where life is left bare, the camp set up by the
deportees in the locked territory between the Israeli and Lebanese forces—
which they called Mukhayyam al-ʿAwda, the "Camp of Return"—became a
focal point of political action. Both Hezbollah and the Iranian Revolutionary
Guards forged close relations with Palestinians in the camp; this relationship
proved critical in shaping the tactical abilities of Palestinian resistance groups
in the 1990s and 2000s and launched some of the deportees into political lead-
ership positions. The snowy mountainous camp attracted intense international
media attention and diplomatic pressure eventually forced Israel to shorten the
expulsion period. Overall, the deportees spent twelve months on this mountaintop. Geopolitics, mobility, political agency, temporality, and even climate
played significant roles in shaping the no man's land inhabited by the 415 Palestinians in southern Lebanon.

How, then, can a study of abandonment account for these spatial, temporal, and political contingencies? How can we write abandonment that is not
abstracted into metaphysical realms or extended to the degree that it loses
sight of those experiencing its sharpest effects? The answer is partly found
in a more rigorous engagement with the care that is withdrawn, as well as
the care that remains once the sovereign turns away. Abandonment appears

as deeply visceral, a haptic experience that makes its marks on bodies and matter, on relations and symbolic representations. Spatializing abandonment brings to the fore a granular and situated understanding of its actualities and its effects on bodies, environments, and objects. This regards the obvious marks of physical degradation and injury, as well as more subtle traces that are coded into seemingly innocuous fabrics of life. Uncaring has, in other words, a place.

Tracing no man's land and the logic of uncaring is not, however, just a matter of empirical rigor. The critical task requires a constant movement from the grounded realities of life and matter toward a rethinking of the conceptual conventions that set the limits of inquiry. Borrowing Athena Athanasiou's formulation, we could think of this problem by distinguishing between abandonment as "being" and abandonment as "becoming" or "being made."[3] "Being abandoned" relates to an almost primordial, foundational condition in the constitution of the subject, whereas "becoming abandoned" assumes an ensuing, derivative process of deprivation, abdication, and exposure. As the spaces documented throughout this book attest, this task is both intellectually significant and politically urgent.

More specifically, what is required is a clearer and more precise distinction between uncaring and established ways of understanding abandonment. To begin with, the radical uncaring I write about here diverges from late modern forms of neoliberal governance in which the state seeks to free itself from the various responsibilities of maintaining its subjects while "conferring upon those subjects themselves the daily obligations of self-maintenance and self-regulation."[4] As Elizabeth Povinelli observes, late liberal abandonment never fully abdicates care. It is instead driven by deep care, although that care is directed at maximizing economic and cultural values, so long, of course, as they flow from subordinate to dominant groups.[5] Transferring the responsibility of care to nonstate actors or to individuals has radically upended political structures and left millions adrift, bereft of basic services and securities. But care still remains, even when it is administered—poorly, cynically—by others.

Second, uncaring is not simply synonymous with biopolitical abandonment. The latter results from structures and institutions that are deeply invested in the care for human life, even though this care often manifests in violence, exploitation, and death.[6] Camps, plantations, and colonies are the quintessential sites of these violent abandonments.[7] More recently, humanitarian interventions and bordering practices have led to the policing of life in service of securitizing the nation-state. But almost every aspect life in these spaces—the camp, the border zone—is regulated to an extreme degree: calories are counted, productivity is measured, and movements constantly monitored.[8] This is not uncaring; if anything, it is a modality driven by excessive care, by forms of care that intrude, punish, and violate. The condition that emerges in the spaces I write about is related but importantly different: Uncaring entails a more profound severing of any pretense of responsibility or concern toward a clearly defined space and the lives entangled with it. It is abandonment without care.

Plotting a fuller history of no man's land—and the sovereign logic of uncaring that governs it—makes it impossible to confine analysis to metaphysical or existential contemplation. Instead, we must confront an utterly granular reality of uncaring: messy, historically specific, and politically grounded. At heart are the stories of those who abandon, those subjected to abandonment's realities, and the spaces where abandonment rules supreme.

3

Gestures of Uncaring

Abandonment is the foundational act of no man's land. What constitutes abandonment is far less obvious, though, ranging from spectacular evacuations and massive troop withdrawals to seemingly almost invisible acts, like the elimination of a postal code. Such acts of state are one way of documenting and thinking through abandonment. Gestures are another: some look away, and others go to great lengths to renunciate. Whether they are expressed through a sovereign refusal to extend protections or through the more mundane aestheticizations of violence, the gestures of abandonment are more than metaphoric. They reveal logics of power that are deeply embedded in the operational context of governance, so subtle as to seem trivial.[1] Gestures can also, as Erin Manning points out, "creat[e] sites of dissonance, staging disturbances that open experience to new modes of expression."[2] Uncaring emerges from such gestural inquiry as an embodied form, partly performed by organs of the state but often imperceptibly lodged in shrugs, raised eyebrows, and blank stares.

There is no grand manifesto of uncaring. Formal declarations, governmental policy papers, and legislation rarely state an overt intention to abandon lands and lives. Like in early photographs of no man's land, uncaring appears obliquely, in the multiple ways it forms habits and postures, fleetingly appearing in myriad practices and materials of everyday life. What follows is an effort to mark a few gestures of uncaring, small acts that can too easily be shrugged off, dismissed as minor moments in more consequential geopolitical dynamics. Yet in the absence of other, more explicit markers, a shrug can plainly signal the edge of care.

Looking Away

"Dead zone" is a phrase many Cypriots use to refer to the UN-controlled strip that partitions the island. The term is not solely intended to memorialize those who were killed during the intercommunal conflicts of the early 1960s and the Turkish military invasion in 1974. As the architectural and urban critic Stavros Stavrides observed, for so many Cypriots, "dead zone" is a direct expression of loss, a lamentation of a space severed from life. Residents of Nicosia in particular, he writes, "understand the buffer zone as a tangible indication of a process through which part of their city was killed, deadened."[3]

Such expressions of loss are often intimate and personal. When this powerful experience is shared, it circulates mostly among family members and close friends.[4] This is not to say that the dead zone is somehow mute or invisible in the public realm. It requires, though, sharper attentiveness to features that are perhaps less obvious. Dead ends, for example, are a striking reminder of the dead zone: Dozens of streets and alleys in the city end abruptly with barricades made up of an assortment of stacked barrels, concrete walls, barbed wire, metal gates, and elevated guard positions. This assemblage has become all too familiar in the material composition of violent geographies around the world. However, those who live in Nicosia don't spend their days staring mournfully at the barricades. In fact, over the years, the fortified positions and barriers have gradually faded from sight, melted into the materiality of the city around them, almost to the point that they seem not to be there at all.

This invisibility can be jarring. I once met a group of local researchers at a small bar on Manis Street in Nicosia's Old City. The weather that evening was warm, and we sat outside at one of the tables that spilled into the quiet alley in front. About an hour into our conversation, I realized that the white wall behind us was a concrete barricade that marked the edge of the dead zone. The very possibility of placing tables out into the road in front of the bar depended on the fact that there was nowhere for vehicles to go. At different points on the wall, someone placed red and green planters with lush vines drooping down beneath thick coils of barbed wire.

On the one hand, the indifference with which everybody around went about drinking in such close proximity to the most obvious marker of conflict in Cyprus is utterly predictable. Stavrides suggests that these casual urban integrations of the dead zone into everyday life manifest what Georg Simmel describes as "blasé attitude," although urban apathy in this case is rooted in a very different context. In his 1903 essay, Simmel describes the indifference that is produced by "violent stimuli" of the modern capitalist metropolis.[5] The leisure of having a drink under the barbed wire of the dead zone is made possible, instead, by the overbearing presence of a highly militarized environment. When violent rupture and loss are inescapable in this way—their blunt markers literally blocking the movement of bodies and lines of sight across the city—willful blindness of this sort becomes an essential coping mechanism. Looking away is one response to the intractable violence of the dead zone and to the political stalemate that has left the island divided for decades.

Everyday apathy, however, is not just a matter of individual indifference. During a visit to Cyprus in 2014, I met with Angus Loudon, who was then chief of staff of the UN peacekeeping forces and commander of the British contingent. We sat in a large, sunny office at the UN headquarters, adjacent to the abandoned Nicosia Airport. "Of course the dead zone isn't dead," he said. "It's full of activity and life, but it does have a morbid reputation." Loudon, a tall Scotsman for whom this would be the last deployment before retirement, expressed the view of someone whose time was consumed with overseeing over eight hundred soldiers from twenty-six countries who surveyed, patrolled, and invested substantial resources in the infrastructural upkeep of the zone.[6] Apart from a few farmers with special permits to access fields and pasture, UN personnel are the only ones who move freely and regularly within the dead zone.

But the blue UN flags have come to symbolize the intractability of the partition and the paralysis imposed by the status quo that emerged after the 1974 Turkish invasion. Even though the mandate of UN force was to restore "normal conditions," their ongoing presence in and preservation of the Buffer Zone removes any urgency to resolve the core issues of the conflict, a conundrum that UN officials are not oblivious to.[7] If, on a micro scale, a hipster aesthetic enables young Cypriots to turn their back on the fortified barricades of the Buffer Zone while having a drink, the presence of UN peacekeepers allows political leaders in both parts of the island to adopt similar gestures of looking away. When the international forces clear woodland to prevent wildfires, chase poachers, and even remove rubbish, all other parties can allow themselves to care less. This abdication of sovereign care and everyday indifference go hand in hand in keeping the dead zone dead.

It may seem counterintuitive to linger specifically on the act of looking away. Historically, after all, no man's land was subject to all range of visual surveillance, monitoring, and documentation. Few spaces were recorded as extensively as that space between the trenches of World War I, with thousands of lenses documenting in unprecedented detail its most minute features. Official photographic documentation supplemented other practices of surveillance, from charting and mapping to ballistic calculation diagrams, in addition to millions of photographs, sketches, and drawings produced by soldiers on the front lines for personal rather than tactical use. If anything, this was a space of hypervisibility, often a catastrophic archive of overexposure, as I discussed at length earlier.

Yet the production of invisibility—through gestures that render a space beyond sight and therefore beyond care—is inherent to the visual order that governs no man's land. As Gil Hochberg documented in the context of the Palestinian-Israeli conflict, concealment plays a critical role in producing violent visual regimes.[8] She specifically notes erasure, denial, and obstructions of sight as powerful mechanisms that enable and sustain the willful obliviousness of most Israelis to the lives of Palestinians under occupation. Yet when considering the ways that uncaring lodges itself into the minute, gestural habits of life, we must also remain attuned to more rudimentary practices of concealment, to improvisatory acts like the planters that were placed on the concrete barricade. This is not a laborious act that requires extensive planning or forethought. Not much is needed, it seems—a string of fairy lights over mismatching furniture—to turn the barbed wire into merely another prop in a shabby chic scenery that could easily be found in Lisbon or Los Angeles.

Gestures are minor, merely a matter of posture, the subtle twist of the hand or tilt of the head. One of many nearly imperceptible gestures, looking away seems inconsequential; it is a fleeting moment, but one in which uncaring is revealed as habit. Yet when the abdication of care becomes inseparable from the most minute bodily tendencies, it also becomes harder to recognize, let alone undo. Uncaring becomes an intractable condition, beyond the realm of action and transformation. Gestures of abandonment reach their most perilous effects when they foreclose the future, stifling the ability to imagine alternatives, to peer through the barbed wire or even possess the curiosity to do so. Foreclosure operates in an utterly political realm, but it neuters the impetus for political action. Turning away allows the dead zone to emerge as a lamentable but still tolerable condition that does not necessitate urgent response. Once the dead zone stops being recognized for the violence it harbors, when it becomes a mere spectacle or is reduced to an aesthetic prop, it also forecloses the possibility of change. In these slightest of gestures—the blank stare, the turning of the head—a zone is not only proclaimed dead but also deemed beyond resuscitation.

Renouncing

On October 4, 2015, in the frenzy of sorting out logistics before heading out of Cairo, my friend and longtime collaborator Alasdair Pinkerton got a thirty-nine-word email from an official at the Egyptian embassy in London.

He wanted to let us know that our request to enter Bir Tawil, an unclaimed territory situated on the border between Egypt and Sudan, was rejected. The precise message is worth citing in full (all typos in the original): "I am soory to inform you that the Egyptian authorities in Cairo informed us that they are not going to be able to acoomodate your planed visit to Egypt and grant you the required permissions to continue your journey."

This message marked, in more than one sense, the dead end of a six-thousand-mile journey we undertook in the autumn of that year. Our hope, intentionally phrased in the naivest terms, was to find no man's land. And rather than confine ourselves to the archives, we purposely sought others—artists, forest rangers, political activists, UN peacekeepers—who were able to offer living insights into what the space is and why it matters. We set off from London and traveled through Western Europe, south into the Balkans and across Cyprus. Our final destination was Bir Tawil, a trapezoid-shaped territory on the Egypt-Sudan border, which to this day remains unclaimed by both countries. In quite a literal manner, by rejecting our request, the Egyptian authorities marked the end of the road for our research expedition, forcing us to conclude our journey at a desert checkpoint on the outskirts of Aswan. It was an inglorious spot surrounded by piles of dumped construction waste and flying plastic bags. More than four hundred miles from our intended destination, we were forced to do a U-turn and head back.

On the face of it, we simply joined a long tradition of expeditions that failed to reach their destination, although unlike many of our predecessors, we did not die trying. The moment when an expedition is forced to turn back has become a recurring and conventional motif in the canon of expeditionary tales, and aside from its dramatic effects, it seems to offer few critical insights. However, there was a longer process of exchange and negotiation that preceded this singular moment, which reveals a largely overlooked facet of international relations and state politics: the active unmaking of territorial claims.

In our case, the laconic message was the last in a months-long series of correspondences and conversations undertaken in an effort to receive Egyptian approval for our request to reach Bir Tawil. One element that became obvious during the process was the bewilderment of many Egyptian officials about our destination. Several times during phone calls and face-to-face meetings, our interlocutors—embassy officials, staff at the Egyptian Cultural and Educational Bureau in London—admitted complete ignorance about Bir Tawil, and they had no clue who would even be in a position to grant access to it. In one of these conversations, a secretary at the Egyptian Cultural Bureau admitted she had never heard of the place, but she added: "This sounds like a fun trip. Can I join?"

This recurring bewilderment and bureaucratic confusion are partly due to the murky demarcation of Egypt's southern border. At its core was an 1899 British-Egyptian treaty, which set the border between Egypt and Sudan along the Twenty-Second Parallel.[9] Three years later, however, another document was drawn up by the British. This one noted that a mountain area just south of the Twenty-Second Parallel was home to the nomadic Ababda tribe, who were considered to have stronger links with Egypt than with Sudan. The document stipulated that henceforth, this area—Bir Tawil—should be administered by Egypt. Meanwhile, a much-larger triangle of land north of the Twenty-Second Parallel, named Hala'ib, abutting the Red Sea, was assigned as grazing land for tribes who are largely based in Sudan and thus came under Sudanese jurisdiction.[10] Because of its proximity to the coast and its potential mineral wealth, both countries claimed Hala'ib, and consequently neither has sought to extend its sovereignty over Bir Tawil. It is a historical maze, but from it, a no man's land was born.

For Egyptian officials, our request posed a rather peculiar dilemma. In one phone conversation, a secretary at the Egyptian embassy in London who knew about the southern border and its sensitivities said that he could not issue us a permit to access Bir Tawil because Egypt does not recognize the border territory as part of its sovereign jurisdiction. "This isn't ours, so I can't say you can go," he said. Alasdair was tempted to point out that, by the same token, if Egypt cannot permit access to Bir Tawil, neither can it restrict it, but he kept this observation to himself.

This candid statement from the embassy official reveals a curious relation to no man's land more broadly. There is a vast and extremely diverse scholarly corpus that explores the long history of sovereign claims over territory, the myriad forms it takes, and the challenges it faces by forces of globalization or internal fractures. No man's land shifts this debate in a different direction—from claim making over land to practices of renunciation and processes through which sovereign abdication manifests. In Bir Tawil, this renunciation is driven by geopolitical calculation; elsewhere, tactical military considerations or catastrophic environmental degradation prompted the intentional withdrawal of conventional sovereign presence. No man's land always emerges out of such forms of willful abdication of care and denial of responsibility.

On the face of it, renunciation is not new. Throughout history there have been numerous cases in which territorial claims were ceded as part of broader land treaties, often in exchange for other economic or political assets. But the abandonment of no man's land is not a case of simple exchange of one asset for another. Uncaring, as it is considered throughout this book, is different in that it radically devalues clearly defined space and severs any pretense of sovereign responsibility. Uncaring, in short, results in ultimate disposability.

Severing

The separation wall is the first thing you see at the entrance to Sheikh Sa'ad. Having lived in Jerusalem for years, I've seen its towering concrete slabs numerous times, but here, the wall seems to appear out of nowhere. The narrow road swerves down a steep hill through the densely built streets of Jabal Mukaber, the adjacent Palestinian neighborhood. And then, suddenly, there it is. Trash is the other inescapable feature that dominates this space, piling on both sides of the road and covering the slopes of the hill. Only the area marked off for the military checkpoint stands out for its cleanliness. It is also the only place where pedestrians are able to walk on a proper sidewalk rather than the unpaved side of the road. Not that there is much space along the road either, since it is the only place where vehicles can park. In the summer of 2014, during one of my visits to Sheikh Sa'ad, I walked from my car toward the checkpoint alongside a well-dressed, middle-aged couple. It was Ramadan, and they were going to see family on the other side of the checkpoint, carrying with them a large tray of sweets. The man wore dark blue, neatly pressed trousers, but by the time we got to the gate, they were visibly dusty. He did his best to brush the dust off. "Look," he said, "we have to walk through trash. The indignity of it all."

In many ways, this chaotic scene is emblematic of almost every Palestinian neighborhood in East Jerusalem; everyday city life under occupation. Going by visual cues alone—the trash, the crumbling infrastructure, the ever-present surveillance and oppressive enclosures—it would be nearly impossible to distinguish one side of the wall from the other. As a space that is ostensibly governed by a unique logic of uncaring, is Sheikh Sa'ad really that different from other parts of Palestinian Jerusalem?

Like many places documented in this book, the predicament of Sheikh Sa'ad is partly a matter of historical chance. In 1967, Israel annexed approximately seventy square kilometers of the West Bank to Jerusalem and proclaimed the area subject to Israeli law. The city's new boundary cut through the Arab a-Sawahra area, which comprised several villages on the southeastern periphery and created an artificial distinction between the legal status of its respective residents.[11] Jabal Mukaber was included within the new Jerusalem city limits and its inhabitants recognized as "permanent residents" of the city. Some were also issued Israeli IDs. Sheikh Sa'ad, however, remained formally under the military regime that governed the occupied West Bank.[12] The boundary, as delineated, was nothing more than a line on a map; for the most part, residents' lives were not altered as a result of this exercise in draftsmanship. Family relations, employment patterns, and commercial ties between Sheikh Sa'ad and the adjacent neighborhoods to its west remained as they had been before the Israeli occupation. Only following the general closure imposed on the Occupied Palestinian Territories in 1993, and especially after the outbreak of the Second Palestinian Intifada in 2000, did it become clear that the division was to have far-reaching consequences.

Since the wall enclosed the neighborhood on the hilltop, only residents who held a blue Israeli IDs or residency cards could cross the checkpoint with relative ease into Jerusalem. The checkpoint often closes without warning, and even when it is open, it can take over an hour or more to get through during busy periods. Nevertheless, being in possession of the right document means that schools, universities, and hospitals are within reach. Nihad, a teacher who lives in Sheikh Sa'ad but works at a high school in Jabal Mukaber, got into the habit of carrying his family's garbage with him every morning because rubbish isn't collected in Sheikh Sa'ad and is usually burned in large containers. In the internal hierarchy that the Israeli regime created, Nihad's blue ID means he is relatively better off. Approximately half of Sheikh Sa'ad's residents held green IDs issued by the Palestinian Authority, which meant they were largely dependent on a convoluted permit regime managed by the Israeli Civil Administration. Work permits and access to education and health-care facilities were all managed through a byzantine system of requests, proofs, forms, and authorizations.[13] The trials of the living also apply to the dead. For generations, Sheikh Sa'ad relied on the cemetery in Jabal Mukaber for its burials, given the lack of space in the crammed neighborhood. When I last visited, grieving families are forced to apply for a permit from the Israeli Civil Administration to bring the body of the deceased through the checkpoint. As the Israeli authorities usually grant permits for only fifty people daily from Sheikh Sa'ad, many family members are unable to join the traditional rituals of mourning.

Yet even these conditions that endemically hinder access to basic services and freedoms are hardly out of the ordinary. The Israeli regime in the Occupied Palestinian Territories has normalized the relegation of entire populations to life on the "threshold of catastrophe," even if it inflicts these harms with varying intensities.[14] What makes Sheikh Sa'ad unique in this Israeli matrix of control is not the invasive or punitive forms that govern it; numerous other places experience these harms more acutely. Instead, Sheikh Sa'ad stands out because it captures an extraordinary sovereign effort to normalize its abandonment.

In early April 2020, shortly after Israel imposed strict national lockdown measures to stave off the COVID-19 pandemic, the main water pipe into Sheikh Sa'ad burst. Even after it was cut off from Jerusalem by the wall, the neighborhood remained reliant on the city's municipal water company. However, when residents called for the burst pipe to be repaired, they were told that the pandemic posed a grave risk to engineers and that the municipality would not be able to resolve the issue. No one seemed concerned that Israeli stay-at-home policies meant Sheikh Sa'ad was without water, that they exacerbated existing shortages of fresh food and put health services beyond reach. When the Palestinian Authority imposed its own lockdown in neighborhoods under its control, even using the treacherous road into Palestinian areas farther east was no longer an option. "The neighborhood is turning into an island," one resident texted me. Later the same day, he called to say that things were getting desperate: "We're being suffocated. We can't breathe."[15] It was eventually up to one of the residents, Daoud, to bring his tools and fix the pipe himself. It took another week and urgent appeals from human rights organizations to force the military to open the checkpoint again and allow minimal services to resume.[16]

This sequence of events, one of so many, distills the logic of uncaring as well as its less obvious ambiguities. The denial of basic resources and the indifference to the consequence of this denial, is not intended to punish the residents of Sheikh Sa'ad. There is no corrective or coercive intention behind the refusal to aid. It is driven, instead, by systematic abandonment that undoes the fundamental relation of care between a sovereign regime and those subjected to it. As was acutely evident during those ten days in Sheikh Sa'ad, uncaring results in lives left precariously exposed.

But what if the sovereign wields care not toward benevolent ends but as part of a punitive logic of policing, restriction, and violence? For most Palestinians, encounters with the care of the Israeli state often take the latter, punitive form. In light of that, being relegated to a space of uncaring may also offer some reprieve from the violent expressions of care, from invasive surveillance and acute restrictions that dominate almost every aspect of life. Home demolitions, for example, have become a pervasive expression of the restrictive spatial regime in Palestinian neighborhoods of Jerusalem. Between 2000 and 2017, the Israeli authorities demolished 112 houses in Jabal Mukaber after they were deemed to be built without necessary legal permits. During the same period, only one home was demolished in Sheikh Sa'ad.[17] Speaking to several family members whose home was under the threat of demolition in Jabal Mukaber, I asked about Sheikh Sa'ad. "Over there they have freedom," one of the men said. "But they're paying a heavy price for that freedom."

The abandonment of Sheikh Saʿad and its isolation from the rest of Jerusalem restricted the mobility of its residents and their access to basic services. But the same logic also spared the neighborhood from one of the most insidious expressions of sovereign control. This is the Janus face of uncaring: it is a naked form of abandonment that has no interest in punitive correction, in financial gains or political advantage. The engineers who refused to repair the water pipe to Sheikh Saʿad, the housing inspectors for the municipality, and the military officers who ignored pleas from residents all contributed, in their own way, to the systemic logic that set Sheikh Saʿad unambiguously outside the realm of care.

Shrugging Off

General Enrique Mora came prepared for our meeting. For nearly two hours, in a wood-paneled board room at a military academy in the north of Bogotá, the retired head of the Colombian armed forces offered a detailed historical review of the violent conflict in the country. Assuming a professorial posture, he was keen to address the strategic conditions and calculations that led the Colombian state to abandon a large region in the center of the country. In November 1998, the newly elected government of President Andrés Pastrana sought to end the violent conflict that had ravaged Colombia for decades. To facilitate peace talks with FARC guerrilla forces, Pastrana agreed to designate an area of over twenty-six thousand square miles, larger than Switzerland, as a safe zone for rebel forces. The population of this region, approximately 150,000 people, had no say in the matter. As far as the state was concerned, FARC was the region's de facto ruler. The withdrawal only made that official. For more than three years, until February 2002, the area was formally known as the Zona de Distensión, roughly translated as the de-escalation zone. Most people in the region, however, refer to it as *el despeje*, "the clearance."[18]

Mora oversaw the withdrawal of troops from five municipalities that constituted the area, although he was keen to stress that the decision to remove government forces was taken by the president despite the military's objections. As he saw it, "there was a great deal of naivete" behind the withdrawal and demonstrated lack of understanding of the real intentions FARC. The guerrilla, Mora insisted, were simply using the process to regroup and strengthen their military capacity and the trafficking networks that funded their operations.

Mora remembered in great detail the withdrawal of the infantry battalion from the town of San Vicente del Caguán, despite early promises that town centers would remain under government control. For most of our conversation he was standing at a whiteboard and often accompanying his narrative with bullet points and sketched timelines. He recalled how the military withdrawal was soon followed by a decimation of other representatives of the state—police, judges, prosecutors. In his telling, FARC used the freedom it was granted in the Clearance Zone (known formally as Zona de Despeje de San Vicente del Caguán) to gradually close in on the country's capital. For its own part, the Colombian military used that period to initiate a major strategic restructuring program, but Mora remained convinced that the Clearance Zone was a failed experiment. In many respects, his position echoed familiar critiques of Pastrana's policies, but the process seems to have affirmed those who doubted the process: negotiations with the guerrilla ultimately collapsed.

At the end of our meeting, as I was gathering my notes and getting ready to leave, we spoke briefly about his time as Colombia's ambassador to South Korea. He noted that several times during his tenure, he had visited the Demilitarized Zone that divides the peninsula. When I asked whether he saw any similarities between the DMZ and the Colombian Clearance Zone, he was quick to dismiss the parallel. "Korea's Demilitarized Zone was the product of war and a covenant made and led by the military. But it was a war situation, a real war," he explained. The Colombian region was just abandoned to the control of the guerrillas.

Our conversation came at the end of a three-week research trip that was mostly spent in the former Clearance Zone, where I met people in communities that experienced it firsthand. I wondered out loud whether the parallels to Korea are found not in strategic levels of policy but in the mundane experiences of farmers who lost their fields or villagers living in fear of another escalation. It was about the shared experience of being abandoned. After a few long seconds of awkward silence, the general shrugged.

This silent gesture did not appear in the audio recording of the meeting, but years later, I am still struck by it. In the Greek, *gerere*—from which *gesture* is derived—means "to bear," "to carry," but also "to show," "to reveal," "to perform the function."[19] Mora's shrug was revealing. It was indicative of a deeper political logic that wrote off 150,000 people in five municipalities for over three years, not through a genocidal plan of elimination, but simply through a minor gesture—individual, nearly imperceptible—that articulated in the most unambiguous manner the complete absence of care.

4

Rock Bottom

Rarely is it possible to follow, almost in real time, the making of no man's land. Abdication can seem protracted and hidden in geopolitical wrangling and diplomatic machinations. Yet uncaring is a concrete reality in Rukban, an encampment housing tens of thousands of displaced Syrians stranded in the no man's land between Syria and Jordan. This chapter documents how this place was transformed from a remote desert crossing to a space governed by extreme abandonment, by a deliberate and calculated refusal of any sovereign power to care for its inhabitants. Rukban reveals, in the most concrete terms, the logic of uncaring in our political present.

It was an error, but as errors go, it was a telling one. The transcript of a conversation between US Ambassador James Jeffrey and Josh Rogin, a *Washington Post* columnist, at the 2019 Aspen Security Forum, replaced the name Rukban with "rock bottom."[1] Syrians began arriving in the remote desert region of Rukban in 2013, fleeing the violence that was raging across the country and hoping to cross the border into Jordan. Yet years later, "rock bottom" seems an accurate description of the situation that evolved since.

Getting to Rukban requires a lengthy and perilous journey through the southern Syrian desert, but for two years, until late March 2015, it was one of the only open border crossings into Jordan. Those fleeing the battles in eastern Syria, primarily from rural parts of eastern Homs province, had few alternatives, and a growing network of smugglers was there to facilitate their journey while profiting off their need.[2] Already coping with hundreds of thousands of refugees, Jordan began imposing greater entry restrictions in the Rukban crossing. These applied specifically to Palestinians fleeing the Syrian battles, who had to undergo lengthier vetting procedures. As a result, thousands of people found themselves stranded near the crossing for extended periods. Provisional dwellings were set up, and an encampment emerged approximately a kilometer south of the Syrian border, adjacent to the large earthen berm that runs parallel to the border. By mutual agreement, the Syrians and the Jordanians had erected berms on their territory an equal distance from this section of the borderline, creating a no man's land in between.[3] From 2015 to mid-2016, as more people were fleeing areas under Islamic State control and the multiple-sided military campaign that was expanding throughout eastern Syria, the population of the camp grew from several thousand to an estimated seventy thousand.[4] A city emerged in no man's land.

During this early period, aid trickled into Rukban from Jordan, with some additional supplies being smuggled through the Syrian front lines. Yet following a suicide attack that killed seven Jordanian soldiers at the Rukban crossing in June 2016, the Jordanian border was completely sealed.[5] Unable to cross south into Jordan, and fearing violent retaliation from the Assad regime if they made their way back north, those in Rukban were trapped. Conditions in the camp were already harsh, but the closure of the border blocked what little aid had been able to reach it before then. Citing heightened concerns over the presence of terrorist forces in Rukban, Jordan allowed only two aid deliveries in the year following the attack, and only a handful in the years since.[6] Diminishing access to clean water, food, and medicine was accompanied by a collapse in personal safety and security, with increasing reports of violence amid growing competition between militias for control over residents' lives.[7] "Starving to death, no—but it's gotten to a dangerous point," Sheikh Muayyad Muhammad al-Obeid, head of Rukban's refugee affairs council, said in a 2017 interview. "A person needs to turn vicious to eat. There's no work, so where does he go, he needs to eat . . . stealing, looting, begging—that's what things have come to here."[8]

Harsh enclosure regimes, almost complete dependency on humanitarian aid, and the increasing precarity of life are not particular to Rukban. Is it, therefore, just another iteration of the catastrophic archipelago of camps that has come to define the early part of the twenty-first century? Practitioners working in Rukban were wary of drawing such parallels. "I'm not sure *camp* is the right word, to be honest," Juliette Touma, UNICEF's spokesperson in Amman said. "So, I'd look for another word—between quotation marks, 'berm' or 'the area between Jordan and Syria,' but it's not a camp."[9] Such hesitation is not just about semantics. In a conversation we later had, Touma explained that Rukban doesn't have any of the systems and infrastructures that sustain other camps. Official avenues of recourse and assistance offered in other camps by either government agencies or nongovernmental groups, limited as they may be, are simply unavailable in Rukban. "Here it's like a dead end," she said.[10]

What emerges in Rukban is a systematic and extreme abdication of care, which sets it apart from myriad other spaces of incarceration and exclusion. Like other places throughout this book, abandonment is not a matter of failure or accident, but a premeditated consequence of deliberate abdication of care and the duties that it is assumed to entail.

Rather than the action of a single sovereign, the abandonment of Rukban is the result of a wide geopolitical power struggle. When, in 2016, US forces captured the al-Tanf border post a few miles east of Rukban, Syrians fled to the area in large numbers hoping that the American presence would offer greater protection from the violence elsewhere. A fifty-five-kilometer "de-confliction zone" around al-Tanf was established in June 2017, which one researcher described as "an isolated bubble of Coalition-held land, jutting out into the Syrian desert from the tri-border area."[11] In practice, American and Syrian rebel forces retain effective control of the area. Yet like all other state actors, the United States has so far refused to assume responsibility for Rukban. Since seizing the al-Tanf base, the United States has taken measures to prevent any violation of the zone's perimeter but at the same time has rejected direct responsibility to care for Rukban. Ambassador Jeffrey reiterated this position at the Aspen Security Forum, where he argued that the United States could not provide humanitarian assistance, lest it give the impression that its forces would stay in al-Tanf "forever." According to Jeffrey, those trapped in Rukban have no right to American aid. He suggested that if the American government does feed the people, Russia would argue that the United States has become an occupying power, which would trigger legal obligations to the camp's residents.[12] Interests abound, but care for Rukban remains in short supply.

When asked to comment on the situation in Rukban, Bill Frelick, director of the refugee program at Human Rights Watch, called the idea of a "no man's land," where no state is responsible for the rights of those fleeing conflict, a "legal fiction." "Where a state exercises control over people, they have a responsibility to protect and uphold the rights of those people. You can't declare a stretch that's a rights-free zone," he added.[13] Frelick is correct to point out that a no man's land lacks any formal legal status. But the assumption that such spaces are somehow designated as "rights-free zones" misses the critical challenge that no man's land poses. Looking through hundreds of official statements made about Rukban by state actors determining its future, one would be hard pressed to find a single statement that explicitly rejects the rights of those trapped between the Syrian and Jordanian forces. Take, for example, a series of joint statements made by the Russian and Syrian Coordination Headquarters in the spring of 2020, as the coronavirus pandemic was spreading in encampments for internally displaced Syrians.[14] Although the texts are an explicit part of the Russian-Syrian effort to lay the blame for Rukban's plight on US obstruction, they repeatedly mobilize the promise of care as an inherent component in the obligation of the Syrian state to its subjects. The rights of those trapped in Rukban are never simply denied, but they can be ensured only outside Rukban, in the territory fully controlled by the Syrian regime.

Rights, at least nominally, are recognized. Yet no actor with sovereign claims over Rukban, or one with de facto control over the territory in which it sits, has accepted the responsibility to protect those rights and ensure they can be exercised. In other words, the fundamental relation of care, which assumes the sovereign duty to manage life, has been severed.[15] Care was to be provided by either someone else or somewhere else. Jesse Marks, who worked for the UN High Commissioner for Refugees in Amman when conditions in Rukban deteriorated following the 2016 border closure, described the geopolitical debate surrounding Rukban as an "example of states casting off responsibility. . . . [A]rguments are being made as to why the state is absolved of its responsibility to help these people. Which is what truly makes it no man's land."[16]

From Siege to Abdication

Rukban is not, of course, wholly unprecedented. In an extensive analysis of Israel's logic of rule in the Occupied Palestinian Territories, Ariella Azoulay and Adi Ophir focus specific attention to the abandonment of Gaza.[17] They document Israel's refusal to accept responsibility over the territory and, specifically, to recognize a duty of care toward its large refugee population.[18] Dispelling any assumption that this is a recent development, they recall a caricature published in an Israeli newspaper after Israel occupied the Gaza Strip in 1967, which portrayed Palestinian refugees as people trapped inside a football, with Egyptian, Syrian, and Jordanian feet kicking it to and fro. However, while the abdication of responsibility was inherent to both the Egyptian period of governance in Gaza (1948–1967) and the first decades of the Israeli occupation, the second Palestinian Intifada that erupted in 2000 turned abandonment into an official Israeli policy, a policy made explicit by the 2005 withdrawal of Israeli military ground presence and the removal of several thousand Jewish settlers.

Rather than simply a policy of indifference, the abandonment of Gaza in the years that followed the Israeli redeployment constituted a complex and invasive system of rule: lines were drawn around and through the crammed territory to designate and differentiate intensities of securitization and restrictions of mobility. Who can move, how far, and for what purpose are still issues of prime concern to Israeli officials. Israel continues to monitor the territory's population through numerous parameters that calculate health, nutrition, employment, and access to goods.[19] Despite the 2005 elimination of the Israeli Civil Administration—the military bureaucracy that managed everyday life in the strip since 1967—Gaza's electrical grid and telecommunications are still reliant on Israeli suppliers. Yet as Azoulay and Ophir point out, the extensive networks of governance were paralleled with a drastic narrowing of the sovereign relations to those under its control: "No longer perceived as a subject with an identity who must be subjugated but also cared for, the Palestinian was tagged as a client of humanitarian aid, a hunted person, a name on an elimination list, a dot on the electronic display in an operations room or a military pilot's cockpit. Despite having shirked its duties towards some of its subjects, the Israeli regime did not relinquish the sovereign's ultimate right: the authority to take life."[20]

Despite its violence, the regime of abandonment in Gaza is predicated on the simultaneity of military force and the biopolitical management of life through an extensive humanitarian operation. It is this humanitarian apparatus that enables the Israeli regime to abdicate its care for Gaza by effectively taking on the duties that would have otherwise been part of the sovereign state obligation. Humanitarian aid organizations, in turn, have been internalized into the Israeli rule over Gaza, enabling Israel to maintain the strip on the "brink of catastrophe." Azoulay and Ophir situate Gaza in a threshold condition in which controlled scarcity is not a failure of governance, but a normalized mechanism that allows only the bare minimal human existence. "This kind of governance through catastrophization," they conclude, "is a new component in a new economy of violence."[21]

On the face of it, there are clear parallels between Rukban and the realities of life in Gaza. Both feature similar conditions of besieged existence and almost complete dependency on external aid, which, in both cases, is weaponized as a means of exerting political pressure and achieving geopolitical ends. Albeit by different actors and in distinct geopolitical circumstances, abandonment has been normalized into a system of rule. No longer an indication of political failure or error, abandonment functions as an organizing principle for a whole set of political practices, mechanisms, and procedures, structuring discursive and physical environments. In short, it has effectively become a governing logic.

This shift is indicative of a broader normalization of abandonment as part of contemporary modalities of what Ophir defines as the "catastrophic state."

"For the providential state formation," he writes, "the abandonment of a designated population is always an aberration of the system; for the catastrophic state formation, it is the fundamental rule upon which the system rests."[22] Along with destruction and exclusion, abandonment is conceived here as a disaster-producing apparatus that is employed and administered by the catastrophic state. Contrary to the spectacular violence that was responsible for the spread of disasters in premodern times—plagues, floods, genocidal wars—abandonment produces disasters through absence, by the catastrophic state's systematic withdrawal of care and renunciation of obligations toward a population under its governance. As such, it is often highly elusive yet also more pervasive: it appears in a broader array of political configurations and is not confined solely to the most obvious and extreme cases of the twentieth-century totalitarian state.

There is, however, a critical difference that sets Rukban apart from Gaza and numerous other spaces like it, zones that have been reduced to almost absolute dependency on humanitarian aid. Put simply, care functions differently in each of these spaces. The regime of abandonment that governs Gaza is deeply invasive and utterly involved: it administers the most minute aspects of life, calculating calories, births, and unemployment rates; it monitors movement, intensities, and proximities; and it concerns itself with the full spectrum of materialities that constitute every space—from the density of vegetation on the surface and fishing practices out at sea to wind directions and their effect on potential "incendiary kites" set off by Palestinian protestors to ignite fields of Israeli communities across the fence that surrounds Gaza. In this guise, abandonment is folded into a punitive logic of siege: its existence depends on the presence of the sovereign, the constant investment of resources and the continual involvement in the management of life, even if that life is kept enclosed at a distance and held on the verge of catastrophe. Israel, in other words, never severed its care for Gaza, violent and punitive as its care indeed is.

Rukban, in contrast, encapsulates uncaring in its most naked form. Conceptually, it reveals a different relation between abandonment and care. As noted before, both beneficent and malevolent shepherds wield care in forging their relationship with their flocks: the good shepherd uses care toward providential ends and the bad shepherd wields it in the service of punitive violence, cruelty, and, in its extreme, genocidal ends. One makes life, the other takes life. Despite their obvious differences, care remains a central pillar in both, underpinning the relation between sovereign and subjects. In Rukban, as in other spaces of uncaring that are documented throughout this book, abandonment emerges as a systematic abdication of care, almost to the point at which it is severed altogether. Unlike the Syrian regime's violent effort to use humanitarian logics to solidify sovereignty elsewhere in Syria,[23] Rukban is explicitly defined by the absence of aid and the almost complete refusal to allow humanitarian assistance from reaching those trapped on the border. When, in mid-August 2019, a UN convoy was finally allowed into Rukban, it brought with it no food, medical supplies, or other essentials. Instead, its mission was to assess the willingness of people to return to areas under the control of the Syrian regime.[24] In doing so, it reinforced the particular logic of Rukban's abandonment: anyone seeking care can hope to find it only elsewhere.

Humanitarian Purgatory

Just because the sovereign abdicates its care does not mean that others cease to try to fill the voids left by its withdrawal. But uncaring as it is considered throughout this book is not reducible to neoliberal delegation of care to market forces of capital, nor is it the result of structural state weakness that cripples its ability to extend resources and assert its care. In all cases, the ruling apparatus possesses the capabilities of providing care and at times, an interest in doing so, but instead chooses to abandon. Those who remain in the space of uncaring are left to fend for themselves, often relying on alternative networks of support: armed groups, criminal cartels, aid organizations and intimate kinships have all emerged in the spaces I document here, on their own or more often, in tandem. At times, though, the state not only abdicates its care for a given territory and its population but also seeks to ensure that others won't be able to care in its place. That is the case in Rukban.

Explaining the refusal of state actors to resolve the paralysis engulfing the camp, one diplomat noted that Rukban is deliberately kept "on the verge of catastrophe." It was a practical diagnostic rather than a political analysis: the last major convoy reached the population trapped in the camp in early February 2019.[25] The reduced and intermittent presence of the few humanitarian organizations that managed to continue operating after the Jordanian border was closed in 2016, ceased almost completely two years later. A UNICEF-run clinic on the Jordanian border was the sole address for medical emergencies, but it, too, was forced to shut when coronavirus precautionary measures were introduced in the first weeks of the pandemic. To avoid starvation and overcome severe medical shortages, those trapped in Rukban came to rely exclusively on smuggling networks operating from Palmyra. A market that operates in the northern part of the encampment reportedly sells medicine, food, and nonfood items, but at exorbitant prices.[26]

At its peak, Rukban housed over seventy thousand internally displaced

Syrians with no reliable means to provide for their basic needs, yet the camp never became a major humanitarian hub. Instead, and this has become a specific challenge since 2016, Rukban stands out because it lacks almost any access to humanitarian aid. In other international emergencies, humanitarian groups are the ones that are assumed to pick up the pieces when the state cannot or will not. As the past half century has demonstrated time and again, this is a deeply problematic prospect. Reducing entire populations to mere recipients of aid can itself become a catastrophic governing logic that strips people from their political subjectivity and agency. In turn, dependency on aid can be used to exert political pressure and gain geopolitical advantage, to penalize and to incentivize. While these critiques of humanitarian logic are important, what is striking is that Rukban's population doesn't seem to merit even that type of response. The people there exist below the threshold of humanitarian intervention, not because their catastrophe is illegible or insignificant, but because humanitarian intervention—even if it is delegated to others—requires a minimal extension of care. The overarching logic that governs Rukban, in contrast, is radical uncaring.

Aid encapsulates the radical abdication of care in Rukban, and all actors in the region have been implicated in this power play. Since closing the border, Jordan has maintained that Rukban is in Syrian territory and therefore the responsibility of the Syrian government.[27] Two months after the border was closed, Jordan agreed to allow a single shipment of food and hygiene kits, but even then, it sought a mechanical solution that would keep direct contact to a minimum. Two seventy-meter-high cranes were brought to the border and hauled the parcels across.[28] The UN World Food Programme, which funded and organized the delivery, released a statement thanking the Jordanian government and military for facilitating the drop-off. Distribution, the statement added, would be monitored remotely from the Jordanian side of the border. These elaborate administrative and logistical procedures reveal a rather blunt reality: the people of Rukban were deemed, quite literally, untouchable.

The mechanics of aid delivery—the refusal to allow for even minimal human contact with those trapped in Rukban—captures a deeper political logic that systematically abdicates care in clearly defined spaces of abandonment. Jordan is not alone in wielding this logic; every other state actor that operates in the region seems to have eagerly embraced this position, even if their actions don't take the blunt form of a large yellow crane. Since the early days of the conflict, the Syrian regime highlighted its aim of reasserting full sovereignty over its territory, especially regaining control of its borders.[29] However, claims for legitimate territorial sovereignty were never met with a willingness to fulfill fundamental duties of care. Through its control of all major transportation routes crossing the desert, the Assad regime effectively blocks all regular humanitarian access to Rukban. With backing from Russia, the Syrian regime justifies the blockade by arguing that militant groups and rebel militias have found shelter in the region and will pose a threat to aid conveys entering Rukban.[30]

Since humanitarian aid was halted, Rukban's residents have depended almost solely on smuggling routes that brought in food and medical supplies from regime-held territories. Mouaz Mustafa heads the Syrian Emergency Task Force (SETF), a nongovernmental organization based in Washington, DC. In addition to supporting civil society efforts across Syria, SETF has smuggled basic goods into Rukban. Mustafa says that the regime's recent crackdown on smuggling has been catastrophic. Before, smugglers would use what means they could to bring goods from Damascus into the camp, often paying off guards at regime-run checkpoints. Prices were still inflated and quality control nonexistent. But they made do amid the stalemate over access to Rukban between the United States, Syria and Russia. Then, in autumn 2019, guards stopped accepting bribes. Experienced and well-networked smugglers are no longer able to access Rukban through their typical routes. One of two bakeries in the camp had to close, and residents have taken to mixing water with stale bread in lieu of flour.

Care is not completely absent but tactically withdrawn. In mid-February 2017, Russian and Syrian officials announced the opening of "humanitarian corridors" that would provide access and support to the thousands of internally displaced Syrians who were trapped on the border. The access points were set up at the northern edge of the fifty-five-kilometer de-escalation zone that surrounds Rukban. Slick promotion videos posted on social media by the Russian Defense Ministry proudly feature the "reception centers" or "reconciliation centers," as they are referred to by Russian outlets. Guarded by Russian military police forces, each of the two centers included medical facilities and a registration tent with neat rows of white plastic chairs facing the desk of a Syrian government official. This kind of performance of bureaucratic competence and the capacity to deliver care is more than mere cynical propaganda. It charts the exact line where care ends and no man's land begins. It articulates both the abdication of care from the territory that lies to its south, and it signals to those residing on the border that their only hope of accessing humanitarian aid must involve a return to areas held by the Assad regime. According to the Syrian state, those in Rukban who want care can access it, but only outside the space of uncaring.

It is worth spelling out more explicitly what counts as care in this case. A statement from the Russian and Syrian Coordination Headquarters suggested that every Syrian who wishes to enter the government-controlled territory will find that "the doors are always open. All necessary conditions for a decent accommodation have been already created. Refugees from the al-Tanf zone will be provided with the necessary humanitarian, medical and social assistance."[31] The implication is that care is not confined to addressing medical needs and providing humanitarian services, but extends to social and material necessities like housing. Care is a promise that foundational needs of security, health, and well-being will be provided and assured; care is the promise of the social contract.

But reentering the realm of care also means that one is once again at the mercy of the same ruling apparatus that has used care to its most catastrophic ends. Specifically, since the early days of the conflict in Syria, the promise of medical care was used by the regime to torture and kill thousands who were suspected of participation in opposition activism.[32] Leaving Rukban means submitting to the mercy of this care. Residents still inside Rukban testified that cell phone communication with returnees is virtually cut off once they cross into government territory. They spoke of families separated upon arrival, with women and children held apart from men.[33] Reports have suggested that some of those who have left Rukban and returned to regime-held territory were subjected to detention, forced conscription, and even death.[34] These harms, which have become so routinized in the Syrian regime's logic of governance since 2011, are not antithetical to care. Instead, they demonstrate how care and violence are conjoined almost to the point that they are no longer distinguishable.

Given the harms that potentially await them on the other side of the "humanitarian corridor," it is perhaps not surprising that those who remain in Rukban would rather contend with the harsh realities of uncaring. It is a cruel choice: stay in purgatory or try your chances in hell.

One response to this reality, in which those who have been pushed beyond the realm of care meet neither the threshold of humanitarian subjects nor that of political agents, is to assume that they have been reduced to mere bare life. But even the violent reduction of human life to sheer survival—the sovereign stance of "letting die"[35]—requires at least a minimal effort to quantify the conditions that sustain life, to monitor and regularly ensure that life is maintained and that death on a mass scale is avoided. As Achille Mbembe argues, modernity is premised on a plethora of "death-worlds" in which whole populations are subjected to "conditions of life conferring upon them the status of living dead": plantations, colonies, concentration camps.[36] In some of these spaces, monitoring and regulation of life is carried out by the ruling apparatus itself, by state bureaucracy, by police or military forces. In other cases, care is delegated to others, from private contractors to aid agencies and humanitarian organization. Either way, in all these geographies of terror and death, the management of life or its disposability is ultimately bound up in the extension of care, even if care often takes atrocious forms.

Rukban's residents are not reduced to "bare life" in this care-full biopolitical sense. As a place where care has been abdicated to the extent that it constitutes a system of rule, no one knows precisely how life is sustained. When I asked, "smuggling" was often the short answer, but smuggling networks are hardly based on careful assessments of needs and resources. Calculation and close surveillance are replaced by rumor, speculations of profit, remote pleas, and distant guessing.[37]

What is life beneath the threshold of humanitarianism? What is life that cannot even be cared for even as a recipient of aid and simultaneously poses no imminent threat that would merit urgent military responses? Answering these questions confronts us with distilled uncaring that has turned into a system of governance, a political logic that also dictates the actualities of uncared lives and uncared spaces. How we develop meaningful knowledge about the realities of uncaring is a question in and of itself.

Caring at a Distance

Information about Rukban has been increasingly difficult to obtain and even harder to verify. Journalists and researchers working for international agencies have been prevented from entering the encampment itself, and a closed military zone imposed by the Jordanian authorities blocks access even to its southern vicinity. Information gathered by the last convoy organized by the Syrian Red Crescent in February 2019 was solely limited to gauging the willingness of Rukban's residents to return to regime-held regions. Other aspects of life were outside their mandate. Several aid workers I spoke with noted that even raising the humanitarian plight in Rukban has become impossible in Jordanian policy circles; breaching this unwritten code could jeopardize an organization's ability to continue to operate in the country. In other emergency contexts, the veneer of humanitarian crisis has been enough to cover over a general condition of abandonment.[38] When it comes to Rukban, though, even uttering humanitarian concern is a breach of protocol. Care has become taboo.

When no access is allowed, how can we know what happens in Rukban and places like it? Increasingly, remote sensing technologies have become a common tool for researchers, UN agencies, and aid groups. Carrying the promise of forensic accuracy and scientific verifiability, high-resolution satellite imagery and other remote sensing systems are mobilized to assess the conditions in the camp and highlight the urgency of action to address them. Specifically since the 2016 closure of the border into Jordan, groups like Human Rights Watch and Amnesty International have been able to draw international media attention to the situation in Rukban by releasing a series of satellite images and aerial heat maps that captured the growing number of dwellings on the border.[39] A group of scholars even used Rukban to test new artificial intelligence tools that detect refugees tents with greater precision, in hopes of providing "humanitarian organizations effective information for camp-site planning, field operation, and rescue effort."[40] An analyst who previously worked for one of the major aid agencies told me that the only way she was able to monitor the severity of the situation in the encampment was by counting new graves in the cemeteries that were visible in satellite images produced by UNOSAT and private firms. Yet such efforts merely highlight a fundamental crisis: the inability to access the camp in the first place. The increasing reliance on remote forms of documentation emerges directly in response to absence on the ground and the urge to generate knowledge that compensates for this absence.

The urge to remotely document no man's land has a longer history, dating back to its iconic emergence in World War I (fig. 6). It was during this war that the space between the trenches became an object of photographic interest, partly due to its inaccessibility. As I detailed in chapter 1, the war incubated new ways of seeing, "training the eye" to observe and extract tactical knowledge from a space that was otherwise ruined almost beyond recognition.[41] Over a century later, attempts at "visualizing the invisible" continue to carry an implicit promise that the hard-to-reach will be reached.[42] As Paul Saint-Amour points out in his analysis of reconnaissance optics and rhetoric that emerged out of World War I and II: "Conventions of documenting the real are constructed by strategic and compensatory exaggerations that become naturalized, even normativized, over time. While indulging frequently in fantasies of comprehensive and totalizing representation, they also illustrated the dependence of such fantasies upon site-specific, partial, relativistic acts of perception."[43]

What is at stake here is not so much the changing technologies of representation through which abandonment is refracted and understood. Instead, I wonder whether the growing dependency on remote sensing technologies is indicative of the very condition of isolation that is integral to the political logics of abandonment: the isolation of Rukban means that even those who are hoping to compensate to some extent for all that has been abdicated, are only able to do so from a distance. Remote imaging can assist in calculating

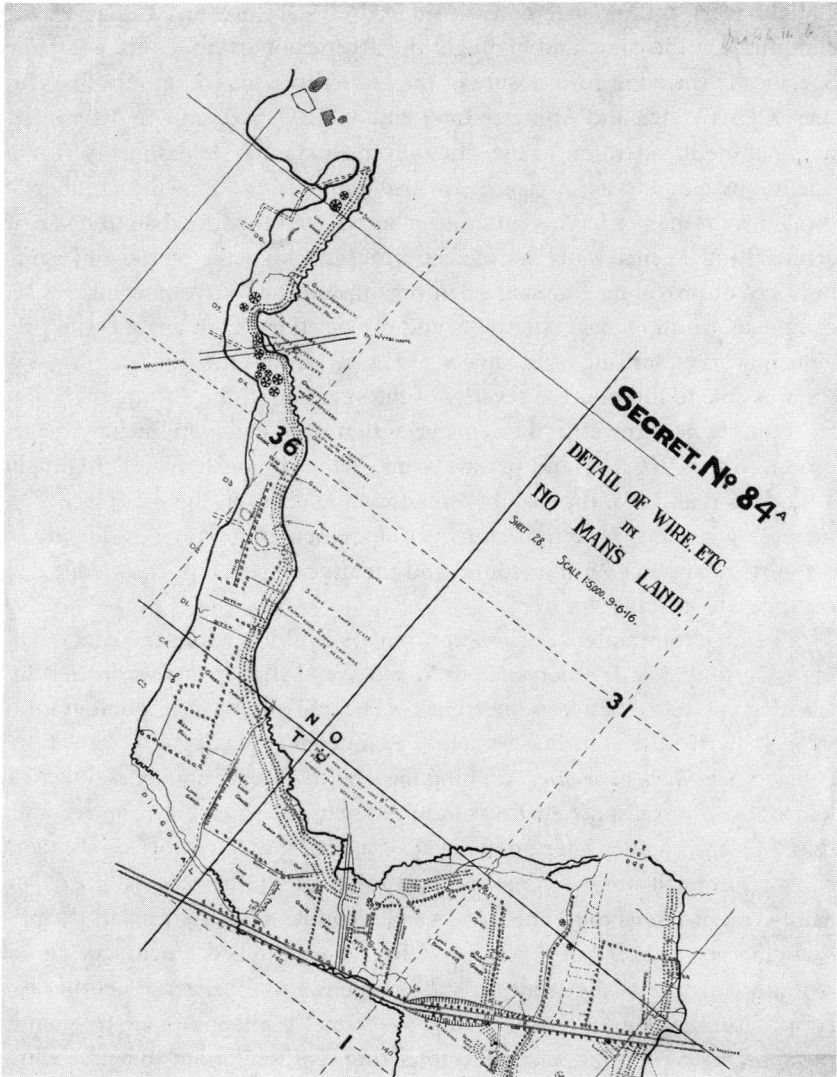

FIGURE 6. Sector map of the Western Front. Note that this map lists specific sections of barbed wire, as well as turnip and bean fields. Ordinance Survey, 9 June 1916.

dwelling density and counting new graves. But the details that can be seen from that distance solidify tropes of passive suffering by a faceless "displaced population" that dwells and dies somewhere, far away, on the Syria-Jordan border.[44] Its resolution and chosen frame leaves out the presence of exactly those forces that have created the space of abandonment in the first place—

the ongoing Syrian, Russian, American, and Jordanian refusal to extend care either in the immediate form of aid or through a more comprehensive attempt to relocate over ten thousand people from the desert berm to safety. Precisely because they are so effective in sanitizing the appearance of uncaring, the same remote sensing images have become a favorite illustrative tool in press releases by the Russian Defense Ministry.[45]

The fact that information is increasingly gauged remotely does not mean that Rukban has been completely blacked out. Several groups have begun to mobilize social media platforms to deliver regular updates from the camp and send pleas for international intervention. Improvised media centers like the *Voice of Rukban* use social media campaigns, including a series of short videos featuring women and men, most with their faces concealed by an abaya or a keffiyeh, asking the world to intervene on their behalf, thus enabling them to leave the camp for safety. However, the dominance of powerful tribal leaderships and outright intimidation by competing armed groups imposes self-censorship and skews the information that does make it out. A small number of journalists continue to report on the camp and rely on individuals still residing in Rukban, although conventional routes of independent verification are nearly impossible to follow. I, too, encountered similar hurdles in my research. Early on, I had to admit to a senior colleague in my department that I was unable to confirm the identity of some of those with whom I was in touch. There was a likelihood that some may have been associated with organizations prescribed by the UK government as terrorist groups. It was better she heard it first from me, just in case the British security services came asking questions.

Spaces of uncaring present a peculiar epistemological challenge. Their abdication is often intertwined with an assumed inaccessibility, with distance and danger that, in turn, need to be overcome to produce a rigorous understanding of abandonment's political logics and its effects. Yet the very tools that are so often invoked to overcome this distance only highlight how limited the effort is. To put it simply, the remoteness of remote imagery is the very condition of possibility that uncaring relies on. Care, after all, requires proximity, the same proximity that is made impossible by the abdicating apparatuses in the first place.

Cruddy Abandonments

When the state severs the fundamental relation of care toward a given space and those who inhabit it, as the Syrian regime has done in Rukban, the consequences are dire. But Rukban exists exactly because tens of thousands of people fled the murderous care of the state, preferring the precarities of life in a desolate desert region over the certain violence inflicted by the Assad regime, or by numerous other groups involved in the fighting. This is not to imply that Rukban is spared from violence or that those who inhabit it are passively enduring the violence inflicted on them by external forces. Politics saturates this space: at last five opposition groups have established themselves in Rukban and have carved out specific areas of dominance in the encampment.[46] Smugglers have also exploited the dependency of Rukban's population and reports have proliferated of recruitment of child soldiers, domestic violence and underage marriages, all gendered and intimate forms of harm that I return to at length later.[47]

The intimacy of abandonment was also a story that Omar, a young man living in Rukban since 2016, insisted I hear. In a lengthy exchange of phone messages, made necessary because the signal was never strong enough to sustain an uninterrupted call, he lamented all that gets lost in most depictions of Rukban. Media preoccupation with international wrangling over responsibility for the camp on the one hand and graphic depictions of harm and suffering on the other miss the intimate realities of life that are not spectacular or obviously urgent. Although he works as a pharmacist in the camp, selling medication that is still smuggled into Rukban in small amounts, his concern was not medical per se. "One child came to this camp when he was six years old. Years have passed and we are still in the camp. This means that this generation of children are deprived of education and become ignorant. This child cannot learn after becoming this old . . . Many high school students have their dreams gone and their studies gone. When I got out of the small village I grew up in, I was enrolled at the Institute of Nursing and Anesthesiology. But my dreams were lost when I was displaced. The future that I dreamed of is lost."[48] Even dreams are not safe from the corrosive effects of uncaring.

Uncaring produces more than violence and the proliferation of harms. The resolution of satellite images cannot capture this, but the systematic abdication of sovereign care brings to the fore a different register of care. It is a "place-based ethics of care," to use Karen Till's formulation, a form of care that is not confined to the relationship between sovereign and subjects.[49] Instead, this register of care prompts people to open improvised schools and places of worship, to foster communal relations and expanded networks of support. One of the schools in Rukban was built out of mud bricks and a roof of corrugated iron sheets, but someone took the time to paint small colorful murals that brightened up the earth-brown walls. This is not an anecdote or a detail. Documenting the space of uncaring cannot lose sight of humbles acts of life that emerge once care is withdrawn. The following chapters seek to move even closer to the humble spaces where living and dying actually take place. Our understanding of abandonment, its political stakes and consequences, requires such attention, even to the murals that pop up when you reach "rock bottom."

PART III

Beyond Care

The following chapters venture into the darkness of abandoned space, documenting what happens once care is withdrawn, leaving lives and lands exposed. If abandonment constitutes no man's land, exposure is its outcome.

History, however, hasn't always parsed abandonment from exposure so clearly. The origins of abandonment are often traced to the Roman legal category of *expositio*, which designated an abdication of a family's responsibility toward a child.[1] This form of abandonment-through-exposure—leaving a child to die in a designated public place—was well established in Greco-Roman policies of eugenics. In *Politics*, for example, Aristotle argues for a law that would permit infanticide of any child born with deformities. Exposure to him almost always means an abandonment to death. But late Roman sources suggest that abandoned children often did not die but were rather enslaved or used for prostitution.[2] This dark economy of abandonment that transforms bodies into commodities highlights the slippage between *expositio*—the abandonment of life—and *derelictio*, a parallel category that designated the abdication of claims over material property.[3] Jewish sources debating the concept of *hefker* are equally attentive to the enmeshment of bodies and objects. One Talmudic debate, for example, concerns the status of an enslaved man whose owner dies and cannot emancipate him through ordinary procedures; the man's freedom therefore depends on an extraordinary court intervention (*hefker beit din*).[4] Enslavement reduces the subject to property, but the Talmudic debate emerges exactly because it recognizes that abandonment (*hefker*) is a condition of unique vulnerability in which even the protections assigned to commodities—for example, forms of violent care that rule the labor force in plantations or penal colonies—no longer apply. Exposures in the space of uncaring therefore challenge the boundaries dividing bodies and the material worlds: shrapnel tears through skin, poisons are inhaled and enter the bloodstream, chemicals are absorbed into soils and radiation alters cellular structures. These are often the stories exposure exposes.

Harm, loss, and death are often the consequence of exposure, a condition that sees life left to confront the elements or the wrath of others. It is a condition that not only puts the body in harm's way, but also more profoundly dissolves the boundary between the body and the space that surrounds it. For the most part, it is a catastrophic dissolution, even if catastrophe happens beyond sight. But the analysis comprising this section suggests that if we are to venture closer into the darkness that often shrouds abandoned lands, exposure may emerge as more than just an experience of naked vulnerability and the harms endured in its wake. Historicizing exposure through the contingent processes that constitute it, sheds new light on the space of uncaring: rather than a dead end, no man's land can become a catalyst for the creation of new relations between self and others and between the body and the world. From this affirmative exposure, the space of uncaring can also be rethought as an incubator of political action and possibility. At the same time, recognizing the granular effects of exposure also foregrounds its deeply uneven impacts. Gendered and racialized hierarchies often endure long after sovereign care has been withdrawn, meaning that some bodies are more likely to find themselves exposed than others.

Exposure, when thought of this way, brings into view an intimate and unruly tale of life in the space of uncaring.

5

Exposures

On April 26, 1986, Michael Marder, who was then a young boy, boarded a two-day sleeper train from Moscow to Anapa, a town on the coast of the Black Sea. That same day, a deadly explosion ruptured one of the reactors in the Chernobyl nuclear plant. The trip was intended to spare him from his suffocating seasonal allergies to birch, oak, and other flowering trees. But like millions of others, Mardar was unknowingly being exposed to a large amount of nuclear radiation. Years later, Marder recalled the journey and the events that were taking place in the aftermath of the Chernobyl disaster. In his account, and his is hardly an uncommon stance, such exposure of human bodies cannot but spell pure vulnerability, passivity, helplessness.

Yet Marder's account is noteworthy exactly because he never loses sight of the ways his body was absorbing radiation alongside the bodies of others, "animals and other humans, as well as with plants and the soil that received huge amounts of radiation without anyone being aware of it."[1] Unlike humans, who can flee disasters, vegetal beings, with their roots in the ground, were unable to escape the harmful effects of radioactivity. Yet more-than-human vulnerability is only part of the story. Inanimate beings also appeared more adaptable. Soybeans experimentally grown in Chernobyl's radioactive environment have displayed drastic changes in their protein makeup, enabling them to improve their resistance to heavy metals and improve their carbon metabolism.[2] When we refuse a narrow anthropocentric perspective, exposure still entails vulnerability, but it also signifies a condition of being in the world and being with others, including other beings. It was "exposure in common."

Pure vulnerability and radical commonality seem irreconcilable. Yet exposure, as it gradually unfolds in this chapter—and with different emphases, in the chapters that follow—not only holds this multiplicity but also, in fact, derives its critical significance from it. Several scholars have highlighted the critical tension that exposure entails, but it is particularly meaningful in the spaces at the heart of this book. If intentional withdrawal of sovereign care leaves life adrift, exposed to harm and hazard, the space of uncaring also harbors the concomitant condition of sheer openness that allows new commonalities to be created. It generates encounters with others that, without this exposure, would be far less possible. Documenting the realities of life in the space of uncaring constantly holds these multiplicities and follows those who have to navigate the terrain between them.

Dark Exposures

Calamity is often the opening chapter in the tale of exposure. The Chernobyl Nuclear Plant Zone of Alienation (Зона відчуження Чорнобильської АЕС), commonly known in English as the "Exclusion Zone," was drawn around the damaged nuclear reactor in Chernobyl by the Soviet military shortly after the 1986 explosion, and it designates a restricted area of 2,600 square kilometers. More than 5 million people live in areas of Belarus, Russia, and Ukraine that are classified as "contaminated" with radionuclides due to the Chernobyl accident. Among them, about 400,000 people lived in more contaminated areas—classified by Soviet authorities as areas of strict radiation control. Of this population, 116,000 people were evacuated in the spring and summer of 1986 from the "the exclusion zone and the zone of absolute (mandatory) resettlement" to noncontaminated areas. Another 220,000 people were relocated in subsequent years.[3] Normal habitation of the area was prohibited and normal services were withdrawn. To date, fewer than 200 people reside in the zone.

On the face of it, exposure was the obvious threat authorities sought to mitigate: less than three hours after the initial explosion in Reactor 4, a disaster headquarters was set up and roadblocks erected to prioritize emergency responders. Simultaneously, residents were warned to remain indoors. Soon after, more severe measures were added to these initial delineations of risk space, constituting a months-long containment effort often referred to as the "liquidation." Helicopter pilots dropped sand, clay, and lead to seal the reactor's core; soldiers were tasked with removing graphite debris from roofs; and a team of Russian miners filled an excavated void under the reactor room with concrete to prevent it from burning into the underground water system.[4] This volumetric effort later included damming of water sources, a technological infrastructure for the monitoring of radiation, and sanitary posts for the decontamination of workers' clothing, as well as more conventional uses of fences, barbed wire, barricades, and checkpoints.

But the use of *alienation* in the Exclusion Zone's official title hints at less visible ruptures in the life fabric of individuals and communities medically and economically affected by the event. The abandonment of the Exclusion Zone and its intense enclosure couldn't fully keep exposure at bay. In a detailed study of Chernobyl's impact on Ukrainian forms of citizenship, Adriana Petryna illustrates how "exposure," as a condition of vulnerability to violence and death, continued to plague those who were forced to evacuate their homes following the accident.[5] The "deep intrusion of illness onto personal lives," she writes, "fostered a type of violence that went beyond the line of what could be policed."[6] Her account illuminates how the persistent damage (to bodies, ecologies, and atmospheres) was also made into a resource, into social protections, forms of citizenship and informal economies of health care and entitlement. Exposure, as either peril or potential, is never fully confined by the strict enclosures of no man's land.

Yet the evasive quality of exposure, which allows it to lodge itself so persistently in the ill and wounded body, also produces new enclosures. The wife of one of the first responders who was exposed to extreme levels of radiation described the bio-chamber in which he was placed during his hospitalization in Moscow and the extensive quarantine measures that isolated the man from the medical staff. To complete his dehumanization, one nurse referred to the dying man as "a radioactive object with a strong density of poisoning. . . . That's not a person anymore, that's a nuclear reactor."[7]

The radical unmaking of the human body to the extent that it is no longer distinguished from the original space of disaster, is exposure's most violent effect. When medical and public health scholars consider exposure as the "contact between misplaced matter and flesh," they naturally place primacy on the human body.[8] Yet if we closely examine how the space of uncaring brought about the exposure of lands and lives, this prioritization of the human seems incongruous with the calamity that these spaces feature. Animate and inanimate matter becomes intractably entangled, often catastrophically so. Describing the no man's land between the trenches of World War I, the German cultural historian Bernd Hüppauf documents the material decomposition that violent exposure brings about: "A series of pictures taken over a long period of time shows regions of forests, which slowly begin to clear until only stumps of trees remain. Even those disappear under continuous bombardment, and finally, all that stays are a plane of black and dark tones of grey, rooted up ground without any contours, and mud interspersed with the remainders of combat-actions."[9]

The human body is almost absent from this description, but for good reason. The nature of mechanized warfare pulverized the no man's land of World

War I and almost all that was in it. The consequence was utter and violent exposure: trees were slashed, the earth was churned, and bodies were crushed, often leaving no recognizable trace. Writing about this exact space six months after the Armistice, the French senator Paul Doumer described "a desert, a zone of death, assassination and devastation. . . . There are corpses of horses, corpses of trees covering corpses of men."[10] Exposure, in this context, refuses the prioritization of the human body, not just as a critical prompt toward the intersections of human and more-than-human life, but because the violence that it entailed often resulted in the physical annihilation of that body altogether.

Horror was one reaction to this catastrophic dissolution of the boundaries between body and space. Some, however, found a regenerative force in this exposure. In *Der Kampf als inneres Erlebnis* (The Battle as Inner Experience), Ernst Jünger describes how the *Fronterlebnis*—life on the edges of no man's land—dissolves the boundary between body and space, transforming the soldier into an integral part of a frontline ecology: "There, the individual is like a raging storm, the tossing sea and the rearing thunder. He has melted into everything."[11] This is not a traumatic subjection of the body to mechanized war, but, as Jeffrey Herf notes, an almost erotic rebirth and transfiguration of men into a new, improved community of the trenches that will lead the creation of "new forms filled with blood and power [that] will be packed with a hard fist."[12] Rather than resort to nostalgia for a pastoral reindustrialized era, in the no man's land, Jünger discovers a landscape where body, machine and soil are fused to form "magnificent and merciless spectacles."[13]

If the Western Front provided the urtext of modern no man's land as a space abandoned between warring parties, Chernobyl is paradigmatic of late twentieth-century spaces where catastrophic environmental conditions force a radical withdrawal of conventional human habitation and normal functions of governance. Obviously, there are important distinctions that set the two apart. Abandoned spaces locked between opposing warring forces are spatially designated through blunt performances of power (fortified trenches, barbed wire) and a temporality of urgency and immediacy (evacuations in the face of clear and visible danger). Catastrophic environmental degradation, like the one that forced the abandonment of Chernobyl, rarely appear spectacular or urgent. In fact, they sometimes never appear at all, at least not to the unsuspecting onlooker. Temporally, these are forms of harm that take decades and even centuries to make their mark. Spatially, they seep into subterranean strata, cluster in atmospheric layers well beyond human view, or transform submolecular composition of life and living environments. As such, these

PLATE 1. A UN surveillance tower overlooking the Buffer Zone that runs through the historical heart of Nicosia, Cyprus, 2015. Photographer: Elliot Graves.

NANZE GEFONSEN
GEGENUBER VOH
SCHULHAUS IN OSTER-
FERNEBO

C. Hesse- Honniger

Gysinge, 31 Juli 87

PLATE 2. Cornelia Hesse-Honniger: Head and thorax of soft bug from Gysinge, Sweden. © DACS 2025.

PLATE 3. Mishka Henner. "Via Traversagna Nord, Vecchiano Pisa, Italy." From *No Man's Land*, 2011–2013.

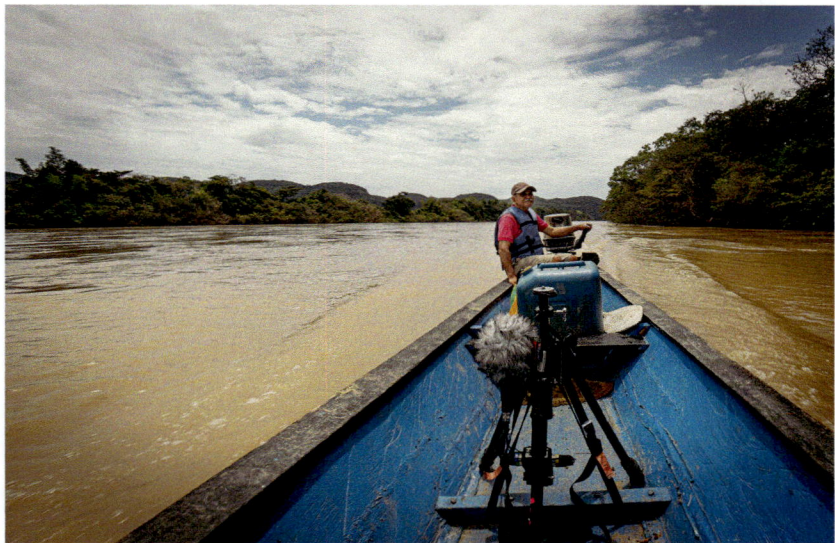

PLATE 4. Isaías Sánchez Castaño steering his canoe up the Guayabero River, Colombia, 2018. Photographer: Elliot Graves.

PLATE 5. Unexploded shells from World War I rest against the mossy trunk of a tree planted in the "Red Zone," the areas hardest hit during the war and deemed beyond repair. Verdun, France, 2015. Photographer: Elliot Graves.

PLATE 6. A stretch of forest cut down to grow coca. After a violent government crackdown on coca cultivation, cacao trees were planted to provide income to local farmers. Meta, Colombia, 2018. Photographer: Elliot Graves.

processes rarely trigger the same urgency of response and remediation. Rob Nixon famously described this as "slow violence," meaning "violence that occurs gradually and out of sight, a violence of delayed destruction that is dispersed across time and space, an attritional violence that is typically not viewed as violence at all."[14]

Not all exposures are created equal. War and environmental catastrophe generate very different conditions of harm; they unfold at a different pace and demand different responses. A history of no man's land that spans long historical periods, political contexts, and geographical scales risks glossing over critical differences simply by viewing these spaces as generalized sites of exposure. I think of exposure, instead, as a valuable conceptual lens that sharpens attention to the consequences of abandonment, to spaces where life is regularly stripped of conventional protections. And while exposures are not confined to no man's land, it is there that we encounter them in their bluntest and most horrific form.

It is sometimes hard to think of no man's land beyond the disastrous exposures of the human body. The scene of bodies and machines mangled beyond recognition in a muddy wasteland looms large over this space. But how can we seriously think about this condition of exposure when flesh is no longer coterminous with the body? How do we understand fleshy exposure when confronted with such images of disfigured matter? Partly by expanding the historical corpus we interrogate, moving away from the Great War as a paradigmatic reference point. Without a doubt, that war remains a critical juncture in the genealogy of uncaring. But in over a century since, uncaring has emerged well beyond the confines of militarized space and its histories. Like radiation that invisibly lodges itself in cells and leaves its marks on DNA sequences long after the fact and thousands of miles from its initial points of impact, exposures to the harms of uncaring finds its way well beyond the barbed wire and military barricades.

Infinitesimal Harms, Distant Exposures

Within a week of the nuclear accident in Chernobyl, enhanced radiation levels were reported thousands of miles from the site of the explosion, as far as the United Kingdom to the west and Scandinavia in the north. More than four million people were exposed in the former Soviet Union alone to nuclear particles that were carried into the atmosphere and seeped into the soil and groundwater. Exposure proved hard to contain, but when endured remotely, scientists often deemed its residual harms to humans as "insignificant."[15] But how would exposure to that same dose affect a one- to six-millimeter bug larva feeding on contaminated plant juices for three months while it developed into a mature insect?

It was a question that, in the days following the accident, nagged at Cornelia Hesse-Honegger, a Swiss artist who was trained as a scientific illustrator. Having documented morphological deformities in insects exposed to X-ray radiation in labs, she was looking at the catastrophe from a unique vantage point. A friend who was a student at the Nuclear Engineering Laboratory of the Swiss Federal Institute for Technology gave her detailed information about the accident three days after the first news reports. She was not convinced by the experts and policy makers who were eager to alleviate public concerns about the risks from the fallout. "My scepticism about the general all clear," she later recalled, "was due to the fact that, as far as I could see, what happened a Chernobyl was hardly different from what the geneticists induced artificially in the laboratory. It was an involuntary 'outdoor' experiment."[16] Using a report issued by the Swiss government on the distribution of the radioactive cloud, Hesse-Honegger found that the highest amount of radioactive material fell in Sweden, especially in the region of Gävle. "And that," she writes, "was where I wanted to go."[17]

She arrived in Sweden in the summer of 1987, just over a year after the breach of the Chernobyl reactor. As a scientific illustrator, drawing was her form of critical observation and documentation. She therefore immediately began sketching, starting with foliage near her hotel that oddly turned rusty red at the height of summer, or a lilac branch with deformed leaves. The following day, as she turned her attention to bugs, her alarm grew. "One bug had a peculiarly shortened left leg, while others had feelers like shapeless sausages, and something black grew out of the eye of another bug."[18] Once back in Switzerland, Hesse-Honegger continued to collect insects and flora, documenting further deformities. But when she tried to share her findings with geneticists and entomologists in Sweden and Switzerland—almost all men—her findings were dismissed. In addition to faulting her methods of collection and analysis, they rejected the hypothesis that the mutations she documented were the result of exposure to nuclear fallout. It ran against the scientific consensus at the time, which assumed that doses in these regions were far too low to induce changes to hereditary genetic material.[19]

The paintings, mostly watercolors, that emerge from these studies are deceptive. At first glance, they are instantaneously bracketed by the conventions of scientific illustration. Those who went to school several decades ago might associate this aesthetic with posters in lab classes that, more recently, have

popped up as paraphernalia in vintage shops. They are curios. Yet a more patient observation reveals the injury that lies behind the delicate nature of the
watercolors: a leaf deformity that seems to shred its surface, or an insect feeler
that appears to have been torn out. Aside from minimal descriptive text, no
explanation is given in the paintings themselves. Hesse-Honegger leaves it to
the viewer to realize that there was no natural storm that brought about these
injuries.

    During the research for this book, I often returned to these images. Scaled
up several times their original size, I find the violence endured by the insects
and plants documented in them hard to bear. Astrid Schrader aptly describes
this sense, following Derrida, as "abyssal intimacy," a heightened awareness
and proximity mixed with a sense of something wholly other.[20] This entails a
broad shift in the relation to the drawing. As an artist, Hesse-Honegger has
long sought to push against the conventional perception that sees drawing
and painting as a "secondary representation of what is already understood."[21]
In the hierarchies of knowledge production that are still dominated by scientific truth regimes, her illustrations "fail" to register as evidence or analysis.
By this conventional measure, drawings matter far less than the object they
depict. But this is partly what lies at the heart of Hesse-Honegger's critical
effort. In her pictorial process, drawings are research, a space where collection, observation, analysis and dissemination intersect. Viewing these images
likewise calls on the spectator to shift from their conventional position as a
passive recipient, to a different, more active stance. The abyss in "abyssal intimacy" may indicate a sense of radical difference but just as much an invitation to turn intimate observation into critical reflection.

    Why care, then, for injured insects and mutated plants? For one, these im-
ages chart a more expansive geography of exposure's violence. Although they
seemingly state the obvious about the perils of nuclear technology, the body
of the insect or plant segment are clearly located: Gysinge, Sweden; Gösgen,
Switzerland; Pripyat, Ukraine. Each of the paintings offers a focused snapshot
from the wider expanse of the radiation cloud and the damage it left in its
wake. In doing so, the paintings transport the viewer further away from the
a clearly demarcated zone of disaster to a diffuse geography of exposure. Second, they stretch out the temporality of harm. Once exposure begins to transform DNA sequences and chromosomal compositions, it can no longer be
confined to the spectacular moment of the catastrophic event—a war, an accident. Instead, it becomes hereditary and endemic, lasting decades and centuries. "Slow" has often been invoked to address these instances in which exposure (to toxins, depravation, violence) results in endemic harm.[22] But scale

is just as important as pace here: infinitesimal doses translate into visible injury once the creature exposed is small enough, only a few millimeters long. Third, the materiality that bears the imprints of exposure is often too small or too mundane to merit care, unless it is prompted by deliberate intention and a mediating practice. Put differently, while Soviet (and later Ukrainian) authorities were heavily invested in managing the accident and its myriad effects, this care was largely anthropocentric, a concern for human life and environmental dimensions that support it (i.e., removal of contaminated soil, monitoring water sources). No one seemed to care about insects. They appear, as Hugh Raffles put it in his *Insectopedia*, "So tiny, so damaged, so irrelevant."[23] Hesse-Honegger's images, and importantly, the way she employs drawing as process, foreground this intention: look longer, look closer, look farther.

Different Lights

Exposure bears an implicit promise of clarity and resolution. As the opposite of concealment, it assumes a revelation of hidden truths once they are aired out in the open. Yet as Peter Sloterdijk argues, the twentieth century witnessed the weaponization of air itself, first through chemical warfare and later through nuclear radiation. Exposure became an inherent part of warfare, displacing "destructive action from the system (here: the enemy's body) onto his environment—in the case at hand: the air milieu in which enemy bodies move."[24] The catastrophes of the past century have made exposure into a toxic and often deadly condition. Its potential as an illuminating and untethered condition seem to have been overshadowed once the chlorine gas clouds drifted across the Ypres no man's land on April 22, 1915.

Recovering a radical openness and potentiality within conditions exposure requires attentiveness to different histories, but just as much, an attentiveness to different lights. I borrow this latter formulation of "different lights" from the photographer elin o'Hara slavick and her work in Hiroshima, which traces the relationship between radiation and the visual language of photography. In her work, slavick uses different practices to document places and objects that survived the atomic bombing. In one series, everyday objects that survived the nuclear explosion and were kept in the vaults of the Hiroshima Peace Museum—a comb, petal of dead flowers or a bottle deformed by the immense heat of the explosion—were placed on an X-ray film. Once exposed to sunlight, the radiation still stored in the objects left a white trace on the film surface.[25]

For slavick, exposure is both a problem and a process in her work: On the one hand, residual radiation remains, invisible to the naked eye, in countless objects and places; these objects were exposed to radioactive particles, but the exposure remains hidden. That is the problem. Yet the same radiation that is stored within these objects also causes the imprint to appear. The process slavick employs brings to light this invisible residue. Her work with autoradiography involved placing A-bombed objects on X-ray film in light-tight bags for a period of ten days. Without external light, the objects caused abstract exposures on the film—spots, dots, cracks, and fissures. Catastrophic exposure to atomic energy during an event that happened decades ago became the condition of possibility for seeing, in a new light, the violence that lingers.

In quite a similar manner, exposure emerges as both a problem and a process in the space of uncaring. First, knowing that lives are stripped of sovereign care belies the multiplicity of beings exposed in this process. The work of Hesse-Honegger and slavick is a reminder of multiple lives exposed, how different beings—animate and inanimate—are relegated beyond the realm of care. Historically, the space of uncaring was most visibly recognized not through the exposure of human life, but through the vast tracts of exposed earth, spaces stripped of vegetal and animal life by bombardment, neglect, and corrosive toxicity. As I discuss at length later, land and nonhuman life often bear the imprint of exposure long after the initial moment of abdication. As such, the surface of a leaf may offer a testament of uncaring that is just as profound, if not more so, than a policy brief from a military general.

This is also part of the conceptual process that this discussion prompts. We cannot wish away the calamitous consequences of exposure. But reclaiming its meaning as a condition of clarity, commonality, and openness is ethically important and politically urgent, first and foremost because that is an essential part of life in spaces subjected to systemic abandonment. Once sovereign care is withdrawn, individuals and communities can do more than merely cope with and endure exposure—to the elements, to violence, to depravation and environmental degradation. Much like slavick, who has sought to "utilize exposures to make visible the unseen, to reveal what is denied and hidden," many of the stories that unfold in this book document the ways exposure has been politically mobilized for claiming agency and catalyzing change.[26] Some have even found refuge in no man's land. Despite the risks, they fled other places to make a home in the space of uncaring exactly because it enables life freed from the violence of the state outside it. For them, exposure retains a critical dimension of promise rather than simply designating a condition of pure vulnerability. The historiography of no man's land, which remains largely consumed with war and largely populated by masculine protagonists, may be radically altered if we take seriously this nuanced conceptualization of exposure, but it will be richer for it.

The following chapters consider other registers of life exposed once sovereign care is systemically withdrawn. Yet the caring practice of Hesse-Honegger and slavick prompts critical questions that are deeply consequential for any understanding of more explicitly political logics of sovereign uncaring: If the harms of exposure find a way to escape the enclosures that surround zones of uncaring, where else should we look? What carries the harms when they don't take the form of nuclear particles? What flesh ends up bearing their violent imprints?

These are critical concerns for this project as a whole. They may help us redefine what is at stake in the study of sovereign abdication and the realities of life that emerge in its wake. But they also highlight how no man's land, the space where uncaring becomes a governing logic, is profoundly porous, almost to the point where it loses its specificity. It might become, once again, a metaphor that can be placed anywhere. I am not interested in redrawing the lines around no man's land or to conceptually police its boundaries. Border guards and custom officers are better suited to impose definitions and regulate meaning. Instead, we should turn attention to the myriad ways the spaces of uncaring intensify and exacerbate exposure, as both a condition of naked vulnerability and the potential for radical openness.

6

Left to Die

In 1962, Ghassan Kanafani wrote about three Palestinian men seeking a future, an escape from the hopeless present of their lives in an Iraqi refugee camp. Each of the men carries a story of forced exile, of a home lost and the weight of personal regrets and dreams. The novella, *Men in the Sun*, takes place a decade after the Nakba, the Palestinian catastrophe of 1948, and follows the men's attempt to reach Kuwait and the promise of work in the booming oil economy.[1] It is midsummer, and in their desperation, the three men agree to join a water-tank truck driver who is willing to take them through the blazing heat of the desert, across the border. To avoid inspection at the border points, the men hide inside the empty metal tank. At the Iraqi crossing, the men barely make it out of the inferno of the metal container alive. However, at the second crossing, while they are still inside no man's land (which Kanafani describes as the "unknown region") the driver, Abul Khaizuran—himself also a Palestinian—is held up by the border guards. They ignore his urgency and take joy in frivolous chatter, mocking him for a supposed affair. By the time he is finally able to drive far enough away from the border post and reopen the metal tank, the three men have suffocated.

Death takes place in the hermetic darkness of the empty water tank. Kanafani does not venture into the darkness of the tank in the three men's final moments and it remains sealed from the border guards' view and that of the reader. Only once the truck is far enough from the border post is light shed on the catastrophe that took place in the minutes it was delayed. Darkness also envelops the disposal of the bodies at the end of the novella, as Abul Khaizuran discards them at night in a Kuwaiti garbage dump. In this darkness, he cannot see their features or tell them apart. On the face of it, such darkness stands in stark contrast to the blinding light, the relentless sun, and deadly heat of the desert the men are crossing.

But harms taking place out of sight are inherent to the production of violence in the space of uncaring. By relegating their death to the enclosed dark space of the water tank, Kanafani removes it from the deliberate actions outside. In other words, it was not sovereign decision that killed the men but intentional inaction or the prevention of action.[2] Moreover, at no point in their journey do they come into direct contact with official agents of the state. Instead, they interact with numerous others—smugglers, landlords, even foreign tourists. Yet they are beyond the care of the state. To be clear, the sovereign in the novella is not a benevolent force, and its interventions will offer no relief: if discovered, Kanafani clarifies, the three men would be executed, as would the driver smuggling them. "This is indeed," Maria Margaroni writes, "the most profane and banal death that Agamben talks about, an un-heroic, unaccountable death that simply occurs in/because of abandonment."[3]

In no man's land, exposure to harms happens beyond the realm of care, in the darkness beyond sight. When light is allowed in, it is often too late. Kanafani published his novella in 1962, narrating fictional events that took place in the decade or so before then. Over half a century later, thirty-nine Vietnamese nationals were found dead, locked inside a refrigerated lorry container that was driven to the United Kingdom from Belgium. According to preliminary police reports, they froze to death inside the refrigerator unit where the temperature can drop to below twenty-five degrees Celsius.[4] Only at the point of contact with the industrial complex of the border—inspectors, shipping contractors, dockers, and customs officers—was the horror brought to light, at an inconspicuous industrial park in southeastern England. Harm took place before that, in the darkness between the sovereign perimeters, the darkness that is not only devoid of light but also, more importantly, devoid of care. Care made an appearance too late, but that wasn't a matter of timing. Instead, it was a reminder, if one was needed, of all the spaces where people are left to die not as a punishment or by mistake, but as a matter of course, without intervention or interruption.

State of Exposure

On May 28, 2008, Omar Abu Jariban, a thirty-five-year-old Palestinian from the Gaza Strip city of Rafah who illegally entered Israel, was seriously injured in an accident while riding with a friend in a stolen car. He was diagnosed with neurological head injuries, internal bleeding, and multiple bone fractures and was hospitalized in the Sheba Medical Center, near Tel Aviv. While in the hospital, he also suffered from pneumonia.

Two weeks after the accident, Abu Jariban was prematurely discharged from the hospital, into the custody of Rehovot police officers—barefoot, with a urinary catheter still in place, still using adult diapers, in need of further medical care and rehabilitation and appearing confused. Abu Jariban was registered as anonymous in hospital records, and the cost of his care was charged to the hospital itself. This partly explains the hospital's eagerness to transfer him prematurely into police custody. As the Rehovot police station commander told an investigating officer, "the hospital only sought to vacate the bed."[5]

Unable to walk, Abu Jariban was wheeled into the police station on an office chair. When later that day the Israel Prison Service hospital said it had no room for him, it was decided that he would be driven to the West Bank. Two officers held his arms and pushed him into the back of a police car, while a third folded his legs in. En route, they stopped at another police station, but the electronic database that would have allowed them to confirm his identity was inoperative. The policemen drove to a West Bank military checkpoint, but the commanding officer refused to take responsibility for Abu Jariban. The same scenario repeated itself at another checkpoint north of Jerusalem.

At 2:50 a.m. Abu Jariban was taken out of the car on Highway 45, between the Ofer army base and the Atarot crossing point. One of the police officers subsequently testified: "Together with the volunteer, we took the detainee out of the car and placed him behind the safety railing so that he wouldn't be hurt. He wasn't removed very far from the road—he was left in a place where he would be able to hitch-hike a lift. We made a report and then drove off." The police investigator asked him to clarify his reasoning about the suspect's ability to get a lift on a speedy highway. The officer replied: "I expected that cars would stop at the side of the road, that someone would take him in and give him a ride. All told, he is one of their people and the Arabs are known for their solidarity."[6]

The policemen apparently did not know that Palestinian vehicles were blocked from travelling on this road. Abu Jariban was left to his own devices, wearing his hospital gown and with his discharge papers in his pocket. The catheter was still with him. He was barefoot. The policemen left neither food nor drink with him; they reported back that they had completed the mission. Two days later, on Sunday morning, June 15, 2008, a pedestrian discovered Abu Jariban's body. He had died of dehydration.

Only two police officers, of the dozens who came into contact with him, were charged and convicted with negligent homicide. Jerusalem District Court

Justice Yoram Noam concluded in his sentencing that "the appellants' negligent behavior . . . undermined basic and universal human and moral values, when they abandoned him [Abu Jariban] to his destiny in the dark of night." For their act, the two were sentenced to twenty-one months in prison.[7]

Numerous events took place from Abu Jariban's accident to that moment when he was left exposed in "the dark of night." Yet for the court, abandonment occurred only at the very final act of leaving Abu Jariban on the side of a West Bank road. Abandonment was assigned a singular time and space. But the abdication of responsibility and exposure to harm began long before that, in the banality of administrative misregistration and premature discharge at the hospital. Dozens of people—medical staff, police officers, and soldiers— came into contact with Abu Jariban, and none interpreted his suffering as urgent enough to prompt action. Furthermore, the damage to Abu Jariban's body had an unmistakable materiality, including the absent slippers, the office chair used to wheel him into the police station, and the safety railing he was hauled over. The infrastructure of roads and network of checkpoints, their convoluted organization and differentiated legal administration—all part of the labyrinthine mobility regime that is so inherent to the Israeli control over Palestinian space—were as implicated in the conditions of his exposure as his legal-political status as a Palestinian noncitizen under an occupation regime.[8]

Omar Abu Jariban was left to die because—more than just being callous or cynical—no one who could care cared enough to do so. Like so many of the processes I follow in this book, uncaring is an inherent component in a wider political logic of governance. Its consequences are rarely overwhelming death tolls and expansive material destruction. More often, it emerges as a chronic abdication of responsibilities that percolates into microscales of bureaucracy, mundane materialities, and spaces on the side of the road. Bluntly illustrating this, the testimonies of those who came into contact with Abu Jariban reveal his exposure not as a metaphor for vulnerability but as an utterly material and somatic experience. When asked how he could have discharged a patient barefoot, the physician who signed the hospital release documents said, "I don't have a stock of slippers."[9] In court, one of the three police officers who drove Abu Jariban to the West Bank offered an equally illuminating explanation: "My eyes are not your eyes. I dealt with migrant workers, the poorest. We used to take Africans with their smell all barefoot. To me it doesn't scream out that he's barefoot and wearing a pajama. I was apathetic."[10]

The political present comprises myriad petty acts of abandonment that might never register as spectacular or explicitly violent. Like all the components that preceded Abu Jariban's death, these petty acts are bureaucratic, infrastructural, banal in their materiality, and generated through inaction, delay, and indifference, as much as through deliberate deeds.[11] Punishment or error don't explain this proliferation of abandonment into everyday life, even though the Israeli state has mastered the differential distribution of care among a stratified polity. Omar Abu Jariban was left to die not because of neoliberal restructuring of health-care services or the adoption of what Lisa Stevenson calls "anonymous care," "a regime of care that requires life to become an indifferent value—that is, a regime in which it doesn't matter who you are, just that you stay alive."[12] Nor was it a result of security calculations that seek to justify state violence to live up to Foucault's injunction: "Society must be defended."[13] Instead, a man was left to die because no one who crossed his path cared to prevent it. The logic of uncaring that ultimately led to Omar's death is not totalizing or omnipresent, but when it appears, it implicates multiple actors, institutions, and materialities, making it simultaneously elusive and pervasive.

There is one additional factor that makes the events surrounding the death of Omar Abu Jariban significant to this effort to document and better understand the logic of uncaring. Unlike most processes I follow in this book, his exposure may have been the result of this logic, but it took place outside any strict boundaries that mark out a specific space where this uncaring rules. The geography of uncaring in this case spans multiple spaces, locations, and even modes of transportation, but it was never confined to a clear zone. As such, it may seem like an outlier. My stated focus, after all, was specifically on those spaces where uncaring has crystallized into a dominant governing logic, zones clearly set apart from normative space of sovereign governance. Moreover, the impetus for a critical reevaluation of no man's land was partly its transformation into a floating signifier, its assignment to a whole variety of spaces and conditions, almost to the point that it has lost any analytical significance. What, then, links the abandonment of Omar Abu Jariban—in an otherwise inconspicuous stretch of highway—to the specific concern here with the space of uncaring?

A search for no man's land is not a search for absolutes. Much like the administration of care, the management of uncaring requires attention to degrees and intensities. Perfectly controlling exposure and confining its effects to a clearly marked zone is often the fantasy of the abdicating sovereign. It is the state who would like to solidify the belief that the sovereign territory is the ultimate harbinger of care. For better or worse, it often is. However, the mutated leaves and injured insects in Cornelia Hesse-Honegger's oeuvre are testimony to the catastrophic failure of this fantasy and the ease with which harms travel far beyond the enclosed no man's land. The contours, as I discussed at length in chapter 2, are always more porous than the sovereign state would like us to believe. What these injured bodies and damaged surfaces nevertheless reveal are the political logic of uncaring and the exposures it brings about.

The challenge, to my mind, is not to determine where no man's land starts and ends. An approach of this sort will blind us to what is actually at stake in this study, namely, understanding the real consequences of systemic sovereign uncaring. To be sure, the most acute effects of uncaring are still likely to be felt within the no man's land, in zones where uncaring has morphed into a foundational logic of governance. But following the way its effects, its aftershocks and radiation clouds are felt over time and space, means that this project can do more than just provide a cartography of sovereign care and its absence.

Flesh: Exposure Joining Body and World

Exposure is hardly foreign to the vocabulary of no man's land. In 1917, the poet Wilfred Owen titled one of his best-known war poems "Exposure," a worm's-eye view of life on the edge of no man's land. Instead of bullets, ice and snow appear as lethal forces. Frost envelops skin and mud alike, blurring differences not only between life and matter but also between the living and the dead. Four times the poem repeats the refrain "But nothing happens," a reference to the paralysis of war and its futility. Indeed, the phrase concludes the last stanza of the poem, which depicts an excursion into no man's land to bury the dead; "all their eyes are ice," Owen writes, although it is unclear if those are the eyes of the dead or of their freezing undertakers.

Owen's war poetry captures the deadly natures of exposure, how it violently undoes the protective certainties of boundaries and cohesions. As so many scholars have documented in the century that followed World War I, exposure has only proliferated, as more lives are left bare, stripped of rights, protections, and possibilities. When considered in this light, exposure opens a rather bleak political horizon—one that is not entirely foreclosed but whose potential is hardly promising.

Decades later, another man wrote another poem from another no man's land. Muhammad Fu'ad Abu Zayd was born in 1935 in the town of Qabatiya near the city of Jenin, in the West Bank, and early in life he joined the Muslim Brotherhood. After studies at Damascus University, he taught high school for eighteen years, first in Jordan and then in Jenin. In 1977, he began working in the religious bureaucracy in the West Bank and was appointed mufti of the Jenin Governorate in 1996. At the same time, he served as a preacher in various mosques, including Al-Aqsa in Jerusalem. In 1992, he was one of the 415 Palestinians who were deported by Israel to Lebanon.

Having begun writing poetry in the 1970s, he continued to do so throughout his year in the mountainous no man's land of southern Lebanon. Several of Abu Zayd's poems from this time were published in a volume entitled *Heartbeats in Marj al-Zuhur* (*Nabaḍāt qalb fī Marj al-Zuhūr*).

In one long narrative poem, "The Cry of the Deportees" (*Nada' al-Mub'adin*), written a month after his arrival in southern Lebanon, Abu Zayd documents the harsh conditions that he and his fellow deportees encountered. As in Owen's poem from the Western Front, the visceral exposure to the elements features as a central experience of life in no man's land. Exposure once again seems to dissolve the clear distinctions between body and space, but not as a deadly rupture of the body that leaves it teetering on the brink of death. Instead, exposure is part of the metaphoric power of the poem; personifying inanimate landscapes—naked land, craggy hills, mountain peaks—becomes a form of strength, adaptability and resolve:

> They set up camps on the naked land
>> and refused to live like chased-off refugees.
> They resolved to remain in the craggy hills,
>> with willpower amply provided by their Lord . . .
> Their skin stings with the bitter cold,
>> but their slogans—such is the will of God—remain assured . . .
> Food was scarce, but still their voices repeated:
> "God is great! Our resolve will never die!"
> Their fuel depleted, but never their resolve,
>> while snow clouds gathered and loomed above them . . .
> Surrounded by mountain peaks on every side,
>> like the mountains, their resolve grew solid.[14]

Recasting exposure as a condition of openness and potential was not achieved only through poetic devices within the text. Numerous footnotes allude to occasions in which this and other poems were read out loud to a large audience of deportees in the camp. These acts of public readings became important moments of exposure to others, of being and creating with others. It was an affirmation of political vitality and action in a space that all too often is associated with fragmentation and deadly paralysis.

Poetry was only one creative practice adopted by the Palestinians locked in no man's land. Within days of setting up the camp, the deportees established a strict routine in which each person played a role in the fight for daily survival. They established various committees that split up routine tasks and made efforts to enhance the religious and cultural foundations of their lives. With infrastructural support from a nearby village, they built a cafeteria, a library, and Ibn Taymiyya University, an institution that offered courses in Palestine studies, language, professionalization, Qur'anic recitation, and karate. In a study of the large documentary archive that emerged from the camp, Keith Feldman and Emily Drumsta point out that at least nineteen writers produced more than thirty books, all but two of which were about the camp—including several collections of poetry, a yearbook for the university, documentary photomontages, and social-scientific analyses of life in the camp.[15]

One book by the Lebanese photojournalist and writer Sa'id Ma'alawi, *The Eagles of Marj al Zuhur: The Daily Struggles of the Palestinian Deportees, in Words and Images* (1994), provides an extensive documentation of life in camp, as well as a small portrait of each deportee. Ma'alawi refuses the visual conventions that constrict the depiction of Palestinians as either threats or victims. Instead, he turns his camera toward the very means of cultural production from which this kind of exposure emerges in the first place. One photo in the book is captioned "A camera crew from the television channel CNN International films and broadcasts live from the camp. This step had a significant impact in showing the true scope of the deportees' suffering." Part of what military occupation wields is a command over what is made visible and to whom. Haim Weiss, who was an officer in the Israeli army and at the time was stationed near the deportees' camp, recalled that the region was referred to as the "containment zone" with strict limitations on media access.[16] But in the Lebanese no man's land the Palestinian deportees transformed exposure from a vulnerability into an empowering instrument of political action and expression.[17]

It is not surprising, perhaps, that a group of activists organized itself when confronted with such severe circumstances. Many of the men who were deported in 1992 experienced firsthand the violent realities of Israel's military occupation and the political resistance to it.[18] However, organizing effective political action in the streets of a city—even a city under occupation—is more easily done than at an isolated mountain camp between opposing military forces. What stands out to me in the tale of the Marj al-Zuhur camp is not so much the novelty of political practices or the effectiveness of resistance strategies, but how it questions the very concepts through which we understand no man's land and the realities of life in it.[19]

In Marj al-Zuhur, the space of uncaring became, quite literally, a new vantage point; from the mountaintop camp set up between Lebanese and Israeli troops, many things were seen differently. Even when the state performed an explicit act of abandonment, literally leaving hundreds to fend for themselves, exposure was never reducible to mere defenselessness, precarity, or utter vulnerability. Instead, exposure was a way of seeing anew, another form of uncovering that brought about illumination, an ability to observe, to recognize and be recognized. These are facets of exposure that are rarely central to critical debates of political or economic abandonment, yet time and again they appear as inherent qualities of the space of uncaring.

Jean-Luc Nancy is often cited for his influential work on the juridico-political theorization of abandonment and the exposure of life to the force of the law. Many efforts to theorize systematic processes that leave entire populations defenseless and susceptible to harm drew important lessons from this critique. But Nancy also offers a very different understanding of exposure in his work on community and the philosophical possibility of being-in-common. For Nancy, community is not something that can be presupposed as a ground of being; as totalitarianism does in positing a fundamental essence to the community. Instead, for Nancy, community requires stepping outside of oneself. In his formulation, being exposed means "having to do with an outside in the very intimacy of an inside."[20] This is an affirmative understanding of exposure that does not end with the withdrawal of protections and its assumption of inherent vulnerability. Instead, what is opened here is the potential existence of commonality and community.

The Palestinian camp in Lebanon was designed as a microcosmic showcase of a utopian Islamic society: self-organized while spiritually and practically linked to an international *umma*; steadfast and grounded without losing sight of other spaces, concrete or symbolic; religiously pious while embracing creative practices and media acuity. No man's land became an incubator of alternative political horizons that, spatially and ideologically, existed outside the claim of the territorial nation-state. The activists who resided in this zone demonstrated and actualized what Grant Farred calls an "axiomatic politics": "the refusal of politics as the predetermined meeting in the middle—the ameliorating of extremes, the art of settling for, of the middle as the place where, in fact, no politics takes place."[21] This edge of territory, which was also the edge of care of the Israeli state, was where these experiments could materialize, even if fleetingly.

This political embrace of the abandoned edge is what was so explicitly embodied in the no man's land of Marj al-Zuhur. But this willingness to step out and form meaningful action with others is just one part of the political potential harbored in the space of uncaring. Celebrating outcast spaces of collective action alone will provide a very partial understanding of no man's land as a significant political space.

As Abu Zayd writes in his poem, a politics of affirmative exposure begins to emerge in the relation to others and the formation of new communities. Affirmative exposure can also inhabit a more intimate encounter between the body and the world, as in the immediacy of skin stinging from cold. In the concluding chapter of his expansive interrogation of biopolitics, Roberto Esposito develops the potential of affirmative exposure as an unmistakably embodied condition. The violent biopolitics of genocidal regimes, he argues, is obsessed with limiting exposure (to threatening Others); it exposes life only for the sake of its annihilation. Alternatively, Esposito follows Merleau-Ponty in introducing flesh as a mechanism that holds the potential for deconstructing the genocidal foundations of biopolitics. As the line that is in common between the body and the world, flesh refers to the "sensibility of things," all that connects us to others—beings, materialities, and intangible affects that surround us.[22] Once the flesh is seen not as an "abject zone of exclusion that culminates in death but an alternative instantiation of humanity," to borrow Alexander Weheliye's formulation, exposure can bring about an embodied, relational, and affirmative politics in no man's land, one that might even thrive in the space of uncaring.[23]

Exposure opens a much richer and more nuanced political horizon. In the space of uncaring, the haptic, sensual, and fleshy are not secondary to the act of politics; they are its deepest expressions. Far from abstract musings, fleshy exposures illuminate critical political conditions that surface throughout the archive of no man's land—from the corporeal poetics of the Western Front and the catastrophic porosity of Chernobyl's radiated bodies to the subversion of visual politics by the deportees in Marj al-Zuhur. They are also the space from which a different political horizon might open, one that reveals potential histories and yet-to-be-foreclosed futures.

7

Disorders

We can suffer abandonment but also find immense joy in acting with abandon.[1] It is perhaps not a coincidence that no man's land becomes a space where radical experimentations can flourish: When the sovereign turns its back on the space of uncaring, alternative visions can begin to materialize. The dual potentiality of exposure, at once an indication of the capacity to act and the "hardest and bitterest experience possible," runs through this chapter and throughout this book more broadly.[2] Nevertheless, recalling these instances of action, opposition, and experimentation in detail is important exactly because it grounds both possibility and its failures, situating them in concrete realities of political apathy, racial violence and the intractable intimacies of life. My return to these histories of disorder in this chapter is not done naively: Action rarely remedies the fundamental logic that underpins uncaring, nor the harms that it produces. But at the very least, it leaves open the possibility that alternative horizons are not always or completely foreclosed.

Osmotic Space

It seems like a bygone era, but hope rippled across the world in late 2011. The optimism of the people who then gathered to challenge oppressive political and socioeconomic realities subsequently gave way to disillusionment and violence, but it was not utopian, at least in the sense that it was not merely a placeless aspiration. Reclaiming public space became a central tenet of almost all the initiatives that emerged at this time, even when their political goals and historical contexts diverged radically. Lines of confrontation were largely drawn along competing spatial-economic logics, between those who sought to remake the (mostly urban) commons and a political elite that valorized the enclosure and privatization of these spaces in the name of market efficiency, austerity or "security concerns." All this is well documented and rather familiar. What happens, though, when the lines of struggle are no longer drawn along this binary set of competing interests, public versus private, commons versus enclosure? Specifically, what happens once the occupation of space is not pushing against the intrusions of a political system skewed by corporate interests and neoliberal logic, but against the absence of state presence and its refusal to assume even the most fundamental duties of care?

This isn't a thought experiment. In mid-October 2011, a group of Greek- and Turkish-speaking Cypriots began weekly occupations of the Ledra Street/ Lokmaci Gate crossing at the heart of Nicosia's divided Walled City. Through their actions, the Occupy Buffer Zone (OBZ) movement was formed. A month later, the group established a permanent presence "between the two checkpoints," a narrow north-south passage that crossed the dead zone. Tents were set up; a separate area was carved out as a collective kitchen and another for communal meetings. It was a cold winter, and by January, the activists moved into a building adjacent to their encampment. "The old shop of a luggage maker and the larger shop next door on the corner of the formerly vacant part of Ledra/Lokmaci Street, between the two checkpoints, are becoming our activity and events center," a leaflet announced in January.[3] Activists spent the next three months cleaning the building, preparing to expand the activity as the weather warmed up.

It was, to use Olga Demetriou and Murat Ilican's term, a laborious process of "organic rehabilitation."[4] They describe how debris that filled the building was integrated into the activists' spatial and temporal orientation around this small corner of the Buffer Zone. A flagpole on the roof hoisted a Greek flag, prompting debates about its presence in a space that was deliberately anti-nationalist. The flag disappeared after the pole collapsed one night during a storm, or so went the formal explanation. There were more humble interventions that fused the dilapidated materiality of the building into the reconfigured space, from old newspapers and books that were added to a communal library to sandbags that were used to prop up tabletops in the activity center. It can be thought of as an "archaeology of knowledge," Ilican told me when we spoke. "It means that you don't pass something without evaluating it . . . without touching it and feeling it."[5] Rudimentary improvisations like these constitute a place-based ethics of care that is not directed at the symbolic realms of memorialization or healing in the aftermath of violence but is grounded through a politics of direct practice and immediate need.[6]

The scene resembled other occupy encampments around the world, but the location set it apart from the squares and parks that housed demonstrations around the world at the time. In 2008, this small section of the UN-controlled Buffer Zone was celebrated as a central site of diplomatic breakthrough when it was opened as a formal crossing, allowing people, tourists, and shoppers to cross to the other side.[7] Like many officials on the two sides, the United Nations considered the opening a clear achievement: UN officials hung an exhibition documenting it on the walls of abandoned houses that flanked the crossing. Three years after the opening, however, the initial excitement was dimming: diplomatic negotiations toward reconciliation were at a stalemate, and with the biting recession that followed the 2008 global financial crisis, public discourse was becoming increasingly insular and nationalistic. "In Cyprus," OBZ activists noted in their formative statement published two months after the occupation began, "we have not only become used to the discord between us, but have also become used to its creation and re-creation."[8] Occupying the Buffer Zone was a refusal to acquiesce to this state of affairs, to "become used to" the logic of partition, to the perpetuation of enmity and the socioeconomic orders that sustain it. In other words, they were no longer content to turn their back on the dead zone.

Despite its centrality, the location of the encampment built by the activists was not a reclamation of a privatized commons. The administration of neither the Turkish Republic of Northern Cyprus nor the Republic of Cyprus has had any formal foothold in the Buffer Zone since the drawing of the ceasefire lines in 1974. Who, then, were the occupiers reclaiming the space from?

Formally, at least, the UN peacekeeping forces were responsible for policing the Buffer Zone and dealing with the "invasion." In practice, it was much more complicated. Ilican, who accompanied the OBZ activists, recalled the complex maneuvers that surrounded the removal of a protest banner expressing solidarity with a Turkish-Cypriot blogger who documented torture within the ranks of the Turkish army. Although they were positioned only a few meters away, the ceasefire agreement prohibited the entry of Turkish forces into the Buffer Zone. They therefore had to rely on the United Nations to remove the sign. Later that night, the United Nations also supervised as Turkish soldiers confiscated the OBZ generator that was placed closer to their positions, while agents of the Republic of Cyprus secret police were closely monitoring from the south to ensure that the action was not violating the careful status quo.[9] On a daily basis, with the most rudimentary tools—some banners, tents, a generator—OBZ exposed the byzantine administration of the Buffer Zone and the excessive labor it required, which otherwise remained largely discrete.

The presence of the activists was a threat to many of the political myths that helped forge collective identities on both sides of the divide. In the north, the Turkish Republic of Northern Cyprus relies heavily on the Buffer Zone as a border that buttresses the sovereign pretenses of what Rebecca Bryant and Mete Hatay define as an "aporetic state."[10] The crossing points in particular have become key performative spaces, where the Turkish Republic of Northern Cyprus sets up booths to inspect passports of those crossing and stamp them with visas that are not recognized by any other state and are seen as an outright insult by many Greek-speaking Cypriots.

Simultaneously, the OBZ activists exposed the southern Cypriot reliance on the Buffer Zone as proof of enmity and ongoing struggle. There were also more subtle critiques of the sociopolitical and economic structures that preserve the concentration of real property in the hands of a small number of families and, most of all, in the hands of the church. As a whole, OBZ highlighted the deep conservativism of Cypriot society and its aversion to any form of social transgression. Whether viewed from the north or the south, the activists that occupied the Buffer Zone called out the thin facade behind which authority hid. For Slavoj Žižek, "This appearance is essential: if it were to be destroyed—if somebody were publicly to pronounce the obvious truth that 'the emperor is naked' (that nobody takes the ruling ideology seriously . . .)— in a sense the whole system would fall apart."[11] The whole system did not fall apart, but the critique was important nevertheless.

From within the Buffer Zone, activists were able to draw specific attention to the hypocrisies of the reconciliation discourse that gained prominence in the years preceding the occupation. In the very first days of the occupation, the activist received an ultimatum letter from the United Nations stating the requirement to obtain permission for any "bi-communal event or activity" in the Buffer Zone. The protestors' response was unapologetic: "We are not a bi-communal movement or activity, but a peaceful, yet occupying multicultural force." As Ilican observes, the activists' demand for a complete and immediate demilitarization and unification of the island was largely in line with the UN position, making it nearly impossible for the United Nations to take an overtly confrontational stance, at least in the first instance.[12] Later on, when threats of forced eviction became more explicit, the occupiers again called out the contradiction between official UN support for unification and its refusal to accommodate those who actively practice it. One banner, clearly addressed to UN officials, summed this up neatly: "We are here to unite the island. Removing us means you're supporting a divided Cyprus. Make up your mind."

By early April, six months after the first tents went up, the authorities made up their minds. The activists were just about to launch their radio station and music was pouring out the open windows of the cultural center, inviting pass-ersby to come in. There was a sense of joy and freedom; one could act with abandon. "When the state saw that we are not going to be monkeys in a cage and we are actually trying to move outside," Ilican recalled, "that's when they destroyed us." On the night of April 7, 2012, an antiterrorism unit of the Cy-priot police raided a building inside the Buffer Zone where OBZ activists set up the cultural hub. Unusually, the Turkish military closed the crossing to the north, blocking the activists' escape route. When police moved in, they did so with full force, arresting at gunpoint twenty-eight people. Seven were beaten and injured during the arrest.

For a brief moment, sovereignty made an appearance in the dead zone. The state suddenly cared. The raid was a spectacular performance of state vio-lence, seeking most obviously to bring transgressive bodies back in line. In-flicting violence on bodies was, however, only one aspect of this resurgent sov-ereign force. Specific effort was made by the police to reinstate the dilapidation that ruled this small corner of the Buffer Zone: Doors, chairs, music equip-ment, and valuable instruments were deliberately damaged when the police squad moved in. Even the chicken coup built by the activists wasn't spared—four chickens were missing, two were dead and seven were found alive.[13]

It is all too easy to see this as merely a predictable fallout from the indiffer-ent use of brute force. But in the dead zone, uncaring is not an aberration, but a condition of possibility. Rather than a failure of the sovereign pastor to ad-minister care—when sovereign violence is understood as merely the acts of a bad shepherd who "disperses the flock, lets it die of thirst, [and] shears it solely for profit"—in no man's land the absence of care is systematized.[14] It is a found-ing, constitutive logic and perpetuates the existence of these spaces. There was no failure in the police raid. The highly trained antiterror unit was perfectly capable of removing the activists with little commotion. Doing so, however, would have deprived the state of the opportunity to reenact the absence of care that sets this space apart from the normative sovereign order of care outside it.

A few days after the violent eviction, OBZ activists returned to the site. For a month, they gathered to discuss their options in the reopened coffee room. Contrary to their earlier ire, neither the Cypriot authorities in the south nor the Turkish military in the north showed any urgency to once again evict the activists or police their activities. It took them many months to gradually resecure the area occupied by the protestors.[15] One could say they didn't care, but that, of course, was the point all along.

Green Line, Black Panther

In 1951, Israel built a set of walls along the edges of the no man's land that ran through Jerusalem to protect residents living in border neighborhoods from Jordanian sniper fire. The sniper walls supplemented the coils of barbed wire and minefields that were already strewn between the Israeli and Jordanian forces. Rough frontier structures of this sort are the hallmark of no man's land, but other elements were lodged into the fabric of the line. From the early days after the partition of the city, state officials made concerted efforts to buttress the urban perimeter with the presence of human bodies, adding to the concrete and wire. "It was not a functional stone wall," Adriana Kemp observed in her description of life in the neighborhoods along the no man's land, "but a living wall of settler-fighters that would protect their personal and national home."[16]

"Settler-fighters" sounds heroic. Indeed, some of those residing on the edge of no man's land did so out of choice. With the typical machismo and sexism of an Israeli army veteran, Shlomo Baum recalled how, in 1955, he was fed up with renting a room from "Jerusalem housewives that counted my showers and the number of 'chicks' I brought home."[17] Using his military knowledge of the line, Baum found an empty home in Abu Tor, a small neighborhood that was split between Israel and Jordan in 1948. Arieh Zachs, an Israeli poet and later a professor of theater and classics at the Hebrew University of Jerusalem, also moved to Abu Tor, attracted by its affordability and tranquility. He lived in the neighborhood from 1963 until his death in 1992. He described his home, which was facing the Jordanian Legionnaires, as the "end of the world."[18]

For others, the edge of no man's land offered a different kind of refuge. Reuven Abergel was seven years old when his family emigrated from Morocco to Israel. Initially, the family was sent to a transitional camp in the north of the country, but with no prospect of work and the absence of a social support network, they decided to flee the camp. They boarded a truck that took them to Musrara, where other relatives already lived, and settled on the ground floor of a house just a block away from the no man's land. "Twelve of us shared a single room," he told me, "but the second floor, which was empty, was too dangerous. It was too visible to the snipers."[19]

Seeking shelter in the shadow of no man's land was not an obvious act. Israeli state authorities in the early 1950s placed great emphasis on the distribution of Jewish immigrants around the country. It was a national strategy that saw the immigrant population from North Africa and the Arab world as a movable asset that can be settled according to political needs and geopolitical calculation. By refusing to stay put, the Abergel family and others who fled the transit camps, turned a story of hegemonic coercion to one of defiance.[20] Most of them had only few belongings—Reuven remembered their furniture consisting of only a couple of metal army beds—but defiance was one thing that traveled with them.

After the partition of Jerusalem, the Jewish population of the city soared, rising 45 percent within two years.[21] Hundreds of homes belonging to Arab Palestinians forced to flee during the war were quickly used to alleviate the severe housing shortage in the city.[22] The homes, however, varied in size, grandeur, and, importantly, their proximity to the front lines. An official hierarchy was therefore established to manage this process: the villas of Talbiyah and the German Colony were allocated to senior government officials, and junior clerks were sent to the humbler neighborhoods of Baq'a and Abu Tor. Newly arrived immigrants from North African and Arab-speaking countries, meanwhile, were concentrated in frontline slums like Musrara and Mamilla.[23] Until the partition of the city, the latter had been wealthy neighborhoods built just outside the Old City walls. But by the early 1950s, the violence had taken its toll. During Musrara's first decades, all its basic services were linked to the eastern part of the city; after the partition, everything was cut off. Electricity was severed, sewer pipes were blocked off, and excrement flowed directly into the no man's land. "Everything between the outer houses of the neighborhood and Damascus Gate on the other side looked like a swamp," Reuven recalled. "The mosquitos were so big that they scared off the birds."[24] The Arab Jews who inhabited these neighborhoods couldn't escape as easily: from one side, they were pushed out to the edges of the urban frontier, and from the other, they were hemmed in by the barricades of the no man's land.

Even if the Green Line that marked the edges of the no man's land in Jerusalem started out as a graphic fiction drawn amateurishly by two generals, it was also a *useful* fiction that gave a colorful articulation to the Israeli state's binary ethno-territorial logics: up to the line, Israel; beyond it, Jordan. Up to the line, Jews; beyond it, Arabs. Up to the line, friend; beyond it, foe. The color of the line set the two conveniently apart and established an aggressive mutual exclusion. But the burden of keeping this fiction alive was not shared equally. Brown and Black bodies of Arab Jews were de facto placed in the line of fire. As such, they doubly inhabited the line: at the same time that they were corporeally complicit in buttressing the myth of territorial cohesion, they were being subjected to its violence. "We were cannon fodder," one woman recalled. "The people in Musrara were cannon fodder."[25]

This visceral sense of abandonment was rooted in the city's hierarchy of care. Simply put, the closer you were to the no man's land, the lesser the care you were deemed to deserve. In Musrara, hierarchy was not only coded into the scarcity of resources or the neighborhood's economic deprivation but also experienced through topography itself. Affluence resided on the ridges—in well-off neighborhoods like Talbiyah and Rehavya. Descending eastward toward the basin that surrounds the Old City walls also meant the gradual disappearance of services and the erosion of infrastructure. Living at the bottom of a steep hill also reflected the social stratification of the city: people in Musrara were, in an utterly physical sense, being looked down upon. If care was completely absent from the no man's land, those living in its shadow palpably experienced its withdrawal, without formally or completely being deemed beyond the pale.

Traveling, then, from the center of western Jerusalem to the no man's land was a journey through the gradients of care. Gradients denotes here the varying extents to which care is applied, including its benevolent provision in the affluent parts of the city, its gradual erosion in places like Musrara, and its almost complete disappearance in the no man's land. As scholars of segregation and inequality have extensively documented, care is never equally applied. But no man's land highlights more than the familiar failures in the provision of care in spaces plagued by racial stratification, neoliberal privatization, or even extreme conditions of genocidal violence.[26] Care, I would argue, is present in these cases even if it is broken, insufficient, or catastrophically intrusive. Instead, no man's land confronts us with the systematization of uncaring and its emergence as part of the spatial vocabulary of governance.

Residing in the shadow of no man's land meant enduring the violent exposure that came with this systematic absence of care. But it was also a refuge, a place to escape to from the strictures of an imperious state and its systemic discrimination of Arab Jews. At times, though, the no man's land was just a spontaneous shelter from the enclosures of poverty and social stigmatization. Now in his seventies, Reuven still recalls his childhood in vivid details. Contrary to most descriptions of life on the urban front, he insisted that "the walls and barricades didn't confine us, and we often found our way into the no man's land." At times this was pure childhood adventure, a test of courage and curiosity. But other reasons drew some children into the no man's land. Seeking respite from the crammed and tense situation at home, Reuven found a ruined house in the no man's land where he could stash books he stole from a shop down town. "At home there was always commotion and stress. It was impossible to find a quiet spot. My 'fort' was the only place I could read."[27] The first book he remembers reading in his no man's land fort was Jules Verne's *Around the World in 80 Days*. The grand adventures of Phileas Fogg were a far cry from the confined realities of life in 1950s Jerusalem, but that is partly what made no man's land a perfect literary escape.

The war that broke out in 1967 and the resulting Israeli occupation of the West Bank radically transformed Jerusalem: from a divided frontier city, it became the center of an Israeli euphoria, with tens of thousands flocking to see the newly occupied eastern part, most notably the Old City and its holy landmarks. With similar zeal, Israeli authorities wasted no time in seeking to eradicate the Green Line. The no man's land was a marker of partition that had to be erased: barbed wire was removed, minefields were cleared, and bulldozers were sent to remove the ruins that littered this dead zone. Having both East and West Jerusalem under Israeli control also meant that neighborhoods that until then lay at the urban frontier, in the shadow of no man's land, found themselves at the heart of the so-called unified city. As land values soared in the new inner city, neighborhoods adjacent to the old ceasefire line became the target of mass evictions, making way for lucrative gentrification projects and construction of valuable commercial property.[28] The houses of the Musrara neighborhood were set to be demolished to make way for the construction of tenements for Jewish immigrants from the Soviet Union.[29] Arab Jews who lived there for two decades were now being evicted. In the effort to eradicate the no man's land, the removal of mines and barbed wire went hand in hand with the racialized displacement of bodies. All were disruptive reminders of the rift that had until then carved through the city.

Enter the Black Panthers. In 1971, four years after the war, the Israeli Black Panther Movement emerged as the most radical effort to date to challenge Israel's ethnic, socioeconomic, and political hegemony. Traditional chronicles of the Black Panthers focus on the growing frustration among young Arab Jews at their racialized disenfranchisement and marginalization by the country's Jewish European elites.[30] These accounts trace the Panthers' emergence to their first demonstration in March that year, which quickly turned violent and solidified their mass public appeal. To date, no other protest movement has gained similar resonance.

But these familiar accounts of the Black Panthers often downplay the fact that many of its activists originated from Musrara. Their formative years were spent in the shadow of no man's land, a space that was not just a backdrop of childhood memories or merely where experiences of discrimination, marginality and antagonism were first felt. The no man's land played a more direct role in the political formation of the Black Panthers, although that took place at a moment when the no man's land was seemingly becoming obsolete. After the 1967 war, as the walls and fences were coming down, the no man's land not only opened new spaces for capitalist creative destruction under the guise of urban renewal and postwar reconstruction, but also opened— quite literally—new horizons, socially and politically. "You could see farther,"

Reuven told me. He was talking partly about the landscape that opened in front of him and partly about the more-than-ocular ability to encounter others and be acknowledged by others. It was a moment of political reckoning, and it took place in the no man's land.

Shortly after the war, young men from Musrara used their contacts in East Jerusalem to sell hashish to university students and tourists. These ventures soon developed into joint watermelon stands that were built inside the former no man's land, ramshackle sheds of wood and tarpaulin, where every evening Arab Jews and Palestinians played music and drank together. These encounters with Palestinians and radical left-wing students created a very different kind of exposure: not exposure in its familiar biopolitical sense that leaves lives precariously stripped of fundamental protections, but exposure as an openness and illumination of potentialities that were otherwise foreclosed. Specifically, the watermelon shacks enabled exposure to the radical political thinking of the late 1960s and early 1970s, to ideas of Black Power and the civil rights movement in the United States.[31] This proved critical to the shaping of the Israeli Black Panthers' rhetoric, political agenda, and even their visual symbols—the movement adopted the clenched fist of the Black Power salute as its official banner.

As important, though, was the direct exposure of young Arab Jews to Palestinians. For some, the watermelon shacks in the no man's land provided the ground for a deep rethinking of the basic tenets of Israeli ethno-nationalism and the logics that set Arab and Jew as diametrical oppositions that cannot—indeed, must not—meet.

One of the Black Panthers founding members, Kochavi Shemesh, reflected on this radical shift:

> The Panthers were ahead of Israeli society by a whole generation, and ahead of the Left as well. We had connections with the Palestinian Liberation Organization as early as 1972. We met with PLO leaders and recognized them as legitimate leaders of the Palestinian people. We had talks, and we understood their need for independence and to eliminate the occupation, and we agreed that the problems of [Arab-Jews] and of Arab-[Palestinians] are intertwined. There will be no equality and no chance for Arab-Jews as long as there's an occupation and a national struggle, and on the other hand, the national struggle will not be over so long as Arab-Jews are at the bottom of the ladder, and are particularly [used] as an anti-Arab lever.[32]

Connecting geopolitical, ethnic, and socioeconomic struggles has long been the elusive holy grail of the international Left. For members of the Black Panthers, this was an experiential, almost intuitive link that pushed them to

challenge Israel's core political paradigms of ethnonational enmity and racialized socioeconomic stratification.[33] All this, starting with watermelon shacks
in the no man's land.

The architecture of exposure that emerges here bears little resemblance to
the blunt fortifications of no man's land. They are, after all, just watermelon
shacks: seasonal, rudimentary, transient, and open. In 2012, the artist David
Behar was commissioned to redesign a watermelon shack in the former no
man's land, working closely with Koko Deri, one of the founding members of
the Black Panthers who owned one of the original shacks.[34] It was an agora-
like structure, where exchange and encounter were possible, supplemented
by fruit and booze.

This prelude to the formal emergence of the Black Panthers illuminates
the subtle transformations in the logics of partition and segregation that constituted the no man's land in the first place. As noted before, the fortification
of the Green Line was based on a logic of ethnonational enmity, a physical
expression of a false diametrical opposition between Jews and Arabs, and the
imagined cohesion of a national collective. In turn, the removal of the blunt
architectures of the Green Line exposed what W. E. B Du Bois famously described as the "color line," the racialized structures that reject and violently
retaliate against any transgression of a dominant segregative order.[35] If fortified structures were previously used to segregate Jews and Arabs, the humble
architectures of watermelon shacks in the no man's land functioned as a radical hyphen.[36] They spatially brought together Jews and Arabs. But more profoundly, they raised a possibility of the Arab Jew as an identity that refuses
the racial binaries that underpin settler colonial logics. The space of uncaring was where encounters of this sort were made possible—encounters with
others, but importantly also encounters with oneself, with personal cultural
identities that struggled to find a place outside it. This refusal to accept foreclosed binaries and the opening of new urban and political horizons remains
one of the core facets that conventional histories of no man's land repeatedly
ignore.

As long as these encounters were confined to the watermelon shacks in
the no man's land, the state showed little concern. For two decades Israeli authorities focused almost exclusively on confining this space and perform-
ing its extraterritorial status: marking and retracing the line with barricades
and fortifications that designated no man's land outside the normative sovereign order. This entrenched absence of care was not about to be reversed
overnight. At that brief moment before the no man's land became the site of
massive strategic infrastructural development, while officials were still looking away, critical encounters could flourish.[37]

This is not a story with a happy ending. Many of the watermelon shacks were torn down in the 1970s to make way for a highway that ran along the convenient gap that the no man's land carved through the city. Speeding cars, rather than barbed wire, now bifurcate the Palestinian neighborhoods in the east from the Jewish neighborhoods in the west. The Black Panthers' emergence in the public sphere was similarly short lived. Within a few years the group's work was brought to a near halt by intense police harassment, fatigue, and ideological rifts. The war that broke out in 1973 once again drew the line of aggression along familiar battlefronts. Yet for a brief moment, the Israeli Black Panthers forced a remaking of the relation to self and others in a way that was never done before, and that few have repeated since. This radical action took place in utterly humble architectures of no man's land, which, like a watermelon, emerged in that meeting point between green and red.

Shadows of Care

Five years after Jerusalem was divided by the no man's land, the Palestinian author Emile Habibi used the main crossing between the two parts of the city as the setting for his first story, "Mandelbaum Gate" ("Bawwabat Mandelbaum"). It tells the story of an elderly Palestinian woman who wishes to cross to the Jordanian side to see her daughter who was separated from the family during the 1948 war. Otherwise accessible only to diplomats and UN personnel, the gate was also opened to Christian pilgrims and Palestinians with special permits, often to reunite with family members. While her family kisses her goodbye, the Israeli customs officer issues a warning: "Whoever exits from here never comes back."[38] For the elderly woman leaving her home, her land and her family behind, the no man's land is a space of transition between life and death. But as she slowly crosses the strip of land between the Israeli and Jordanian posts, surrounded by ruined houses and debris, the melancholic scene is suddenly disrupted: ignoring the warning signs and armed officers, the woman's granddaughter runs after her grandmother, across no man's land, for one last embrace. Habibi's narrator sees this as nothing less than a "great miracle": "A little girl cuts across the Valley of Death from which none return. And see, in spite of everything she does come back to us crowned with triumph over the present reality of war, borders, and the Mandelbaum Gate."[39]

What kind of triumph is Habibi writing about? When the story was published in 1954, Palestinians living in Israel were under a military rule that governed almost all aspects of life: employment, political representation, movement restrictions, and confiscation of property. The scene of a child running across the no man's land seems as merely a naive literary anecdote in this context. Most political chronicles of no man's land would stick to more obvious figures of protest. After all, their willingness to stand out, to disrupt the order of things and to command attention makes them obvious protagonists. To an extent, this is understandable: activists and oppositional groups have reanimated the space of uncaring, infused it with political energy and potential. Yet part of what makes these moments significant is their exceptionality, the fact that they uniquely interrupt the normative flow of events. Conversely, for most, everyday life flows through the mundane rather than the monumental. And still, it is the radical and extraordinary that leave a lasting impression: It is the Panthers' demonstrations and their contentious meeting with Golda Meir, the Israeli prime minister, that made it into the historical records, not their childhood games or youthful ventures selling watermelon in no man's land. However, some of the most significant disruptions to the space of uncaring happen not in the limelight but in the shadows.

When sovereign care is withdrawn it leaves lives and lands in the shadow, a space dark enough so that harms go unnoticed, but also a place where restrictions and prohibitions that reign outside are suspended. There, in the shadow, other horizons for action and imagination open up. Hunaida Ghanim noted that in "vernacular Arabic, the term *khayal* is a synonym for *thel* (shadow), but the free translation of *khayal* is, literally, 'imagination': the similar and the imagined. This means that *khayal*—shadow—is not only a reflection of its possessor; it is also an 'engine' that activates his or her free thoughts, reveries, waking dreams and fantasies."[40] What links the story of a young Palestinian girl running across no man's land to hug her grandmother with that of a young Jewish boy reading stolen books in the wreckage that litters this space is exactly the ability to let another kind of imagination fill the space of uncaring. I return to the fantasies that are projected onto no man's land later, but it is worth repeating what is often not obvious: under conditions of systemic marginalization, and racial or patriarchal violence, letting the imagination run wild is no small feat. James Baldwin wonderfully captured this power when he wrote:

> Imagination
> creates the situation
> and, then, the situation
> creates imagination.
>
> It may, of course
> be the other way around:
> Columbus was discovered
> by what he found.[41]

Yet note that in the second stanza of the poem Baldwin questions whether imaginative manifestation alone ever exists. It is an important doubt, especially given the real violence that colonial imaginations unleashed, be it in the North American context Baldwin writes about or the one Habibi writes about in Palestine. Encounters with the space of uncaring are not mere figments of imagination. Instead, those who come into contact with these spaces are themselves formed and transformed. And for those who refuse to conform to the strictures of the colonial, patriarchal state, the space of uncaring also gives a chance to break past the border guards that police their lives beyond its boundaries. The realm of uncaring facilitates a potential encounter with individuals, ideas, and material realities that may be considered otherwise transgressive, although the form of these encounters may not at all resemble the heroics of exploration and "discovery."

Rafi Marziano, who was part of the Black Panthers in the early 1970s, remembers people singing in Arabic in the watermelon shacks where Arab Jews and Palestinians would meet in the evenings. "You need to understand that there was almost nowhere else in West Jerusalem where we could sing in Arabic out in the open," he told me when we walked through his old neighborhood. During the first decades after Israel's independence, Arab music was considered an abject element that had no place in the national culture of the Westernized Jewish state. Despite the large Arab Jewish population that considered it part of its cultural identity, Arab music was not performed in concert halls or as part of the repertoire of mainstream orchestras. Even Israeli Hebrew radio stations rarely played it.[42] In the no man's land, in contrast, no one policed the performance of culture. No one cared whether a Jew sang in Arabic, and people sang with abandon.

A song, a hug, a meeting with someone from the other side of town—such are the small disorders that are carried out with great care, and for the most part, may be unimaginable anywhere but in the space of uncaring.

8

Man's Land?

Scantily clad women on the edge of a road, standing or sitting on plastic chairs, at times alone and at times in pairs. They are surrounded by luscious green vegetation and wide-open skies. And while their bodies are largely exposed, their faces are blurred.

This is perhaps the first hint regarding the origin of the images that make up *No Man's Land*, a project by the artist Mishka Henner: it is an eerie collection of photographs based on images appropriated from Google Street View, each documenting sex workers in Italy and Spain. Men—the clients—are absent, making the women the only humans populating the landscapes. Trash, however, is abundant, scattered in roadside ditches and lay-bys, dotting fields and olive groves. Detritus is also transformed into a makeshift architecture that offers the women shade or a place to sit: an old couch, a discarded tractor tire, a plastic bucket (see plate 3). "Aesthetically," Henner noted, "what drew me was this lush green landscape punctuated by these women and trash everywhere. Discarded trash, discarded lives."[1]

Trash is only one visual cue that sets these southern European wastelands apart from the Arcadian landscapes that populate neoclassical paintings of the very same regions.[2] Other elements scar the surface of the images, directing attention from the subjects caught on camera to the technologies that produce these images in the first place. When Henner began working on the project, in 2011, the imagery produced by Google Street View cameras and the software used to generate its three-dimensional effect was relatively rough, still a ways away from the seamless experience it purports to offer users a decade later. Henner consciously incorporates these "defects": "What I loved about working with Street View is that all the glitches are there- the imperfection, the traces, sometime even traces of the speed of the car when the edges are blurred. There's movement. . . . All of those things interrupt this kind of really pure reading of the image."[3]

Smears and blurred markings have had an intimate relation with the production of no man's land. They turn neat, abstract lines on paper into wide stretches of territory on the ground. But through Henner's visual practice, the imperfections and blurs are no longer considered just as fateful errors. Instead, they call attention to other bodies, harms, and technologies that are all too often rendered invisible.

No man's land, according to most chronicles, is populated by men who fight over it, are killed and wounded in it, and at times agonize over its horrors. Men are almost always the protagonists of these tales even though they are often tormented and deeply scarred protagonists; masculinity itself was one of the casualties of the Great War. Yet even if the shattered landscape between the trenches profoundly destabilized masculine notions of identity, sexuality, and gender, no man's land was still largely a man's land.[4] Women, in turn, are relegated to the peripheries of this militarized "theater of operation": they appear as the refugees fleeing the front lines; they serve "in the rear" as nurses in field hospitals and dressing stations; or more often, they exist even further afield, supporting the war effort through labor and love while waiting "back home" for news from the front. The English term *no man's land* literally places man at its center.

Yet like other harms, abandonment is never distributed equally, nor is it evenly experienced. Once no man's land is no longer considered solely through the obvious battlefields of World War I, the scene of violence that emerges from these spaces can no longer be reduced to masculine bodies exposed to the brute force of mechanized war in a wasteland of shattered earth and debris. In the spaces of uncaring, abandonment's effects are most acutely felt by those already facing deeply rooted systems of exploitation and domination, from patriarchal strictures to racist orderings. Historically, the state has helped uphold these exploitative orders, but its withdrawal offers little remedy or refuge. Intimate violence lingers, even when its impacts are far from view, relegated to back rooms and side roads.

The no man's land that emerges from Henner's photographic practice invites us to see these spaces in stark new light. First, he refuses the visual tropes that have solidified the spaces in Western cultural imagination in the past century. The images he extracts from southern European side roads bear little resemblance to the spectacular landscapes of smoldering debris and scorched earth. But the images invite us to ask what uncaring actually looks like in the twenty-first century and where it takes place, whether it might be just as endemic in the brownfield lands surrounding towns and cities in southern Europe where women make a living on the side of small roads.

Second, Henner's work conceptually prompts us to see no man's land as inextricably gendered. Women are clearly at the center of these images, but the project poses a more profoundly critical challenge to the ways we think of gendered abandonment. Most critical efforts to document the exposure of women to systematic forms of political abandonment still retain the state in its familiar position as the arbiter of care and life. It is an important corpus that highlights how contemporary systems of care fall short, prove inadequate, callous, greedy, or outright punitive.[5] These are urgent concerns. But what happens when the state isn't simply clumsy or cruel but is intentionally seeking to renunciate all pretense of care? What perpetuates such gendered harms in spaces of radical uncaring?

These questions prompt us to seriously consider abandonment as a concrete, embodied, and intimate condition rather than an abstract political constellation. Available vocabularies of lives stripped bare in spaces of legal exception and states of emergency often fail to capture more mundane routines and everyday existence where the harms of uncaring are not constant and catastrophic, but sporadic, selective and ordinary. Closely followed, it also confronts us with mechanisms that work to conceal its harms and deny their existence. While other harms are etched on to the surface, gendered exposures like those documented in Henner's *No Man's Land* are often blurred, coded, and obscured by indifference and complicity. This chapter follows these blurred patches in the history of no man's land, not to correct the record—it was never incorrect—but to push against the dominant gendered topology that situates women at the periphery of this space, at the edge of the edge of care.

"When the State Left": The Story So Far

Doreen Massey memorably describes space as "a simultaneity of stories-so-far."[6] In no man's land, however, stories are often all that remains, when the destruction of war wipes out even the traces of war itself. Most stories of no man's land revolve around such spaces of iconic catastrophe, with their smoldering ruins and lunar wastelands. Other stories of no man's land, though, have few physical markers to hang on to: the state withdraws with haste, with little fanfare, and even less concern to what and who is left behind. There are stories to be told about this too, although they aren't told as often, and when they are, they articulate the grand politics of uncaring through small places and small things. These stories assemble abandonment through mundane objects, inconspicuous economies, and improvised infrastructures, which don't always result in good stories—exhilarating, action-laden, setting villains versus heroes. Instead, such stories risk appearing insignificant or parochial. Yet through these unspectacular sites and faded objects, the state of uncaring emerges as a chronic assemblage that finds its way into the most intimate spaces, marked on bodies and routinized to such an extent that it is barely worth retelling.

Here's one, abbreviated story: La Cooperativa, a village in Colombia's western Amazon got its name from the cooperative kiosk around which it emerged. There were a few farms growing mostly maize, but not much aside from that. *Then the state left.* The guerrilla moved in, coca cultivation boomed, and the wild years began.

A lot gets lost in this condensed version—the backstory, for one: Yes, the state withdrew its forces, creating the Clearance Zone and leaving it to the control of the Fuerzas Armadas Revolucionarias de Colombia (FARC), but there was also a pervasive sense that the spaces abdicated never truly belonged to the Colombian state. In many respects, the Clearance Zone only made formal what was a decades-long reality of state neglect, indifference, and marginalization. The state never functioned as a competent proprietor of sovereign care. But this official designation mattered: it marked the first time the Colombian government formally abdicated territory and, with it, shirked its responsibility of care toward those who inhabited the space. The Clearance Zone territorialized what Michael Taussig has called Colombia's moral topography, that is, a set of hegemonic representations that set the supposedly civilized Andean highlands and people against the country's savage hinterlands.[7] From the mountains, those who inhabited the Clearance Zone were regarded as dispensable, if they were regarded at all.

Abbreviations also omit the storyteller. Don Gonzalo, a tall man in his early fifties, arrived in the region four years before the government's withdrawal. He was escaping "the mafia" and found work on a nearby farm that he later purchased. We crossed paths in 2017, just outside La Cooperativa on a sweltering afternoon. He was riding a large brown horse and was curious to see two outsiders walking down a farm road three hours from the nearest town. Standing in the sun, I told him about my interest in the village and in life during the years of the Clearance Zone. It turned out that he was the vice president of the community and had some stories he could share, so we agreed to meet after work in one of the bars.

"There was nothing here," he said that evening, "not even a road. The beer used to come on the back of a mule, and it was never cold because there

was no fridge in the village." A pit dug in the ground behind the kiosk became an improvised solution, keeping the beers buried away from the heat
outside.

However, once the Clearance Zone was announced and the threat of government incursions into the region was lifted, cultivation of coca boomed.
Thousands of people migrated to work in the coca fields and in the "kitchens" that processed coca leaves into cocaine. As FARC commanders gained a
monopoly on violence, they wasted no time in transforming the tiny hamlet.
Within months they had widened the cattle track into a dirt road that led to
the nearby town of Vista Hermosa. Supplies began to flow more easily into
the region. By 2000, fewer than eighteen months after the government abandoned the region, La Cooperativa was showing all the hallmarks of a boom
town. Beer, Don Gonzalo recalled, was one sign that things were dramatically changing. Rather than local Colombian beers, *Polar* was being imported
from Venezuela, and *Monterrey*—his personal favorite—was shipped from
Guatemala. Mules also fell out of favor with the arrival of stolen Toyota Land
Cruisers and Ford Explorers, SUVs favored by local FARC commanders who
no longer had to shelter in the forests.[8]

The arrival of beer and big cars complemented other tropes of boom and
glut. Money was a dominant feature: over breakfast of *caldo de pescado* in the
town of La Macarena, several boat mechanics and fishermen recalled with
some nostalgia the large canvas bags full of cash that were regularly offloaded
onto trucks that drove down to the small dock. For most people, though, glut
was a rather more humble affair. Doña Consuela, a woman who owned one
of the two bars still open in La Cooperativa, remembered that in 2000 the
first elementary school was opened and a doctor set up a clinic in the village.[9]
Both were rare amenities until the Clearance Zone was established, and neither survived its dissolution: the doctor fled, fearing retribution for his ties
to the guerrilla, and as families moved away, there were not enough children
to keep the school open. In the space of uncaring that was formed once the
state left, life was able to thrive, exactly because the care of the Colombian
state took, at best, the form of callousness and indifference. More often, it was
pernicious and imposed through brute military force.

For Peter, who drives his *línea* on the Macarena-Vista Hermosa route—
more a cattle path than a road—abandonment is deeply engrained into these
red-clay tracks.[10] He was a young boy during the early 2000s, but his father
was one of the first drivers to inaugurate the route that runs through the Serranía de La Macarena national park. Peter owes his livelihood to that road,
one of many roads the guerrilla paved as strategic supply routes to support
their rapidly expanding cultivation of coca.

Building the roads was hard work, often done as punishment for transgressing the rules set out by FARC. Anything from theft and drunken behavior to infidelity and even gossip carried a punishment. Makeshift tribunals were set up ad hoc, and verdicts were handed out by the local commander, often measured by the length of road one was forced to clear or repair. Once, as we were waiting for a barge to take us across the Guayabero River, Peter told me about a wealthy rancher who exceeded the number of forest hectares he was allowed to clear for his cattle. The local commander set him a stretch of road to fix, but the rancher sent a few of his farm workers to do it in his place. Several days later the man was dragged out of his house at gun point and spent the next few days working the road under the personal oversight of the guerrilla. "The red dirt of these tracks is soaked with blood," Peter said.

During our long drives we would often pick up children on the way back from school, deliver horse feed to a local farm, or drop off tools to be fixed by one of the mechanics in town. The red tracks led to stories, to the histories of those residing in the region and to the stories of those who were no longer there. Abandonment was a long story that was never just about existential angst. Instead, it was a tale about a school closing down or an acre of forest burning or the assassination of local community leaders and the indifference of the government. Stories, even when they are fragmented, broken, anecdotal and loosely connected, paint a multifaceted picture of uncaring as it takes concrete form and place. Such stories also gave the process traceable histories, political contexts and cultural vocabularies rather than abstract it into a general political or existential theory.[11]

"When the state left" is the zero point in the story of no man's land. It marks historically and conceptually the moment the state abandons any pretense of care. In Colombia, these stories convey the tale of an uncaring state, a community left to fend for itself and that remains ostracized for its alleged ties to the guerrilla. With no grand monuments to indicate the Clearance years, stories often cling to mostly innocuous markers—a boarded-up house or a collapsing bridge—that gave them a rhythm and place. These humble traces narrate hurt and injury but also the resignation of those who expect little from an uncaring state. "We lived together, unless you screwed up," Consuela said when she recalled the forced labor on the roads.

Usual stories, however, take us only so far. The theme of collective endeavor and experience partly emerges from the stigmatization of the region's residents as criminals, guerrilla collaborators, and enablers.[12] But it also implies that all those subjected to the state's abandonment somehow constituted a homogeneous group, at least in the sense that they were equally left exposed to a state of uncaring. This flattening of intricate social nuances ignores the deep structures of inequity that persist even in the absence of state apparatuses that produce and reinforce these hierarchies, from schools to the courts and state security forces. In particular, gendered violence is conspicuously absent from conventional accounts of life in the Clearance Zone. It is as if the antagonism toward the state, the experience of abandonment, and the harms that were unleashed in its wake consumed all other social relations and frictions.

Even when they are omitted from most accounts and recollections, gendered experiences of harm are never simply erased from the space of uncaring. They lodge themselves into places that preserve both the imprint of bodies and the forces they are subjected to. To be clear, this is not a melancholic poetics of space, but a tangible set of physical marks that exceed the stories so far, sometimes because they are too painful to recall or because of the utterly unremarkable state of their "repositories," ruined, dilapidated, and abandoned surfaces.[13] Far from obvious, these are very often only fragments in the material sense of ruins and rubble, broken parts of a larger whole, a system or structure that may no longer seem intact.[14] But fragments are also punctuation marks in a seemingly familiar tale of abandonment that no man's land endemically and violently produces. When I heard them, these caesuras halted the flow of telling, arresting the conversation with an uncomfortable silence. At times, though, this was a starting point of other stories that populate no man's land with other spaces and other bodies.

What follows is an attempt to document two gendered structures of harm that underlie the state of uncaring. Both are deeply entwined but point in importantly different directions. The first traces gendered violence as a structure of governance. In the space of uncaring, harms and injuries produced by abandonment are not aberrations of the governing structure but are normalized as part of its system of rule. When narrated by those subjected to its harms, it often emerges as a rupture, an external incursion on life and its social orders. A second understanding of gendered harms and their role in the space of uncaring shifts the attention inward, to the proximities of neighbors, to familial bonds and networks of friendship. Gendered abandonments can no longer be externalized as the sole act of state or the quasi sovereigns that emerge in its absence. Instead, it confronts us with intimate complicities, modes of being that sustain gendered abandonments in everyday routines and mundane exchanges. If systems of rule change over time—different banners, different guns, different uniforms—the complicities of uncaring illuminate the endemic harms that remain in abandonment's long wake.[15]

Gendered Abandonments I: Systems of Rule

One way of confronting gendered abandonment is to externalize it, to peg it onto systems of rule and structures of authority that have long sustained the gendered violence of the patriarchal state. The Colombian state may have formally designated the Clearance Zone beyond its realm of care, but others were keen to ensure that patriarchal orders remained intact.

When FARC took over the Clearance Zone, it initiated a campaign of "social cleansing" that governed every aspect of life, even the most intimate. This was not a chaotic campaign of violence unleashed indiscriminately. Instead, it was a set of stipulations—*reglas de convivencia*—published by FARC commanders and constituting one of the most important documents in the sparse archive of the Clearance Zone. Within days of the establishment of the Clearance Zone, compulsory assemblies in each village and town in the region were convened at which rules were read out. Public realms of law and order were integral to these assemblies, but the stipulations also encroached on the most intimate realms of domestic life: infidelity was a punishable crime, as were domestic abuse, sexual violence and even gossip. The state left, but patriarchal strictures of gendered regulation were there for all to see, pasted onto walls and trees, distributed as pamphlets and at times painted onto rocks.

But posters rip and paint fades. By the time I arrived in La Cooperativa, in 2017, the boom years were a matter of memory. From nearly a thousand residents during the Clearance years, only a dozen families were still living along the dirt road that ran through it. There was a kiosk, a bakery, and a couple of bars that blasted *vallenato* tunes to the few customers who played pool in the evenings.[16] But beyond the central cluster of inhabited houses, La Cooperativa bore the hallmarks of a ghost town, with dozens of buildings lying disused and in different degrees of decay. It was less than a year after the peace between the Colombian government and FARC, and I joined a group of scholars led by Diana Ojeda, a feminist geographer and friend, to attend a gender workshop at a guerrilla demobilization camp nearby. When we first drove through the village, the dereliction was striking.

The next morning, viewed up close, the dilapidated buildings contained an entire material archive of a Colombian boom town gone bust. In one bar there were heaps of empty La Costeña beer bottles and a 2002 calendar with fading images of horses still hanging in the kitchen. There were three abandoned clubs, with wooden dance floors visible under the thick layer of dust, and handmade mirror mosaics to spruce up the clapboard walls. At the *discoteca* Noches de Maravilla a disco ball was still hanging from the corrugated iron roof. A bar on the western fringe of the village had a professional pool table, so heavy that it required the owner to reinforce the floor, its green velvet surface soaked with water and partly covered by moss.

Among the abandoned houses in La Cooperativa, a small building almost at the edge of the village stood out from the rest, not only because it was at the very top of the hill. Its exterior was painted pastel blue on which someone had added a colorful mural of flowers, a bird, two half-moons, a setting sun, and a large red heart pierced by a black arrow. Even though it didn't make much sense, the mural was eye-catching. The faded script entwined in it read "En el placer está el sueño," roughly translated as "in pleasure is the dream." On the balcony wall, another small mural was slightly more suggestive: "Mi fruto prohibido Adán y Eva" ("My forbidden fruit, Adam and Eve"). The words were neatly drawn around a large apple. Walking onto the porch and into the narrow corridor that led to the rear quickly dispelled the mural's hazy naivete. Single wool-stuffed mattresses were still on the floor in each of the three small, windowless rooms. There was just enough light for Laura, my research assistant, to take a few photographs, but only because the wooden wall slabs have warped and detached from the frame since the place was abandoned. Whose bodies were made into "prohibited fruit" that can be coveted by those who frequented this establishment?

It took a couple of beers that evening for Don Gonzalo to mention the women who came to work in La Cooperativa's local brothels. It was the first and almost only time this would be acknowledged explicitly; sex work, and sexual violence more broadly, had very little place in tales of life in the Colombian Clearance Zone. "There was prostitution," Gonzalo said, "but it was clandestine, not formal. It was a man's world." Women, he said, were brought in from larger cities outside the zone—Bogotá, Villavicencio, Granada—and would stay for a few days. As if to balance the impression this would have given, he added that the girlfriends of local guerrilla commanders—"the bosses"—also had many lovers.[17]

Of course, it wasn't just a man's world. Many women already lived in the region when the Clearance Zone was declared, and many others came in search of work or even safety from the violence that raged outside. These women tell other stories of the Clearance years, stories of parenting, and mothering in particular, that painted life in the region in darker hues. "You had to develop two sets of eyes, one at the front of your head and one at the back," a woman told me once, recounting her fear that her children would be recruited into the guerrilla, a sentiment expressed by numerous others. At the office of the Colombian National Park Service in Vista Hermosa, a staffer recounted at length how the guerrilla threatened to kill her husband and recruit her young son and daughter. When she refused to allow it, she was held for six weeks in a rural farmhouse while the local guerrilla commanders deliberated whether she should be executed for her insubordination. Yet when asked whether she knew of any women who came to work in prostitution in the Clearance Zone, her response was brief: "Yes. It makes me sick."[18] There was nothing more to say about that. She quickly veered back to the violence experienced by girls recruited as child combatants to the *guerrilla*.

This moment of impatient dismissal says a great deal about the economy of violence in the space of uncaring. Some harms are more valuable than others; they are considered worthier, socially legitimate, and hence speakable and deserving of public acknowledgment. Recruitment of children to the *guerrilla*, for example, is an experience that can be narrated as part of a broader story of national conflict and class struggle, the suffering endured by campesinos for generations, and the sacrifices they made while trapped between the state and the *guerrilla*. With child soldiers, there is someone external to blame. Sex work, and the economic networks of sexual violence that sustain it, broach a sphere of violence that cannot as easily be mapped onto recognized coordinates of political struggle.

Sexual violence entails exposure to harms, but it is a dark exposure, often confined to a domestic geography that is conventionally considered distinct from the public sphere of politics and geopolitical struggles.[19] Addressing the challenge of accounting for these harms, Nayanika Mookherjee points out that sexual violence in violent conflict is not simply silenced but continues to exist as a "public secret." It cannot be narrated overtly, she argues, only invoked at specific moments of intersubjective exchange as scorn.[20] To say "It makes me sick," was an expression of that scorn but also an admission that this secret was still active and visceral, generating a stark bodily reaction nearly two decades after the fact. This kind of public secrecy that suppresses sexual violence in communal memories, Mookherjee writes, "makes it indispensable to the operations of power and subservience because it enchants a community into silence and shame."[21] Suppressing the presence of sex workers in the historical narrative of the community made it easier to maintain one's own moral facade: someone else had the power, the power to care and control; they are the ones to blame.

To a large extent, this is a valid stance. Once the Colombian state abandoned the region, FARC was eager to incorporate the performance of sovereign care into what Ana Arjona calls "Rebelocracy," a social order in which armed groups intervene beyond security and taxation—how people can dress, their sexual behavior, their use of alcohol and other mind-altering substances.[22] And much like the Colombian state, FARC's performance of care was enacted to police, often violently, a heteronormative social order.

In this sense, the blunt statement "it makes me sick" can be understood much more literally, specifically because of what sickness often entailed under the rules that governed the Clearance Zone. According to testimonies gathered shortly after the zone was formally abolished, HIV/AIDS was rapidly spreading in the regions under the control of the guerrilla. In response, obligatory HIV tests were imposed on the local population. The Twenty-Seventh Front of the FARC allegedly began a campaign of mass testing in the municipal area of Vista Hermosa, which includes La Cooperativa, to detect who was HIV-positive. Reportedly, twenty thousand people were forced to submit to the tests, at times at gunpoint, and to pay for them themselves. Those who tested positive were forcefully displaced from the region, as were the few openly gay men and even male hairdressers whose profession was enough to mark them as a moral threat.[23] This is a familiar performance of biopolitical care, but it emerges out of systemic uncaring.[24] The state may have turned away, but the regulation of life was still inseparable from the governance of heteronormative orders.

In much the same way, brothels and sex work were not a moral aberration but integral to the wider political economy of the Clearance Zone. Although it was an economy that was always deemed criminal, illicit, and transgressive, it also involved numerous others at different degrees of proximity. Like the widespread cultivation of coca and the arms trade that sustained FARC's decades of military struggle, the brothels were part of a geography of violent exploitation, common enough to merit regulation. According to one set of rules set by the guerrillas, "bringing in prostitutes" was an offense that carried a severe fine of one million pesos, but some evidence suggests that prostitution was tacitly tolerated and even regulated through compulsory medical examinations and even taxation by FARC.[25] In many respects, this resembles a well-documented phenomenon of military prostitution, where sex work is harnessed to serve armed forces.[26] Yet the particular realities of the Clearance Zone extract this political economy from the grid of state care and its deep links to neoliberal globalization and the political economy of violent conflict.[27] Instead, it foregrounds its existence in a specifically localized social order and systems of rule that have been explicitly severed from the conventional logic of state care.

There is some comfort in seeing gendered abandonments as solely the result of externally imposed systems of rule. Blame is more easily assigned. Yet there is a subtler dynamic that produces and sustains these harms, one that does not view abandonment as the sole act of state or the petty sovereigns that emerge in its absence. Instead, it resides much closer to home, in the intimate realms of complicity.

Gendered Abandonments II: Complicities

Some abandonments don't leave grand traces. Mishka Henner pointed to the
smears and imperfections that scar the surface of his images, traces of technologies that produce this space and so easily remain unaccounted for and
unaccountable. As a region controlled by a guerrilla group that has mastered
the art of camouflage and tracelessness for its very survival, the Colombian
Clearance Zone left very few material remnants of the wholesale sovereign
abandonment that produced and governed it. Silences and deflections that
surround gendered abandonments narrow this scarce corpus even further.
The brothel in La Cooperative was not a brothel, one woman insisted, "it was
a motel."

Until, that is, someone points at the scar without secrecy or shame.

I was sitting on the front porch of Arelis and Paisa at the center of Yarumales, a bucolic village of fourteen houses set along a single dirt track at the
very heart of the former Clearance Zone. It was late spring in 2019, and by
then, I'd been coming to Yarumales for extended visits for four years. I've met
and spoke to everyone there (granted, fewer than thirty people). I've walked
up and down its single road hundreds of times. There were always new stories, though, and that afternoon they were recalling the sadistic violence that
a local guerrilla leader, Rodrigo Cadete, was spreading in the region. They
told of Cadete's gruesome killings and his insistence on hanging the dismembered bodies of his victims from trees.[28] Arelis, then in her early forties, never
lost her measured tone when describing these horrors, and although her ten-
year-old daughter was sitting with us, it didn't seem like we were broaching a
sensitive topic. Given the openness of the conversation and the fact that my
research assistants, Laura and María Teresa, were sitting with us, it felt like a
good moment to ask about the brothels.

"You often describe the violent history of this region, and you've always
been open about that," I said, feeling like I was walking on eggshells. "But
there's something no one seems to be willing to talk about—the brothels and
the women that were working there."

"Which brothel?" she asked, again, completely unperturbed. "The one we
had here in Yarumales?"

Her answer caught me off guard. No one had ever mentioned a brothel
before. The thought that I'd missed a space like that in such a small place was
bewildering.

"We can go see it now if you want," she said.

And there it was, five houses down, seemingly impossible to miss. A large,
two-story building painted dark blue and green on the riverbank, at the very

FIGURE 7. A room in the Yarumales brothel, 2019. The chambers contained a bed made of wooden planks and a small back door for those embarrassed to enter through the front. Photograph by the author.

entrance to the village as you cross the bridge. It now stood empty, not an uncommon sight in the region after the collapse of the coca industry. At street level was a typical bar space with two pool tables. Another floor was built further down along the slope that descends toward the river, invisible from the road. Six narrow rooms faced a balcony with a serene view of the river, but none had any windows. In each, wooden planks were hammered together to form a rudimentary bunk, the only furnishing in the rooms (fig. 7). The most notable feature in each room was a small back door that led to the storage room of the bar.

"Those clients who didn't want to be seen going in from the street could pretend they were going into the bar," Paisa explained.

Some of the details they noted confirmed Don Gonzalo's recollections from La Cooperativa. Women were brought in from cities and would stay for a few days at a time. But Arelis had more intimate insights. The women would come for three days, usually for the weekend, and would meet customers for fifteen minutes each, sometimes seeing more than twenty men in a row. The going rate was one hundred thousand Colombian pesos.

"I often thought this might be very difficult for them," she said as we walked back out onto the road. "But when I asked them, they would say that you get used to it." Arelis didn't look like she believed that.

When gendered realities of exploitation and harm are this close to home, it is much harder to externalize them into a largely abstract system of rule. You cannot just blame the state or the rebels. As Arelis plainly noted, her own father used to occasionally frequent the brothel. Encountering abandonment up close forces us to contend with its endemic nature, the ways it seeps into the most intimate realms and engulfs a wider set of relations: friends, fathers, brothers. It requires, in other words, the knowledge by intimate others and their acquiescence, if not their active involvement; in short, it demands complicity.

In legal and moral discourses, complicity designates culpability and a liability for the perpetration of an act. Its vilifying effect is all too familiar in the spaces that are documented throughout this book: most commonly, it appears as a denigrating allegation made by the state—painting those who have been confined to the spaces of uncaring as collaborators with subversive oppositional forces. It sees those abandoned as responsible for their predicament. Complicity also critically circulates within abandoned communities, appearing as an accusation leveled at neighbors or acquaintances for alleged political disloyalty.[29] In Colombia, the stakes are even higher: complicity can get you killed. As an attribution of guilt, it continues to be deeply entangled with a long history of brutal violence, from extrajudicial killings to the more recent assassinations of communal leaders in rural regions of the country. Understood solely as a vilifying accusation, complicity seems to offer a rather bleak critical horizon.

Yet complicity may present a more nuanced engagement that connotes juridical culpability but also a potential for answerability and the ability to respond. Complicity shifts the critical vocabulary in two important ways: First, it directs attention away from seemingly straightforward accounts of resistance and domination toward what Fiona Probyn-Rapsey calls a "tangled sideways reading of complicity as a condition of relations and encounters between Others."[30] Second, and this is particularly significant given the specific language used to describe the effects of gendered violence, complicity is not reducible to the discourse of guilt and shame that often dominate accounts of past violence. Whereas guilt and shame are vertical, individualized, and deep, complicity is horizontal and has pervasive breadth—as in a network. Christopher Kutz explicitly links complicity to the concreteness of social existence, arguing that the "hidden promise of complicity is the conception of community upon which it draws: a world where individuals shape their lives with others, in love mixed with resentment, and in cooperation mixed with discord. Such a world is no utopia, which suggests that it can be made real."[31]

In his study of the relationship between South African intellectuals and the apartheid system, Mark Sanders specifically contrasts complicity with one of the quintessential gestures of uncaring. What is entailed in this process, he writes, is exactly "not washing one's hands but actively affirming a complicity, or a potential complicity, in the 'outrageous deeds' of others. Once cultivated, this sense of responsibility would, in the best possible worlds, make one act to stop or prevent those deeds."[32] Taking his cue from the discussion of moral responsibility in the Truth and Reconciliation Commission, which introduced the term *little perpetrator*, Sanders points out that the "projection of complicity through an owning of the 'little perpetrator' is, however, the ethico-political response available to anyone."[33]

I am not wholly convinced that the ethical-political imperative to actively prevent harms is indeed as readily and equally available to anyone, primarily because such preventative response depends on one's relative position in existing orders of privilege and subordination. Yet prevention is only one expression of one's complicity, a practice belonging to "the best of all possible worlds." In less perfect worlds, like most of those documented in this book, the politics of complicity is at best a politics of thrown-togetherness, where encounters with others are up close and intimate, with all the friction and unease that they so often involve. Put simply, uncaring is harder to perform at such close quarters: can you wash your hands of "outrageous deeds" when they take place next door or are performed by your father?

When it is this close, it is impossible to peg gendered harms onto the uncaring state or the ones who sought to fill the void it left behind. Complicities that produce gendered violence rely on diffuse networks of intimacy and subtle economic relations, but diffusion and subtleties should not be mistaken for an absence of harm; it is only harm that circulates differently. Complicities illuminate the capillary flow of harms, exposing multiple others to its violent effects. In an extensive record of gendered violence experienced by LGBTQ+ survivors of the armed conflict in two Colombian municipalities, Colombia Diversa, an organization that promotes and defends LGBTQ+ rights, captures these capillary flows, how they circulate through a community and expose all those they come into contact with, directly or indirectly, to harm.[34] One of the report's core case studies focuses on the small town of Piñalito and details the violence encountered by Verónica and Jenny, during the Clearance years.[35]

For years, the two lived together and worked in a salon that Verónica owned. The business provided a degree of economic stability, serving coca workers, guerrilla combatants, and even local FARC commanders. However, both also defied the strict heteronormative expectations in this rural region: Verónica currently identifies with their feminine name and as a gay man; Jenny identifies as a trans woman. Threats, stigma, and intimidation were a constant part of their life, but once the state formally abandoned the region, life became significantly more perilous. In the spring of 2000, a friend who was also in the ranks of the guerrillas warned them that several women combatants were looking to drive them out of town for allegedly having sexual relationships with FARC men. Then, one morning in April, they awoke to find graffiti on the walls and doors of the house bearing the message "Verónica has AIDS." The accusation would have been enough to get them expelled from Piñalito.

Neither Verónica nor Jenny knew who had sprayed the graffiti, but each had their suspicions. It could have been men from the *guerrilla* with whom they had had sexual relations; some of the encounters were consensual, they said, but both had previously experienced sexual assault. Jenny even said that it could have been a boyfriend Verónica had at the time, who was HIV-positive and would have claimed that he had caught it from Verónica. Verónica did not confirm that version and instead commented that they had once talked about HIV in the beauty salon where they were working and anyone who heard them could have misinterpreted the conversation.[36]

The morning the graffiti appeared, a group of guerrilla fighters arrived with instructions to take the two to a FARC camp located on the other side of the Güejar River. They thought they were going to be executed. When they arrived, they were received by Pitufo (Smurf), the Twenty-Seventh Front's second-in-command, who forced them to write a list of all the members of the LGBTQ+ population, "including those still in the closet," whether they were militiamen or local workers in the coca plantations.[37] Putting together the list was not only an information-gathering exercise; as Jenny pointed out, it was also a means of asserting "control" over the townspeople.[38] The two had little option and gave away the names of all those with whom they had had sexual encounters. They were released on the condition that both undergo an HIV test in a nearby town.

Their ordeal wasn't over. Later that morning, a guerrilla came to the beauty salon to look for them again. He asked them to accompany him into town. At the soccer field, Pitufo had put on cardboard the list of the men betrayed by them. Other people from town gathered to read the list. When Verónica and Jenny showed up, people started shouting abuse, pelting them with rocks and calling for them to be expelled from town. A friend advised them to leave the town at dawn the following day, when inspections at FARC checkpoints might not have been as rigorous, but they feared that even that might be too late. By early evening they boarded a bus heading north, leaving all their belongings behind. At the last guerrilla checkpoint, as they were about to exit the Clearance Zone, they showed a travel note Pitufo gave them. The guards waved them through.

An estimated three hundred thousand people across Colombia were internally displaced in 2000 alone.[39] Many of them were displaced from the Clearance Zone, and many headed there after being forced to flee their homes elsewhere. Despite its ubiquity, Verónica and Jenny's story illuminates a diffuse terrain of uncaring: the harms that the two experienced had no single source from which it emerges, nor can its effects be easily confined to a single object. Although they were the main target of this sequence of gendered harms, violence cascaded across the community that surrounded them. The forced HIV testing ordered by FARC resulted directly from the initial list Jenny and Verónica drew; anyone testing positive would likely face a similar fate of forced displacement. In other words, complicities reveal the capillary circulation of uncaring across the social terrain rather than it being solely a sovereign act. Second, and directly related, complicity blurs any clear line setting victims and perpetrators as diametrical oppositions. Jenny and Verónica were at once on the receiving end of violent public scrutiny—exposed by hushed rumors and blunt graffiti—and the assumed source of intimate knowledge that exposed others. While gendered abandonment involves one's direct exposure to harms, it also cannot be wholly individualized; it involves the intimate exposure of others and the intimate exposure to others.

Rather than undoing the logic of uncaring, complicities seem to reinforce it. Specifically in such instances of social abandonment that are rooted in deeply entrenched structures of prejudice, complicity proliferates harms: As long as men were able to covertly experience sexual encounters with Verónica and Jenny, exposure to difference was tolerated.[40] Once it was out in the open, exposure—and intimate exposures in particular—produced a violent backlash. Luis Fernández, a Colombia Diversa lawyer who documented gender-based violence, described the social contract of exploitation as one that relied on secrecy: "People's approach was 'I don't want you here, unless you are here for satisfy my sexual desire.' In all other social interactions, the attitude is 'you do not exist, we have no deal, we do not know each other publicly, I never came here.'"[41] When they were forced to break the public secret, Verónica and Jenny also lost the fragile protections they relied on to live as gender-nonconforming individuals. Any semblance of care was gone.

If gendered abandonment is the consequence of social orders policed by

sovereigns or petty sovereigns, and at the same time enforced by the complicities that circulate across the social terrain, how can this structure of uncaring
be broken? In other words, is there an ethical-political response to gendered
abandonments that can recuperate the sense of responsibility and the ability
to respond that Sanders talks about? By this point, it should be clear that this
is not a plea for the return of sovereign care per se—an ideal many Colom-
bians would regard with equal degrees of derision and dread—but rather an
attentiveness to small, fleeting acts that might call into question the immuta-
bility of uncaring.

Refusals; or, A Memorial to Gendered Abandonment

Political theory in the past half century has offered frustratingly few tools for
understanding abandonment through its specifically gendered impacts and
implications. When the deeply uneven effects of abandonment do take center
stage, they emerge from important work of scholars committed to closely
documenting the lives of those exposed to the violence of late modern capitalism, resurgent imperialism, and more recently, the chauvinist-nationalist
state. None offers a convincing framing of abandonment that allows us to simultaneously maintain a clear view of gendered violence and its logics, without subsuming it to the care-control nexus wielded by the state and the agents
acting on its behalf. Put differently, we might ask which vocabularies can we
consider to understand gendered violence that emerges in the wake of radical
abdication of care?

I want to draw on a Jewish genealogy of abandonment that rarely appears
in Western political and theoretical accounts. It outlines a potential understanding of abandonment that is at once attentive to gendered harms and
does not foreclose the subjectivity of those who find themselves beyond the
realm of care. The Talmudic discussion of abandonment (*hefker*) involves a
direct engagement with forms of abdication that take place in intimate realms
of vulnerability and kinship. What stands out in this debate is its focus on the
safeguards that need to be extended to children or women in cases of marriage and death rather than just focusing on their precarity and susceptibility to harm. In one debate, for example, *hefker* is applied to the right of an
underaged orphan girl to refuse marriage:[42] While refusal is recognized in
other cases, this particular constellation leaves the young woman outside the
patriarchal conventions of care that would have been extended to her otherwise by her father or husband. This seemingly parochial discussion stands
out exactly because it directly grapples with the legal and social protections
that vulnerable individuals are entitled to by the court and the community.

Invoking *hefker* in this case does not reduce the body of the girl to an own-erless property, but it highlights the potential vulnerability of an individual who finds herself stripped of legal status. The official recognition of *hefker* as a threat to an individual's fundamental autonomy ought to be seen as part of a broader effort to challenge the patriarchal hierarchy that reduces (specifi-cally gendered) lives to commodity.[43]

While the Talmudic debate offers important ethical orientations, direct-ing our attention toward instances of revived agency and responsibility, it also urges us to avoid confining abandonment to realms of metaphysical or exis-tential contemplation. Instead, it veers the critical inquiry toward concrete re-alities in which gendered abandonments take place. I've noted earlier in this chapter the difficulty of tracing gendered abandonments, the often-too-faint marks they leave on the landscapes of uncaring. But that is not to say they aren't there. Contrary to the statist architecture of abandonment that marks the edge of care—militarized checkpoints, brute barricades, and barbed-wire fences—gendered harms are encoded into more discrete and humble forms. The Jewish concept of *hefker* provides a critical reorientation toward spaces that other political theories of abandonment largely overlook. Rare glimpses into these material remains—the stifling windowless rooms, the dirty mat-tresses, sixty men over a weekend—illuminate the intimate proximity of un-caring that cannot be kept at a distance and need to have a place in our con-ceptual vocabularies of abandonment.

All this still doesn't answer the question of response and the ability to in-terrupt the social networks that enable uncaring. What does it mean to re-fuse gendered abandonment and remain responsible toward others in the way that the Talmud asks? Given that the crumbling architecture of gendered harm is, also, an architecture of shame, even acknowledging what takes place is hard to do. At times, this shame has a material form, like the small doors in the back of the brothel rooms that allowed clients a clandestine entrance and exit. The doors allowed some to maintain a facade of normative social order while effectively removing the unease of one's overt involvement in routine acts of exploitation. Shame stifles action, in particular action that requires confrontation or opposition.

There is another response though, one that does not succumb or acqui-esce to social orders and the shame of complicity. It took place in 2010, right in front of the brothel in Yarumales, in broad daylight on the single dirt road that crosses the village. The brothel was owned by a man named Pedro, who used to come to the village from Villavicencio, five hours to the north. His wife, Jennifer, never knew about her husband's work as a brothel owner or his long relationship with one of the women working for him, with whom he also had a child. When Jennifer discovered what was happening during her husband's business trips, she came down to Yarumales. Pedro's Toyota truck was parked just outside the building, and Jennifer doused it with petrol and set it on fire. The building was her next target. Setting it on fire would have burned down the entire village, given that the wooden houses are only a few feet apart. Residents pleaded with her, and an agreement was finally reached: Jennifer would spare the brothel building, but the place would be shut down, never to be opened again.

Pedro's burnt Toyota is still there, at the entrance to Yarumales as you cross the bridge. No one bothered towing it away, but that's only befitting. At least half a dozen burnt cars and trucks are scattered around this tiny hamlet, left there as FARC forces fled the Colombian army's assault in the region in the mid-2000s. The cars function at tacit monuments that tell the story that everyone seems to be eager to tell: "when the government left." That is the tale of sovereign uncaring.

But I wonder whether Pedro's burnt car is also a different kind of monument, one that attests to the gendered harms that happened in abandonment's wake. Much like the Talmudic debate on gendered *hefker*, it emerged out of a refusal to externalize gendered violence and pin it solely to a state that shirks its duty of care. Community, intimate relations, and proximate others were all complicit in the harms taking place in the brothel on the riverside. It took one woman to force them out of their uncaring, to remind them that the fire that might consume the brothel would burn their houses too.

PART IV

Wild Country

During World War I, a legend arose out of the real-life horrors that took place in the no man's land between the trenches. Paul Fussell described it as "finest legend of the war, the most brilliant in literary invention and execution as well as the richest in symbolic suggestion," and like many tales told and retold, it has had several variants.[1] The recurring core of the legend warned of scar-faced and fearless deserters banding together to live deep beneath the abandoned trenches and dugouts that made up the no man's land. According to some of the more gruesome versions, the deserters scavenged corpses for clothing, food, and weapons. One of the earliest versions of this tale, James Deutsch notes, appeared in a 1920 memoir, *The Squadroon*, by the British cavalry officer Ardern Beaman.[2] One scene in the book takes place in the no man's land of the Somme, where Beaman had seen a group of escaped prisoners disappear. He is, however, warned against sending a search party into the devastated trench system, which, according to his interlocutor, "was peopled with wild men, British, French, Australian, German deserters, who lived there underground, like ghouls among the mouldering dead, and who came out at night to plunder and to kill. In the night, an officer said, mingled with the snarling of carrion dogs, they often heard inhuman cries and rifle shots coming from that awful wilderness, as though the bestial denizens were fighting among themselves."[3]

This story, in different variations, appears throughout the following century. Later iterations of it even make their way into the *New York Times'* opinion page. In a 2006 piece, James Carroll noted how World War I deserters refusing to fight "had organized themselves into a kind of third force—not fighters any more, but mere survivors, at home in the caverns. Dozens of them, perhaps hundreds. Human beings caring for one another, no matter what uniform they were wearing."[4] According to Carroll's interpretation, the deserters were like angels, taking care of those who had fallen into the safety of the underground caverns—acting as a sane alternative to the insanity of war.

The tale of the wild deserters of no man's land, whether in its devilish guise or its more angelic version, is a telling account. For Fussell, it captures a universal shame about the abandonment of the wounded between the lines and the fantasy of flagrant disobedience of authority.[5] Osbert Sitwell, who reluctantly served as an officer in the Grenadier Guards during the war, speculated that this was a myth created by the wounded themselves, "as a result of pain, privation, and exposure."[6] Both point to the hope implicit in the story, that there might be some fantastical refuge from the horrific catastrophe of the war. Fantasies of flight are hardly unheard of in situations of extreme confinement, oppressive regimentation of life and the constant presence of impending violence. What strikes me, however, is that the tale of the deserters' community situates this refuge specifically in the no man's land, hardly a space of tranquility and solace. At least to some, this was a preferable alternative to life just outside it.

I think of fantasy both through its more established forms as a psychic condition and a literary genre but also, and primarily, as a political affect. Jacqueline Rose notes that the political efficacy of fantasy has often been dismissed from the political rhetoric of the Left, "because it is not serious, not material, too flighty and hence not worth bothering about."[7] In a masterful historical study of World War I, Eric Leed expressed such reservations about fantasy, "which has too many connotations of escape from the real and problematical into the unreal."[8] Instead, he opts for "myth," which offers greater focus on social and cultural contexts. Even Edward Said rejects the association of Orientalism with merely an "airy European fantasy," juxtaposing fantasy with a crafted body of theory and practice that merits critical attention.[9] Yet fantasy, Rose argues, far from being the antagonist of public, social, being—or relegated to a mere flight of imagination—"plays a central, constitutive role in the modern world of states and nations."[10] Fantasy may be projected toward a distant realm that does not (yet) exist, but the effects of this projection are utterly real and consequential.

Territorial sovereignty, specifically through its imperial and national manifestations, retains a powerful gravitational pull on the form and function of political fantasies. What Donald Pease refers to as the "structure of desire" that underpins fantasies is all too often tethered to the bounded geographies of the state.[11] The state and its territory is the canvas onto which political fantasies are often projected. What happens, though, at the edge of these confined territorialized fantasies? What fantastical regimes govern those spaces that have been disavowed by statist sovereign structures?

The space of uncaring pushes this political fantasy to the limits. While never completely divorced from the sovereign territories of the state, fantasies that surround these spaces are nevertheless distinct from it. Specifically, although no man's land fantasies seem to resemble the political imaginations of borderlands or frontiers, the latter are never subjected to the same willful absence of care by which no man's land is constituted. In fact, frontier fantasies are always directed at an eventual conquest, a very different prospect from the abandonment and radical uncaring that produces no man's land. If there is a resemblance to be drawn, it is between fantasies of uncaring and the fables of pirate utopias, with their romanticized allure of escape from the strictures of state and the normative impositions of social order.[12] Fantasies that swirl around the space of uncaring draw from the anarchic spirit of this genre, but a close examination reveals the more nuanced links between fantasy and violence, between the dreams projected onto this space and their sober realizations.

Dread and desire densely populate the fantasy of no man's land: they shape its cultural forms in literature, poetry, and visual culture. Much like colonial fantasies of discovery and conquest, they tell us a great deal about those who fantasize, their hopes and fears, probably more than they reveal hidden truths about exoticized elsewheres that are the subject of fantasy. But as I have found time and again, fantasies of no man's land are just as much about action as they are about imagination. They shape lives and livelihoods, spark conflict, and often lead to great disillusion. Fear is a case in point: intuitively, apocalyptic visions of a zone plagued by disaster triggers evacuations and flight. But fear drives people—and not only people—*into* the space of uncaring in search of refuge and the potential for escape. They seek shelter not only from violence in its bluntest physical form but also from other plights and deprivations— poverty, discrimination or a repressive regime. Rarely do fantasies come true in full. The lives entangled with these spaces expose not only the fantasy and the attempts to realize it but also, importantly, what is left in its wake.

9

Terra Fantastica

Refuge, Rebels, Fish, and Fear

A century after World War I and thousands of miles from the Western Front, the refuge of no man's land came up again. I was on a wooden canoe going up the Guayabero River in central Colombia. Isaías Sánchez Castaño, a sixty-year-old boat mechanic from the town of La Macarena was steering the canoe along the northern riverbank, occasionally slowing down to enthusiastically point out tortoises and birds that rested on the branches (see plate 4). It was still early in the autumn rainy season, but the river was already fast flowing and murky with mud. To the north, we could see the Serranía de La Macarena rising above the trees. This geological formation at the northwestern edge of the Amazonian Basin was formed 1.7 billion years ago, and it is known in geology as a craton—a stable portion of continental crust that has survived the geological cycles of merging and rifting of continents. The mountain range is a kind of Noah's ark from which many of the species that are part of Amazonia and the Andes originated.[1]

Isaías arrived in the region as a young boy in the mid-1960s when his family fled from the city of Villavicencio, about three hundred kilometers to the north. They were part of the second wave of Andean peasants who found in the Amazonian lowlands a different kind of Noah's ark, a haven from both the paramilitary groups that forced them off their lands and the escalation of conflict between the government and newly formed guerrilla movements, most notably the Revolutionary Armed Forces of Colombia–People's Army—FARC-EP—founded in 1966. Isaías recalled those early years with an obvious tinge of nostalgia, describing "pure virgin mountains," a river brimming with fish and forests teeming with wildlife. The isolation that sheltered wildlife in what was then a remote frontier region also drew those who were internally displaced by the violence. When they arrived, he told me, "this place was called El Refugio, because people sought refuge here. People who had trouble outside began looking for these spaces where there was no authority."[2]

A refuge was also our destination. We were heading to El Cajón ("the box"), a set of rapids flanked by narrow rocky banks. Because of heavy rains, the current in the rapids was ferocious, forcing us to moor the canoe downstream and proceed for a mile on foot. Isaías wanted to show me a faded warning sign that was painted in the early 2000s on the face of a rock by the rapids. At least two layers of paint, first red and then retraced in blue, were used to mark the message, which read, with some typos, "Fishing Is Prohibited in El Cajón." That point in the river sits almost at the exact boundary between two large national parks—La Macarena in the east and Tinigua to the west—but the sign wasn't painted by the Colombian park service. In bold yellow, next to the warning, was the signature of the authors: FARC-EP.

Rebel forces have had a long history in this region. In 1955, communist and liberal peasants who escaped government bombardments in Andean regions such as Marquetalia and El Pato settled in several localities nearby. The very foundation of FARC was decided in April 1966 at the Second Guerrilla Conference, which took place on the banks of the Duda River, just a few miles to the north. Given that Colombian state presence in the northwestern Amazon was scarce at best, FARC turned the region into its central base of operation, fewer than two hundred miles from the capital of Bogotá. For the most part, the population of the region had been left to fend for itself, with almost no government investment or meaningful state support. The state was nowhere to be found, but that was exactly the allure for those fleeing its violence.

The sign in El Cajón is a rare physical remnant of a short period during which the region's abandonment by the Colombian state was not just a fact of life, but a formal policy. El Cajón sits almost exactly at the heart of the Clearance Zone that was abandoned by the Colombian government to the control of FARC in 1998. The thought that one of the most powerful guerrilla forces in the twentieth century concerned itself with fishing regulations may seem perplexing, but the faded sign warning against fishing was part of an elaborate set of rules FARC imposed in territories under its control (fig. 8). These rules, which I discuss at length in the previous chapter, included the regulation of political activity and the local economy, but also a whole set of environmental elements, including limitations on deforestation, hunting, and fishing.[3] These decrees were commonly issued by local FARC commanders, but they gained a much more formal status once the Clearance Zone came officially into force. And far from being secondary to other rules governing the social and political realms of life, environmental regulations were some of the first orders issued.[4]

FIGURE 8. A sign on the Guayabero River that reads Fishing Is Prohibited in El Cajón / FARC EP, 2018. Photographer: Elliot Graves.

For Isaías, fishing restrictions in El Cajón were just a matter of common sense, as it is well known as a spawning site for large river fish. It was the same, he told me, for the prohibition on fishing with dynamite, which indiscriminately kills everything in the blast radius. In more than one way, El Cajón was a microcosm of refuge: a haven for fish, much like the region as a whole became a destination for peasants fleeing violence and guerrilla fighters seeking shelter from Colombian military incursions.

Refuge zones, as James Scott famously pointed out, have offered an escape from the strictures of state and coercive labor for at least two thousand years.[5] Scott describes the formation of such spaces in geographically remote regions where obstacles hindered the state's ability to establish and maintain authority. Within these "nonstate spaces," subsistence routines and social organizations were crafted specifically to thwart their incorporation into state territory. "There," Scott concludes, "in regions beyond the state's immediate writ and, thus, at some remove from taxes, coercive labour, conscription, and the more than occasional epidemics and crop failures associated with population concentration and monocropping, such groups found relative freedom and safety."[6] It is tempting to see refuge zones as havens of safety, somehow isolated and protected from the orders of violence that govern life in spaces more central to the imagined geography of the state.

But all too often, "refuge zones" are portrayed merely as a response to existing threats or coercions emanating from either a colonial power or the state. As Silvia Espelt-Bombin noted in her historical anthropology of Amerindian spaces in the Brazilian Amazon, the label of "refuge" ignores a much longer history of life in these regions that often predates colonial presence. "A space of refuge is self-contained, limited, and safe," she adds, yet "none of this was the case for the lands and waters under consideration."[7] Viewing refuge zones as sites of safety and regenerative potential belies the far reach of violence and its insidious presence in such spaces. I note these critiques not to dismiss the importance of refuge to the space of uncaring, but to avoid a rose-tinted view of these regions. The critical challenge lies in productively retaining these tensions of power, where violence is inherent to the search for safety.

When we headed back from El Cajón in the early afternoon, Isaías turned the engine off so we could talk while floating downriver, because his soft voice was easily drowned by the rattle of the outboard motor. At first, he spoke fondly of the river, about the abundance of fish he used to easily gather when he was younger. But other things crept into his story, disrupting the bucolic reminiscing. The riverbanks that demarcated stories of escape and refuge (for fish, for his family) were also telling a less upbeat story. "Farmers have been cutting down the forest and the roots aren't holding the banks anymore," he said. As the banks collapsed, several farms built along the river had to be abandoned, forcing the farmers to clear out even more forest inland. In some parts of the river, only a single row of trees remained along the banks, barely concealing large swaths of land cleared for cattle grazing. "Once there was the forest," Michael Taussig wrote in a succinct summary of the political changes that transformed Colombia's rural landscapes. "Then came the cattle. Everyone loves cattle. There is something magical about cattle. From the poorest peasant to the president of the republic, they all want cattle and they always want more."[8] Those who cleared the forest don't often take the time to do a thorough job, leaving charred stumps across the exposed expanses. Taussig prefaced his reflections on landscape, society, and politics with a line that was jarring when I first encountered it. "They have no land but no man's-land," he wrote. As we floated past these exposed lands dotted with burnt tree stumps, their similarity to no man's land images from World War I seemed eerie and inescapable.

In conversations I've had throughout the areas that made up the Colombian Clearance Zone, refuge kept coming up. Almost everybody arrived in search of shelter, but violence always came with them. When Isaías was referring to El Refugio, he was in fact using a name first given to a settlement built around an abandoned airstrip used by the Shell Petroleum Company in 1937.[9] The Colombian sociologist and writer Alfredo Molano suggested that

even the trail that led the first displaced peasants into the region was marked
by oil explorers a decade earlier, first for the Tropical Oil Company and then
for Shell.[10] Following in the footsteps of extractive exploration was hardly a
promising trail. The horrors inflicted by extractive industries—first rubber,
then fossil fuels and precious metals—have been well documented and cri-
tiqued. What is striking, however, is that the search for refuge in the footsteps
of extraction explorers foretold a contemporary wave of what Michael Watts
describes as "petro-violence."[11] In the northwestern Amazon, it has taken the
form of terror wielded in the service of multinational hydraulic fracturing
ventures that are increasingly encroaching into the former Clearance Zone.

In some cases, the history of refuge in the Clearance Zone was entwined
not only with extractive exploitation but also with outright murder. In the late
1940s, a fugitive criminal named Hernando Palma terrorized the region for
several years. According to stories I've heard time and again, Palma and his
band extorted the small local population, rustled cattle, and were responsible
for the massacre of an Indigenous Tinigua community that resided not far
from El Cajón. Sixto Muñoz, the last remaining native Tinigua speaker, recalled in a 2013 interview the horrors of that event: "He locked them all up in
his ranch, tied them up and killed them one by one—shooting target, burning
them alive and killing pregnant women and what they had in their bellies.
It was heartbreaking."[12] The Colombian historian Claudia Leal noted in an
extensive ethnographic account of the region's history that information about
Palma remains scarce, alive mostly in personal recollections and stories circulating around the community for decades. From the stories, Palma emerges
as "a sinister phantom that lives scattered in the memory of inhabitants."[13] A
violent phantom that haunts and disrupts the comforting fantasy of refuge.

The challenge, in a way, is not to seek a typology of fantasies in the space
of uncaring—refuge here, violence there. Instead, it is to trace in the historical records of such spaces the simultaneous existence and intricate relation
between the two nodal political imaginations. A few hours up the river from
El Cajón, above the banks of the Duda River, a biological research station
operated between 1986 and 2002 (Centro de Investigaciones Ecológicas, Macarena). It hosted a large international group of researchers and became one
of the most important centers for rainforest research in Latin America. Pablo
Stevenson, a biologist from Los Andes University in Bogotá, worked in the
station for several years doing his doctoral research. But when we met at his
small university office, he was quick to dispel any romantic notions of a natural sanctuary: "The abundance of monkeys in this region is not natural. The
density of primates is down to many factors, from soil fertility to abundance
of food sources. But it is also because the Indigenous peoples in the region,

who used to hunt these monkeys, were all massacred."[14] Even the sign pro-
hibiting fishing in El Cajón took on a very different meaning in his account.
Rather than a river sanctuary, it was a private hunting ground for guerrilla
commanders. "During the Clearance Zone years, Mono Jojoy [the commander of FARC's Eastern Bloc] went over to the site with a group of his men
and shot hundreds of fish, simply because they could."[15] Refuge and violence
are constantly entangled in these tales, but rather than prying them apart, the
space of uncaring forces us to seriously consider their co-constitution and the
particular political conditions they produce.

Fantastic creatures of all kinds filled the space of uncaring, from giant cat-
fish to fugitive gang leaders who pillaged and massacred. Despite one being
a nostalgic idealization and the other violently haunting, the beasts share a
single political order: both owe their existence to a political logic that system-
atizes sovereign abdication of care.

In Colombia, the failure of the state to meet its basic duties of care is in fact
not a failure at all. Instead, it is a consubstantial aspect of sovereign power relations that routinely designates populations and spaces beyond the realm of
care. In a powerful analysis of this logic, the Latin American historian Marco
Palacios conjures other kinds of mythical monsters. "The monster that Co-
lombians face," he writes, "is not Thomas Hobbes' Leviathan, which requires
that all be equal before it, but an *imaginary Leviathan*, precisely because this
environment of equality does not exist nor has it ever existed in Colombia."[16]
If the Leviathan is the mythical monster of sovereignty, what are the fantastical beings that thrive under the political logic of abandonment?

Instead of a definitive answer, a midway postscript of sorts: Hernando
Palma, the murderous gang leader who terrorized the region that later became the Clearance Zone, was killed on the banks of the Guayabero River by
a man whose wife and daughter were murdered by Palma's group.[17] His body
was tied to an old wreckage of a plane that crashed nearby. It was then thrown
into the river, just a short walk from the giant fish of El Cajón.

Seeing Things

"He's drunk," my research assistant Laura said quietly about the man at the
table next to us.

Although it was still early in the morning, he was already in a talkative
mood. He wanted to tell us all about his years fishing the rivers near the town
of La Macarena, where we were staying in 2017. But his story went further
than that, beyond the challenges of a dwindling catch or even the risk of

chance encounters with the guerrilla that could end in the confiscation of a boat. What he really wanted to talk about were his alien sightings: when he was fishing at night, he would see flying saucers that would appear suddenly and disappear just as quickly. He had a couple of empty beer bottles next to him, so Laura's assertion seemed plausible, and besides, extraterrestrial life seemed beyond the remit of even my rather loose sense of what I was after in that first visit to Colombia.

Five weeks later, I was once again in La Macarena, this time a neighborhood of Bogotá that bears the same name. I was meeting Carlos Arturo Mejía—known to everyone as "Caturo"—who set up the biological research station on the Duda River with Japanese colleagues. Now in his late 1970s, slim and soft spoken, Caturo remains somewhat of a legendary figure among Colombian scientists, many of whom still carry fond memories from their time at the research station. Friends would also visit the station, taking advantage of the chance to enter a part of the country that would have otherwise been almost inaccessible, partly due to its remoteness and partly because of guerrilla dominance across the region.

Caturo and I first met one early evening at a coffee shop not far from his house. At a certain point during our conversation, a man walked over to greet Caturo. Eduardo was a journalist and a longtime friend who spent a few weeks in the late 1990s with Caturo at the research station. In the evenings, he recalled, he would often go up to sit on a ledge above the station that had great views of the river and the dense forest the stretched beyond it. "It was a great spot to kick back at the end of the day, relax, smoke a joint," he said with a wide smile.

"You know, if you're interested in the Zona de Distensión, there's a great story I have to tell you," he added. "One evening, after dark, I was on that ledge when I suddenly saw a circle of light appear above the pitch-black forest in the distance. It looked like a flying saucer in the haze, and then, in an instant, it disappeared. I couldn't believe my eyes. I ran back to the camp, but couldn't bring myself to share what I saw. I thought the scientists would think I smoked too much weed." The following night, he ventured back to his vantage point, and after a while, his sightings recurred: in the distance, an illuminated sphere in the low-hanging clouds above the canopy. Was he really seeing UFOs? "The best part came later," he said, "when I finally mustered the courage to tell others what I saw. It wasn't flying saucers." But the explanation was fascinating nonetheless: as coca cultivation proliferated in the rebel-held region, so did "kitchens" for processing and producing cocaine. In the process, wet cocaine paste had to be dried before it could be ground into powder, and placing powerful heat lamps under the wet substance was one solution. Often, the beam would shine upward, hitting the low clouds above the rainforest and creating a round circle of light. From a distance, it would look like a Bat-Signal of sorts, or a flying saucer.

Even though there were no green men, this story populates the space of uncaring with a particular fantastical quality that touches on the formation of political power itself. "Hobbes's Leviathan is mythical yet also terribly real," Michael Taussig noted in an interview following the publication of *The Magic of the State*.[18] It was in that book that Taussig argued that "any engagement with that thing called the state will perforce be an engagement with this heart of fiction, the very script of whose very real and grave purpose presupposes both theatre and spirit possession."[19] The state undoubtedly still needs its fantastical incarnations and would like to keep alive imaginations of its monsters and its mythical spirits, primarily because they help narrate and make sense of the order of violence: for Hobbes, the violence of the state of nature is handed over to the Leviathan state, with its promise of contractual sublimation of this violence. Invoking the monster entails invoking the basic order of governance on which its subjects can rely, or as Hobbes put it, "peace at home, and mutual aid against their enemies abroad."[20] Though very narrowly defined, and despite its diabolical association, the Leviathan today remains the most familiar mythical embodiment of sovereign care.[21] What happens to the fantastical, then, once the sovereign turns away, clearly designating spaces beyond the realm of its care?

Hobbes named his sovereign state for a biblical sea monster, but there seems to be nothing monstrous in the famous 1651 frontispiece of *Leviathan*.[22] However, the image that adorns the cover of *De Cive* (On the Citizen), which Hobbes published nine years earlier, at least at first sight offers a glimpse into this fantastical space beyond the sovereign realm. It sets out a stark juxtaposition: in the left panel stands a statuesque, classic feminine figure Imperium (sovereign jurisdiction) overlooking an orderly scene of productive labor. The opposite panel, Libertas, depicts the original state of nature, represented by a fortified rudimentary village, a violent manhunt and dismembered limbs. This scene is epitomized by the figure of an American "savage." Wearing a feathered skirt and armlets, the long-haired Indigenous figure is assumed to be a woman, but her lined face and muscular, slightly hunched body, defy the conventional features of European femininity. The figure's chest is concealed from view, adding to the androgynous appearance. Their left arm seems to dissolve into a serpentlike creature as it embraces a long bow. The juxtaposition of the two figures is reflective of Hobbes's wider political theory and the contrast he sets between civil subjection and "that liberty, which all men have to all things, to wit, naturall, and savage, (for the naturall state hath the same proportion to the Civill, I mean liberty to subjection, which Passion hath to Reason, or *a Beast to a Man*)."[23]

Does this depiction of the New World as beastly and savage capture the precise relation of uncaring that constitutes no man's land? In other words, is the Amazonian figure of the savage native an early incarnation of the political monster of uncaring? The relation that Hobbes establishes between the two realms—Imperium and Libertas—relegates the latter, societies outside the "ordered" system of European states, into a prepolitical condition of savage anarchy. Such strategic reduction became a convenient pretext for colonizations yet to come. As Robert Nichols has argued, such "references to the 'state of nature,' become, after Hobbes, a primary tool that serves to circumscribe conceptually, represent symbolically, and defeat politically, the Amerindian peoples."[24] In short, a great deal rested on the discursive mechanisms, from vast prospects of economic extraction to the self-fashioning of Western identity. Given all that was at stake, it would be more accurate to say that fantastic figures of savagery in the New World, like the one on the frontispiece of *De Cive*, were a consequence of too much caring—desires of conquest, extraction, and imperial expansion—rather than inhabiting what I see as the condition of sovereign uncaring that governs no man's land.

I do not mean to gloss over the fact that reducing Indigenous populations to the "state of nature" also meant relegating them below the threshold of political subjectivity. The atrocities that were justified in the name of such cosmological hierarchies are always important to return to, partly because they did not spare the Indigenous peoples of northwestern Amazonia, the same region that would, in the late 1990s, be designated for the Clearance Zone. But to my mind, the monster of uncaring has different features from those of the *colonos* who ventured into Colombia's Amazon basin in the early part of the twentieth century.[25] And it certainly did not take the spectacular form of a vicious ghoul or an angelic being. Its elusiveness is partly due to its banal appearance, to the fact that, most often, there is nothing extraordinary about it.

I got glimpses of it throughout my research for this book, almost always in polite settings of offices and conference rooms, in correspondence and the testimony of those who held official positions. Daniel García-Peña, who headed Colombia's Office of the High Commissioner for Peace between 1995 and 1998, offered one of those glimpses. Daniel was a generous interlocutor, sharing insights from internal deliberations as well as his critique of Colombian decision-making during the negotiation with FARC in the late 1990s. But when I asked whether any of the cabinet meetings considered the fate of those who would be left behind once the Colombian military withdrew from the

Clearance Zone, his answer was illuminating. "Let's not forget that the area in the five municipalities was already under FARC control," he said, emphasizing that "the whole idea that the armed forces abandoned the area" was only a talking point of those who opposed Pastrana's effort to reach an agreement with FARC. "The general overview [among policy makers] was that since FARC controlled the region for so long, the local population was necessarily FARC sympathizers."[26] In other words, the state never abandoned the region because it never possessed a real foothold there in the first place. Implicit in his answer was the fact that the fate of approximately 150,000 people was of no serious concern.

Defined by absence and deprivation, the image of uncaring that emerges from this sovereign gesture is fantastical exactly because it is largely devoid of clearly traceable features—a monster without a face or a body. Without these, it is much harder to translate this political logic into a recognizable cultural emblem, like the figures that adorn Hobbes's frontispieces. Yet as the Colombian anthropologist Margarita Serje argues, the very notion of the absent state—the Leviathan that has no foothold in the "Other Colombia" (*otra Colombia*) is perhaps the most monstrous trick of all: "This popular notion functions as a smoke screen; it serves to cover up all sorts of intrusive interventions and abuses by the state-elites in the mythically lawless lands."[27] Even if uncaring possesses a spectral, ephemeral quality, its consequences are nevertheless concrete and, as this book documents time and again, unambiguously monstrous.

The Leviathan might pull back, but monsters don't disappear; abandonment only unleashes other fantastical creatures. Like other political monsters, the tales of giant fish and extraterrestrial spaceships, of murderous bandits and Eden-like sanctuaries, are more than eccentric oddities. "The monstrous body is pure culture," Jeffrey Jerome Cohen notes in his first of seven "monster theses": "A construct and a projection, the monster exists only to be read: the *monstrum* is etymologically 'that which reveals,' 'that which warns.'"[28] In some articulations, the monsters of no man's land signal a primordial fear of dystopian chaos in which one is left completely vulnerable. In their more bucolic version, they express the desire for refuge, a desperate fantasy of flight, not to violence, but from it. Despite pulling in seemingly different trajectories, all the fantastical creatures that populate the space of uncaring emerge exactly because the monster of the Leviathan state is no longer there.[29] Their appearance embodies the potential regression to a state of nature, in the form of either the return of violence that is no longer tamed by the sublimating promise of a social contract or the emergence of a bucolic ideal of shelter.

Still, fantastical fables of no man's land are worth retelling exactly because they often appear outlandish, the figment of an overactive imagination or too many beers. Rather than shrug them off, the fantasies are revealing; the very etymology of the word is traced back to the Greek *phantasia*, the process by which all images are presented to us. And so many people were eager to share, during a long taxi ride or over a beer, their own outlandish tales. It wasn't only because I was a naive outsider. The proliferation of the fantastic in these spaces became a way of comprehending what remains beyond reach, what was too frightening or too heartbreaking to recall otherwise. But this physical inaccessibility often frustrated any factual verification. I never found out, for example, whether crates full of cash were really buried in the Colombian jungle by FARC rebels as they hastily fled the Clearance Zone. Imaginations of this sort nevertheless still expose anxieties and aspirations, very real forces that explain some of the lasting allure of no man's land.

Kings of No Man's Land

Here's a story you may have heard before: a tale of an empty, unclaimed land in the middle of a remote desert, supposedly holding great quantities of untapped gold. What follows is equally predictable: someone (usually a man) sets out (usually from Europe) to "discover" this land (usually with some combination of scientific prowess, military might and financial means) and does so after overcoming trials and tribulations ("hostile" environments or populations). Despite its longevity, this tale is still in circulation, conjuring new variations on a well-worn theme. And yet it is also a tale worth revisiting, exactly because it captures the particular entanglement of White identity and White violence with contemporary spaces of uncaring.

Fame and fortune are the most obvious elements keeping tales of discovery and conquest alive. Another, less obvious, force helping these stories retain their allure regards their ability to sustain what Clive Gabay calls the "mythologised historical genius of Whiteness."[1] In their most familiar iterations, fantasies of discovery rest on a civilizational hierarchy that positions the destination, typically Africa, as culturally and economically inferior to the point of departure. Such accounts paint Africa as emptier, more savage, more childlike, less modern, and less civilized than the West. The specifically tired trope of the "failed state" highlights the incapability or unwillingness to implement Western models of sovereignty in Africa.[2] When it is understood as merely a chaotic, ungoverned space, no man's land fits neatly into this mold and, in turn, allows a (commonly White and male) protagonist to introduce "order" through systems of capital accumulation or civilizational paternalism.

This chapter begins with this seemingly familiar process as it unfolds in an outlandish race between two men—a Russian and an American—both laying claim to Bir Tawil, a territory on the Egypt-Sudan border, as their kingdom.

In their retelling, Bir Tawil is unclaimed and uncared for. Yet what makes these fantasies of White and masculine conquest important is the way they invert uncaring: rather than simply seen as an attribute of inferiority (a lack, or flaw, a space that is "less than"), uncaring is a quality to be coveted, an object of desire. Put simply, uncaring is exactly what makes Bir Tawil so valuable and, in many respects, preferable to Western political orders that have been repeatedly trumpeted as paragons of the international system. I start, therefore, by following how Bir Tawil became this object of desire that draws out contemporary White fantasies of conquest and extraction, emancipation, and self-realization. Through the story of competing claims over a remote desert territory, the space of uncaring enables the recuperation of White masculinity at a moment when its vitality is no longer taken for granted in Western politics, economies, and societies.

It would be a mistake, however, to see the race for Bir Tawil as solely a tale of two White Western men and their idiosyncratic scramble for conquest in Africa. Considering Whiteness as a system of privilege and a related set of norms that serve to reinforce that privilege also requires an equally candid reflection on White scholarship, its tools, and the pitfalls it needs to navigate, especially when it is committed to grounded research.[3] The second section in this chapter confronts these challenges, not to offer easy solutions, but to chart some of the impasses that politically and ethically defy resolution. Put simply, my own work cannot be detached from longer traditions of Western scholarship and its cultures of exploration. It is exactly these lineages that have contributed to the formation of the "mythologised historical genius of Whiteness," often while erasing the presence and experience of those who do not fit its conventionalized regimes of truth. That is the starting point for the third section of this chapter, which brings to the fore spaces, experience and knowledge that Whiteness repeatedly seeks to erase. Written in four fragments, it foregrounds other dreams and other practices that make Bir Tawil meaningful through local communities, networks and practices. While it refuses to understand the space of uncaring as solely a figment of White fantasy, it also highlights the constant proximity of White violence.

The Race for Bir Tawil

Sometime even a king has trouble with his travel plans. Dmitry Zhikharev— or as he introduced himself when he first reached out to me, "Dmitry the First, King of Bir Tawil"—hadn't realized that the ferry service from Egypt to Cyprus was canceled in 2013 following the escalation of the Syrian civil war. His "royal carriage," a Dacia Duster SUV, was suddenly stranded after completing a sixty-seven-thousand-kilometer journey from Moscow, through Morocco to South Africa, and then north, to his prized destination, Bir Tawil. Mission accomplished. But getting himself and his partner, Mikhail Ronkainen, back home to Russia proved a much harder task: even when the car was driven to Israel, from where it was supposed to be shipped to Turkey, the engine broke down and had to be completely replaced. "Just my luck," he told me. "Of all the places we've been through, it had to break down in the most expensive country in the region."[4]

Despite his extensive travel record, Zhikharev's journeys are not motivated by cultural curiosity, the love of remote natural landscapes, or even the hope of escaping Moscow winters. Nor, it seems, is he an explorer in the classic colonial sense, serving an ever-expanding empire by seeking new geographical frontiers. Instead, his wanderlust serves a different passion: amateur radio operation. In the milieu of shortwave radio enthusiasts, Zhikharev is somewhat of a celebrity for his dedication to broadcasting from the most remote places on earth. Among the 112 countries he has operated in are North Korea, Yemen, Libya, and Sudan. "Everywhere I go some shit happens after that. I go to Libya—boom, there is a war. I go to Yemen—boom, there is a war. So, everyone puts two and two together and, like, 'Shit, wherever Dmitry goes to, some shit happens.' But I have nothing to do with it. Somehow it just works this way."[5]

Radio enthusiasts divide the world into forty geographical zones, and operators compete to establish two-way contact with operators located in as many other zones as possible. Zone 34, which includes Egypt, Libya, Sudan, and South Sudan, is the most sought after, primarily because the heavy restrictions on the operation of shortwave radio in those countries. Zhikharev first heard about Bir Tawil when he was operating in South Sudan in 2011. He was initially lured by the prospect of setting up a transmission station where none existed before. But what he had in mind was more than a radio competition. What he saw was the chance of being recognized as a "radio entity." When we spoke, he recalled the neutral zone between Saudi Arabia and Kuwait that became a coveted transmission point for radio enthusiasts in the 1980s and 1990s. "Some of the people operating from those zones were considered [by the radio operator community] as entities, like a new country!" he said, omitting the fact that the neutral zone was abolished when the two countries partitioned it in 1970. Radio signals apparently drew a different map, which seemed to matter more than the geopolitics of international treaties.

On this shortwave atlas, Zhikharev's proclaimed his "kingdom" by setting up a new call sign, 1U4UN. Even this was carefully chosen, imitating the call sign of the UN amateur radio club, 4U1UN. Much like license plates on motor vehicles, call signs associate their operators with a specific country. A convoluted system of international regulations govern the allocation of call signs, but a specific range remains unassigned and has become an electromagnetic zone of unrecognized states and breakaway regions. For example, call signs with the prefix 1B are used by operators in the Turkish Republic of Northern Cyprus, a de facto state recognized only by Turkey; separatists in Chechnya use 1C as their call sign prefix. During his first two visits to Bir Tawil, Zhikharev operated a mobile shortwave radio from his tent, but to solidify his presence in the airwaves, he made another trip to Bir Tawil in February 2016 and erected a radio beacon on top of a nearby mountain. Linked to a solar panel and completely autonomous, the beacon transmits a Morse message in regular intervals: "This is the kingdom of Bir Tawil, 1U4UN."[6]

Transmission was the first step, but reception proved much harder. Some radio enthusiasts were clearly taken by Zhikharev's escapade in Bir Tawil, although others pointed out that as long as he remains unrecognized by shortwave radio governing bodies, he "doesn't count."[7] Even family and friends struggled to share their sovereign's enthusiasm. When he first crossed the administrative line into Bir Tawil, Zhikharev used his satellite phone to call his wife back in Moscow. "I called her and said, 'Hey, you're talking to the king now.'" Her concerns, however, were rather less regal: "What did you do to the computer at home?" she asked, "I can't open any files." Hoping for a more supportive response, he phoned his office and declared, "This is King Dmitry calling!" His colleague who picked up again had more pressing things on his mind. "Listen," he said, "this is not the time. We have a problem with the ruble and inflation. Yeah, sure, it's good, King Blah Blah Blah, but this is not the time to talk cause I'm really pissed off and stressed. We have our own shit to take care of."[8]

To disprove the skeptics, Zhikharev purchased a whole set of domain names containing "Bir Tawil" and, for $4,000, registered the territory at the Russian trademark and patent office.[9] A website is still under construction but already opens with a slideshow that invites visitors to "discover the kingdom" with its ominous "extreme conditions" and the promise of "billions of stars" every night. A timeline charts Bir Tawil's origins in ancient Nubia, through the Ottoman and British conquests in the region, its unclaimed status as no man's land, and its rebirth in 2014 with "HRM Dmitry I as a Ruler and Mika Ronkainen as Duke of the Southern Territories."[10] In the first slide, Zhikharev is shown from some distance standing on a hill of rock and sand with a vast desert landscape behind him, while Ronkainen, a few meters to his right, is hoisting a pole bearing the flag of Bir Tawil.[11] When I first noticed the flag in one of the videos Zhikharev posted from Bir Tawil, I mistook it for the

Prussian flag—a horizontal white stripe on top of a black one. But when asked
about the banner's design, the explanation was rather more literal: "Russians,
white people, in the black continent. It's easy." A Moscow-based firm was commissioned by Zhikharev to design the flag, along with other sovereign essentials, from the official seal to a passport.[12] More mundane objects were also
harnessed to prop up the kingdom's legitimacy, like a blue Russian post box
that Zhikharev made sure to bring along with him on his latest trip: "You
know, one of those hanging on the wall that say почта, 'post.' . . . That's the
first thing you do. The first thing you do is have a post office, because that's
how you have an address, that's how it's officially claimed because you have a
post office, like anywhere. Like North Korea."

Zhikharev talks about Bir Tawil with obvious confidence and describes
his claim over it as a matter of fact. He has invested significant personal resources into the endeavor, and takes pride in the paraphernalia that is at once
a product of this project and a proof of its success. After all, he has a flag, a
passport emblazoned with the golden emblem of his kingdom and his very
own post box.

Yet throughout our conversations, his assuredness was inseparable from
his frustration with everyday life in Moscow. During one of our phone calls,
while Zhikharev was stuck in Moscow's rush hour, he was dismayed when
other cars were driving against traffic. He was late to the hospital to pick up
his seven-year-old son, while others were blatantly flouting the law. Watching
this scene, he admitted, "At some point you think, damn, I can just do better
than anyone else who's around me."[13] In his kingdom, he noted with unapologetic self-satisfaction, he would prevent women from driving. "We are the
only country [that does that] now, because Saudi Arabia allowed women to
drive. My wife hates the idea. And I said listen: we provide a driver to every
woman. It's funny but still."[14] In our very first conversation several months
earlier, Zhikharev hinted that what lay behind that inconclusive "but still,"
behind the jokey comments and crude misogyny, is his own political disillusionment. Asked why he wanted to control Bir Tawil, he answered: "Why not?
We can't control our own country then why not control somewhere else?"[15]

Zhikharev is not alone in claiming the crown of Bir Tawil. Like a cliché
Cold War plot, his nemesis is an American armed with his own fantasies and
an origin story befitting a fairy tale. In an account that, for a short while, received widespread media attention, Jeremiah Heaton, a farmer and entrepre-
neur from Virginia, promised his daughter Emily one evening that he would
make her a princess. To live up to his promise, Heaton decided that the only
way to bestow royal status on his daughter was to make himself a king. After
considering his options, he set his sights on Bir Tawil.

His journey through Egypt is described with familiar tropes of hardships overcome, local guides, and, in some versions, a camel caravan, all leading to a ceremonial flag planting on the top of a rugged hill. Even that latter gesture bore almost-perfect symbolism, as it was done on June 16, 2014, the day of Emily's seventh birthday. By November that year, Heaton's story was bought by Disney. In *The Princess of North Sudan*, the studio was hoping to "focus on the father-daughter relationship and use [it] as a jumping-off point for a fantastical adventure."[16] Once news of the production began circulating, criticism mounted and the film was frozen, although Disney still maintains the story rights.

While the filmic fantasy was put on hold, Heaton remains as committed to his bigger dream of a kingdom in the desert. If his Russian rival has taken incremental steps to prove his presence on the ground and on the airwaves in the hope of being recognized as a sovereign radio entity, Heaton admitted he has not set foot in Bir Tawil since his initial visit. Instead, he paints a vision that blends benevolence, scientific innovation, and neoliberal entrepreneurship into a libertarian utopia. In one essay he states his intention of eradicating hunger and famine by becoming "the Elon Musk of agricultural development," with vertical farming powered by solar energy in the place of electric cars.[17] To fund this elaborate plan, Heaton first launched a crowdfunding campaign that offered supporters various incentives: from a $25 honorary title to the naming rights for a future international airport or the capital city, which would cost $1.7 million.[18] When the appeal failed to generate any meaningful support, Heaton shifted his efforts to lobbying the Egyptian and Sudanese governments. In August 2018 he met with Sudan's ambassador to Washington, accompanied by a retired marine colonel who currently works as a defense lobbyist and two Saudi American businessmen. The meeting focused on Sudan's international business interests rather than on Bir Tawil.[19] Geopolitical sensitivities, he realized, were likely to prevent any official recognition of his sovereign claims. Neither Egypt or Sudan cared for Bir Tawil directly, but they cared immensely about what such a recognition could trigger.

Once diplomacy failed to advance his cause, Heaton pitched ambitious development projects like solar farms and banking services, in return for what he describes as "recognition through the functional means of a business contract."[20] The kingdom's energy business would be supplemented by massive server farms "where reporters can share information the way WikiLeaks works. That's basically a repository for free speech, a repository for transactions and that sort of thing." He planned an airfield that could become a hub for distribution of aid, where NATO and USAID could "know that supplies won't be stolen, pillaged." Most recently, Heaton launched a cryptocurrency called

Neap Coin as yet another way of fundraising, again, with limited success.[21] Over five years after first planting his flag, Heaton admitted that setting up a kingdom is harder than he first thought: "It's just difficult. It's not easy at all."

Nevertheless, Heaton seems undeterred. He sets his libertarian vision of individual freedom untethered from the confines of government against a backdrop of violence and repression. Seeing the instability that plagues many African countries, he seeks to create "one place in Africa that was that shining example of what can happen when commerce and trade are allowed to occur freely, and you don't have any religiosity dictating things, no political unrest, no infighting." He critiques other micronations that have begun issuing citizenship to anyone who can afford a relatively small amount. In contrast, he strives for a more lucrative polity that is supposed to bring with it utilitarian stability: "We're only focusing on citizenship of people right now who are high net-worth individuals who can help us advance the project through their own finances. Having a country that's centered on business and doesn't have the social liabilities . . . we don't want to get into the business of building schools for people, and that sort of thing, at least not right now."

Heaton's narrative is perplexing in its contradictory facets: Disney fairy tales, server farms ensuring unrestricted free speech, and unregulated monetary instruments supported by massive solar fields all in the service of the eradication of hunger and the supposed benefit of those in need, although the poor won't in fact be allowed into the future kingdom. All these fantastical grand plans are conjured, mostly, from his farmhouse in Virginia, thousands of miles from Bir Tawil. Heaton vehemently rejects accusations that his actions represent a contemporary form of colonial intrusion. But at least in one respect, his pursuit of a remote unclaimed desert territory fits a well-established genre of stories told about faraway fantastical lands. Julie Sanders notes how armchair travel fantasies from the seventeenth century satisfied desires for power and possession and expanded an understanding not of foreign lands but of "home" and "self."[22]

Like European fantasists in the early modern period, Heaton's desire for freedom and territorial autonomy emerges out of a sense of disillusionment and loss of agency closer to home. Long before he laid claim to Bir Tawil, Heaton twice ran unsuccessfully for a congressional seat in his Virginia district.[23] "We're living in an age of overreach," he told me, sounding exasperated by regulations and restrictions imposed by government and "corporate overlords."

Fantasies of a desert kingdom with its emancipatory promises are directly rooted in anxieties of White, middle-class privilege that no longer goes unchallenged or taken for granted. In his fantastical kingdom, all this uncertainty can be done away with. Drawing on the most obvious American precedent, Heaton clarified that, in Bir Tawil, "we're not going to police anything. It's gonna be the Wild West. That's fine." Such nostalgia for the American frontier paints this particular political fantasy in bright colors of freedom, prospect, and unshackled potentiality. When all these seem foreclosed in twenty-first-century rural Virginia, Bir Tawil offers a readily available space onto which these fantasies can be transplanted.

Conjuring the Wild West is fanciful, but it is also telling. Like his predecessors' fantastical projections of vast domains emerging from the "unclaimed" wilderness of the American West, the political fantasy that drives Heaton never fully rids itself of the violence of settler colonial expansion. Displacement and mass killing that took place in the settler frontier of North America are never acknowledged as integral to Heaton's fantasy, but their potential is always looming. "This land is barren land," he told me, trying to counter some of the criticism he faced: "There's nobody there. I've kicked nobody off. There are no houses there, and I have not impacted a soul by doing what I'm doing."

Although its terrain is indisputably rugged and currently has no permanent settlement, Bir Tawil isn't empty. Its very existence as a cartographic anomaly emerges out of official recognition of nomadic practices in and possession of it. Colonial bureaucrats understood that the line drawn in 1899 along the Twenty-Second Parallel to separate Egypt and Anglo-Egyptian Sudan failed to address the Ababda and Beja people's irregular movements across this wide swath of land. The Administrative Line of 1902 corrected this and explicitly recognized tribal affiliations to distinct regions along the border. Specifically, it acknowledged the Ababda people's presence in and use of Bir Tawil.[24] Far from legalistic minutiae, these details highlight Bir Tawil's role within a recognized Indigenous system of life that has not disappeared, even after the territory was explicitly renounced by Egypt and Sudan. Reducing complex histories and subtle use practices to "barren land" fits all too well into settler colonial discourse that is often followed by the violence of dispossession.

Heaton adopted the legal concept of terra nullius—a territory that has no recognized claims of ownership—to justify his claim, comparing the desert territory to a volcanic island that has popped up "in the middle of international waters."[25] But Bir Tawil is not an island. By invoking the concept of terra nullius, Heaton mobilizes, perhaps unknowingly, one of settler colonialism's most obvious instruments of violence, used to systematically nullify Indigenous forms of land ownership and tenure.[26] He rejected any link between the Ababda people and Bir Tawil, arguing that they concentrate hundreds of miles to the north. Even more direct forms of dispossession were inherent to his plans. In our conversation, I pointed out that, far from a desert island, Bir Tawil is currently home to thousands of Sudanese miners prospecting for gold, a fact he was fully aware of: "I'm not worried about those people once we get to Bir Tawil. With the power of the US dollar I think we can co-opt them out of the mining industry and help them set up, to be able to spend time with their families in Sudan, do agriculture, do whatever."[27]

In some fantasies, there are no monsters, at least not of a mythical or supernatural kind. Zhikharev had to cut short one of our conversation because the elevator in his apartment building wasn't working and he had to help his wife carry the baby pram down the stairs—hardly living up to his regal credentials. The morning we last spoke, Heaton told me he was exhausted after spending the previous day building a skateboard ramp for his son. After our call he was going to a Fourth of July barbecue at a friend's house. Fantasies of an independent desert kingdom have not, apparently, made him abandon the national rituals of his current home. Despite their rivalry, both see their kingdom in no man's land in escapist terms, a break from their otherwise mundane lives in Moscow and Virginia. But Zhikharev's search for recognition is largely confined to the governing bodies of shortwave radio and his fellow radio enthusiasts. In his fantasy, there are no bulldozers, no airfields or massive mining operations. Importantly, his fantasy does not result in dispossession. Conversely, there was something matter of fact about the way Heaton described the eventual removal of Sudanese miners from his future kingdom. What happened to them and their livelihoods, or to the ancestral links of the Ababda, seemed secondary. It seemed like he didn't care, which makes him, in this odd competition, the true king of no man's land.

Destination Temptation; or, Why I've Never Been to Bir Tawil

Blue barrels filled with sand or concrete that form a barrier across a narrow street in Nicosia, an Israeli soldier at a checkpoint, an email from the Egyptian embassy in London refusing travel permits. Dead ends appeared almost at every turn while researching this book. Being turned away was often frustrating and disappointing. Once access was denied, arguing was rarely an option, not only because the decision was unlikely to be reversed, but also because arguing is a privilege few have in such situations.[28] Doris Rivera, a Colombian social leader who escaped to the FARC-controlled Clearance Zone in 1999, described to me once her constant fear of crossing the many paramilitary checkpoints that surrounded the zone, common sites of summary executions. I recall her account here not to draw superficial parallels but to recognize that a fixation on "getting there" can easily prevent us asking whose mobility is in question and why we want to get there in the first place.

Being turned away doesn't prevent you from trying again. In the spring of 2022, seven years after our first request to reach Bir Tawil was refused by the Egyptian authorities, my friend and collaborator Alasdair and I arrived in Sudan. Travel restrictions imposed to control the COVID-19 pandemic had been eased slightly in the months prior, but the country was still grappling with the aftermath of a military coup and the collapse of the nascent transition toward democracy that started after the 2019 ousting of Omar al-Bashir. Large demonstrations were taking place daily in cities across the country, met with deadly police violence. But it was a brief window that finally allowed me to speak to those for whom Bir Tawil is more than an empty canvas onto which Western fantasies are projected. Hundreds of thousands of Sudanese were digging for gold across the northern regions of the country, and as many as four thousand were seeking their fortune in Bir Tawil itself. Not accounting for their stories and experiences would have been antithetical to this book's fundamental effort to understand the space of uncaring not as an abstract political constellation, but as a living place. Moreover, it would have problematically followed a pattern of White writers documenting White conquest in Africa, whether for scientific ends, strategic calculations, or sheer adventure. Going to Sudan was a way to insist that Bir Tawil not be seen solely through the eyes of an American and a Russian, as a mere object of White fantasy.

To be clear, White fantasies are consequential, sometimes catastrophically so. Both Zhikharev and Heaton offer valuable insights into the aspirations and trepidations that plague Western geographical imaginations and how those imaginaries are projected onto contemporary no man's land. But stopping there would have made this a rather parochial discussion. Not that being "on the ground" offers an assured antidote to the ingrained provincialism of White experience. There was an inescapable irony in the fact that Alasdair and I were two White men seemingly retracing the journey of two other White men. It was impossible to undo the basic facts of who we are. The only thing we could control was how we went about doing the work that we do—specifically, by not going to Bir Tawil.

An abandoned station on the railway line connecting the long stretch of desert between Wadi Halfa and the town of Abu Hamad was as far as we got. In recent years, the station has become the main refueling spot for miners working across the northeastern desert. Bir Tawil was only another three hours' drive north, but there was little to gain from the purely symbolic act of setting foot. If anything, it was exactly that act that needed to be avoided. First, because refusing to set foot dispels any fantasy of conquest that still persist, even subliminally, in practices of field research and, relatedly, in the heroics associated with the figure of the explorer. Put rather crudely, if you can't get there, you can't claim to own it. Second, against the conventional focus on the isolated moment of arrival and the singularity of the destination (with its highly conventionalized choreographies and documentary practices[29]), what is proposed here is a subtler attention to multiple encounters and expressions of uncaring that intersect in and around Bir Tawil, many of which are not confined to a strict perimeter.

Finally, and perhaps most importantly, no one invited me. This may sound like a prosaic reason not to travel somewhere that has been on my mind from the very first stages of this project, but throughout my work on this book, I never arrived anywhere unannounced. I relied on the hospitality of others, and through their hospitality, I came to see how they negotiated my presence with otherwise invisible forces that regulate and govern the space of uncaring. But hospitality must begin with a willingness to host, to welcome a guest—a foreigner—with all the perils that an invitation like this entails. Hospitality, as Derrida famously notes, is intrinsically linked to law and to violence;[30] time and again, I have learned that this is not simply an abstract proposition. Two of my hosts in Colombia, whose repeated hospitality was often generous beyond their means, were targets of assassination attempts. As I have discussed elsewhere in this book, when the state abdicates a given territory and those who reside in it, it also unleashes other forces that, often violently, impose their own internal order on the space and its population. My presence almost never went unnoticed, and often it was the task of my host to explain it, with some risk to themselves and others around them. In Sudan, a country that has seen the deadly consequences of many White men arriving uninvited, venturing into Bir Tawil without clearly knowing that my presence there would be welcomed was a line I could not cross.

And still, sitting in the shade of a hut where we met with miners who were digging across the region, the temptation of the destination was hard to deny. As Alasdair pointed out at one point, Bir Tawil was, after all, only a few hours away. Recognizing the temptation was important, a reminder that we are not untethered from the violent expeditionary histories that have, fundamentally, been obsessed with the conquest of the destination and myths of masculine heroics. Yearning for the space of uncaring, whether it is in search of an escape from the confining stricture of the state or even as an intellectual concern, was a privileged preoccupation. Inescapably, it was bound with a White fantasy of an unclaimed desert territory that awaits to be "discovered" intellectually. Even if we could have made it, this was a siren song worth resisting.

White fantasies of territorial "discovery" (in Africa in particular) are almost always propped up by Black knowledge and Black labor. Europeans who ventured across the continent in search of scientific discovery or territorial conquest often depended on local guides, cooks, drivers, and porters for their very survival. And while such local knowledge was often a matter of life and death, many of those who shouldered these tasks did so under duress. Rarely did they choose to undergo the hardships of exploration. At the same time that White fantasies relied on the work and knowledge of others, it also laboriously sought to erase this inherent dependency. Reading the archives of German colonization in West Africa, John Noyes describes the ox wagon used by settlers as a "writing machine" that marks with its movement a triumphant narrative of pioneering and European expansion. But this movement, he notes, is all too often predicated on tracks that were already there and are immediately overwritten. It is, Noyes writes, a tautological gesture: European expansion retraces "a mark which is always already there, and whose priority is erased in its retracing."[31]

It is hardly a surprise, therefore, that for Zhikharev and Heaton, the journey to claim Bir Tawil is largely described as a tale of individual triumph, a venture into the empty desert in search of an unclaimed land. Each makes a passing mention of local guides, but the details are vague. No Sudanese or Egyptians are mentioned by name, and none appears in the many images that accompany their websites and media reports that document the rivaling escapades. One of the most widely circulating photographs features Heaton holding his flag with a barren desert stretching behind him; another image shows Zhikharev and his friend, Mikhail Ronkainen, in a similar posture.

When we went to Sudan, Alasdair printed those images and brought them with us; we thought they might offer an illustration of what was otherwise a rather outlandish story of two White guys and their competing claims over a border territory in northeastern Africa. An hour into the drive out of Khartoum, Al handed the photographs to Nazar, a young Sudanese who had organized our arrival and gotten us through the convoluted bureaucracy of Sudanese visas and permits. It was only thanks to him that we were able to get into Sudan, and our entire work in the field rested on his logistical experience and deep knowledge of the country. It took Nazar only a quick glance as the photograph of Zhikharev to start laughing.

"You know what's missing from this photograph?" He asked. "Me! . . . I was the one who took this picture!" (fig. 9).

FIGURE 9. Nazar, holding a photograph he took of Dmitry Zhikharev and his companion in Bir Tawil, 2022. Photographer: Alasdair Pinkerton.

For Zhikharev's first two visits to Sudan, Nazar was the one who arranged almost every aspect of his journey to Bir Tawil. Beyond permits and visas, he liaised with drivers and purchased fuel, cooked food, and built the camps along the way. He translated and, when needed, was also the designated photographer. As the one holding the camera, Nazar was left out of that widely circulated photograph. None of the captions ever credits him. This was exactly the kind of thoughtless erasure that White fantasy tries to perform, consigning Black knowledge and labor on which it heavily relies into a nameless and faceless background. This is far from novel. Several scholars of imperial and colonial history have explicitly sought to subvert the veneration of the explorer as an individualized expert. Instead, they highlight the critical importance of "go-betweens" and Indigenous expertise in "the brokered world" of imperial knowledge making.[32] In the case of Bir Tawil, there is no need to comb through the archive in search of such marginalized histories, forms of knowledge and biographies. What is needed, instead, is a conscious expansion of the frame; the faces, voices, and experiences of those who were previously hidden or edited out are right there.

The Desert Edge: Four Fragments

Roughly nine hundred kilometers divide Khartoum from Bir Tawil. Covering that distance entails a movement through the gradients of sovereignty—from its obvious performances in the country's capital to the point where any pretense of sovereign care is left behind. The following four fragments follow this movement, documenting how uncaring is a condition that unfolds gradually and almost imperceptibly. It is also a movement from a clearly defined space that confines uncaring, to a more diffuse political condition that sees uncaring seep into wider political geographies of the state. Bir Tawil may be the no man's land where sovereign care is altogether abdicated. But along the way it becomes clear that cracked surfaces, defunct infrastructures and damaged lands all bear the imprint of uncaring, its violence and the hopes that it harbors.

I. INFRASTRUCTURE OF DISENCHANTMENT

An asphalt road traces the eastern bank of the Nile from Khartoum up to the northern gold-rush frontier. Until recently, this was the only road connecting Sudan to Egypt, in a country that already has one of the lowest road densities in Africa and the world.[33] Regular checkpoints are set up along the road, every hundred kilometers or so. At each one, a copy of a travel permit, which took several days and bribes to obtain back in Khartoum, is handed over to an official who may be wearing a police or military uniform or sporting just a football jersey emblazoned with a Chinese logo. Several times, the document was accepted without any inspection; once, the young official who walked up to the car briefly inspected the permit, but held it upside down. A road tax of one thousand Sudanese pounds is also charged for the journey, although additional payment may be required at each checkpoint, depending on the whims of local officials. Outside the capital, the road was the only space where one regularly encountered the trappings of the state and its petty sovereigns.

Roads are supposed to be technologies of integration, and the integration of a national territory in particular. In Sudan, where the Nile has functioned as the central spine running through the national territory, roads have only recently attained a greater role in this regard.[34] Yet integration is often most visible through its disruption, through blockages and ruptures. One of the most visible acts of defiance against the military coup of 2021 involved a blockade of the main export route from Sudan into Egypt. A spokesperson for the opposition "Resistance Committee" noted how road blockades were one of the few tools available to the protestors to fracture the country and isolate the coup leaders in Khartoum.[35] Roads are thus not just material forms, but also promises toward a future that is often uncertain and unclear.[36] But for roads to integrate territory, they actually need to be materially intact. Only their material surface gives tangibility to immaterial (through undeniably powerful) imaginations of territory and political community.

What, then, is the power of a crumbling, pothole-ridden road like the one linking the capital to the northern states? Seif, who drove the car we were traveling in, had to constantly swerve to avoid the craters that dotted the road. There is one speed camera for the entire road, and offenders are pulled over at the nearest checkpoint to pay a fine. Seif joked that there was no need for a speed camera, given that no one could drive more than half the speed limit. Nazar, who spent days sorting out payments for travel and tolls, found it less amusing. "Where is the money going?" he asked, and as an answer, gestured toward his shirt pocket, gesturing to someone pocketing public funds. From its very early days, Nazar was deeply involved in the protest demanding democratic transition in Sudan and repeatedly noted his disillusionment with the blatant corruption of state officials. "It wasn't like this in the past," he said. It wasn't clear which era he was longing for, but his disillusionment with those in power was palpable.

Writing about similarly broken down and fractured spaces in Peru, Penny Harvey and Hannah Knox suggest that crumbling, cracked, and pothole-strewn roads invoke "an awareness of all of those extended relations which have failed to cohere to produce a tangible material infrastructure."[37] The disintegration of the road—the impact of the potholes and the constant need to swerve and slow down—was a repeated jolt, a rude awakening from the promise of the state as a providing, generative entity rather than a purely deductive power that is there to tax, fine, or arrest.[38] As one travels north, farther away from the capital, the broken road and the boorish checkpoint personnel are a manifestation of the state's diminishing intensity. It is a "road register," to use Kathleen Stewart's term, that offers a material crystallization of both the structures and fantasies of state thinking.[39] This is not a register of a "failed" or "dysfunctional" state; for a small elite, the state functions all too well. For most, especially those outside the capital, it has never provided the basic forms of regulation, governance, and protection that are the assumed attributes of modern sovereignty. Instead, what this crumbling road registers are the fading moments of sovereign presence, the scarce spaces in which formal performances of state care still take place. Such appearances punctuate ever-increasing swaths of territory ruled by the uncaring state, where indifference and callousness are the common dispositions.

These are also sources of deep disenchantment with a state that system-atically fails those subjected to it. Such indifference, Rukmini Bhaya Nair writes in her analysis of Indian postcolonial rule, is perhaps the most com-mon substance "that postcolonial institutions of all sorts, and most especially institutions of government, are engaged in manufacturing."[40] Moreover, she importantly reminds us that even when uncaring is systematized into a logic of governance that is deeply enmeshed in the fabric of the state, it is not dis-tributed equally. In other words, uncaring has a geography where it appears in its most distilled form: "Indifference belongs unarguably to border coun-try, to these shadowlands of postcoloniality."[41] With this in mind, it is perhaps not surprising that thousands are using this crumbling road on their way to the northern gold regions. Fortune, they hope, lies somewhere in the desert ahead, in the border country where care officially ends.

II. TRACKS OF EMPIRE

Approximately five hundred kilometers from the capital, the paved road ends at the town of Abu Hamad. The town sits at the center of the great S-shaped bend of the Nile, as the river turns sharply southwest. It is the gateway to the mining fields surrounding it, and one of the main hubs for equipment, machinery and chemicals used by mining companies in the area. There is also a thriving market that services small-scale prospectors. Aside from the shops selling pickaxes, shovels, and outdoor cooking stoves, there are smaller billboards around town that target this artisanal end of the extractive logis-tical chain, advertising specialized scales able to weigh minuscule nuggets, the kind that most artisanal prospectors will try to sell off from their desert explorations.

From here on, there are no roads leading north, only sandy tracks. An-other infrastructure nevertheless crosses the desert: the now-defunct railway line that runs from Wadi Halfa on the border with Egypt to Abu Hamad. Like many railways, the tracks set out the direction of imperial conquest and vio-lence; in this case, it was the British effort to retake Sudan from the control of the Mahdi, Muhammad Ahmad. Herbert Kitchner, who took over the com-mand of the British-Egyptian forces in 1896, used the rail line as a pivotal component of his military push south.[42] This infrastructural "triumph" paved the way for the British advance and the decisive battle near the city of Om-durman in 1898, in which eleven thousand of the Mahdi's army were killed and sixteen thousand injured—although the number of actual fatalities was significantly higher owing to the neglect and execution of the wounded.[43] Now that the trains have stopped running, the tracks and telegraph poles that

FIGURE 10. Station 6 on the Wadi Halfa–Abu Hamad railway, Sudan, 2022. Photographer: Alasdair Pinkerton.

stretch along them still offer a navigation aid through a region that comprises vast and largely featureless desert plateaus.

Old train stations built by the British and later used by the Sudanese national rail company still stand at regular intervals along the line. Without trains to service, most stations were abandoned, their structures left as crumbling remnants of colonial pasts and postcolonial promises. Out of the ten stations between Abu Hamad and Wadi Halfa, only one—Station 6—remains inhabited, solely because it serves as a refueling station for miners working in the desert (fig. 10). Although the Sudanese rail company has offered to rent the old station structures, most of those who set up businesses on site opted to build their own structures, turning Station 6 into a small hamlet comprising two dozen buildings. The original station structures are primarily used as public toilets. Almost every basic service is offered here, from dry provisions and sweets, to water and diesel. There is a shop offering satellite phones and internet connection, a place to buy a goat and have it butchered, and a small mosque. There are also, of course, several stalls to sell gold nuggets.

Abdu, who worked as a ticket master for thirty years while the trains were running, sells tea and coffee to those passing through. We sat in the shade of his large shack that was built using old train tracks and spoke to men who came in throughout the day. Most were young, in their late teens and twenties, working for small-scale mining crews in the area. One man, however, stood out. He was older, in his forties, freshly shaven and neatly dressed in a polo shirt rather than the white galabia that was worn by almost everyone else. He worked for a Russian mining firm that has a concession a few miles east. Our conversation started out cordially, but after a few minutes, the tone changed.

"Ask them where the gold is," he said to Nazar.

Jokingly, Nazar translated the question. We laughed, but the guy did not. After an awkward moment, Nazar asked him why he thought we knew where to find gold given that we were two foreigners who have never been to Sudan before. The guy answered without hesitation.

"They built the railway, so they know where the gold is," he said.

He explained that a few kilometers north, in a place called Bir Murad, the British are rumored to have discovered a large gold cache and used the railway to transport the hoard south to Khartoum. It was then supposedly shipped off to England. Sudanese workers who helped dig the treasure were all killed. Before traveling, we had printed an early map of the Egypt-Sudan border, with the location of Bir Tawil marked out. What we thought of as a visual aid in generating conversations, was, for our interlocutor, subtle proof of our ill intentions. For him, there was only one reason for two White guys to show up and ask about everyday life out in the desert: we were out to mine gold. We were on an extractive mission just like so many White people who came through here before us, laying rail tracks on their march south while leaving the bodies of thousands of Sudanese in their wake.

III. A CALCULUS OF DREAMS

Ratios. It takes six shovel loads from a massive loader tractor to yield a single gram of gold. Most prospectors head out with only the most rudimentary tools—metal detectors, shovels, pickaxes. Without the use of mechanical equipment, they are likely to detect only nuggets found on or close to the surface. While purchasing heavy mechanical equipment is likely to be well beyond their financial means, bulldozers, excavators, loaders, and diggers are all readily available to hire closer to the exploration sites. In fact, the only billboards one sees when arriving in Abu Hamad are those advertising local dealerships for heavy machinery, each with a large image of a tractor or truck, uniformly painted bright golden yellow.

Quantities. One shovel of a large loader can lift over a ton of soil. Immense amounts of earth need to be dug, crushed, sifted, and discarded to extract miniscule amounts of gold. Small-scale prospectors begin gold exploration by scanning the surface using handheld metal detectors. For some, the search relies on an equal measure of technology and divine ordination: They believe nuggets are planted by a godly being that only certain ordained prospectors are destined to find.[44] Others use the more chaotic *taminjeri* method, a term borrowed from the Arabic title for the Tom and Jerry cartoons. Like the never-ending wild chases of the two animated figures, prospecting is understood as nothing more than a random pursuit.[45] Either way, surface scanning is only the first step. Once gold is detected on or near the surface, more extensive scraping follows. A tractor removes approximately a foot of topsoil, pushing the ground into a series of mounds. The scraped earth is then scanned again with metal detectors. Nearly two decades of scraping have altered the landscape of the northern desert, with the natural plateaus that stretch between dark rocky hills now featuring endless rows of scrape mounds. Some are freshly dug, still featuring the plowed toothmarks of the bulldozer shovel. Older ones are already covered in a layer of sand that softens the edges of the small, bulldozer-made geological formations.

Percentages. Fifty percent of any gold found goes to pay for heavy mechanical equipment, and an additional 5 percent is taxed by local officers stationed at key market locations where nuggets are sold (fig. 11). From the remaining 45 percent, prospectors still have to pay workers on their crew, as well as the expenses of food, fuel, and water. Even before they set foot in the desert, prospecting entrepreneurs rely on family and community networks to provide the needed investment to purchase basic equipment and reach the increasingly remote regions where gold has yet to be exhausted. These debts have to be repaid, and some profit margin needs to be maintained to support families who stay behind. Official figures are nearly impossible to come by, but according to one estimate, approximately 14 percent of Sudan's population is dependent on the artisanal mining industry.[46] Given their minuscule margins, it is frightening to realize how many dreams and fears are carried on the pickup trucks loaded with men heading north into the desert.

IV. PARCELS AND PARAMILITARIES

There is a lot of desert in Sudan, but even the desert is increasingly out of bounds.

After it lost oil revenues to the newly independent South Sudan in 2011, Sudan was plunged into economic turmoil. Gold, which has been mined in the region for nearly five thousand years, emerged as an available resource

FIGURE 11. Bulldozers waiting to be hired by small gold-mining crews in Station 6, Sudan, 2022. Photographer: Alasdair Pinkerton.

that could provide much-needed access to foreign currency. In addition to signing dozens of concession agreements with international investors, the Sudanese government also began purchasing gold from artisanal gold miners and prospectors at above market rates, with the main intention of ensuring foreign currency flows. From the early days of the scramble for gold, Sudanese state maintained an ambivalent position with regard to artisanal mining, primarily because it remains a sector that is harder to regulate and tax. The Mineral Wealth and Mining (Development) Act of 2015 was the most recent attempt by the Sudanese state to establish a legal framework for governing extractive resources and economies.[47] The act designates all mineral resources as the sole property of the state and prohibits all forms of exploration, prospecting, and mining without a government license. In other words, it both bans artisanal mining and criminalizes those engaged in small-scale gold production outside the purview of the state. In practice, it had little effect and millions across the country joined the rush for gold.[48] As state authorities were increasingly forced to contend with civil unrest in more populated regions, their capacity and motivation to enforce an outright ban on this activity dropped.[49]

Although the state does little to curtail artisanal mining, parceling out the

northern desert through concessions and contracts remains a powerful political tool through which territorial order is projected. Given the near impos-
sibility of providing regular governing presence in the vast expanses of arid
and largely uninhabited land that stretches between the Nile valley and the
Egypt-Sudan border, it is easy to see the allure of drawing neat lots that can
be quantified and leased at market rates. With a few lines on a map, the state
is able to project a sovereign order without any need for physical presence
on the ground. This process is not unique to Sudan. Revisiting the colonial
history of tin mining in Nigeria, Gavin Bridge and Tomas Fredriksen point
out that while private companies "probed the underground to determine the
richest properties and calculate production costs, the colonial state aspired
to a more ambitious epistemic grasp of the territory, one that sought forms
of knowledge functional to administration and the production of social order."[50] Put simply, speculative partitioning and concession drawing was a way
to territorialize the state, exactly in those spaces that otherwise elude other
performances of state control.

At times, though, desert parcels emerge as more than sources of foreign
currency or instruments of territorial consolidation. At the right moment,
they also offer a geopolitical lifeline. The brief transition toward democracy
that began after Bashir was deposed in 2019 also saw a relaxation of the international sanctions against Sudan, including its removal from the US State
Sponsors of Terrorism list. However, improving relations between Sudan, the
United States and European Union quickly stalled following the military coup
of October 2021. Sudan once again found itself largely isolated, and gold was
one of the few assets it could leverage in seeking new strategic partnerships.
Gold was also what Russia was eager to purchase at that very moment. One
part of a wider Russian strategy that sought to insulate its economy from the
vulnerability of currency reserves to US sanction regimes involved the sharp
increase of gold reserves since the early 2000s.[51] After the 2014 invasion of
Crimea, and in the run-up to the 2022 invasion of Ukraine, gold was seen as
largely beyond the reach of international sanctions and, therefore, a source
of revenue that could keep the Russian economy afloat at a time of extreme
isolation.[52] It was a shopping spree that spanned Africa—including Mali, Bur-
kina Faso, and the Central African Republic—but Sudan proved an especially
eager vendor.

On the eve of Russia's 2022 all-out invasion of Ukraine, a Sudanese delegation headed by Mohammed "Hemedti" Hamdan Dagalo happened to be in
Moscow for an official visit. Hemedti, who emerged from the military take-
over as the country's de facto vice president, commands the Rapid Support
Forces (RSF), a large government militia with deep reach into the country's

gold industry. It is now the main conduit for Russian presence in Sudan, and its gold-mining sector in particular.

A shadowy partner was also spearheading the Russian side. It is hard not to get lost in the maze of Russian companies and subsidiaries involved in Sudan's gold extraction—among them M-Invest, Kush E&P, and Meroe Gold—but all seem to be linked to the Russian oligarch Yevgeny Prigozhin.[53] Before his death in a 2023 plane crash, Prigozhin led the Wagner Group, an opaque private military company that helped the Kremlin extract natural resources and support oppressive regimes around the world. Wagner has been especially active in Africa. Hundreds of Wagner mercenaries have been working in Sudan for years, training and fulfilling specialized security tasks. Wagner formed close ties with the RSF in particular and was also involved in the deadly suppression of antimilitary protests.[54]

In February 2022, RSF and Wagner forces staged a joint incursion into the area surrounding Jabal Sufar, close to Sudan's border with Egypt. Several witnesses we spoke to noted that the forces were heavily armed. It was rare for paramilitary groups to venture into these remote borderlands, and the presence of Russian mercenaries was even more unusual. A small number of mining companies have operated in the region for over a decade, but it was mostly prospected by several hundred artisanal miners. Once the militias arrived, they informed the miners that Jabal Sufar was to be used solely by a Russian mining operation and ordered them to leave the area. "People were angry. They were kicking us out of our own land," said a young man who was present when the events took place when we met him and other local miners a month later. Another miner who sat with us explained that the anger was erupting partly because this was the ancestral home of the Ababda people; "dar el Ababda."[55]

Local miners and Indigenous tribes increasingly find themselves between the rock of large mining corporations and the hard place of armed militias. In the search for gold, private companies and paramilitary groups have deepened their involvement in the northernmost fringes of Sudan. Faced with impending violence, the Ababda people, who have traversed the border regions for centuries, are being forcefully pushed off their ancestral lands and increasingly toward the one parcel that remains explicitly outside the Sudanese state's push for the marketization and securitization of the desert: Bir Tawil.

Miner Dreams

During research in a small community in the north of Sudan over a decade ago, the anthropologist Sandra Calkins already noted how "everyone was

talking about gold, dreaming of new wealth and prosperity."[56] For hundreds
of thousands of people in the northern desert alone, this dream is still alive
today. Pickup trucks race across the sandy plains, their beds packed with a
dozen or more men. Some of the prospecting parties we met included boys
in their early teens, some even younger. Carrying bare necessities that will
sustain them in the desert for several weeks and basic tools, they head north
chasing that age-old dream of striking gold. Some will join existing small
operations or replace crews that have been out working while others will try
their luck in new locations. Some travel on their own, hitching a ride on a
supply truck going north, and will wait in remote refueling stations to find
work with a local crew. One young man studying for an English degree at the
University of Khartoum traveled out into the desert during his summer break
as a way of funding his studies.

Gold miners dream of gold. This statement seems utterly obvious, but
such dreams are meaningful insofar as they sharply break from fantasies of
the state, of a nation's progress through collective projects of modernization
and civic participation. Instead, they are fed by individual desires for wealth
and prosperity. These seemingly prosaic motivations are also expressions of
exasperated subjects that have grown increasingly disenchanted with the failed
promises of an uncaring state. They give rise, instead, to "a sort of image of
the entrepreneurial figure of the prospector, who appears to be freed from
normative constraints that normally weigh upon his engagements with land
owned by others."[57]

That, in a nutshell, is the greatest draw of the space of uncaring: it offers a
place where dreams of uninhibited prospect can flourish, even if they never
materialize. For thousands of Sudanese who travel from across the country,
Bir Tawil captures, in the most distilled manner, the potential of stepping out
of the formal realm of sovereign care, beyond the violence, harassment, corruption, and callousness that otherwise govern Sudan.

On the face of it, such dreams of escape and freedom may not be that different from the ones that Zhikharev and Heaton express when they talk about
Bir Tawil. They, too, saw it as a space uninhabited by the state, its restrictions
and its violence. It is tempting to see the space of uncaring as a place where
White fantasies and Black dreams find a shared surface. The only problem,
of course, is that the former always comes at the expense of the latter.

If there are parallels to be drawn, it is between the two self-proclaimed
kings, the British imperial forces that retook Sudan in the late nineteenth century, and the soldiers of fortune working for the Wagner Group. The latter are
the latest iteration of White violence in Africa, dedicated to an endeavor that
sheds any other pretense apart from the extraction of wealth and resources

by any means necessary. In this constellation, local populations can either assist this extractive project or face its eliminatory violence.

In *Out of Darkness, Shinning Light*, Petina Gappah rewrites the story of David Livingstone's search for the origins of the Nile, through two African narratives, one of Halima, a cook, and the other through the eyes of Jacob Wainwright, a servant on the expedition. Early in the novel, Halima expresses her incomprehension of the entire pursuit, telling the Scottish doctor to go back to his country "because the Nile has been here since time began, and it will be there after you and I are in the soil, and what will you do then, because the Nile won't care about whether you know where it begins."[58] Indeed, White fantasies of conquest in "unclaimed lands" are often vacuous and futile. But just as often, they are violent, covering and displacing other dreams and other ways of practicing those spaces. Now, as ever, the space of uncaring seems especially enticing to those whose fantasies quickly turn into nightmares.

States of Nature

Plants will gently gag the silent scream of things. Where there was devastation and abandon, there will be a forest.

MICHAEL MARDER, *The Chernobyl Herbarium*[1]

When John Masefield visited the front lines of the Somme several months after the British offensive of July 1, 1916, the poet struggled to discern details in the landscape that opened before him. In his notes from that visit, only a few grim objects stand out in the desolate landscape. Masefield observes some rotting sandbags, relics of battered black wire and wooden crosses marking the graves of men who charged through this open field. This bleak view is contrasted with a "vast heap of dazzlingly white chalk, so bright that it is painful to look at."[2] In the months preceding Masefield's visit, more than one million people had died along the Somme in one of the most destructive battles in human history. Yet Masefield's observation of the chalk pile in front of him points attention not only to the extent of the catastrophe that took place there but also its depth.

Many accounts of World War I battles focus on the horror of soldiers going "over the top," climbing out of the trenches and starting the charge toward the enemy's position on the other side of no man's land. Out in the open, many were gunned down within seconds. But in the run-up to the British offensive at the Somme, Royal Engineer tunneling companies began a vast mining operation, creating a series of underground passages that would reach the German positions. Miners went to great lengths to ensure the operation was carried out in silence: men worked barefoot and lined the floor of the tunnels with sandbags filled with chalk from the bedrock they were tunneling through. Handheld bayonets were used for the digging, and the dislodged rock was carefully caught to prevent it from hitting the ground.[3] By the end of the operation, a total of sixty thousand pounds of explosives were placed in two chambers and the tunnels leading to them. Though the tunnels did not quite reach the German frontline, the explosion of the mines created a "wave" of earth nearly fifteen feet high that buried nearby German trenches and the troops within them.

The explosives were set off at 7:28 a.m. on July 1, 2016, two minutes before the official start of the British offensive. Cecil Lewis, a British pilot who flew an observation mission approximately two miles away just as the mines were being detonated, later recalled the scene:

> We were over Thiepval and turned south to watch the mines. As we sailed down above all, came the final moment. Zero! At Boisselle the earth heaved and flashed, a tremendous and magnificent column rose up into the sky. There was an ear-splitting roar, drowning all the guns, flinging the machine sideways in the repercussing air. The earthly column rose, higher and higher to almost four thousand feet. There it hung, or seemed to hang, for a moment in the air, like a silhouette of some great cypress tree, then fell away in a widening cone of dust and debris. A moment later came the second mine. Again the roar, the upflung machine, the strange gaunt silhouette invading the sky. Then the dust cleared and we saw the two white eyes of the craters. The barrage had lifted to the second-line trenches, the infantry were over the top, the attack had begun.[4]

It was destruction of geological proportion. The explosions pried the earth open, turning the bedrock into topsoil.[5] Detonating the mines marked just the starting point of a battle that lasted well into the early months of winter, bringing into stark view the war's dynamic of destruction. Approximately one billion artillery shells were fired, the prime instrument in the decimation of the landscape and its radical transformation. Watercourses that were extensively shelled flooded surrounding areas and over time, were transformed into vast marshes; more than 1.25 million acres of forest were lost, leaving vast expanses of bare land.[6] A report in *The Statist* magazine from 1920 described how "nothing remains of the once flourishing forests save a few blasted tree trunks whose blackened and naked branches symbolize the desolation that meets the eye for miles on all sides."[7] Understandably, numerous writers and chroniclers of the war felt compelled to document this violently transformed landscape, but often the war had altered the very material composition of the soil in mostly invisible ways. According to some assessments, up to one-third of the munitions fired did not detonate, with many artillery shells sinking, intact, into the muddy ground.[8] Shrapnel from munitions that did explode saturated the soil with metal particles (see plate 5). Heavy metals and arsenic from chemical munitions added yet another layer of ground contamination; some sites are so contaminated that they remain bare to this day.[9]

The introduction of new, high-impact armaments into the battlefield resulted not only in extensive destruction of land and natural environments, but also in the unprecedented brutalization of the human body that made distinctions between corpse and surroundings often impossible. Life was lost on an unprecedented scale, but the destructive forces unleashed in the war meant that many bodies were no longer recognizable or recoverable. As Paola Filippucci describes this horrific scene, bodies were "disfigured, shattered and scattered, blown into the air and around, obliterated so completely that by the end of the battle there were thousands and thousands of missing."[10] This regarded not only human life, but also innumerable lives of animals and plants. Writing about it six months after the Armistice, Senator Paul Doumer described "a zone of death, assassination and devastation. . . . There are corpses of horses, corpses of trees covering corpses of men."[11] Bodies and the lands that surrounded them were pulverized to such an extent that neither was distinguishable from the other, and neither bore any resemblance to "living" matter. Bluntly summing the desolation he witnessed in the narrow strip that made up the no man's land of the Somme, Mansfield explains, "Chalk, wire, stakes, friends, and enemies seem here to have been all blown to powder."[12]

This landscape of total destruction was novel and perplexing. The vocabulary long used to convey the soothing qualities of natural environments seemed obsolete and inadequate. In literary accounts written shortly after the war, no man's land appears as a featureless expanse, so much so that it is depicted not as the muddy plains of northern France, but as a newly formed sea or desert.[13] Mary Borden, who ran field hospitals in the Western Front, found in this landscape a wholly new natural formation, what she describes as a wet desert, "as if a great wave had just receded, leaving the muddy bottom of the earth uncovered."[14] Although she can spot no sign of life on the hybrid surface, she nevertheless imagines the kind of life such unnatural nature might incubate: "Perhaps a new race of men has been hatched out of the mud, hatched like newts, slugs, larvae of water beetles. But slugs who know horribly, acutely, that they have only a moment to live in between flood tides."[15] Literary fiction was no refuge either. Opening his story "The Nightmare Countries," the Irish writer Lord Dunsany recalls some of the haunted lands that populate the writing of Poe, Coleridge, and Swinburne. Readers, he suggested, draw great pleasure from the dreaded lands that occupy the writers' pages exactly because "you can banish them by the closing of a book." The same was not possible when it came to the landscapes of the war. "In France," he writes, "the nightmare countries stand all night in the starlight; dawn comes and they are still there. . . . [T]he lost lands lie unburied, gazing up at the winds; and the lost woods stand like skeletons all grotesque in the solitude; the very seasons have fled from them."[16]

Time and again, chronicles of World War I describe how mechanized modern war resulted in the "indiscriminate and total annihilation of every-thing."[17] No man's land is the epicenter of destruction. Once care is with-drawn, natural environments are destined for assured devastation: flora and fauna will be crushed along with bodies and machines; all that is left is a dys-topian cyborg ecology of fractured geological formations and soils composed of organic matter, metallic fragments and toxic chemical residues. Even when it is surrounded by vast infrastructures and technologies of modern war, no man's land itself is a space ruled by chaos and cataclysmic indiscriminate vio-lence; a "state of nature" that devastates nature.

Yet there was another sense to the state of nature that rules no man's land, one in which the natural world reigns supreme. It, too, emerges out of the landscape of total annihilation but sees nature thrive in the post apocalypse from which humans have been banished.[18] In "Master of No Man's Land," a morbidly satirical description of this nascent fantasy of a posthuman Eden, Dunsany describes a miraculously thriving swede plant growing in the space between the trenches: "It grew as you never saw a swede grow before. . . . . It lifted its green head and gazed around No Man's Land. Yes, man was gone and now it was the day of the swede."[19] The destruction of nature around that thriving swede is never forgotten, making a brief appearance with the men-tion that "the trees went." But the survival, and even the flourishing of the swede and the weeds that emerge in its surroundings illuminates a radically new ecological future that might emerge from this ruined landscape: once humans withdraw, nature will repair itself and regain the vitality that was so badly damaged by the violence of war.

The century since the end of the World War I has seen the ruins of late modernity accumulate all around us, from spaces of nuclear aftermath to the decay of postindustrial cities and the ever-expanding geographies of en-vironmental catastrophe. Perhaps unsurprisingly, the proliferation of ruins brought with it a fascination with the ability of nature to revive, to "return to the 'good mother,'" as Georg Simmel put it in his 1911 essay *The Ruin*.[20] No man's land seems as just another iteration of this seductive promise that hu-man withdrawal will somehow allow nature to reemerge out of the ruin, to "make whole what has been smashed."[21]

Exactly because it is the quintessential site of death and destruction, there is an understandable lure to the thought that no man's land can become a refuge for nonhuman life. In fact, this view seems to gain traction exactly when natural habitats have come under growing pressure from catastrophic events and slower processes of extractive development and climate-related ecosystem collapse. One recent articulation of this state of nature insists that, "despite its deadly character and its status as an active war zone, [the Korean

DMZ] is a haven for nature. Through its exclusion of humanity, the DMZ has welcomed other species—plant and animal—that have reclaimed it as their own."[22] Numerous similar texts refer to the wolfs roaming freely in the Chernobyl Exclusion Zone or the former death strip that ran along the route of the Iron Curtain, now comfortingly rebranded as the European Green Belt.

Yet the archive of no man's land reveals a longer and more complex relationship to ideas of wilderness, natural preservation, and revival. As I have noted earlier in the book, at the same time that uncaring removes protections and exposes to harm, the absence of care also offers refuge from the violence that reigns outside. Put simply, the space of uncaring always features this tension between risk and refuge. Nineteenth-century expeditions to the western United States were among the first to associate territories visited only by war parties with a refuge for game animals. In August 1806, near the confluence of the Platt River with the Mississippi, the American military explorer William Clark noted in his diary: "I have observed that in the country between the nations which are at war with each other the greatest numbers of wild animals are to be found."[23] A few decades later, another army officer, Richard Irving Dodge reported that a disputed territory between the Sioux, Crow, and Pawnee tribes "became a debatable ground into which none but war parties ever penetrated. Hunted more or less by the surrounding tribes, immense number of Buffalo took refuge . . . where they were comparatively unmolested remaining there summer and winter in security."[24] While these accounts are written from the perspective of American surveyors observing violence between Indigenous peoples, the spaces of relative safety they describe must be understood in a settler colonial context of mass bison slaughter throughout the nineteenth century and the violent displacement of Indigenous populations.[25] If spaces between warring parties offered relative refuge, it was only because they were set apart from the violence that ruled around them.

What, then, is the state of nature that governs the space of uncaring? The critical challenge is not to parse imaginations of absolute annihilation on the one hand, from those of a bucolic, posthuman return of nature on the other. This is not a choice between two mutually exclusive states of nature. Several literary scholars have made a similar argument. Drawing on the work of Laurence Buell, Ursula Heise sets out the ways in which literary and aesthetic modes of apocalypse and pastoral are mutually constituting, illuminating how Edenic narratives of a return to an undisturbed world serve as an "imaginary countermodel" to a discourse of a corrupted, toxic earth.[26] The brief analysis of colonial narratives in North America suggests that this is indeed the case, that environmental cataclysm and natural idyll coincide and co-constitute the same place.

I think, though, that there is more that a return to no man's land can offer. Contemplating how to live in the "end times" of climate and ecological catastrophe, Bruno Latour suggests that such an endeavor must begin by facing "the apocalyptic dimension of which we are the descendants—the apocalypse that we have imposed on the other collectives and that is falling back on us today." He then goes on to ask: "Can we relearn to live in the time of the end without tipping thereby into utopia, the utopia that has beamed us into the beyond, as well as the one that has caused us to lose the here below?"[27] I wonder whether a move from the "*time* of the end" to no man's land—the space at the edge of care—may offer some initial paths of engagement, specifically with the critical effort not to lose the here below.

Troubled Earth

José and I were standing on a narrow balcony facing southwest, just as the sun was setting into the dense canopy that stretched in the valley below. As the community leader in Yarumales, José was in charge of the local motel, a two-story wooden building painted blue and green that stood at the top of the hill overlooking the village. From the second floor, a picture-perfect view unfolded in front us: the silhouette of trees dark against the luminous orange sky, with the dense ambient sound of insects and birds completing the serenity and beauty of the landscape. It was 2017 and my first visit to Yarumales, which also meant that my naivety and ignorance were impossible to hide.[28] "It is such a tranquil view. A lot of people have told me about this forest around here," I told José. There was hope behind that statement, hope that this line of trees was a stark contrast to the vast tracts of forest that were being cut or burned down at a rapid pace throughout the region.

José, a tall thin man with a gentle demeanor and a kind smile, took a few seconds to reply. "Yes, it's beautiful. But there's a lot of blood under that forest," he said eventually.

A few months earlier, the peace agreement between the Colombian government and FARC was ratified, allowing thousands of FARC guerrilla fighters to come out of remote regions where they had sheltered during decades of conflict. Public debates over the merits of the peace deal were still raging across the country, but many environmental groups were already raising the alarm that the demobilization of FARC forces will expose previously untouched regions to rapid development; the peace deal, they argued, will spark a war on the forest. Activists and organizations that I spoke to before arriving in Yarumales expressed similar concern. Although it was formally reoccupied by the Colombian military in 2002, the former Clearance Zone and the two national parks that made up the majority of its territory—Tinigua and Macarena—were of specific concern. In their telling, the presence of the *guerrilla* helped deter, or at least slow, the expansion of uncontrolled development that will inevitably come at the expense of the forest.

In the years since, this narrative has only entrenched. Peace, one article in a prominent scientific journal warned, "is destroying Colombia's jungle," citing a government analysis that found a 44 percent increase in deforestation in the year of the peace accord.[29] Deforestation is undoubtedly accelerating.[30] With deep political ties to large land owners and corporate interests, the conservative government of Iván Duque, which took power in 2018, did little to temper the expansion of industry—cattle farming, agribusiness, and resource extraction—into areas previously held by FARC. But what is often lost in the rallying cries to protect the forest is the violence that took place beneath the canopy.

On the evening of my arrival in Yarumales, a community meeting was called. I was asked to introduce myself and explain my research—not many people bother to stop here, let alone stay for any meaningful period. People came at the end of a long day of work, but when they heard I was interested in the history of the Clearance Zone, many wanted to speak. One after the other, they talked about the abandonment years, of being overlooked and disregarded, of the school that closed and the bridge that was never repaired after a jet bombed it in 2002. One of the bombs never exploded and was proudly displayed in the corner of the bar where we were meeting; when José showed it to me earlier in the day, he joked that it was a memento from "the last government visit to Yarumales." Many of the events recalled that evening took place years prior. But the time that passed did not blunt the sense that anyone who has made a home in this former FARC-held region, was written off. If they were at all part of an official discussion, it was only when they were being referred to as illegal "invaders" and "squatters" in the national parks, or in more sinister terms of guerrilla sympathizers whose presence threatened the fragile ecosystem of the parks with coca cultivation and cattle grazing. That the nearest doctor or school were more than an hour drive away, or that extortion by local armed groups was rife, was hardly worth mentioning when residents met with government representatives. Officials knew, but no one seemed to care.[31]

There is an image that repeats itself in many of the documents and reports on environmental degradation taking place in former FARC-held territories like Yarumales. This image appears in different variations, but it almost always includes an open landscape dotted with charred tree stumps, remnants of a rainforest that was felled and then set on fire to prevent it from rejuvenating. At times, it includes a figure of a man carrying a chainsaw, but in other iterations, cows are seen grazing. It is a picture that has become part of the visual canon of environmental degradation, an iconic marker of the brutalization of lands that, until recently, were still "out of bounds," untouched and protected by the presence of armed insurgent forces that found shelter under the thick canopy.

Although its explicit subject matter is ecological catastrophe rather than war, it is striking to note the similarity between the images and the photographs that seared no man's land into popular imagination after World War I. Like the images from the war, it aims to generate a sense of shock. Yet I find a deep melancholia in these images of blackened tree stumps, in the Freudian sense that their repetition produces not an empowerment of the viewer to act, but a paralysis and inability to move forward from the loss.[32] It was Susan Sontag who famously argued that the act of photography seeks to keep things as they are, "at least for as long as it takes to get a 'good' picture," which is fundamentally "an act of non-intervention."[33] For Sontag, that often means acts of photography are complicit with the forms of human suffering they document.

Yet it is important to qualify the precise function of this environmental melancholia. What emerges in much of the discourse that surrounds those who resided in the Clearance Zone, and those who still reside in areas formally held by armed insurgency forces, is not a straightforward policy of non-intervention. Environmental reports and policy documents are explicit and detailed about the kind of action they are calling upon from readers and wider audiences. Action, they claim incessantly, is urgently needed: to protect the forest, save endangered species, salvage ecosystems, and avert climate catastrophe. And yet, when read from the humble "down below" of Yarumales, the spectrum of action called for focuses primarily on the charred limbs of trees rather than the bodies of peasants. The latter rarely feature unless they are the ones wielding the chainsaw. Put differently, there is a lot of care that goes toward these scarred environments. But for those who have made a home in these spaces and endured systemic abandonment throughout their lives here, care seems to be in short supply. From the outside, communities like the campesinos who live in Yarumales are seen as culprits in the destruction of the rainforest and as a hurdle that ought to be removed if nature is ever going to regain its lost vitality. As the local community leader, José often faced the ire of government agencies and environmental groups. In their eye, he was the villain. Most of the time, though, campesinos in Yarumales weren't seen at all.

FIGURE 12. José "Marranito" Valdés at his now-abandoned farmhouse on the outskirts of Yarumales. The heavy machine-gun chain was left from the battles that raged on the farm in the early 2000s. Photographer: Laura Pardo.

Being rendered invisible by a violent state means you can hope to be spared its harms. That is what drove so many to seek refuge in this FARC-dominated region in the first place. It also means that the state is unlikely to extend any protections to those who exit its realm of care. I starkly remember being stopped at a military checkpoint just outside the town of La Macarena, one of the main municipalities that comprised the Clearance Zone and now a booming tourist destination. A large military base adjoins the town, and patrols around it are common. But this show of force largely ends once you enter the Macarena National Park north of the town. As the sergeant who stopped us put it, "From here onward, you're on your own." It was a blunt statement, and one that was also misleading. While there is almost no effort to police the vest area that stretched north of us, it was not outside the state or divorced from it.[34] It remained a product of state logic, but a logic of intentional and calculated abdication.

Such explicit delineation of uncaring—demarcating where care ends and where the presumed space of untamed nature begins—has direct and violent consequences. In December 2018, less than a year after we stood at that checkpoint on the way to Yarumales, José was shot (fig. 12). He was heading home on his motorcycle when a would-be assassin fired at him from close range. Hit in his upper arm and pelvis, he veered off the road and down a steep hillside. Yarumales is a small, tight-knit community, but it took a long while for neighbors to note his absence and even longer until he was found after walking, wounded, for eighteen hours through the forest. He nearly bled to death, but unlike over five hundred community leaders and activists who have been assassinated in Colombia since 2016, he survived.[35] After a lengthy period in the hospital, José was advised to leave the region. If he wanted the care of the state—security, health care, financial support—he would have to go elsewhere.

Environmental organizations had nothing to do with José's assault or similar attacks that took place in the region. Those responsible were likely affiliated with a local armed group that was described to me as "a bunch of thugs who got hold of guns." In fact, many environmental activists face similar threats, including many who reside in the region.[36] The question, for me, is not who bears the greater brunt of violence. What seems more consequential is the enduring utopian view of areas constituting the Clearance Zone as undisturbed, pristine natural environments—*selva virgen*—that, since the demobilization of the guerrillas, are in fact the epicenter of an environmental dystopia, from the collapse of ecosystems to radical change in regional climate patterns that will permanently prevent the revival of the rainforest.

This narrative performs a double erasure: First, it ignores a much longer history of violence that is inextricably intertwined with environmental degradation. Areas that comprised the Clearance Zone have seen this up close, from early twentieth-century oil explorations and waves of colonization in the decades that followed, the displacement and murder of the Indigenous Tinigua people, and the years of guerrilla armed dominance in the region.[37] Yet an equally egregious act of environmental and social violence was the fumigation campaign carried out under Plan Colombia, a strategy to eradicate "illicit crops" under the banners of the two main global wars of the early 2000s: the so-called war on drugs and war on terror. In addition to damaging peoples' health and destroying the considerable biodiversity in these regions, fumigation has placed unprecedented pressures on the social fabric of Indigenous groups and campesino communities. It was an extreme expression of what Margarita Serje describes as a "geopolitical imagination" of Colombia's peripheries, one of many devices "for the bleeding of landscapes and the brutalization of peoples who, to all intents and purposes, are considered to be dispensable, expendable, disposable."[38] It is historically impossible and politically shortsighted to separate destructive policies toward natural habitats from abusive modes of social exploitation, of surplus extraction and enforced compliance. Assassination, extortion, deprivation of services, indifference, stigmatization—all make up the thick reality of the here below, and they happen, as José experienced, among the trees, not just at the trees' expense. What, then, is the pristine moment that is conjured when we talk about the return of nature?

The second erasure concerns more explicitly the state of uncaring. Cultivating greater care for more-than-human life has long been at the heart of conservation narratives. If it is acknowledged at all, uncaring is largely understood as indifference motivated by the endemic tendency of capitalism to generate an "ecological rift" with nature.[39] Uncaring, as it is considered here, exceeds the utilitarian cynicism of capitalist accumulation, exploitation, and extraction. The latter are all expressions of care, even if care takes an invasive and violent form. In any respect, this is not the political logic of radical abdication that governs both human and more-than-human life in the space of uncaring.

Let me ground this argument: During the years of the Clearance Zone, the Colombian state did nothing to prevent harms endured by the local population, in much the same way that it did not stop extensive deforestation that allowed FARC to pave an extensive road system across the region and expand coca cultivation. Bare tracts of land, cut through the thick rainforest and dotted with charred tree stumps, are clearly more palpable than the endemic political realities of uncaring. The two are inextricably intertwined, but such ties require us to tell other stories and other histories that remain attentive to the forest without losing sight of the blood beneath the trees.

Although I encountered the phrase late in the writing of this book, I realize that much of it is written from what Latour calls the "here below." It is a stance that refuses both utopian idealizations of wounded natural environments left to heal once humans withdraw and the dystopian depictions of no man's land as the ultimate manifestation of ecological cataclysm. Without doubt, these imaginations retain a seductive pull.[40] Yet they do little to bring us closer to the realities of life under conditions of systemic abandonment, especially in places that do not command the attention of Western audiences like postindustrial Detroit or Chernobyl. These realities of uncaring that are neither purely bucolic nor simply catastrophic often leave the observer in a frustratingly inconclusive place.

But this much I know: Chainsaws can often be heard buzzing around Yarumales, meaning a tree is being cut down. In a small village of fourteen houses, where everyone knows one another by name, that is also a sign that, out there in the forest, a neighbor is still alive.

Under the Green Cover

Throughout this book I've been grappling with the harms that proliferate in the space of uncaring. Some of these take the form of catastrophic destruction that was unleashed in World War I, the extensive annihilation of land and life I describe in the opening of this chapter and throughout this book. But nature has its own way of documenting the imprint of uncaring, the harms it inflicts and the durations of that harm. Very often natural environments document the aftermath of uncaring and its lingering effect, not just its brute, violent impact. In these instances, harm is corrosive and chronic, but just about bearable, prompting no urgency of response. It is a condition tolerable enough as to not generate care. That is also how uncaring makes its imprint onto natural environments. Rather than a spectacle of environmental apocalypse, nature appears under duress.

Writing about the ongoing reverberations of colonial history, Ann Stoler describes duress as "a relation to a condition, a pressure exerted, a troubled condition. . . . It may bear no immediately visible sign or, alternatively, it may manifest in a weakened constitution and attenuated capacity to bear its weight."[41] There is immense value in thinking with duress. But Juanita Sundberg is right to point out that we "need categories other than debris, ruins or ruination"—categories Stoler often returns to—if we are to redirect our analytical attention away from the dominant imaginations of no man's land and its natures.[42] Debris, ruins, and ruination are certainly part of the lexicon of abandoned environments, but duress may point us toward subtler pathways that perhaps bring us analytically and ethically closer to the topos of harm.

I am thinking, for example, of decay. In the areas that comprise the Chernobyl Exclusion Zone, a space that often attracts glossy stories of nature's return in the absence of regular human habitation, decay feeds a melancholic pleasure.[43] That is partly what makes it easy for popular accounts to celebrate the packs of wolves running through the empty streets of Pripyat. Yet decay takes a very different meaning when you venture into the forests that surround the damaged reactor. Recent studies have shown that fallen tree trunks within the Exclusion Zone are not decaying at the rate they normally would. Decomposers—organisms such as microbes, fungi, and some insects that drive the process of organic decay—have yet to recover from the high radiation levels that followed the 1986 accident.[44] Fallen trees, therefore, remain abnormally intact decades after they have fallen. This is not "slow violence" in the sense that Rob Nixon writes about, an attritional violence that is often not recognized as violence at all.[45] Instead, it is the violence of frozen time

itself, a form of harm that targets the "material afterlife of rotting and decay."[46]
This is how harm registers when natures are under duress, harms that are at
once pervasive but nearly impossible to detect when our analytical purview is
confined to either environmental degradation or its antithesis, a paradoxical
condition of "collateral conservation" in zones of withdrawn human activity.[47]

Elsewhere, insects are not absent but overly abundant. They are what eats
away at the facade of environmental resurgence. Immediately after World
War I, attempts were made to document the scale of destruction along the
front. Based on "destruction maps" drawn by the French Geographical Institute, officials divided the entire area affected by the war into three zones
designated by the severity of the damage. The most severely affected parts
were designated as the Red Zone (Zone Rouge) and referred to regions of
"total destruction," with almost no remaining infrastructure at the end of the
war. This zone required the most intense intervention, from the removal of
human remains, to neutralizing the decomposing animal cadavers and per-
forming extensive demining campaigns. During a visit to one of the enclosed
regions in 1921, a minister was confronted by locals who demanded the rapid
rebuilding of their farms. The local mayor argued that the "wasteland which
recalls the war and all its horrors" should not be tolerated and that abandoned land would simply be breeding ground for "vipers, foxes, badgers and
boars which would destroy crops up to 10 km away."[48] For those who lost
their homes and land, the return of wildlife was no reason for celebration, yet
lacking resources to rehabilitate these vast areas of destruction, the French
government opted to dedicate almost five thousand acres of the Red Zone to
a massive forestation project. It was to become a large commemorative forest,
a place of solace and rejuvenation in the aftermath of war, while simultaneously serving a more practical purpose: encasing toxic soils, bodily remains,
and unexploded munitions within a lush green sarcophagus.[49]

The project was partly funded by German war reparations, and for a short
while, seedlings of spruce and pine were shipped from Germany in large concrete planters, using the same train lines that brought soldiers and supplies
to the front lines only a few years prior. A few of the planters can still be
found, covered by a layer of moss, in the thicket of the century-old wood.
It was, according to Jean-Paul Amat, the "zero point of regeneration," proof
that it was possible to rapidly regenerate a forest, circumventing biochemical
processes that might otherwise take decades and centuries for a mature forest
to flourish.[50] Initial forestation efforts made use of trees that could tolerate
nutrient-poor conditions like pine and spruce.[51] Conifers planted across the
Red Zone have a growth cycle decades faster than oak or other hardwoods,
making them highly efficient in covering the scars of the war, but not entirely.

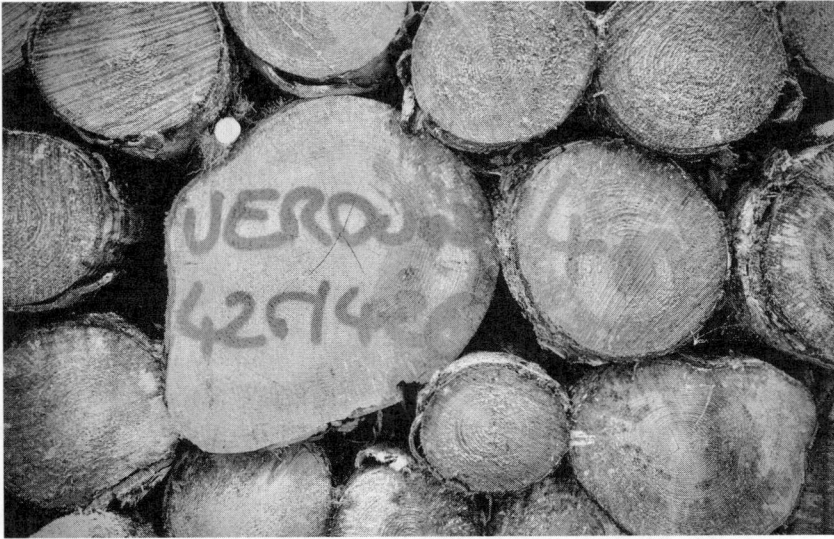

FIGURE 13. Logs of black pine waiting to be transported from the industrial forests in Verdun. Much of this forest covers the heavily contaminated "Red Zone" of the World War I no man's land. Photographer: Elliot Graves.

Despite early protestation of French veterans who feared the newly planted forests threatened to erase the landscape of war and its memory, conifers discourage undergrowth and ensure that features like trenches and shell holes remain visible.

Trees became embedded in the landscape of memory that formed in the Red Zone (fig. 13). Large groves of pine and spruce trees were planted around the iconic 1923 Ossuary Monument, which commemorates the Battle of Verdun and contains the remains of approximately 130,000 French and German soldiers, as well as the largest single French military cemetery of World War I with 16,142 graves. Trees fill the horizon in all directions when you stand at the top of the small hill where the ossuary is located. As Michael Marder noted when writing about Chernobyl, the lush, dark-green canopy soothed the catastrophe beneath it, hushed "the silent scream of things."[52]

Beyond the sites that are most commonly visited and featured in commemoration ceremonies, vast parts of woodland planted in the Red Zone are a commercial forest. The Office National des Forêts, which manages these forests, has used the fast-growing conifers as a major source of revenue. Yet in recent years, thousands of conifers planted in the Red Zone have been infested with bark beetle, a small insect that attacks and kills live trees. The French forestry service is forced to cut down infested trees in a process that is aptly referred to as *l'abbatage*, which carries the double meaning of "felling" and "slaughter."

François Martig, an artist who spent several days with me on my first visit to the region in 2015, pointed out that a deeper logic ties the monoculture conifer forests to the war that preceded it. Unlike tree species that were indigenous to the region before the war—hardwood like oak and beech—conifers are significantly more uniform in shape and hence easier to mechanically handle, from felling through hauling and processing. Optimization of value and the minimization of divergences from a set standard are the foundational elements of timber extraction. Plantations that occupy most of the Zone Rouge are designed to eliminate any divergence from the norm, an industrial-technocratic logic that Vandana Shiva famously described as a "monoculture of the mind."[53] As we were walking through the woodlands of Verdun, Martig noted that the forest all around us was planted only to be chopped off for profit, a disposable forest: "It is ironic that the quintessential site of mechanized war is currently home to this kind of mechanized nature."

Now the forest is under duress. The commercial conifer woodlands that covered the Zone Rouge, are decimated by bark beetle. Historical attempts to rapidly cover up the space of uncaring, to soothe the open wounds of lives lost and lands broken, are gradually being undone. What were once green dense forests increasingly feature vast patches of brown-dead evergreens that can only be cut down. What is left is the exposed space of uncaring where life was disposed of on an unimaginable scale; human life reduced to cannon fodder, trees turned to sawdust.

It is a fleeting moment. Steps are already underway to introduce new tree varieties that will enhance biodiversity of the forest and potentially better withstand the stresses of a warmer, drier climate. Tree species that are dying en masse in the southern European heatwaves of recent years are relocated to the still-cooler north, turning the devastated earth of the former no man's land into a future environmental shelter. The pendulum continues to swing between ravage and refuge. But for now, replanting has yet to cover the barren plots left where dead woods have been felled. A recent visitor commented that one site that had been cleared resembled "a lunar landscape." Equating the damaged space between the trenches to the cratered surface of the moon is one of the persistent clichés of no man's land, although in this context, a potentially insightful one. Until trees once again cover the old battlefields, one can see the cratered, broken land of uncaring, a land still under duress of past and recent slaughters.

Care Returns

I grew up in no man's land. When I was ten, my family moved to a new suburb built halfway between Tel Aviv and Jerusalem, in the former strip that divided Israeli and Jordanian forces until 1967. Even though it was often mentioned, no adult thought to explain what this peculiar designation, "no man's land," meant. It was only stated to make it clear to whomever was listening that we were not "in the occupied territories." Living in Israeli settlements built in the Occupied Palestinian Territories was considered politically unthinkable for my liberal-minded parents. No man's land, though, seemed to leave us untarnished by a complicity in the violence that governed the lives of Palestinians living under Israeli military occupation. In the moral geography of late 1980s liberal Israeli Jews, no man's land was on the right side of the line.

As a child, of course, I had to navigate my own way through this terrain of history and power. Our house was at the very corner of the neighborhood, beyond it lay just a field of seasonal sunflowers, watermelon, and wheat. As kids, my brothers and I frequently rode our bikes down the dirt track that crossed the field, exploring the craggy hills on the other side. In the very first summer we discovered, with some excitement, a small Border Force base at the other edge of the field. As far as we could tell through the thicket of bushes that surrounded it, there wasn't much there aside from a couple of dusty tents, an asbestos shed, and a bored guard at the gate. Bullet casings were strewn all around, and we would often kick around the gravel for a long while to see who could find an unusual one. That seemed a more gratifying task than to ask why a Border Force base was there in the first place. If we were to believe our parents, this was still very much "the center of the country" and the border was somewhere else, far away.

Deeper in the hills, where we ventured to walk the dogs and build camp-fires with friends, it was easy to be overtaken by the serenity of the place. In winter particularly, the rocky slopes would soften with lush grasses dotted with cyclamens and anemones. Yet even there, markers of violence were all around us. On a yellow rusty sign, the words "Firing Zone" were just about legible, and a shell casing would occasionally rest, hollowed, between the rocks. It was a space saturated with violence, but we simply walked past, oblivious.

Then there was an entire other layer that was even harder to decipher, a coded landscape of pain and loss that remained silent to us until much later. Hidden in a gully, surrounded by an old orchard of almonds and pomegran-ate, we came across a single wall, the only one left standing as the rest of the structure collapsed around it. Whose house was this? Whose trees? What made them leave and where were they now? Trivial questions that, back then, were never asked. We were, after all, in no man's land, on the right side of the line.

Ajanjoul is the name of this small Palestinian hamlet, home to five fami-lies who made a living off the almonds, figs, and wheat they grew. Along with most of Palestine's central district, the village was occupied in July 1948, and all its inhabitants were forced to flee. A year later, when the 1949 Armistice Agreement drew the lines that separated Israel and Jordan, the village re-mained trapped between the lines, in no man's land. For nearly two decades, residents of the village were denied the right to reclaim their homes, not be-cause their land was annexed, but because it was deemed beyond the realm of sovereign care. No other explanation or justification was needed, simply because no sovereign authority saw it within its jurisdictional domain. Those who tried to visit their homes and the fruit trees they left behind were shot, labeled "infiltrators" to their own ancestral land. Blocking the return had no grand strategic utility or political calculation. Israel, after all, had no claim over this territory, was not intent on demolishing the village or using its empty houses to settle Jews. The state profoundly didn't care about this place; all it sought was to ensure that no one else was allowed to care for it either.

After nineteen years, the state came back into no man's land, but care did not return with it. After it occupied the West Bank in 1967, Israel turned the former no man's land into a military training zone. Soldiers trampled through the orchards and terraces that were laboriously cultivated over generations; they fired at the emptied houses that still remained intact, gradually seeing to their collapse. If there was use at all to everything around, it was only as cannon fodder. By the time I walked up the gully that leads to this small vil-lage, not much was left. "The place had been lost and so had its name," wrote the Israeli author S. Yizhar in his unflinching description of Arab landscapes and the ways they were obliterated beyond recognition.[1] Even when I grew to intimately know this place as well as I knew my own backyard, for years I could not name it, nor could I account for its past. I repeated what I was told, that this was no man's land. In fact, this lasting designation was a subterfuge, a placeholder that justified our comfortable unknowing and complicit uncaring.

Uncaring is often a habit that's hard to kick. It lingers long after formal designations are removed, taking with them the barbed wire and watch towers. Uncaring lodges itself in hearts and minds, in willful indifference to the pain of others whose lives were deemed less worthy. It easily conjoins other technologies of evasion and abdication of responsibility, what Uri Ram described as "ways of forgetting" through which responsibility is shirked and troubled pasts are effaced.[2] But unlike deliberate acts of physical demolition or symbolic erasure, the uncaring state has no pretense to punish or correct, to extract value or gain advantage. It seeks, instead, to disavow and ultimately sever sovereign responsibilities. Long after Israel occupied these spaces, my ignorance was proof that uncaring was remarkably effective, so much so that it erased the traces of its own operation.

For the Palestinians who were driven from their homes and have never been allowed back, sovereign uncaring is a present-tense condition. It proves remarkably resilient, far outlasting the time and space of no man's land. As refugees residing mostly in the occupied West Bank, descendants of the village are prohibited from visiting their ancestral land without rarely issued permits. In the eyes of the Israeli state, their claims have been nullified.[3] Zochrot, an Israeli organization of Arabs and Jews working to signpost the Palestinian past and its violent eradication, sought permission to place signs marking the depopulated villages in the region. Lawyers working for the Jewish National Fund—which now owns the land—turned down the request.[4] Nothing could be allowed to disturb the comfortable indifference that continues to rule in this space, nearly half a century since the no man's land was formally consigned to history.

This, to me, is a terrifying prospect: The state might return, but care does not.

End Zone

It is hard to fathom life adrift, cut off from basic services and elementary protections that have become so closely associated with the modern state. Without doubt, many around the world—maybe most?—have become accustomed to a state that so often fails to fulfill many of its duties of care. Just as many have come to expect worse, confronting regimes that wield care in the service of punitive violence, cruelty, and, in its extreme, genocidal ends. Yet the underlying assumption that the state cares remains stubbornly intact. The moment when one realizes that the state turned its back and abandoned any pretense to care is often jarring; initial disbelief is followed by indignation.

This moment was perfectly captured when a team of reporters from the radio show *This American Life* set out to document the harsh realities of asylum seekers trapped in a makeshift camp on the US-Mexico border, in the town of Matamoros.[5] Early on, Ira Glass, who hosts the show, speaks to an American volunteer nurse who set up a medical tent in the camp. After she described efforts to build a purification system that will provide clean water, Glass asks whether she is the only one organizing this. "Yeah," she answers. "Not the government? . . . Not the UN?" he proceeds, his voice becoming more strained. "Nope," she replies. But it is Glass's subsequent monologue that reveals not only the supposition that sovereign care will somehow be there, but the crushing realization that care is absent not by fault, but by design: "I have to say, this is the thing that hit me hardest in Matamoros. You have thousands of people stuck there, right on our border, two big governments—the United States and Mexico—one of them, of course, a lot richer than the other, and nobody's looking after these people with food and water and shelter, except a bunch of volunteers who raised their hands and said, we cannot ignore this."[6]

When faced with the despair and deprivation that result from the calculated withdrawal of state care, it is only natural to point to the power that has caused the condition in the first place. We rightly demand that governments act: send aid, open the border, intervene to stop violence. What we are really asking is for them to care, and to extend that care to those who have been deprived of it. Yet to many I've spoken to in researching this book, this desire to see sovereign care reinstated can seem bewildering. For those who reside in spaces of endemic uncaring—some for years, even decades—the prospect of care returning does not simply spell the longed-for provision of services, extension of protections or even the mere semblance of stability. Instead, it is the prospect of care returning with the full force of a punitive state and its vengeful agencies.

This is how the Colombian Clearance Zone came to an end. In January 2002, after months of stalled talks between the government of Andrés Pastrana and FARC rebels, the president instructed the Colombian army to retake the region that was left to guerrilla control three years earlier. The following day, over action-movie soundtracks, national television played scenes of jubilant soldiers waiting for instructions to reoccupy the five municipalities that made up the Clearance Zone. But days passed, and the order to advance had yet to be given.[7] Frantic efforts by international envoys, church leaders and negotiators from both sides sought to salvage the peace process. But a month later, FARC hijacked a passenger plane, targeting a senator who was on board. For the government, this was the last straw. Within hours, Pastrana launched the massive military incursion that would end the Clearance Zone.

But something else happened in the six weeks of uncertainty between the first announcement and the final entry of the Colombian military. Immediately after the president first declared his determination to retake the Clearance Zone, FARC wasted no time and began evacuating its forces from the main towns in the region. As their natural stronghold, the jungle was far safer. One of the main guerrilla bases, located just outside the town of La Macarena, was hastily abandoned. Soon after, locals used this brief interregnum and raided the site, taking whatever they could. In the private quarters of FARC's Eastern Bloc commander—widely known by his nickname, "Mono Jojoy"—they found an elliptical trainer, a grand ornate bed, and a bust of an influential guerrilla leader. The elliptical and the bed were loaded onto a vehicle and driven off. Someone decapitated the sculpture. Everyone was confident that within hours the military would swarm the region and no one would care about an exercise machine and a bed. But the military never came. Instead, the guerrillas returned to find their base ransacked and in the retribution that followed, nine people were killed. One woman, María, slept a single night in Mono Jojoy's grand bed before she was executed.

People in the town repeatedly told me of these events. They were seared into the collective experience in the region. In people's recollections of the waning days of the Clearance Zone, they blame the guerrilla for the violence, or even the victims themselves, who dared defy the rules set out by the rebels. Yet in dozens of conversations, no one ever mentioned seeking help from the Colombian state, whose forces were only two hours away. In these recollections, people don't factor the state as a party to these events, but this is not to say that anyone was under the impression that the government was somehow in the dark about what was going on. Throughout the existence of the Clearance Zone, frequent visits by candidates for public office, journalists, and human rights organizations meant that the regular violations of human rights in the region were common knowledge, an integral part of public and political debate.[8] Despite knowing, government forces held back during those critical days and allowed vindictive violence to unfold without interruption.

Everything that happened during those final days of the Clearance Zone took place under the watchful eye of an uncaring sovereign, a state that rules not through the use of violence, but through withdrawal and abdication. The state knew, even if it didn't care. What is so striking about this decision is the fact that the state derived no value or benefit from it. It was a form of abandonment that brought no tactical advantage or monetary reward; the state was not keeping its distance to punish the local population or coerce them to disavow political alliances. Put bluntly, no general or paramilitary commander ever asked, "Is intervention worth it?" because this question already assumes that such an intervention has quantifiable value and potential returns: strategic, economic, or moral. Each of the realms has its own ledger of abandonment; each sets its own terms on whether or not the abdication of care is "worth it."

Conversely, when the Colombian state held back and allowed punitive killings to occur, it operated according to a different logic of abandonment, a radical abdication that severed any pretense of sovereign care toward those subjected to it. Again, it is worth stating clearly: Abandoning 150,000 people in the Clearance Zone was not premised on cost-benefit calculation. Without doubt, it was borne of other concerns and interests, from geopolitical calculations to internal political pressures. But the local population was never factored into these calculations of potential gains and assessment of risks. They were, as I describe earlier in the book, simply shrugged off.[9]

Eventually, a few days later, care did come back, but violence came along with it. In the following months and years, state violence toward the local population in the region increased sharply, most notably through the use of "false positives," extrajudicial killings of mostly poor young men in rural regions that were presented by the Colombian army as guerrilla casualties.[10] Less spectacular harms also became routine in the wake of the state's return: In Yarumales, the concrete bridge that FARC built was bombed, cutting the village and the surrounding farms from their agricultural land. In La Cooperativa, the doctor fled after receiving death threats from paramilitary groups that were establishing control in the region. Soon after, the school closed. The indiscriminate aerial spraying of pesticides devastated coca trade in the region but also destroyed lives and livelihoods. Residents who sought work elsewhere in the country found themselves shunned and stigmatized, accused of being guerrilla sympathizers. The Clearance Zone was gone, but many had to face the harsh realities of state-sponsored social marginalization and a campaign of political terror.

The waning days of the Clearance Zone capture how care returned and how such returns are often tenuous, unpredictable, and fundamentally violent. Care flickered on the horizon and then faded away. When it returned, however tentatively, it proved a poisoned chalice: the thousands who fled to the Clearance Zone to find refuge from the violent care of the state, found themselves once again contending with its controlling and coercive effects. In dire times it is only natural to wish for the state to come to care for us. No man's land carries a warning: careful what you wish for.

It has been over seven years since Omar arrived in Rukban. I've never met him in person because I could never reach the camp, and he cannot leave, but over the years, we have exchanged thousands of messages. When conditions deteriorate and life in the camp becomes even more unbearable, he sends a text message or a link to a Facebook post. These might describe the death of child during a heatwave or widespread malnutrition when the Syrian government blocks smuggling routes. Sometimes he would ask how the book is coming along. In a recent exchange, I told him that I was in the last stages of writing, and that the conclusion grapples with the possible return of the state, with the potential that sovereign care might once again be extended to spaces of uncaring. There was no answer for a while, but he eventually replied. Waiting for care to return to Rukban, he said, "means it will take a very long time until your book is finished."[11]

Regarding the longevity of uncaring, history may prove Omar right. In Jerusalem, the no man's land survived for nineteen years, ending only with a war whose consequences still plague the city. The Buffer Zone continues to divide Cyprus after nearly five decades, while Bir Tawil remains locked between Sudan and Egypt over a century after a confused line drawn on a map demarcated it as a border enclave. Rukban may be similarly intractable. Syria and Jordan remain largely sanguine, finding it easier to abandon Rukban rather than invest the effort and resources needed to care for the thousands who continue to reside in it. Periodic calls in UN meetings to address the "dire need for assistance in Rukban" continue to be minuted, but as more recent humanitarian concerns come to dominate international agendas, Rukban seems to slip down the priority list.[12] There is no reason to think that the coming years will see this trend reversed. Weighed against the alternatives, most sovereign forces will find it is easier not to care.[13]

Omar dreams of going back one day to his home town, Homs. He hopes to complete the medical degree he was forced to abandon in 2016, to be part of a community that is more expansive than the one he has in the camp. All that can happen only if he is able to leave Rukban, to escape the space of uncaring to which he has been confined for years. But what if this uncaring is not limited to the fifty-five-kilometer zone that surrounds Rukban? What if it travels with him?

The remoteness of Rukban creates a false sense that the realities governing it are somehow an outlandish aberration of political orders, an anomaly of the international system and centuries-old presumptions about the role and responsibilities of the sovereign state. Rukban, we would like to tell ourselves, is simply the catastrophic creation of a monstrous regime, yet another part of Assad's authoritarian violence that systematically kills, imprisons, tortures, and displaces millions. Only this kind of regime can turn its back on thousands of people in this way, creating a place governed by sheer callousness and indifference.

Yet what if Rukban's abandonment is a model rather than an aberration? What if the logic of uncaring that governs it is at play well beyond the remote desert of southeastern Syria? Rukban, like most places in this book, is clearly demarcated. Cartographic lines and blunt fortifications enclose these spaces of uncaring, setting out where they begin and where they end. Yet uncaring travels easily. Far from being a warning about a perilous future of normalized abandonment, uncaring is already part of a diffuse geography with no clear perimeter keeping its corrosive effects at bay. As Estella Schindel has documented, the logic of uncaring now underpins the policing of migration across North Africa. She notes how Moroccan security forces capture migrants trying to reach Europe, load them onto buses, and drive them out to the desert near the border with Algeria.[14] What begins with an act of forced population dispersal—an inherent instrument in the sovereign care-as-control tool kit—ends in lives set adrift. Once people disembark, the buses turn around and drive off along with the security personnel. Care ends.

Spaces of uncaring paint a dark horizon. From afar, they reveal an almost dystopian disintegration of political relations and the assumed certainties they carry. The task is not to reawaken the Leviathan, to make it care again—if indeed it ever did. The harms of uncaring are rarely undone when a caring state sets once again its heavy foot in no man's land. More often, harms proliferate and violence continues.

Instead, the task we face is to recommit ourselves to other ways of being in abandon. The Jewish tradition of Shmita comes to mind. Recurring every seven years, Shmita fosters numerous practices of care through release: forgiving debt, resting land, abolishing property claims.[15] The longtime environmental activist Rabbi David Seidenberg posits that Shmita asks us to practice abdication in a way that can redefine social relationships in a profound manner. "Only in such a society," he writes, "where 'property' does not designate the right to use up what one owns, but rather a kind of fleeting relationship to what one cares for, can people learn the true meaning of justice."[16] More recently, as part of their struggle to save an urban forest in Atlanta, the radical Fayer Collective wrote that accepting the demands of Shmita "is to renounce our pride and its violences, to rectify human error and malice not through a positive solution, but by asking, 'For once, can we just not?'"[17] What emerges here is an "ethics of renunciation," to use Achille Mbembe's poignant phrase, a set of "liberating losses that open onto other registers of life and relation."[18] Abandonment here is imbued with lively potentiality that is not subsumed by exposure to harm. It is cyclical and recuperative, without ever losing sight of the violence that saturates human relations to other beings around us.[19]

"It's like they live on a second planet," Omar wrote to me, referring to American Special Forces who occupy a base only a few miles from Rukban but refuse to offer critically needed water, food, and medicine. They probably don't know about Omar's dreams, or care. Perhaps you will.

That is another response to the state of uncaring. It's a response that is somewhat more prosaic, in the sense that it requires the recuperation of story-telling and transmission. It relies on practices of intimate listening and vulnerable observation that may break our heart, but it may also bring us closer to those who reside in uncaring, to those who live and die in no man's land.[20]

Acknowledgments

The generosity of many people made this book possible, many more than I am able to list here. Some offered direction when I reached dead ends, and others walked me through checkpoints or showed me a forest path covered by the overgrowth. Although this book is concerned with the space of uncaring, with abandoned lands and lives, it comes to light only because of the immense care of friends, family, and colleagues.

My dear friend and longtime collaborator Alasdair Pinkerton has his boot prints all over this work. It was during a drive with Al in 2013 in the mountains of southern Spain that the question of no man's land first came up. His creativity, wisdom, and humor have filled the many miles we covered together since. Chum—I only wish I was a different writer to fully author this with you! Elliot Graves was there from the start of this journey, pushing me to think about other ways of telling the stories of no man's land. His photographs and generous creative advice have been invaluable, as is his friendship.

Although I emailed him out of the blue, Daniel Ruiz-Serna generously shared his work on Colombia, which made it possible for me to reach otherwise inaccessible resources. He was also extremely kind to introduce me to many others who opened their doors and their hearts. Throughout my research in Colombia, Diana Ojeda shared her wisdom, enthusiasm, and endless patience. Her unwavering commitment to collaborative work continues to inspire me. When I first arrived in Bogotá, Erna Von Der Walde provided a crash course in history that was profound beyond anything I could have hoped for. Thank you, Adrián, for introducing us, and for so much more! Caturo and Adelaida Trujillo Caicedo made me feel at home when I really needed it, and they added facets to the book that would have remained invisible to me otherwise. I cannot begin to express my gratitude to my research assistants over the years in Colombia—Laura Pardo, Laura Castrill, and María Teresa González. With immense patience and wisdom, you helped me unlearn and relearn.

Many colleagues and friends offered advice and support throughout many years of researching this book. Louise Amoore, Ben Anderson, Colin McFarlane, Olga Demetriou, Elizabeth Johnson, Jonathan Darling, Helen Wilson, Jeremy Schmidt, and Lauren Martin read early sections, offering careful advice and encouragement. I'm also grateful to Gavin Bridge, Phil Steinberg, Joe Painter, Nayanika Mookherjee, Harriet Hawkins, Christopher Johnson, William Schaefer, and Marc Schachter, who shared invaluable suggestions or simply allowed me to talk things through. Mark Griffiths, Craig Jones, Jesse Proudfoot, and Oded Zipori have been dear friends. I'm sure you will be delighted we can talk about other things now. Lauren Wright was a major presence in the first years of this project, and I am so grateful for it all. I'm deeply indebted to Oliver Belcher and Yoav Ronel who read extensive parts of this book over the years, offering thoughts and immensely needed encouragement. Your wisdom and friendship mean the world to me. Judah Grunstein carefully read and commented on the entire manuscript at a critical moment; your generosity is humbling. Ayala Ronel reminded me to never forget that this book actually needs to matter to people, and I can only hope it does. She remains one of the most courageous people I know.

I have been inspired by mentors who showed me the numerous ways of being a scholar. I am proud to be a student of Anthony Julius, who remains endlessly generous with both critique and kindness. Louise Bethlehem has been an intellectual guide and interlocutor since my days as a lost undergraduate. Her belief in me is humbling. Over the years, Jay Winter, Derek Gregory, Ariella Azoulay, Adi Ophir, and Rachel Pain repeatedly offered advice and support. Their scholarship and knowledge remain an inspiration. Lynn Staeheli has been a colleague, friend, and mentor for many years. Her wisdom, questions, and comments were guiding lights at critical junctures of this project. More than anything, Lynn was never afraid to call me out, to know when I was taking a shortcut or playing it safe for no good reason. Her untimely death in 2020 remains an immense loss.

Immense gratitude goes to Susannah Engstrom, who believed in this book from our very first conversation, to Katherine Faydash, and to everyone else at the University of Chicago Press who made this book happen.

Research for this book was generously supported by Royal Geographical Society's Thesiger-Oman International Fellowship, Durham University, Royal Holloway University of London, and the University of Denver Marsico Visiting Fellowship. Special thanks goes to Catharine Souch, Susan Schulten, and Adam Holden for their support and belief in the project. Parts of this research were presented over the years at the University of Arizona; University of Colorado, Boulder; University of Denver; University of Victoria; University of Grenoble; University of Oxford; Cambridge University; Hebrew University in Jerusalem; University of London; Aristotle University of Thessaloniki; and Durham University. The many questions and suggestions I've received during these exchanges have helped make this book richer than I could have done alone. I have also benefited from the knowledge and support of staff at Bibliothèque Mazarin, Paris; Bibliothèque Centre Pompidou, Paris; Devon Institute, Exeter; Literary and Philosophical Society, Newcastle; the British Library; and the Warburg Institute.

My family never ceases to amaze me with their unconditional love and tenacious care for what I do. They posed some of the hardest questions and strongest disagreements during the writing of this book, and it is better for it. My parents, Daphna and Zeev, my brothers Eylam, Elad, and Amit, and their partners Yam, Daria, and Yasmin are my bedrock. Aramit Lotem and Meir Kraus provided a loving space of sanctuary and deep introspection. Growing up, I often crossed a field that used to be part of an old no man's land between Israel and Jordan to reach the house of my friend, Ido Dweck. He remains a soulmate who shows me how things are built, not only how they are destroyed.

Jen Bagelman has been my best friend, my sharpest intellectual interlocutor, unwavering supporter, and the most inspiring companion I could have ever hoped for. She reminded me to be accountable, taught me that fun is a very big part of every plan, and gave me courage to follow my heart. This book is dedicated to her.

Notes

Introduction

1. I consciously refuse the scholarly tendency to hide behind what Engin Isin describes as "masks of impartiality and disinterest." Working on this book, I was always an engaged interlocutor, and in doing so, I was rarely alone. I write about my own presence and the presence of others who were with me—friends, colleagues, collaborators—to the extent that our presence is often part of the story, of the event of storytelling and of its transmission. On so many levels—ethical, political, and practical—that will become clearer as the book unfolds, hiding was never an option. Nor should it be here, on the page. Engin F. Isin, "A Labour of Love (the Right to Philosophy)," *Citizenship Studies* 27, no. 3 (2023): 422–26, https://doi.org/10.1080/13621025.2023.2171256.

2. For an excellent short ethnography of Sheikh Sa'ad and the taxi collective, see Oren Kroll-Zeldin, "Institutional Separation and Sumud in Jerusalem's Periphery," *Jerusalem Quarterly* 73 (2018): 101–16.

3. Dorit Beinish, Eliezer Rivlin, and Edmond Levi, HCJ 7337/05 Mouhammad Naif Shakir & 28 others v. Military Commander in Judea and Samaria (Supreme Court of the State of Israel: High Court of Justice 15 March 2010).

4. Maria Margaroni, "Care and Abandonment: A Response to Mika Ojakangas' 'Impossible Dialogue on Bio-Power: Agamben and Foucault,'" *Foucault Studies* 2 (2005): 36; Giorgio Agamben, *Homo Sacer: Sovereign Power and Bare Life* (Stanford, CA: Stanford University Press, 1998), 51.

5. Ephraim E. Urbach, "Hefker- mashehu al hamosad imekomo bametsi'ut ha-historit" ["Hefker"—On the Place of "Derelictio" in Historical Reality], *Shenaton ha-Mishpat ha-Ivri: Annual of the Institute for Research in Jewish Law* 6–7 (1979): 17–28.

6. This dual concern has governed the understanding of abandonment for millennia: *derelictio* and *expositio* were early terms in Roman law that addressed the abandonment of property and dependent individuals (orphans, widows), as well as those who fall between these categories like slaves. Adolf Berger, *Encyclopedic Dictionary of Roman Law* (Philadelphia: Lawbook Exchange, 1953). It is far beyond the scope of this book to summarize a full theory of abandonment, a concept with roots in Greco-Roman political theory that have had immense impact on legal-political conceptualization of abandonment in the twentieth century. Instead, the focus

here is on the two main critical spheres that have shaped contemporary understandings and analytical mobilization of abandonment, namely, the critique of neoliberal orders, and abandonment as a central legal-political condition in biopolitical governance. I have discussed the theoretical elements of this genealogy in Noam Leshem, "Spaces of Abandonment: Genealogies, Lives and Critical Horizons," *Environment and Planning D: Society and Space* 35, no. 4 (2017): 620–36, https://doi.org/10.1177/0263775816683189.

7. Naomi Klein, *The Shock Doctrine: Rise of Disaster Capitalism* (London: Allen Lane, 2007). In her work on the lives of Canadian Inuit, Lisa Stevenson develops the notion of anonymous care, "a regime of care that requires life to become an indifferent value—that is, a regime in which it doesn't matter who you are, just that you stay alive." Lisa Stevenson, *Life beside Itself: Imagining Care in the Canadian Arctic* (Berkeley: University of California Press, 2014), https://doi.org/10.1525/9780520958555.

8. All quotes are from Elizabeth A. Povinelli, *Economies of Abandonment: Social Belonging and Endurance in Late Liberalism* (Durham, NC: Duke University Press, 2011), 167.

9. Povinelli, 159.

10. Agamben, *Homo Sacer*; Giorgio Agamben, *State of Exception* (Chicago: University of Chicago Press, 2005); Roberto Esposito, *Bíos: Biopolitics and Philosophy*, Posthumanities Series 4 (Minneapolis: University of Minnesota Press, 2008).

11. For example, Derek Gregory, *The Colonial Present: Afghanistan. Palestine. Iraq* (Malden, MA: Blackwell, 2004); Adi Ophir, Michal Givoni, and Sari Hanafi, *The Power of Inclusive Exclusion: Anatomy of Israeli Rule in the Occupied Palestinian Territories* (New York: Zone Books, 2009).

12. João Guilherme Biehl, *Vita: Life in a Zone of Social Abandonment* (Berkeley: University of California Press, 2005); Geraldine Pratt, "Abandoned Women and Spaces of the Exception," *Antipode* 37, no. 5 (2005): 1052–78, https://doi.org/10.1111/j.0066-4812.2005.00556.x.

13. Achille Mbembe, *Necropolitics*, Theory in Forms (Durham, NC: Duke University Press, 2019), https://doi.org/10.1515/9781478007227. There is a well-established critique of the assumed passivity often associated with the figure of *Homo Sacer* and the way much of this theoretical corpus ignores the agency of individuals even in the most extreme conditions of violence, incarceration, and exploitation. See Nikos Papastergiadis, "The Invasion Complex: The Abject Other and Spaces of Violence," *Geografiska Annaler: Series B, Human Geography* 88, no. 4 (2006): 429–42, https://doi.org/10.1111/j.0435-3684.2006.00231.x; Raffaela Puggioni, "Resisting Sovereign Power: Camps in-Between Exception and Dissent," in *The Politics of Protection: Sites of Insecurity and Political Agency*, ed. Jef Huysmans, Andrew Dobson, and Raia Prokhovnik, Routledge Advances in International Relations and Global Politics 43 (London: Routledge, 2006), 68–83.

14. Enzo Traverso, *The Origins of Nazi Violence* (New York: New Press, 2003).

15. Agamben famously makes this distinction to understand the structure of exception that constitutes contemporary biopower. Giorgio Agamben, *Means without End: Notes on Politics* (Minneapolis: University of Minnesota Press, 2000). Medical violence is a relatively neglected topic in the scholarship on repression, mass violence, and genocide, in spite of its commonality and profound impact on societies. Most research has focused on Nazi doctors and medical scientists, but more recent work has extended, for example, to the role that Syrian doctors have played in that country's violent conflict. Robert Jay Lifton, *The Nazi Doctors: Medical Killing and the Psychology of Genocide*, 4th ed. (New York: Basic Books, 2017), http://catdir.loc.gov/catdir/enhancements/fy0831/2004695065-b.html; Annsar Shahhoud, "Medical Génocidaires in the

Syrian Civil War (2011–2019)," *Journal of Genocide Research* 25, no. 1 (2023): 89–103, https://doi .org/10.1080/14623528.2021.1979908.

16. Since antiquity, the figure of the shepherd functions as a metonym of either divine power (gods) or earthly sovereignty. See Michel Foucault, *Security, Territory, Population: Lectures at the Collège de France 1977–78*, ed. Michel Senellart, trans. Graham Burchell, Lectures at the Collège de France (Basingstoke, UK: Palgrave Macmillan, 2009), 111–26.

17. Foucault, 126.

18. Foucault, 127, 124, 133n32. See also Michel Foucault, "'Omnes et Singulatim': Toward a Critique of Political Reason," in *Power: Essential Works of Michel Foucault 1954–1984* (New York: New Press, 2000), 3:298–325.

19. Michael D. Coogan et al., *The New Oxford Annotated Bible with Apocrypha: New Revised Standard Version* (Oxford: Oxford University Press, 2010), 1210.

20. This verse is from the King James Bible translation, which captures the Hebrew more accurately.

21. Foucault, "'Omnes et Singulatim,'" 321.

22. Foucault, 317, my emphasis.

23. John T. Hamilton, *Security: Politics, Humanity, and the Philology of Care*, Translation/ Transnation (Princeton, NJ: Princeton University Press, 2013).

24. As Hamilton notes, this is true for social contract theory as it is to security software. "We allow our worries to be relocated; we watch them be sent off so that they may be domesticated elsewhere by powers that transcend our own, relatively feeble capacities." Hamilton, 10.

25. Hamilton, 5.

26. Sianne Ngai argues that, indeed, disinterest is internal to interest, "a feeling so low in intensity that it can even be hard to say whether it counts" as affection or disaffection. Sianne Ngai, "Merely Interesting," *Critical Inquiry* 34, no. 4 (2008): 777–817, https://doi.org/10.1086/592544.

27. Following the work of Adi Ophir, I use *evils*—always in the plural—as concrete cases of disvalue, occurrences of offence or inflictions of pain. Adi Ophir, *The Order of Evils: Toward an Ontology of Morals* (New York: Zone Books, 2005).

28. The no man's land of the Western Front during World War I was subject to constant and extensive surveillance, which produced almost daily updates of the exact location of the front lines and the space between them. Yet the frequency of changes along the front meant that by the time maps were printed with the latest survey information and arrived back at the hands of soldiers, they were largely obsolete. See Peter Chasseaud, *Artillery's Astrologers: A History of British Survey and Mapping on the Western Front, 1914–1918* (Lewes, UK: Mapbooks, 1999). See also Derek Gregory, "Gabriel's Map: Cartography and Choreography in Modern War," in *Geographies of Knowledge and Power*, ed. Peter Meusburger, Derek Gregory, and Laura Suarsana (Dordrecht, Netherlands: Springer, 2015). Derek Gregory has been working on the logistics of evacuation in war, and addressed the infrastructures of medical evacuation around the no man's land of the Western Front in World War I for a panel discussion I organized several years ago. Derek Gregory, "Divisions of Life: Journeys from No Man's Land 1914–1918," *Geographical Imaginations* (blog), 28 April 2015, https://geographicalimaginations.com/2015/04/28/divisions-of-life/.

29. Agamben, *Homo Sacer*; Agamben, *State of Exception*. The work of Jean-Luc Nancy had immense impact on the evolution of this conception of abandonment. Abandonment, for Nancy, is an act that delivers over to the sovereign ban, and as such, always exists under the sovereign law: "One always abandons to law." Jean-Luc Nancy, *The Birth to Presence* (Stanford, CA: Stanford University Press, 1993), 44.

30. The major impetus for recentering the debate around ethics of care is Carol Gilligan, *In a Different Voice: Psychological Theory and Women's Development* (Cambridge, MA: Harvard University Press, 2003). On the implications for political theory, see also Virginia Held, *The Ethics of Care: Personal, Political, and Global* (New York: Oxford University Press, 2005), https://doi .org/10.1093/0195180992.001.0001.

31. For Foucault, the territorialization of pastoral power is specifically associated with the Greek god or ruler of the city-state. The Hebrew pastoral relationship, on the other hand, governs a people, not a territory. It governs for the benefit of the people rather than for something external to it like a state. Foucault, *Security, Territory, Population*, 129.

32. During a visit to a border detention facility in July 2019, the US vice president Mike Pence expressed this logic in the clearest of terms: "Every family I spoke to said they were being well cared for, and that's different than some of the harsh rhetoric we hear from Capitol Hill," Pence said. "Customs and border protection is doing its level best to provide compassionate care in a manner the American people would expect." Josh Dawsey and Colby Itkowitz, "Mike Pence Says Migrants Are 'Well Cared For' While Touring Border Detention Centres," *The Independent*, 13 July 2019, https://www.independent.co.uk/news/world/americas/us-politics/mike-pence-migrant -detention-centers-visit-border-camp-trump-mexico-a9003346.html.

33. Eula Biss, *Notes from No Man's Land: American Essays* (St. Paul, MN: Graywolf Press, 2009), 147.

34. Fuerzas Armadas Revolucionarias de Colombia—Ejército del Pueblo (the Revolutionary Armed Forces of Colombia—People's Army) mostly known by its acronym FARC-EP, or FARC.

35. Roderick Impey Murchison, "Address to the Royal Geographical Society," *Proceedings of the Royal Geographical Society of London* 8, no. 5 (1864): 250, https://doi.org/10.2307/1799282.

36. Benedict Anderson, *A Life beyond the Boundaries* (London: Verso, 2016), 154.

37. Ariella Aïsha Azoulay, *Potential History: Unlearning Imperialism* (London: Verso, 2019), 10. Unlearning has been famously a central, if ever-changing component in Gayatri Spivak's critique of Euro-American monoculturalism and its epistemologies. More recently, this practice has been taken up by a growing corpus of decolonial scholars. Though less directly, these have all been deeply influential on my thinking here. Gayatri Chakravorty Spivak, "Can the Subaltern Speak?," in *Marxism and the Interpretation of Culture*, ed. Cary Nelson and Lawrence Grossberg (Urbana: University of Illinois Press, 1988), 271–313; Sara Danius and Stefan Jonsson, "An Interview with Gayatri Chakravorty Spivak," *Boundary 2* 20, no. 2 (1993): 24–50, https://doi.org /10.2307/303357; Madina V. Tlostanova and Walter D. Mignolo, *Learning to Unlearn: Decolonial Reflections from Eurasia and the Americas* (Columbus: Ohio State University Press, 2012), http://muse.jhu.edu/book/24260.

38. As such, the view that these spaces are somehow ownerless is not part of strategic devaluation that will lead to a future reincorporation. This is not merely a repetition of the deterritorialization-reterritorialization dynamic that David Harvey famously talks about. See David Harvey, *The Condition of Postmodernity: An Enquiry into the Origins of Cultural Change* (Oxford, UK: Blackwell, 1989).

39. Unlike its English form, most languages have parallel terms that are gender neutral. I return to discuss the masculine underpinnings of the concept later in the book.

40. Conversation with the author, San Pedro Atocpan, Mexico, 15 August 2015.

41. Michael Taussig, *Walter Benjamin's Grave* (Chicago: University of Chicago Press, 2010), vii.

42. For example, Claudia Leal, *A la buena de Dios: Colonización en la Macarena, ríos Duda y Guayabero* (Bogotá: FESCOL and CEREC, 1995), http://www.bdigital.unal.edu.co/54628/10/95

89272576.PDF; Olga Demetriou, "To Cross or Not to Cross? Subjectivization and the Absent State in Cyprus," *Journal of the Royal Anthropological Institute* 13, no. 4 (2007): 987–1006, https:// doi.org/10.1111/j.1467-9655.2007.00468.x; Anita Bakshi, "A Shell of Memory: The Cyprus Conflict and Nicosia's Walled City," *Memory Studies* 5, no. 4 (2012): 479–96.

43. I learned a great deal from other scholars who have tackled this tension in other contexts. See, e.g., Gregory, *Colonial Present*; Ariella Azoulay and Adi Ophir, *The One-State Condition: Occupation and Democracy in Israel/Palestine*, Stanford Studies in Middle Eastern and Islamic Societies and Cultures (Stanford, CA: Stanford University Press, 2013).

44. Audre Lorde, *Sister Outsider: Essays and Speeches* (New York: Potter, Ten Speed, Harmony, Rodale, 2012), 39.

45. On unlearning with companions, see Azoulay, *Potential History*, 15–19.

Part One

1. Walter Benjamin, "The Storyteller: Observations on the Works of Nikolai Leskov," in *Selected Writings*, vol. 3, *1935–1938*, ed. Howard Eliand and Michael W. Jennings, trans. Edmund Jephcott (Cambridge, MA: Belknap Press of Harvard University Press, 2003), 144.

2. Eric J. Leed, *No Man's Land: Combat & Identity in World War I* (Cambridge: Cambridge University Press, 1979), 19.

3. Arnauld Pierre, *Fernand Léger, peindre la vie moderne* (Paris: Gallimard, 1997), 25.

4. Alex Volmar, "In Storms of Steel: The Soundscape of World War I and Its Impact on Auditory Media Culture during the Weimar Period," in *Sounds of Modern History: Auditory Cultures in 19th- and 20th-Century Europe*, ed. Daniel Morat (New York: Berghahn Books, 2014), 227–56.

5. Dorothee Brantz, "Environments of Death: Trench Warfare on the Western Front, 1914–1918," in *War and the Environment: Military Destruction in the Modern Age*, ed. Charles Closmann (College Station: Texas A&M University Press, 2009), 76.

6. Mishka Henner, interview with the author, 22 October 2018, Exeter, UK.

Chapter One

1. I did this exercise with numerous people I've met during research for this book, from high school students in Cairo to activists in Cyprus and farm workers in Colombia. The results were strikingly similar, despite cultural specificities that are deeply rooted in different languages.

2. Torbjörn Larsson, interview with the author, 14 November 2017.

3. William Orpen, *An Onlooker in France, 1917–1919* (London: Williams and Norgate, 1921), 20.

4. Mishka Henner, interview with the author, 22 October 2018.

5. Henner interview.

6. Raoul Hausmann, "Photomontage," in *Photography in the Modern Era: European Documents and Critical Writings, 1913–1940*, ed. Christopher Phillips (New York: Aperture, 1989), 29.

7. Bodo von Dewitz, "German Snapshots from World War I: Personal Pictures, Political Implications," in *War/Photography: Images of Armed Conflict and Its Aftermath*, ed. Anne Tucker, Will Michels, and Natalie Zelt (Houston: Museum of Fine Arts, Houston, 2012), 157.

8. Paul K. Saint-Amour, "Modernist Reconnaissance," *Modernism/Modernity* 10, no. 2 (16 May 2003): 349–80, https://doi.org/10.1353/mod.2003.0047; Paul K. Saint-Amour, "Applied Modernism: Military and Civilian Uses of the Aerial Photomosaic," *Theory, Culture & Society* 28, nos. 7–8 (2011): 241–69, https://doi.org/10.1177/0263276411423938.

9. Susan D. Moeller, *Shooting War: Photography and the American Experience of Combat* (New York: Basic Books, 1989), 138–39.

10. Susan Sontag, *Regarding the Pain of Others* (London: Penguin, 2004).

11. Simon Grant, "A Terrible Beauty," *Tate Etc.*, no. 5 (Autumn 2005), http://www.tate.org.uk /context-comment/articles/terrible-beauty.

12. Peter Paret, *Imagined Battles: Reflections of War in European Art* (Chapel Hill: University of North Carolina Press, 1997), 108.

13. Paul Nash, *British Artists at the Front. III. Paul Nash* (London: Country Life; George Newnes, 1918), n.p.

14. Walter Benjamin, "Experience and Poverty," in *Selected Writings*, vol. 2, *1927–1934*, ed. Howard Eliand, Michael W. Jennings, and Gary Smith, trans. Rodney Livingstone (Cambridge, MA: Belknap Press of Harvard University Press, 2003), 731–35.

15. Martin Jay, "Walter Benjamin, Remembrance, and the First World War," *Estudios/Working Papers* (Centro de Estudios Avanzados en Ciencias Sociales), no. 87 (1996): 1.

16. Benjamin, "The Storyteller," 144.

17. Peter Sloterdijk, *Terror from the Air*, trans. Amy Patton and Steve Corcoran, Semiotext(e) Foreign Agents Series (Los Angeles: Semiotext(e), 2009).

18. Robert Dixon, "Spotting the Fake: C. E. W. Bean, Frank Hurley and the Making of the 1923 Photographic Record of the War," *History of Photography* 31, no. 2 (2007): 165–79, https:// doi.org/10.1080/03087298.2007.10443516.

19. Frank Hurley, *The Diaries of Frank Hurley, 1912–1941*, ed. Robert Dixon and Christopher Lee (London: Anthem Press, 2011), 73–74.

20. Martyn Jolly, "Australian First-World-War Photography Frank Hurley and Charles Bean," *History of Photography* 23, no. 2 (1999): 149, https://doi.org/10.1080/03087298.1999.10443814.

21. Frank Hurley, "War Photography," *Australian Photo Review*, 15 February 1919, 164.

22. Hurley, "War Photography," 164.

23. Anne-Marie Willis, *Picturing Australia: A History of Photography* (North Ryde, Australia: Angus & Robertson, 1988).

24. Allen Feldman, "Ground Zero Point One: On the Cinematics of History," *Social Analysis: The International Journal of Social and Cultural Practice* 46, no. 1 (2002): 111.

25. Leed, *No Man's Land*, 179.

26. The earliest systematic use of composite photography was made by Francis Galton as early as the 1860s as part of investigations into inherent physiological evidence of intellectual ineptitude, moral depravity, and criminal tendencies. From the 1870s, Galton made increasing use of composite photography as a technical apparatus of eugenics, first by producing portraits of "criminal types" made out of overlaid photographs of different individuals and later through the production of chronological composites with members of the same family. Importantly, composite photography as an instrument of eugenics emerged out of Victorian anxieties about social stability, the effects of industrialization, and changing conditions of urban existence. "At its most extreme," Allan Sekula notes, "the debate on recidivism combined the vagabond, the anarchist, and recidivist into a single composite figure of social menace." Allan Sekula, "The Body and the Archive," *October* 39 (1986): 33, https://doi.org/10.2307/778312. See also David Green, "Veins of Resemblance: Photography and Eugenics," *Oxford Art Journal* 7, no. 2 (1984): 3–16.

27. Georges Didi-Huberman, "Warburg's Haunted House," trans. Shane Lillis, *Common Knowledge* 18, no. 1 (2012): 73, https://doi.org/10.1215/0961754X-1456881.

28. Ann Thomas, *The Great War: The Persuasive Power of Photography*, bilingual ed. (Milan: 5 Continents, 2015); Janina Struk, *Private Pictures: Soldiers' inside View of War* (London: I. B. Tauris, 2011).

29. Gottfried Korff, ed., *Kasten 117: Aby Warburg Und Der Aberglaube Im Ersten Weltkrieg*, 1. Aufl, Untersuchungen Des Ludwig-Uhland-Instituts Der Universität Tübingen, 105. Bd (Tübingen: Tübinger Vereinigung für Volkskunde, 2007).

30. Didi-Huberman, "Warburg's Haunted House," 68. The photographs I refer to here are T4715, T4714, and T3597, all in the Warburg Institute Archive, London.

31. Didi-Huberman, 51.

32. Quoted in Christopher D. Johnson, *Memory, Metaphor, and Aby Warburg's Atlas of Images*, Signale: Modern German Letters, Cultures, and Thought (Ithaca, NY: Cornell University Press, 2012), 12–13.

33. W. J. T. Mitchell, "Method, Madness and Montage: Assemblages of Images and the Production of Knowledge," in *Image Operations: Visual Media and Political Conflict*, ed. Jens Eder and Charlotte Klonk (Oxford: Oxford University Press, 2016), 80.

34. "Jew without a Country Held in Czech Prison," *Jewish Daily Bulletin*, 16 July 1933, 9, http://pdfs.jta.org/1933/1933-07-16_2596.pdf?_ga=2.248628357.362135194.1681144023-1981767255.1681144022.

35. Ariella Azoulay, *The Civil Contract of Photography* (New York: Zone, 2008).

Chapter Two

1. Don Oberdorfer, *The Two Koreas: A Contemporary History*, rev. ed. (New York: Basic Books, 2013).

2. Dean Rusk, *As I Saw It* (Harmondsworth, UK: Penguin, 1991).

3. John P. Glennon, Harriet D. Schwar, and Paul Claussen, eds., "The Commander in Chief, United Nations Command (Ridgway) to the Joint Chiefs of Staff, 26 July 1951," in *Foreign Relations of the United States, 1951, Korea and China*, vol. 7, pt. 1 (Washington, DC: US Government Printing Office, 1983), doc. 472, https://history.state.gov/historicaldocuments/frus1951v07p1/d472; Gerald Segal, *Defending China* (Oxford: Oxford University Press, 1985), 97; Shu Guang Zhang, *Mao's Military Romanticism: China and the Korean War, 1950–1953*, Modern War Studies (Lawrence: University Press of Kansas, 1995), 219.

4. John P. Glennon, Harriet D. Schwar, and Paul Claussen, eds., "The Joint Chiefs of Staff to the Commander in Chief, United Nations Command (Ridgway), 30 June 1951," in *Foreign Relations of the United States, 1951, Korea and China*, vol. 7, pt. 1 (Washington, DC: US Government Printing Office, 1983), doc. 392, https://history.state.gov/historicaldocuments/frus1951v07p1/d475.

5. John P. Glennon, Harriet D. Schwar, and Paul Claussen, eds., "The Commander in Chief, United Nations Command (Ridgway) to the Joint Chiefs of Staff, 27 July 1951," in *Foreign Relations of the United States, 1951, Korea and China*, vol. 7, pt. 1 (Washington, DC: US Government Printing Office, 1983), doc. 475, https://history.state.gov/historicaldocuments/frus1951v07p1/d475.

6. James Brady, *The Scariest Place in the World* (New York: Thomas Dunne Books, 2005), 97, http://archive.org/details/scariestplaceinw00jame.

7. Quoted in Donald Knox, *The Korean War: Uncertain Victory* (San Diego, CA: Harcourt Brace Jovanovich, 1991), 387.

8. Bevin Alexander, *Korea: The First War We Lost* (New York: Hippocrene Books, 1991), 440.

9. Jack L. Cannon, "Attack on Hills 673 and 749," *Leatherneck*, March 1989, 23.

10. Arned L. Hinshaw, *Heartbreak Ridge: Korea, 1951* (New York: Praeger, 1989), 7, http://archive.org/details/heartbreakridgek00hins.

11. Walter G. Hermes, *Truce Tent and Fighting Front* (Washington, DC: Office of the Chief of Military History, US Army, 1992), 86, http://hdl.handle.net/2027/uiug.30112000735826.

12. Hermes, 86.

13. Bill Wilson, "The Fight for the Ridge," Heartland Heroes: Korean War 50th Anniversary Commemoration, 2002, http://www.accesskansas.org/kskoreanwar/stories/story_wilson2.html.

14. Hermes, *Truce Tent and Fighting Front*, 96.

15. Rosemary Foot, *A Substitute for Victory: The Politics of Peacemaking at the Korean Armistice Talks*, Cornell Studies in Security Affairs (Ithaca, NY: Cornell University Press, 1990), 63.

16. Hermes, *Truce Tent and Fighting Front*, 112–21; Foot, *A Substitute for Victory*, 46.

17. Foot, *A Substitute for Victory*, 70–72; John P. Glennon, Harriet D. Schwar, and Paul Claussen, eds., "The Joint Chiefs of Staff to the Commander in Chief, Far East (Ridgway), 14 November 1951," in *Foreign Relations of the United States, 1951, Korea and China*, vol. 7, pt. 1 (Washington, DC: US Government Printing Office, 1983), doc. 707, https://history.state.gov/historicaldocuments/frus1951v07p1/d707; Hermes, *Truce Tent and Fighting Front*, 176.

18. Marijn Nieuwenhuis, "The Invisible Lines of Territory: An Investigation into the Make-Up of Territory," in *The Question of Space: Interrogating the Spatial Turn between Disciplines*, ed. Marijn Nieuwenhuis and David Crouch (London: Rowman & Littlefield Publishers, 2017), 120.

19. Nigel Clark, *Inhuman Nature: Sociable Life on a Dynamic Planet* (New York: Sage Publications, 2010), 95.

20. Adriana Petryna, *Life Exposed: Biological Citizens after Chernobyl* (Princeton, NJ: Princeton University Press, 2002), 2.

21. John P. Glennon, Harriet D. Schwar, and Paul Claussen, "Briefing for Director of Central Intelligence Helms for a National Security Council Meeting, April 16, 1969," in *Foreign Relations of the United States, 1969–1976*, vol. 19, pt. 1, Korea, 1969–1972 (Washington, DC: US Government Printing Office, 1983), doc. 11, https://history.state.gov/historicaldocuments/frus1969-76v19p1/d11.

22. Tim Ingold, *Lines: A Brief History* (London: Routledge, 2008), 160.

23. Martin Jay, "Scopic Regimes of Modernity," in *Vision and Visuality*, ed. Hal Foster, Discussions in Contemporary Culture 2 (Seattle: Bay Press, 1988), 5–6.

24. Israeli Delegation to the Hashemite Kingdom of Jordan/Israel Mixed Armistice Commission, "Remaining Problems on Our Border with Jordan," 11 February 1963, 10, ISA-mfa-Political-000m7dp, Israeli State Archives.

25. Meron Benvenisti, *City of Stone: The Hidden History of Jerusalem* (Berkeley: University of California Press, 1998), 57.

26. "General Armistice Agreement between the Hashemite Jordan Kingdom and Israel," 3 April 1949, UN Doc S/1302/Rev.1, https://peacemaker.un.org/sites/peacemaker.un.org/files/IL%20JO_490403_Hashemite%20Jordan%20Kingdom-Israel%20General%20Armistice%20Agreement.pdf.

27. Benvenisti, *City of Stone*, 57.

28. Benvenisti, 57.

29. "Steinitz Incident (Musrara) 21/1/55," 21 January 1955, ISA-mfa-Political-000m7dp, Israeli State Archives.

30. Justine Clark, "Smudges, Smears and Adventitious Marks," *Interstices* 4 (1995): 4.

31. Walter Benjamin, "Naples," in *Selected Writings*, vol. 1, *1913–1926*, ed. Marcus Bullock and Michael William Jennings (Cambridge, MA: Belknap Press of Harvard University Press, 2003), 416.

32. Andrew Benjamin, "Porosity at the Edge: Working through Walter Benjamin's 'Naples,'" in *Moderne begreifen*, ed. Christine Magerski, Robert Savage, and Christiane Weller (Wiesbaden, Germany: DUV, 2007), 37, https://doi.org/10.1007/978-3-8350-9676-9_7.

33. "In other news" [Od bahadashot], *Al Hamishmar*, 12 May 1950.

34. Rafi Marziano, interview by Yoram Tamir, October 1989, Divided City Folder, Ammunition Hill Archive.

35. *Ma'ariv*, 29 May 1958; *Davar*, 12 June 1958.

36. Ariel Ben Gad, "The City Line in Jerusalem, 1948–1967" [HaKav HaIroni BeYerushalayim 1948–1967] (MA thesis in history, Jerusalem, Hebrew University of Jerusalem, 2018), 53–54.

37. Dan Lindley, "Historical, Tactical, and Strategic Lessons from the Partition of Cyprus," *International Studies Perspectives* 8, no. 2 (2007): 224–41, https://doi.org/10.1111/j.1528-3585.2007.00282.x.

38. AbdouMaliq Simone, *Improvised Lives: Rhythms of Endurance in an Urban South*, After the Postcolonial (Cambridge, UK: Polity, 2019), 3.

39. "Ground Sign Awareness Lesson Plan," *Raytheon Technical Services Company*, Warfighter FOCUS Program, undated, https://studylib.net/doc/6862539/ground-sign-awareness-lesson-plan.

40. Derek Gregory, "The Natures of War," *Antipode* 48, no. 1 (2016): 3–56, https://doi.org/10.1111/anti.12173.

41. Ariela Freedman, "Mary Borden's Forbidden Zone: Women's Writing from No-Man's-Land," *Modernism/Modernity* 9, no. 1 (2002): 1, https://doi.org/10.1353/mod.2002.0006.

42. "The Baramki House," *Late Night Live* (Australian Broadcasting Service, 27 July 2005), https://www.abc.net.au/listen/programs/latenightlive/3355344.

43. Thomas Abowd, "Present and Absent," in *City of Collision: Jerusalem and the Principles of Conflict Urbanism*, ed. Philipp Misselwitz and Tim Rieniets (Basel: Birkhauser, 2006), 334.

44. Wendy Brown, *Walled States, Waning Sovereignty* (New York: Zone Books, 2010). For Brown, the anxiety of the sovereign state is the consequence of unregulated capital flows and religiously sanctioned violence.

Part Two

1. Agamben, *State of Exception*.

2. Agamben, *Means without End*, 24–25.

3. Judith Butler and Athena Athanasiou, *Dispossession: The Performative in the Political* (Malden, MA: Polity Press, 2013), 4–5.

4. Daniel M. Goldstein, "Toward a Critical Anthropology of Security," *Current Anthropology* 51, no. 4 (2010): 487–517, https://doi.org/10.1086/655393.

5. Elizabeth A. Povinelli, "Defining Security in Late Liberalism: A Comment on Pedersen and Holbraad," in *Times of Security: Ethnographies of Fear, Protest, and the Future*, ed. Martin Holbraad and Morten Axel Pedersen, Routledge Studies in Anthropology 12 (London: Routledge, 2015), 31.

6. Anna Selmeczi offers a useful framework for understanding biopolitical abandonment,

a condition that emerges from the paradoxical relationship between a power that aims at the improvement of life and the extent of abandonment it accommodates. Anna Selmeczi, "'. . . We Are Being Left to Burn Because We Do Not Count': Biopolitics, Abandonment, and Resistance," *Global Society* 23, no. 4 (2009): 519–38, https://doi.org/10.1080/13600820903198933.

7. If biopolitics is concerned with the optimization of life, increasing attention has turned to the role of death in the making of sovereignty. For Mbembe, *necropolitics* describes new forms of social existence in which "vast populations are subjected to conditions of life conferring upon them the status of living dead." Balibar, meanwhile, posits that "if Foucault could have seen the way African 'demography' is 'regulated' by the AIDS epidemic (and a number of other epidemics, all monitored by a 'World Health Organization'), he might have ventured to speak of 'negative bio-politics.'" Achille Mbembe, "Necropolitics," *Public Culture* 15, no. 1 (2003): 11–40, https://doi.org/10.1215/08992363-15-1-11; Étienne Balibar, *Politics and the Other Scene*, trans. Christine Jones, James Swenson, and Chris Turner, Radical Thinkers (London: Verso, 2011), 38.

8. Drawing on Zygmunt Bauman's idea of the state as gardener that controls growth and "weeds out" unwanted elements, Claudio Minca points out that the camp was and remains fundamentally connected to ideas of care, custody, and protection that grant it a pivotal role in "improving" the biosocial sphere. Claudio Minca, "Geographies of the Camp," *Political Geography* 49 (November 2015): 74–83, https://doi.org/10.1016/j.polgeo.2014.12.005. For a detailed analysis on how care functions as a technology of border enforcement, increasing the reach of the state to govern more bodies and more spaces, see Jill M. Williams, "From Humanitarian Exceptionalism to Contingent Care: Care and Enforcement at the Humanitarian Border," *Political Geography* 47 (2015): 11–20.

Chapter Three

1. This is what Foucault refers to when he writes that "a well-disciplined body forms the operational context of the slightest gesture." Michel Foucault, *Discipline and Punish: The Birth of the Prison* (New York: Pantheon Books, 1977), 152.

2. Erin Manning, *The Minor Gesture*, Thought in the Act (Durham, NC: Duke University Press, 2016), 2.

3. Stavros Stavrides, "Open Space Appropriations and the Potentialities of a 'City of Thresholds,'" in *Terrain Vague: Interstices at the Edge of the Pale*, ed. Manuela Mariani and Patrick Barron (New York: Routledge, 2014), 56.

4. Scholars like Anita Bakshi and Yael Navarro-Yashin have written extensively about the memory work and affective politics that informed the Cypriot experience of partition. Others have focused more on the material analysis of these fortifications. Karen Till and others have written a brief introduction to this debate, but Wendy Brown's important discussion of the political logic that underscores this walling frenzy in the early twenty-first century remains a critical starting point. Bakshi, "A Shell of Memory"; Anita Bakshi, "Urban Form and Memory Discourses: Spatial Practices in Contested Cities," *Journal of Urban Design* 19, no. 2 (2014): 189–210, https://doi.org/10.1080/13574809.2013.854696; Karen E. Till et al., "Interventions in the Political Geographies of Walls," *Political Geography* 33 (March 2013): 52–62, https://doi.org/10.1016/j .polgeo.2012.11.005; Brown, *Walled States, Waning Sovereignty*.

5. Georg Simmel, "The Metropolis and Mental Life," in *The Urban Sociology Reader* (London: Routledge, 2012), 37–45.

6. According to UN figures, the 2023–2024 The UN Peacekeeping Force in Cyprus's budget was over $56 million, although this included both military and civilian dimensions of the mission.

7. UN Security Council, "Resolution 186 (1964): The Cyprus Question," 4 March 1964, 3, S/5575, http://unscr.com/en/resolutions/doc/186. Thomas Franck, a UN official and later a critical observer of UN operations, noted a similar critique only a decade after the ossification of the status quo in Cyprus. Thomas M. Franck, *Nation against Nation: What Happened to the UN Dream and What the US Can Do about It* (Oxford: Oxford University Press, 1985), 90. For a more recent analysis on this issue see Laura M. Herța, "Peacekeeping and (Mis)Management of Ethnic Disputes: The Cyprus Case," *Studia Universitatis Babes-Bolyai—Studia Europaea*, no. 3 (2012): 59–76.

8. Gil Z. Hochberg, *Visual Occupations: Violence and Visibility in a Conflict Zone*, Perverse Modernities (Durham, NC: Duke University Press, 2015).

9. British and Foreign State Papers, *Agreement between Her Britannic Majesty's Government and the Government of the Khedive of Egypt, Relative to the Future Administration of the Soudan* (London: HMSO, 1902), http://www.heinonline.org/HOL/Page?handle=hein.cow/zzsd0003&collection=cow.

10. Office of the Geographer, Department of State, "Sudan–Egypt (United Arab Republic) Boundary" (Washington, DC: Office of the Geographer, Bureau of Intelligence and Research, US State Department, 27 July 1962); Anthony S. Reyner, "Sudan–United Republic (Egypt) Boundary: A Factual Background," *Middle East Journal; Washington* 17, no. 3 (1963): 313–16.

11. B'Tselem, "Facing the Abyss: The Isolation of Sheikh Sa'ad Village—Before and after the Separation Barrier," Status Report (Jerusalem, February 2004), https://www.btselem.org/sites/default/files/sites/default/files2/200402_facing_the_abyss_eng.pdf; Ir Amim, "Sheikh Sa'ad and the Separation Barrier: Trends in Jerusalem," 29 August 2006, https://sawahreh.wordpress.com/2009/11/12/sheikh-saad-and-the-separation-barrier-trends-in-jerusalem/.

12. On the differentiated citizenship regime in the city, see Danielle C. Jefferis, "Institutionalizing Statelessness: The Revocation of Residency Rights of Palestinians in East Jerusalem," *International Journal of Refugee Law* 24, no. 2 (2012): 202–30, https://doi.org/10.1093/ijrl/ees026.

13. Yael Berda, *Living Emergency: Israel's Permit Regime in the Occupied West Bank* (Stanford, CA: Stanford University Press, 2018).

14. Azoulay and Ophir, *The One-State Condition*.

15. Personal communication with the author, 15 April 2020.

16. See, e.g., Tehila Meir and Hamoked Centre for the Defence of the Individual to Major General Assaf Attias, IDF Civil Administration, "Restrictions on the Movement of Permanent Residents in the Sheik Sa'ad Checkpoint," 6 April 2020, http://www.hamoked.org.il/files/2020/1664210.pdf (in Hebrew).

17. Land Research Center for Arab Studies, "Demolition of Palestinian Houses Displacement Policy: Statistical Summary of Demolition of Housing in East Jerusalem during the Years 2000–2017" (East Jerusalem: Arab Studies Association, 2018), http://lrcj.org/pdf/web/viewer.html?file=Jer_Demo_2000_2017_ARB_S.pdf (in Arabic). For an overview of the Israeli planning policies in Jerusalem, see Rasim Khamaisi, "The Trap of Urban Planning Development in Jerusalem," *Contemporary Arab Affairs* 12, no. 2 (2019): 105–38, https://doi.org/10.1525/caa.2019.122005.

18. It is sometimes referred to as the El Caguán Demilitarized Zone, named after the largest town on the region.

19. P. G. W. Glare, *Oxford Latin Dictionary* (Oxford, UK: Clarendon Press, 1968), 762.

Chapter Four

1. James Jeffrey, US Special Representative for Syria, "The Role of the U.S. in Syria: Planning for the Future," 2019 Aspen Security Forum, interview by Josh Rogin, *Washington Post*, transcript, 19 July 2019, https://aspensecurityforum.org/wp-content/uploads/2019/07/The-Role -of-the-U.S.pdf.

2. A UNHCR statement issued in August 2014 pointed to "worrying signs . . . that the journey out of Syria is becoming tougher, with many people forced to pay bribes at armed checkpoints proliferating along the borders. Refugees crossing the desert into eastern Jordan are being forced to pay smugglers hefty sums (US$100 a head or more) to take them to safety." Adrian Edwards, "Needs Soar as Number of Syrian Refugees Tops 3 Million," UNHCR, 29 August 2014, https://www.unhcr.org/news/latest/2014/8/53ff76c99/needs-soar-number-syrian-refugees -tops-3-million.html.

3. Human Rights Watch, "Jordan: Syrians Blocked, Stranded in Desert," 3 June 2015, https:// www.hrw.org/news/2015/06/03/jordan-syrians-blocked-stranded-desert.

4. Human Rights Watch, "United States: Transfer 70,000 Trapped Syrians," 5 August 2015, https://www.hrw.org/news/2016/08/05/jordan/united-states-transfer-70000-trapped-syrians.

5. Rana F. Sweis, "ISIS Is Said to Claim Responsibility for Attack at Jordan-Syria Border," *New York Times*, 27 June 2016, https://www.nytimes.com/2016/06/28/world/middleeast/islamic -state-jordan-suicide-attack.html.

6. Khetam Malkawi and Omar Akour, "Jordan Commander: IS Expands Hold in Border Camp for Syrians," Associated Press, 15 February 2017, https://apnews.com/6f19357cea4c4dc49 631d4958373fc23; Sam Heller, "What an Unfolding Humanitarian Disaster in a U.S.-Protected Enclave Tells Us About American Strategy in Syria," *War on the Rocks*, 20 November 2017, https:// warontherocks.com/2017/11/16162/.

7. Sara Elizabeth Williams, "World Vision Rattles Aid Groups with Solo Operation for Syrians at Jordan Border," *New Humanitarian*, 24 January 2017, https://www.thenewhumanita rian.org/investigations/2017/01/24/exclusive-world-vision-rattles-aid-groups-solo-operation -syrians-jordan.

8. Quoted in Heller, "What an Unfolding Humanitarian Disaster in a U.S.-Protected Enclave Tells Us about American Strategy in Syria."

9. Quoted in Heller.

10. Juliette Touma, interview with the author, Skype interview, 14 August 2019.

11. Combined Joint Task Force–Operation Inherent Resolve, "Coalition Statement on At Tanf" (Southwest Asia: US Central Command, 8 June 2017), https://www.centcom.mil/MEDIA /NEWS-ARTICLES/News-Article-View/Article/1208008/coalition-statement-on-at-tanf/; Aron Lund, "Blame Game over Syrians Stranded in the Desert," Century Foundation, 18 June 2018, https://tcf.org/content/report/blame-game-syrians-stranded-desert/.

12. Jeffrey, "Role of the U.S. in Syria." Jeffrey's position assumes that adjusting the counterterrorism goals of the US presence in Syria to include protection of internally displaced persons could set a difficult precedent for the Al Hol camp in northern Syria that houses former families of Da'esh fighters. This was challenged by several scholars. See, e.g., Robert Ford and Carolyn O'Connor, "The U.S. Has Legal and Moral Responsibility to Protect Civilians at Rukban in Syria," *Just Security* (blog), 12 August 2019, https://www.justsecurity.org/65773/u-s-has -legal-and-moral-responsibility-to-protect-civilians-at-rukban-in-syria/.

13. Bethan Staton, "Syrians Trapped in Desert No Man's Land," *New Humanitarian*, 9 June

2016, https://www.thenewhumanitarian.org/special-report/2016/06/09/syrians-trapped-desert-no-man-s-land.

14. Interagency Coordination Headquarters of the Russian Federation and the Syrian Arab Republic, "On the Problems of Rukban Camp Disbandment in the Context of Coronavirus Infection's Spread" (Ministry of Defense of the Russian Federation, 26 June 2020), https://eng.mil.ru/en/news_page/country/more.htm?id=12299078@egNews; Interagency Coordination Headquarters of the Russian Federation and the Syrian Arab Republic, "On the Problems of Returning Syrian Refugees and Internally Displaced Persons to Their Homes in the Context of the Spread of Coronavirus Infection" (Ministry of Defense of the Russian Federation: Mission to Syria, 9 June 2020), http://syria.mil.ru/peacemaking_en/info/news/more.htm?id=12296503@egNews; Interagency Coordination Headquarters of the Russian Federation and the Syrian Arab Republic, "On the Problems Hindering the Implementation of Initiative on Refugees and Internally Displaced Persons Return to Places of Their Residence" (Ministry of Defense of the Russian Federation, 28 March 2020), https://eng.mil.ru/en/news_page/country/more.htm?id=12284261@egNews.

15. As noted earlier in the book, such management can seek to either nurture and sustain life or punitively restrict life by exposing it to harm and violence. Either relation is, at its core, a relation of care.

16. Jesse Marks, interview with the author, Skype, 13 August 2019.

17. I was in the last stages of finalizing the manuscript when, on October 7, 2023, Hamas breached Israeli security obstacles around Gaza and launched a widespread attack across southeast Israel. This was followed by a massive Israeli incursion into Gaza that was still ongoing when the book went to press. Given the immediacy of the events, their inclusion and consideration in this analysis seems premature.

18. Azoulay and Ophir, The One-State Condition, 163–82.

19. See, for example, Coordinator of Government Activities in the Territories, Economic Branch, "Procedure for monitoring and assessing inventories in the Gaza Strip" (Submitted to Gisha in the framework of a Freedom of Information Act Petition, AP 2744/09 Gisha v. Defense Ministry, April 2009), https://www.gisha.org/UserFiles/File/HiddenMessages/FOIA_translation.pdf. Control of life-sustaining provisions, including food, water and medical supplies has only intensified since Israel launched a massive invasion of Gaza following October 7, 2023, when Hamas fighters attacked numerous Israeli communities and military installations. According to the World Health Organization, Israel's blockade on aid supplies and ongoing hostilities have brought "The entire population in the Gaza Strip (2.23 million) . . . [to] high levels of acute food insecurity." World Health Organization, "Integrated Food Security Phase Classification, IPC Global Initiative—Special Brief: Gaza Strip," 18 March 2024, https://ipcinfo.org/fileadmin/user_upload/ipcinfo/docs/IPC_Gaza_Strip_Acute_Food_Insecurity_Feb_July2024_Special_Brief.pdf.

20. Azoulay and Ophir, The One-State Condition, 168.

21. Azoulay and Ophir, 175.

22. Adi Ophir, "The Two-State Solution: Providence and Catastrophe," Theoretical Inquiries in Law 8, no. 1 (2007): 136.

23. Reinoud Leenders and Kholoud Mansour, "Humanitarianism, State Sovereignty, and Authoritarian Regime Maintenance in the Syrian War," Political Science Quarterly 133, no. 2 (2018): 225–57, https://doi.org/10.1002/polq.12773.

24. UN Office for the Coordination of Humanitarian Affairs, "Under-Secretary-General for Humanitarian Affairs and Emergency Relief Coordinator, Mark Lowcock: Statement to the

Security Council on the Humanitarian Situation in Syria, 30 October 2017" (Amman, Jordan, 30 October 2017), https://www.unocha.org/sites/unocha/files/statement-and-speech/ERC_USG %20Mark%20Lowcock%20Statement%20to%20the%20SecCo%20on%20Syria%20-%2030 Oct2017%20-%20FINAL.pdf.

25. UN Office for the Coordination of Humanitarian Affairs UN Resident and Humanitarian Coordinator for Syrian Arab Republic and UN Resident and Humanitarian Coordinator for Syrian Arab Republic, "UN in Syria and SARC Deliver Humanitarian Assistance to 40,000 People in Rukban," Reliefweb, 6 February 2019, https://reliefweb.int/sites/reliefweb.int/files/re sources/Rukban2PR_EN_PDF.pdf.

26. Humanitarian Foresight Think Tank, "Jordan and the Berm: Rukban and Hadalat 2017– 2018" (Institut de Relations Internationales et Stratégiques, March 2017), https://www.iris-france .org/wp-content/uploads/2017/03/Sensitive-Jordan-and-the-Berm-1.pdf. Conversations I have held with residents of Rukban confirm this.

27. "The residents of the Rukban camp are Syrian citizens on Syrian soil, which makes dealing with the camp a Syrian and international responsibility and not a Jordanian one," Minister of Foreign and Expatriates Affairs Ayman Safadi said in a meeting with reporters in October 2017. "Jordan will not permit refugees from the Rukban camp to enter the kingdom," he added, "and it will not accept any mechanism for dealing with it that could make treating the situation there a Jordanian responsibility in the future." "Al-Safadi: Jordan Will Not Allow Refugees from the Rukban Camp to Enter the Kingdom," Ad-Dustour, 8 October 2017, https://shorturl.at/ADPRV.

28. World Food Programme, "Cranes Deliver Life-Saving Assistance to Syrians Stranded at Jordanian Border Areas," 5 August 2016, https://www.wfp.org/news/cranes-deliver-life-saving -assistance-to-syrians-stranded-at-jordanian-border-areas. The cranes remained on the border until January 2018 and were partly funded by the Government of the Netherlands and partly by international aid organizations.

29. David E. Sanger and Rick Gladstone, "Defiant Bashar Al-Assad Vows to Retake 'Every Inch' of Syria," New York Times, 7 June 2016, https://www.nytimes.com/2016/06/08/world/middle east/defiant-assad-vows-to-retake-every-inch-of-syria-from-his-foes.html.

30. There are an estimated three hundred to one thousand members of armed groups currently living in and around Rukban in the deconfliction zone, all affiliated with the Free Syrian Army or the moderate opposition. This population includes members of Jaysh Maghawir al-Thawra (MaT), a local partner of US forces at al-Tanf; the Tribes Army, affiliated with the Jordanian Armed Forces (JAF); the Lions of the East; Shuhada al-Quriyatayn; and Forces of Martyr Ahmad al-Abdo (FMAA).

31. Interagency Coordination Headquarters of the Russian Federation and the Syrian Arab Republic, "On the Problems Hindering the Implementation of Initiative on Refugees and Internally Displaced Persons Return to Places of Their Residence."

32. Amnesty International, "Health Crisis: Syrian Government Targets the Wounded and Health Workers" (London, March 2011), https://www.amnesty.org/download/Documents/32000 /mde240592011en.pdf.

33. Ammar Hamou and Madeline Edwards, "In Rukban, Rumors of Dead, Mistreated Returnees Leave Displaced Residents Mulling an Uncertain Homecoming," Syria Direct, 15 April 2020, https://syriadirect.org/news/in-rukban-rumors-of-dead-mistreated-returnees-leave-displaced -residents-mulling-an-uncertain-homecoming/.

34. Amnesty International, " 'You're Going to Your Death' Violations against Syrian Refu-

gees Returning to Syria" (London: Amnesty International, 7 September 2021), https://www.am nesty.org/en/documents/mde24/4583/2021/en/.

35. Which Foucault famously prefaces with "Make live" as the fundamental relation of modern biopolitical logic, superseding a premodern sovereignty characterized by the contrasting power "to make die and let live."

36. Mbembe, "Necropolitics," 39–40.

37. A recent volume, *Seeing Like a Smuggler,* offers a unique perspective on this figure. Once we refuse a state-centric view, the smuggler appears as an immanent figure of the modern nation-states, inherent in the production of social and economic value as well as contesting established conceptions of political order, from borders to citizenship and taxation. Mahmoud Keshavarz and Shahram Khosravi, eds., *Seeing Like a Smuggler: Borders from Below,* Anthropology, Culture and Society (London: Pluto Press, 2022).

38. Israel's policy toward Gaza again comes to mind as one well-documented example of this dynamic, but Alessandro Corso's research on the border regime in Lampedusa provides another detailed analysis of abandonment in a space saturated with humanitarian action. Alessandro Corso, "Lives at the Border: Abandonment and Survival at the Frontier of Lampedusa" (PhD diss., Durham University, 2019), http://etheses.dur.ac.uk/13403/.

39. Human Rights Watch, "Jordan: New Satellite Images of Syrians Stranded at Border," 7 September 2016, https://www.hrw.org/news/2016/09/07/jordan-new-satellite-images-syrians -stranded-border; Amnesty International, "Syria-Jordan Border: 75,000 Refugees Trapped in 'Berm' No-Man's Land in 'Desperate' Conditions," 15 September 2016, https://www.amnesty.org .uk/press-releases/syria-jordan-border-75000-refugees-trapped-berm-no-mans-land-desperate -conditions.

40. Yan Lu et al., "Deep Learning for Effective Refugee Tent Extraction Near Syria-Jordan Border," *IEEE Geoscience and Remote Sensing Letters,* 2020, 1–5, https://doi.org/10.1109/LGRS .2020.2999354.

41. Noemi Quagliati, "Training the Eye: Production and Reception of Aerial Photography during the World Wars," *AUC Geographica* 55, no. 1 (2020): 93–111, https://doi.org/10.14712/23 361980.2020.6.

42. Christoph Koettl, "Visualizing the Invisible: Stranded Syrians in the Desert," *Medium* (blog), 16 September 2016, https://medium.com/lemming-cliff/visualizing-the-invisible-stranded -syrians-in-the-desert-3feccd9707f3. *Hard to reach* is a working definition used by aid agencies to designate communities in need that cannot be accessed "for geographical or political reasons, because of conflict and insecurity, or bureaucratic and legal bottlenecks created by affected states and donors alike." See David Fisher et al., *World Disasters Report 2018: Leaving No One Behind* (Geneva: International Federation of Red Cross and Red Crescent Societies, 2018), 11.

43. Saint-Amour, "Modernist Reconnaissance," 376.

44. In separate contexts, Lisa Parks and David Campbell offer a critique of the unequal power relations constituted by the remote technologies of surveillance that are used to observe vulnerable populations by humanitarian actors. See Lisa Parks, "Digging into Google Earth: An Analysis of 'Crisis in Darfur,'" *Geoforum* 40, no. 4 (2009): 535–45, https://doi.org/10.1016/j.geo forum.2009.04.004; David Campbell, "Satellite Images, Security and the Geopolitical Imagination," in *From Above,* ed. Peter Adey, Mark Whitehead, and Alison Williams (New York: Oxford University Press, 2014), 289–98, https://doi.org/10.1093/acprof:oso/9780199334797.003.0014.

45. "Russian and Syrian Joint Coordination Headquarters Make Another Report on Plight

of the Syrians in the Rukban Camp," Ministry of Defense of the Russian Federation, 12 March 2019, http://eng.mil.ru/en/news_page/country/more.htm?id=12221080@egNews.

46. Editorial Team, "What Do You Know about the Al-Tanf Base?," *Horraya*, 3 January 2018, https://horrya.net/archives/43611; Jesse Marks, interview with the author, Skype, 13 August 2019; see also Lund, "Blame Game."

47. UN Population Fund, "118-Truck Convoy Delivers Urgent Aid to Stranded Residents in Rukban, Syria," 16 February 2019, https://reliefweb.int/report/syrian-arab-republic/118-truck-con voy-delivers-urgent-aid-stranded-residents-rukban-syria.

48. Omar al-Homsi, conversation with the author, WhatsApp, 13 October 2020.

49. Karen E. Till, "Wounded Cities: Memory-Work and a Place-Based Ethics of Care," *Political Geography* 31, no. 1 (2012): 3–14.

Part Three

1. John Boswell, "Expositio and Oblatio: The Abandonment of Children and the Ancient and Medieval Family," *American Historical Review* 89, no. 1 (1984): 10–33, https://doi.org/10.2307 /1855916.

2. Boswell; Mika Ojakangas, "Michel Foucault and the Enigmatic Origins of Bio-Politics and Governmentality," *History of the Human Sciences* 25, no. 1 (2012): 6, https://doi.org/10.1177/095 2695111426654.

3. Berger, *Encyclopedic Dictionary of Roman Law*, 433.

4. *Jerusalem Talmud*, Tractate Gittin, p. 40a.

Chapter Five

1. Michael P. Marder and Anaïs Tondeur, *The Chernobyl Herbarium: Fragments of an Exploded Consciousness*, Critical Climate Change (London: Open Humanities Press, 2016), 22.

2. Marder and Tondeur.

3. Chernobyl Forum, "Chernobyl's Legacy: Health, Environmental and Socio-Economic Impacts" (International Atomic Energy Agency, 2006), www.iaea.org/Publications/Booklets/Cher nobyl/chernobyl.pdf.

4. R. F. Mould, *Chernobyl Record: The Definitive History of the Chernobyl Catastrophe* (Bristol, UK: Institute of Physics Publishing, 2000); Yasuo Onishi, Oleg V. Voitsekovich, and Mark J. Zheleznyak, eds., *Chernobyl—What Have We Learned? The Successes and Failures to Mitigate Water Contamination over 20 Years* (Dordrecht, Netherlands: Springer, 2007).

5. Adriana Petryna, "Biological Citizenship: The Science and Politics of Chernobyl-Exposed Populations," *Osiris* 2, no. 19 (2004): 250–65.

6. Petryna, *Life Exposed*, 216.

7. Svetlana Alexievich, *Voices from Chernobyl: The Oral History of a Nuclear Disaster*, trans. Keith Gessen (New York: Picador USA, 2006), 16–17.

8. Gregg Mitman, Michelle Murphy, and Christopher Sellers, "Introduction: A Cloud over History," *Osiris* 19 (2004): 13.

9. Quoted in Cornelia Vismann, "Starting from Scratch: Concepts of Order in No Man's Land," in *War, Violence, and the Modern Condition*, ed. Bernd-Rüdiger Hüppauf (Berlin: Walter de Gruyter, 1997), 62.

10. Hugh D. Clout, *After the Ruins: Restoring the Countryside of Northern France after the Great War* (Exeter, UK: University of Exeter Press, 1996), 3.

11. Ernst Jünger, *Der Kampf als inneres Erlebnis* (Berlin: E. S. Mittler & Sohn, 1922), 57.

12. Jeffrey Herf, *Reactionary Modernism: Technology, Culture and Politics in Weimar and the Third Reich* (Cambridge: Cambridge University Press, 1984), 74–75.

13. Jünger, *Der Kampf als inneres Erlebnis*, 107.

14. Rob Nixon, *Slow Violence and the Environmentalism of the Poor* (Cambridge, MA: Harvard University Press, 2011), 2.

15. Michael Balonov et al., "Pathways, Levels and Trends of Population Exposure after the Chernobyl Accident," in *Proceedings of the First International Conference "The Radiological Consequences of the Chernobyl Accident"* (Brussels: European Commission, 1996), 238, https://www.osti.gov/etdeweb/biblio/20112742.

16. Cornelia Hesse-Honegger, *Heteroptera the Beautiful and the Other, or, Images of a Mutating World*, ed. Liz Jobey (Zurich: Scalo, 2001), 88.

17. Hesse-Honegger, 95.

18. Hesse-Honegger, 96.

19. In an otherwise enthusiastic review of her work, Martin Kemp noted that the majority scientific view was that Hesse-Honegger's recordings are "statistically insignificant and without correlation to low levels of ionizing radiation." A later study reviewing two decades of biological research following Chernobyl seems to cast Hesse-Honegger's hypothesis in a rather more favorable light, pointing to several cases that prove the association between high and low levels of radiation mutation rates of plants and animals. Martin Kemp, "Hesse-Honegger's Hand-Work," *Nature* 392, no. 6676 (1998): 555, https://doi.org/10.1038/33298; Anders Pape Møller and Timothy A. Mousseau, "Biological Consequences of Chernobyl: 20 Years On," *Trends in Ecology & Evolution* 21, no. 4 (2006): 200–207, https://doi.org/10.1016/j.tree.2006.01.008.

20. Astrid Schrader, "Abyssal Intimacies and Temporalities of Care: How (Not) to Care about Deformed Leaf Bugs in the Aftermath of Chernobyl," *Social Studies of Science* 45, no. 5 (2015): 665–90, https://doi.org/10.1177/0306312715603249.

21. Hesse-Honegger, *Heteroptera the Beautiful*, 7.

22. Nixon, *Slow Violence and the Environmentalism of the Poor*.

23. Hugh Raffles, *Insectopedia* (New York: Pantheon Books, 2010), 29.

24. Sloterdijk, *Terror from the Air*, 24.

25. In addition to autoradiography (capturing on X-ray film radioactive emissions from objects), slavick's practice also includes cyanotypes (natural sun exposures on cotton paper impregnated with cyanide salts), frottages (rubbings), and subsequent contact prints from the frottages, as well as traditional photography.

26. elin o'Hara slavick, "Hiroshima: After Aftermath," *Critical Asian Studies* 41, no. 2 (2009): 313, https://doi.org/10.1080/14672710902809443.

Chapter Six

1. Ghassan Kanafani, *Men in the Sun & Other Palestinian Stories* (Boulder, CO: Lynne Rienner, 1999).

2. Jen Bagelman has written about the systematization of delay in the lives of migrants and asylum seekers. Delay, she argues, is not a failure of the asylum system, but part of the sovereign

violence it inflicts. Jennifer J. Bagelman, *Sanctuary City: A Suspended State*, Mobility & Politics (New York: Palgrave Macmillan, 2016).

3. Margaroni, "Care and Abandonment," 35; the reference is to Agamben, *Homo Sacer*.

4. This was not a unique event. The bodies of fifty-eight people, also Chinese, were found suffocated to death in a Dutch lorry container at Dover, Kent, in 2000. They died during the eighteen-hour journey from Zeebrugge in Belgium.

5. Chaim Levinson, "How Israeli Negligence Led to the Death of a Palestinian Car Thief," *Haaretz*, 17 February 2012, http://www.haaretz.co.il/news/politics/1.1643974.

6. Chaim Levinson, "Court Verdict on Israeli Cops Who Let Injured Palestinian Die Full of Errors," *Haaretz*, 2 March 2014, http://www.haaretz.com/news/national/.premium-1.577368.

7. Yoram Noam, Karmi Mosek, and Moshe Bar-Am, Criminal Appeal 272 44-08-12 Baruch Peretz & Asaf Yekutieli v. Israel Police Internal Investigation Department (Jerusalem District Court, 24 February 2014).

8. Ariella Azoulay, "Citizens of Disaster," *Qui Parle* 15, no. 2 (2005): 105–37.

9. Alon Idan, "Tens of Pixels of Indifference," *Haaretz.com*, 8 May 2012, http://www.haaretz.co.il/news/politics/1.1702532.

10. Quoted in Levinson, "Court Verdict on Israeli Cops."

11. Any reference to deadly banality necessarily conjures Hannah Arendt's observations from the Eichmann Trial. It is well beyond the scope of this book to fully chart the relation between the banality that Arendt identifies in the actions of Nazi bureaucrats and uncaring, but it is perhaps worthwhile making two brief remarks. First, in his trial testimony and in his interview with Willem Sassen, Eichmann insisted he "did not greet his assignment with the apathy of an ox being led to his stall." He was, by his own admission, very different from those colleagues "who had never read a basic book [i.e., Herzl's *Der Judenstaat*], worked through it, absorbed it, absorbed it with interest," and who therefore lacked "inner rapport with their work." Despite the argument of his defense attorney, Eichmann refused to see himself as merely a small cog in the Nazi machine. He cared about his work. His actions were banal in the sense that his care never attained, in Arendt's words, "a faculty of judgement, which rules out blind obedience." Second, and this is a point I made earlier, Eichmann was part of a regime that turned care into a central pillar of a genocidal plan. Nazi concentration and death camps weaponized care to as yet unimaginable degrees: the Nazis were a necropolitical machine that sought to extract as much value as possible from its subjects—documenting and then taking property, labor, knowledge, and biophysical information—before seeking their extermination. On both accounts, the caring banality of bureaucratic evil is distinct from the uncaring I try to contend with here. Hannah Arendt, *Eichmann in Jerusalem: A Report on the Banality of Evil* (New York: Penguin Books, 2006).

12. Stevenson, *Life beside Itself*, 7. On the consequences of neoliberal health-care management in a different context, though with equally catastrophic consequences, see Biehl, *Vita*.

13. Michel Foucault, *"Society Must Be Defended": Lectures at the Collège de France, 1975–76*, ed. Mauro Bertani and Alessandro Fontana (New York: Picador, 2003). We should distinguish this act of "letting die" with extrajudicial killings or the prevention of medical aid that have become part of militarized practice of governing life. The latter are, fundamentally, punitive. Care, in other words, has been weaponized. Letting die, as considered here, is outside this calculative logic.

14. Muhammad Fu'ad Abu Zayd, *Heartbeats in Marj al-Zuhur* [*Nabaḍāt qalb fī Marj al-Zuhūr*] (Beirut: Dār al-Rashād al-Islāmīyah, 1993), 12–13, translated by Emily Drumsta.

15. Emily Drumsta and Keith P. Feldman, "We Deportees: Race, Religion, and War on

Palestine's No-Man's-Land," *Social Text* 34, no. 4 (129) (2016): 96, https://doi.org/10.1215/0164 2472-3680882.

16. Haim Weiss, interview with the author, Jerusalem, 25 April 2014.

17. Drumsta and Feldman, "We Deportees," 98.

18. The deportation took place five years after the outbreak of the first Palestinian uprising, or Intifada, in 1987. This popular, largely unarmed resistance shaped Palestinian politics throughout the 1990s, launching a new generation of political leaders and deeply politicized all spheres of Palestinian life, from education to urban practice. Eitan Alimi, *Israeli Politics and the First Palestinian Intifada: Political Opportunities, Framing Processes and Contentious Politics* (London: Routledge, 2007); Iris Jean-Klein, "Nationalism and Resistance: The Two Faces of Everyday Activism in Palestine during the Intifada," *Cultural Anthropology* 16, no. 1 (2001): 83–126.

19. In their excellent article on the camp, Drumsta and Feldman point to different ways it reflects back on the realities of occupation, its territorial and political logics. They extend and substantiate the point made more briefly by Agamben that I quote earlier in the opening of part 2. No man's land is always, however, inseparable from the logics of the Israeli regime of occupation. The discussion here asks not so much about the ways the camp embodies these logics (which it does), but about what can we learn about no man's land as a specific spatial configuration in and of itself, not solely through its relational qualities. Drumsta and Feldman, "We Deportees."

20. Jean-Luc Nancy, *The Inoperative Community*, Theory and History of Literature 76 (Minneapolis: University of Minnesota Press, 1990), xxxvii.

21. Grant Farred, "Disorderly Democracy: An Axiomatic Politics," *CR: The New Centennial Review* 8, no. 2 (2008): 44.

22. Taylor Carman, *Merleau-Ponty* (London: Routledge, 2008). See also Catherine Mills, *Biopolitics* (New York: Routledge, 2017). Considering exposure from a feminist perspective in the face of radical environmental change, Alaimo offers a similar ethical and political orientation. See Stacy Alaimo, *Exposed: Environmental Politics and Pleasures in Posthuman Times* (Minneapolis: University of Minnesota Press, 2016), https://doi.org/10.5749/j.ctt1g04zkp.

23. Alexander Weheliye, *Habeas Viscus: Racialising Assemblages, Biopolitics, Black Feminist Theories of the Human* (Durham, NC: Duke University Press, 2014), 43.

Chapter Seven

1. I owe this wonderful formulation to Harriet Murav and her generous correspondence with me. She follows this observation in the moving and conceptually urgent *As the Dust of the Earth: The Literature of Abandonment in Revolutionary Russia and Ukraine* (Bloomington: Indiana University Press, 2024).

2. I draw on Agamben's discussion of potentiality, specifically because it recognizes both the more obvious sense of potentiality as capacity, but also the inescapable exposure and vulnerability. Giorgio Agamben, *Potentialities: Collected Essays in Philosophy* (Stanford, CA: Stanford University Press, 1998), 178.

3. Occupy Buffer Zone, "Our Cultural Center" leaflet, January 2012.

4. Olga Demetriou and Murat Erdal Ilican, "A Peace of Bricks and Mortar: Thinking Ceasefire Landscapes with Gramsci," *International Journal of Heritage Studies* 25, no. 9 (2019): 909. https://doi.org/10.1080/13527258.2017.1413673.

5. Ilican, interview with the author, 3 June 2019.

6. In her forthcoming book *Wounded Cities*, Karen Till develops the notion of a place-based

ethics of care more extensively, specifically in the context of memory work. For an outline of her argument, see Till, *Wounded Cities*.

7. Restrictions on movement along the ceasefire line were removed in 2003, but it took another five years of additional negotiations to open this central crossing.

8. Occupy Buffer Zone, "Greetings from the Buffer Zone," January 2012.

9. Murat Erdal Ilican, "The Occupy Buffer Zone Movement: Radicalism and Sovereignty in Cyprus," *Cyprus Review* 25, no. 1 (2013): 68.

10. Rebecca Bryant and Mete Hatay, *Sovereignty Suspended: Political Life in a So-Called State* (Philadelphia: University of Pennsylvania Press, 2020).

11. Slavoj Žižek, *The Sublime Object of Ideology* (London: Verso, 1989), 198.

12. Ilican, "The Occupy Buffer Zone Movement: Radicalism and Sovereignty in Cyprus," 66. In an interview with the *Cyprus Mail*, UN Peacekeeping Force in Cyprus spokesperson Michel Bonnardeaux expressed the United Nations' difficulty in forming a coherent response: "We continue to say they are unauthorised . . . but we sympathise with their goal. We are not the target, and we continue to tolerate and monitor their presence." Patrick Dewhurst, "A Buffer Zone Tent Protest of Many Gripes," *Cyprus Mail*, 18 December 2011, www.cypriot.org.uk/Documents /Haber%2011/27-Kasim.htm.

13. I rely here on Ilican's tally.

14. Foucault, " 'Omnes et Singulatim,' " 301.

15. In the following years, authorities placed steel gates around the crossing, and boarded up some of the buildings that were used by protestors.

16. Adriana Kemp, "Border Space and National Identity in Israel," in *Space, Land, Home* [*Merhav, Adamah, Bayit*], ed. Yehouda A. Shenhav (Jerusalem: Van Leer Jerusalem Institute; Tel Aviv: Hakibbutz Hameuchad Publishers, 2003), 60.

17. Yoram Tamir, *Instruction Material Guidebook: Jerusalem, a Divided City Reunited* [*Hoveret Mekorot Hadracha: Yerusalem Ir Hatzuya she-Hubra La Yahdav*] (Jerusalem: Turjeman Post Museum, 1996), 76.

18. Ben Gad, "The City Line in Jerusalem," 24.

19. Reuven Abergel, interview with the author, audio recording, March 25, 2019.

20. Kemp, "Border Space and National Identity." Other neighborhoods on the cusp of no man's land also offered refuge for those seeking to escape the transit camps. See, e.g., Dvora Hacohen, *Immigrants in Turmoil: Mass Immigration to Israel and Its Repercussions in the 1950s and After* (Syracuse, NY: Syracuse University Press, 2003), 225–26; Reuven Gafni, "Life in the 'Blood Field': Jews, Arabs and Jews Again in Jerusalem's Shma'a Neighbourhood (Sha'ary Zion) 1900– 1970," *Kathedra* 161 (October 2016), https://www.ybz.org.il/_Uploads/dbsArticles/Gafni.pdf.

21. Yehoshua Ben-Arieh and Eliyahu Vager, "Stages in the Development of Israeli Jerusalem between the Years 1948–1967," in *Divided Jerusalem 1948–1967: Sources, Summaries, Key Issues and Aids* [*Yerushalayim ha-ḥatsuyah, 1948–1967*], ed. Avi Bareli, Idan 18 (Jerusalem: Yad Izhak Ben-Zvi, 1994), 94.

22. This process is extensively documented and is well beyond the scope of this book to fully account for. I have dealt with this process in my 2016 book, *Life after Ruin: The Struggles over Israel's Depopulated Arab Spaces*, Cambridge Middle East Studies 48 (Cambridge: Cambridge University Press, 2017); Arnon Golan, "Jewish Settlement of Former Arab Towns and Their Incorporation into the Israeli Urban System (1948–50)," *Israel Affairs* 9, nos. 1–2 (2003): 149–64.

23. Arnon Golan, "Refugees, Immigrants, Abandoned Neighbourhoods: Designing the Urban System of Jewish Jerusalem in the War of Independence and its Aftermath," in *Divided*

Jerusalem 1948–1967: Sources, Summaries, Key Issues and Aids [*Yerushalayim ha-ḥatsuyah, 1948–1967*], ed. Avi Bareli, Idan 18 (Jerusalem: Yad Izhak Ben-Zvi, 1994), 69–90.

24. Abergel interview, 25 March 2019.

25. Anne-Marie Angelo, "'Any Name That Has Power': The Black Panthers of Israel, the United Kingdom, and the United States, 1948–1977" (PhD diss., Duke University, 2013), https://dukespace.lib.duke.edu/dspace/handle/10161/7264.

26. On racial stratification, see Jen Bagelman and Sarah Marie Wiebe, "Intimacies of Global Toxins: Exposure & Resistance in 'Chemical Valley,'" *Political Geography* 60 (1 September 2017): 76–85, https://doi.org/10.1016/j.polgeo.2017.04.007. On neoliberal privatization, see David Harvey, "The 'New' Imperialism: Accumulation by Dispossession," *Socialist Register* 40 (19 March 2009): 63–87; Saskia Sassen, *Expulsions: Brutality and Complexity in the Global Economy* (Cambridge, MA: Belknap Press of Harvard University Press, 2014); Petryna, *Life Exposed*; Guy Standing, *The Precariat: The New Dangerous Class* (London: Bloomsbury, 2014); Povinelli, *Economies of Abandonment*. On extreme conditions of genocidal violence, see Agamben, *Homo Sacer*; Esposito, *Bíos*.

27. Abergel interview, 25 March 2019.

28. Amiram Gonen, "Widespread and Diverse Neighborhood Gentrification in Jerusalem," *Political Geography* 21, no. 5 (2002): 727–37, https://doi.org/10.1016/S0962-6298(02)00018-5; Shlomo Hasson, *Urban Social Movements in Jerusalem: The Protest of the Second Generation*, SUNY Series in Israeli Studies (Albany: State University of New York Press, 1993).

29. Deborah Bernstein, "Conflict and Protest in Israeli Society: The Case of the Black Panthers of Israel," *Youth and Society* 16, no. 2 (1984): 129–52.

30. Sami Shalom Chetrit, *Intra-Jewish Conflict in Israel: White Jews, Black Jews* (London: Routledge, 2009); Yehouda Shenhav, *The Arab Jews: A Postcolonial Reading of Nationalism, Religion, and Ethnicity* (Stanford, CA: Stanford University Press, 2006). For a transnational perspective on the Black Panther Movement and its Israeli iteration, see Anne-Marie Angelo, *Black Power on the Move: Migration, Internationalism, and the British and Israeli Black Panthers* (Chapel Hill: University of North Carolina Press, 2021).

31. Chetrit, *Intra-Jewish Conflict in Israel*; Bernstein, "Conflict and Protest in Israeli Society."

32. Quoted in Chetrit, *Intra-Jewish Conflict in Israel*, 121.

33. Gil Anidjar, *The Jew, the Arab: A History of the Enemy* (Stanford, CA: Stanford University Press, 2003); Oren Yiftachel, *Ethnocracy: Land and Identity Politics in Israel Palestine* (Philadelphia: University of Pennsylvania Press, 2006). See also Shenhav, *The Arab Jews*; Hubert Law Yone and Rachel Kallus, "The Dynamics of Ethnic Segregation in Israel," in *The Power of Planning: Spaces of Control and Transformation*, ed. Oren Yiftachel, Geojournal Library 67 (Dordrecht, Netherlands: Kluwer Academic, 2001), 171–88; Oren Yiftachel, "The Consequences of Planning Control: Mizrahi Jews in Israel's 'Development Towns,'" in *The Power of Planning: Spaces of Control and Transformation*, ed. Oren Yiftachel et al., Geojournal Library 67 (Dordrecht, Netherlands: Kluwer Academic, 2001), 117–34.

34. This was part of an artistic event organized for two years by members of the Muslala art collective, who were trying to reconstruct the watermelon shack as a place for contemporary encounter between Jews and Arabs. For a critical review of this effort, see Meirav Aharon-Gutman, "Art's Failure to Generate Urban Renewal: Lessons from Jerusalem," *Urban Studies* 55, no. 15 (2018): 3474–91, https://doi.org/10.1177/0042098017743682.

35. W. E. B. Du Bois, *Souls of Black Folks* (New York: Dover, 1994).

36. I draw here on the work of Ella Shohat and the analysis that Yehouda Shenhav and

Hannan Hever develop around the concept of the Arab Jew and the political possibility of link-ing the two under the Zionist insistence to set the two as mutually exclusive. See Ella Shohat, "Columbus, Palestine and Arab Jews," in *Cultural Readings of Imperialism: Edward Said and the Gravity of History*, ed. Keith Ansell-Pearson, Benita Parry, and Judith Squires (New York: St. Mar-tin's Press, 1997), 88–105, http://archive.org/details/culturalreadings00keit; Ella Shohat, "Reflec-tions of an Arab Jew," *Against the Current* 18 (2003): 13–14; Yehouda Shenhav and Hannan Hever, "'Arab Jews' after Structuralism: Zionist Discourse and the (De)Formation of an Ethnic Identity," *Social Identities* 18, no. 1 (2012): 101–18, https://doi.org/10.1080/13504630.2011.629517. Thinking this hyphenation through the concrete space of the no man's land situates this conceptual work in the concrete space of the no man's land but also helps historicize specific moments through which this hyphenation was made possible.

37. Israel used the route of the no man's land to first pave a multilane road and later for the route of the city's light rail. These projects linked the city center with Israeli settlements that were built in the north of the city on areas occupied in 1967. See, e.g., Wendy Pullan et al., "Je-rusalem's Road 1," *City: Analysis of Urban Trends, Culture, Theory, Policy, Action* 11, no. 2 (2007): 176–98, https://doi.org/10.1080/13604810701395993; Amina Nolte, "Political Infrastructure and the Politics of Infrastructure," *City* 20, no. 3 (2016): 441–54, https://doi.org/10.1080/13604813 .2016.1169778.

38. The story was first published in the periodical *Al-Jadid* in Haifa in March 1954 and ap-peared later in Habibi's short-story collection *Sudasiyyat al-Ayyam al-Sittah* (The hexad of the six days) in 1970. All excerpts are from the English translation by Stacy N. Beckwith.

39. Emile Habibi, "Mandelbaum Gate," trans. Stacy N. Beckwith, *Short Story Project*, August 1999, https://shortstoryproject.com/stories/mandelbaum-gate/.

40. Hunaida Ghanim, "On the Shadow and Its Shadows," in *Men in Sun*, ed. Tal Ben-Tzvi and Hana Farah (Herzliya, Israel: Herzliya Museum of Contemporary Art, 2009).

41. James Baldwin, *Jimmy's Blues and Other Poems* (Boston: Beacon Press, 2014), 32.

42. Inbar Perlson, *Great Joy Tonight: Arab-Jewish Music and Mizrahi Identity* [*Simha gdola halayla*] (Tel Aviv: Resling, 2006); Motti Regev, "Present Absentee: Arab Music in Israeli Culture," *Public Culture* 7, no. 2 (1995): 433–45, https://doi.org/10.1215/08992363-7-2-433.

Chapter Eight

1. Mishka Henner, interview with the author, 22 October 2018.

2. Christopher Bucklow, "Et in Arcadia Ego: Mishka Henner's 'No Man's Land,'" in *Deutsche Bank Prize Catalogue* (London, 2013).

3. Henner interview.

4. The extent to which the Great War actually altered masculinity is a subject of a long de-bate. A good, though slightly dated, review of this can be found in Lesley A. Hall, "Impotent Ghosts from No Man's Land, Flappers' Boyfriends, or Cryptopatriarchs? Men, Sex and Social Change in 1920s Britain," *Social History* 21, no. 1 (1996): 54–70. Joanna Bourke's brilliant, *Dis-membering the Male: Men's Bodies, Britain and the Great War*, Picturing History (London: Reak-tion Books, 1996) offers an important analysis of the cultural disintegration of the masculine figure and attempts to reconstruct it in the face of the war's devastating effects. Richard Evans offers another important review of changes to masculinity brought about by World War I in "The European Family and the Great War," *Social History* 16, no. 3 (1991): 341–52, https://doi.org /10.1080/03071029108567812.

5. Geraldine Pratt highlights important gendered and racial dimensions that are often lost in conditions of legal abandonment. Another important work in this corpus is Hosna Shewly's analysis of communities living in border enclaves between India and Bangladesh. What I am pointing to here exceeds this important critique, simply because the very legal structures that produce biopolitical abandonment are no longer in place. See Pratt, "Abandoned Women and Spaces of the Exception"; Hosna J. Shewly, "Abandoned Spaces and Bare Life in the Enclaves of the India-Bangladesh Border," *Political Geography* 32 (January 2013): 23–31, https://doi.org /10.1016/j.polgeo.2012.10.007.

6. Doreen Massey, *For Space* (London: Sage, 2005), 9.

7. Michael Taussig, *Shamanism, Colonialism, and the Wild Man: A Study in Terror and Healing* (Chicago: University of Chicago Press, 1987).

8. Gonzalo, interview with the author, La Cooperativa, Meta, Colombia, 26 September 2017.

9. Consuela, interview with the author, La Cooperativa, Meta, Colombia, 26 September 2017.

10. *Línea* refers to a regional transport service operated usually in offroad vehicles that can withstand the rugged unpaved roads.

11. I follow a small but important group of scholars who have begun this effort. João Biehl, for example, draws attention to urban sites that house the social outcasts of contemporary Brazil. Biehl refers to such places as "zones of social abandonment," that is, places that lack medical and governmental attention and are ultimately treated as "dump" sites for the ill, the impoverished, the mentally challenged, the jobless, and the homeless. This stark exploration of social abandonment stands out because it does not assume that abandonment is self-explanatory; instead, it situates this condition in concrete social-historical contexts and spatial forms. Biehl, *Vita*.

12. María Clemencia Ramírez, *Between the Guerrillas and the State: The Cocalero Movement, Citizenship, and Identity in the Colombian Amazon* (Durham, NC: Duke University Press, 2011), https://doi.org/10.1215/9780822394204.

13. Leshem, *Life after Ruin*. Kathleen Stewart's enchanting ethnography of Appalachia has long inspired my research into these seemingly overlooked spaces and the histories they document: *A Space on the Side of the Road: Cultural Poetics in an "Other" America* (Princeton, NJ: Princeton University Press, 1996). Eyal Weizman's work on forensic architectures has taken this concern in a different direction, working in a legal, political, and scientific discourse of evidence and proof. The ruins he and his team are concerned with are also rather more spectacular. See Eyal Weizman, *Forensic Architecture: Violence at the Threshold of Detectability* (New York: Zone Books, 2019).

14. I think of fragments here and elsewhere in this book as both material debris and as a textual form. Holding materiality and textuality in tension produces a more nuanced understanding of fragments. Anne Stoler points at a similar analytical direction in her work on imperial debris. See Ann Laura Stoler, "Imperial Debris: Reflections on Ruins and Ruination," *Cultural Anthropology* 23, no. 2 (2008): 191–219; Leshem, *Life after Ruin*. Others have traced the politically rich materiality of ruined fragments. See Gastón Gordillo, *Rubble: The Afterlife of Destruction* (Durham, NC: Duke University Press, 2014). In thinking through fragments, I'm extremely indebted to Colin McFarlane's work and our conversations on the intersections between our mutual curiosities. Colin McFarlane, *Fragments of the City: Making and Remaking Urban Worlds* (Oakland: University of California Press, 2021).

15. Most commonly, FARC guerrillas have used Russian AK-47 assault rifles. The issue rifles in the Colombian Armed Forces, meanwhile, are the local version of the Israeli Galil and of the Galil ACE, in the 5.56 × 45 mm caliber, produced under license following an agreement signed in

1995 with then Israel Military Industries weapons division, now Israel Weapons Industries. David Oliver and Paolo Valpolini, "The Colombian Military-Industrial Complex," *EDR Magazine*, 28 January 2018, https://www.edrmagazine.eu/the-colombian-military-industrial-complex-2.

16. A popular folk music genre in Colombia, *vallenato* originates from Colombia's Caribbean region but is not hard to come by across the central plains and Western regions of the Amazonian basin. The music migrated into the region with people fleeing violence or searching for work in the booming coca fields of the 1990s and early 2000s.

17. Gonzalo, interview with the author, La Cooperativa, Meta, Colombia, 26 September 2017.

18. Consuelo Herrera, interview with the author, Vista Hermosa, Meta, Colombia, 21 September 2017.

19. This has been the focus of much feminist critique in recent decades. Rachel Pain's work in particular has sought to both draw attention to the geography of violent conflict, and to challenge the hierarchies that continue to situate it beyond (and as inferior to) the political and geopolitical domains. Rachel Pain, "Everyday Terrorism: Connecting Domestic Violence and Global Terrorism," *Progress in Human Geography* 38, no. 4 (2014): 531–50; Rachel Pain, "Intimate War," *Political Geography* 44 (2015): 64–73.

20. Nayanika Mookherjee, *The Spectral Wound: Sexual Violence, Public Memories, and the Bangladesh War of 1971* (Durham, NC: Duke University Press, 2015), 68.

21. Mookherjee, 69.

22. Ana Arjona, *Rebelocracy: Social Order in the Colombian Civil War* (Cambridge: Cambridge University Press, 2016), 28, https://doi.org/10.1017/9781316421925.

23. Office of the UN High Commissioner for Human Rights, "Report of the United Nations High Commissioner for Human Rights on the Human Rights Situation in Colombia" (UN Economic and Social Council, 28 February 2002), https://documents-dds-ny.un.org/doc/UNDOC /GEN/G02/111/15/PDF/G0211115.pdf?OpenElement; Amnesty International, "Colombia: 'Scarred Bodies, Hidden Crimes': Sexual Violence against Women in the Armed Conflict" (London: Amnesty International, 13 October 2004), 50, https://www.amnesty.org/download/Documents/92000 /amr230402004en.pdf.

24. After all, as Foucault notes, biopower is a power "that endeavors to administer, optimize, and multiply [life], subjecting it to precise controls and comprehensive regulations." Michel Foucault, *The History of Sexuality*, trans. Robert Hurley (New York: Pantheon, 1978), 1:139.

25. Arjona, *Rebelocracy*, 185; Ana Arjona, "Civilian Resistance to Rebel Governance," in *Rebel Governance in Civil War*, ed. Ana Arjona, Nelson Kasfir, and Zachariah Mampilly (Cambridge: Cambridge University Press, 2015), 193.

26. For a good summary of military prostitution and its contemporary histories, see Sheila Jeffreys, *The Industrial Vagina: The Political Economy of the Global Sex Trade* (London: Routledge, 2008).

27. Sara Meger, *Rape Loot Pillage: The Political Economy of Sexual Violence in Armed Conflict*, Oxford Studies in Gender and International Relations (Oxford: Oxford University Press, 2016).

28. Arelis and Paisa, interview with the author, September 2019.

29. In Colombia, the use of complicity as a political weapon has a long and well documented history that was specifically wielded against peasant communities in the Amazon region. See, e.g., Taussig, *Shamanism, Colonialism, and the Wild Man*; Ramírez, *Between the Guerrillas and the State*; Erika Rodríguez Pinzón, "Los cambios discursivos sobre el conflicto colombiano en la posguerra fría: Su impacto en la actuación de los actores locales," in *Geopolítica, guerras y resistencias*, ed. Heriberto Cairo and Jaime Pastor (Bogotá: Trama Editorial, 2006), 67–82. For the

emergence of complicity in political struggles within territories abandoned by the Colombian state, see Arjona, *Rebelocracy*, ch. 7.

30. Fiona Probyn-Rapsey, "Complicity, Critique and Methodology," *ARIEL* 38, nos. 2–3 (2007): 68.

31. Christopher Kutz, *Complicity: Ethics and Law for a Collective Age*, Cambridge Studies in Philosophy and Law (Cambridge: Cambridge University Press, 2000), 259.

32. Mark Sanders, *Complicities: The Intellectual and Apartheid* (Durham, NC: Duke University Press, 2003), 3–4.

33. Sanders, 4.

34. Luis Eduardo Fernández Molinares, "Vivir bajo sospecha: Estudios de caso: Personas LGBT víctimas del conflicto armado en Vistahermosa y San Onofre" (Bogotá: Colombia Diversa, May 2017), http://www.colombiadiversa.org/conflictoarmado-lgbt/documentos/vivir%20baja%20sospecha.pdf.

35. The account here is largely based on Colombia Diversa's report and on additional conversations with Luis Fernández, a lawyer working with the organization. Molinares, 38–48.

36. Verónica suffered memory loss following complications from a failed medical procedure. Colombia Diversa researchers verified her information with Jenny and others. See Molinares, 39.

37. The alias of Bertulfo Caicedo Garzón, commander of the FARC's Twenty-Seventh Front.

38. Molinares, "Vivir bajo sospecha," 40.

39. Amnesty International, "Annual Report: Colombia," 2001, 1, https://www.refworld.org/pdfid/3b1de3734.pdf; James M. Shultz et al., "Internal Displacement in Colombia," *Disaster Health* 2, no. 1 (2014): 13–24, https://doi.org/10.4161/dish.27885.

40. In her work on gendered violence in Latin America, Maria Gómez develops a broader definition for prejudice- based violence that does not always fall under the strict legal definition of hate crimes. See María Mercedes Gómez, "Prejudice-Based Violence," in *Gender and Sexuality in Latin America—Cases and Decisions*, ed. Cristina Motta and Macarena Sáez, Ius Gentium: Comparative Perspectives on Law and Justice (Dordrecht: Springer Netherlands, 2013), 279–323, https://doi.org/10.1007/978-94-007-6199-5_8.

41. Interview with Luis Fernández by Laura Castrillano, telephone, 4 May 2020.

42. Boaz Cohen, *Jewish and Roman Law: A Comparative Study* (New York: Jewish Theological Seminary of America, 1966); Aharon Shemesh and Moshe Halbertal, "The Me'un (Refusal): The Complex History of Halakhic Anomaly," *Tarbitz* 82, no. 3 (2014): 377–94.

43. Shemesh and Halbertal, "The Me'un (Refusal): The Complex History of Halakhic Anomaly," 391.

Part Four

1. Paul Fussell, *The Great War and Modern Memory* (Oxford: Oxford University Press, 2013), 132.

2. James Deutsch, "The Legend of What Actually Lived in the 'No Man's Land' between World War I's Trenches," *Smithsonian Magazine*, 8 September 2014, https://www.smithsonianmag.com/history/legends-what-actually-lived-no-mans-land-between-world-war-i-trenches-180952513/.

3. Ardern Arthur Hulme Beaman, *The Squadroon* (London: John Lane, 1920), 186–87, http://archive.org/details/squadroon00beam.

4. James Carroll, "Angels of War," *New York Times*, 10 July 2006, https://www.nytimes.com/2006/07/10/opinion/10iht-edcarroll.2161399.html.

5. Fussell, *The Great War and Modern Memory*, 134.

6. Osbert Sitwell, *Laughter in the Next Room* (London: Macmillan, 1975), 6.

7. Jacqueline Rose, *States of Fantasy* (Oxford: Oxford University Press, 1998), 5, http://www.oxfordscholarship.com/view/10.1093/acprof:oso/9780198183273.001.0001/acprof-9780198183273.

8. Leed, *No Man's Land*, 118.

9. Edward Said, *Orientalism* (New York: Pantheon Books, 1978), 6.

10. Rose, *States of Fantasy*, 5.

11. Donald E. Pease, *The New American Exceptionalism* (Minneapolis: University of Minnesota Press, 2009), 6.

12. Hakim Bey, *T.A.Z.: The Temporary Autonomous Zone, Ontological Anarchy, Poetic Terrorism*, 2nd ed. (New York: Autonomedia, 2003), 95.

Chapter Nine

1. For an excellent English summary, see Daniel Ruiz-Serna, "Enchanted Forests, Entangled Lives: Spirits, Peasant Economies, and Violence in Northwest Amazonia" (master's thesis, McGill University, 2013). See also Víctor Oppenheim, "Geología de la Cordillera Oriental, entre Los Llanos y el Magdalena," *Revista de la Academia Colombiana de Ciencias* 4, no. 14 (1941): 175–81; J. Hernández Camacho, "Una síntesis de la historia evolutiva de la biodiversidad en Colombia," in *Nuestra Diversidad Biológica*, ed. Sonia Cárdenas and Darío Correa (Bogotá: CEREC and Fundación Alejandro Ángel Escobar, 1993), http://agris.fao.org/agris-search/search.do?recordID=CO1999000352; Antonio Olivares and Theobaldo Mozo, *Reserva National de La Macarena* (Bogotá: Universidad Nacional de Colombia and Instituto Colombiano de la Reforma Agraria, 1968).

2. Isaías Sánchez Castaño, interview with the author, Meta, Colombia, September 2017.

3. See, e.g., Sebastián Gómez Zúñiga, "La ecología política de las FARC-EP: Un análisis de las territorialidades, prácticas y discursos de la insurgencia frente a la naturaleza" (Bogotá, Pontificia Universidad Javeriana, Facultad de Ciencias Sociales, 2018).

4. Miro Carmona, interview with the author, La Macarena, Meta, Colombia, 12 September 2017.

5. James C. Scott, *The Art of Not Being Governed: An Anarchist History of Upland Southeast Asia*, Yale Agrarian Studies Series (New Haven, CT: Yale University Press, 2009).

6. Scott, 23.

7. Silvia Espelt-Bombin, "Makers and Keepers of Networks: Amerindian Spaces, Migrations, and Exchanges in the Brazilian Amazon and French Guiana, 1600–1730," *Ethnohistory* 65, no. 4 (2018): 599, https://doi.org/10.1215/00141801-6991253.

8. Michael Taussig, *I Swear I Saw This: Drawings in Fieldwork Notebooks, Namely My Own* (Chicago: University of Chicago Press, 2011), 3.

9. W. R. Philipson, C. C. Doncaster, and J. M. Idrobo, "An Expedition to the Sierra de La Macarena, Colombia," *Geographical Journal* 117, no. 2 (1951): 188–99, https://doi.org/10.2307/1791656.

10. Alfredo Molano, "Aproximación al proceso de colonización de la región del Agri-Güejar-Guayabero," in *La Macarena: Reserva biológica de la humanidad: Territorio de conflictos*, by Fernando Cubides et al. (Bogotá: Centro Editorial, Centro de Estudios Sociales, Facultad de Ciencias Humanas, Universidad Nacional de Colombia, 1989).

11. Michael Watts, "Petro-Violence: Community, Extraction and Political Ecology of a Mythic Commodity," in *Violent Environments*, ed. Nancy Lee Peluso and Michael Watts (Ithaca, NY: Cornell University Press, 2001), 189–212.

12. Juan Pablo Tobal, "El último tinigua," *Semana*, 20 April 2013, https://www.semana.com /especiales/articulo/el-ultimo-tinigua/340475-3.

13. Leal, *A la buena de Dios*, 36–37.

14. Pablo Stevenson, interview with the author, Los Andes University, Bogotá, 12 September 2017.

15. Stevenson interview.

16. Marco Palacios, *Violencia pública en Colombia, 1958–2010* (Bogotá: Fondo de Cultura Económica, 2012), 26, emphasis added.

17. Leal, *A la buena de Dios*, 39.

18. David Levi Strauss, "The Magic of the State: An Interview with Michael Taussig," *Cabinet*, Summer 2005, http://cabinetmagazine.org/issues/18/strauss_taussig.php.

19. Michael Taussig, *The Magic of the State* (New York: Routledge, 1997), 125.

20. Thomas Hobbes, *Leviathan*, Online Library of Liberty (Oxford, UK: Clarendon Press, 1909), 106, http://socserv2.socsci.mcmaster.ca/econ/ugcm/3ll3/hobbes/Leviathan.pdf.

21. For Hobbes, the Leviathan fulfills its obligations toward its subjects "not by care applied to individuals, further than their protection from injuries when they shall complain; but by a general providence, contained in public instruction, both of doctrine and example; and in the making and executing of good laws to which individual persons may apply their own cases." Hobbes, 205–6.

22. Although as Magnus Kristiansson and Johan Tralau note, a close analysis reveals scenes of war in numerous details of the Leviathan frontispiece. Magnus Kristiansson and Johan Tralau, "Hobbes's Hidden Monster: A New Interpretation of the Frontispiece of *Leviathan*," *European Journal of Political Theory* 13, no. 3 (2014): 299–320, https://doi.org/10.1177/14748851 13491954.

23. *Savage* appears as *salvage* in the original English edition. Thomas Hobbes, *De Cive: The English Version*, ed. Howard Warrender, Clarendon Edition of the Philosophical Works of Thomas Hobbes (Oxford: Clarendon, 1984), 2:116, emphasis added.

24. Robert Lee Nichols, "Realizing the Social Contract: The Case of Colonialism and Indigenous Peoples," *Contemporary Political Theory* 4, no. 1 (2005): 46.

25. Catherine C. LeGrand, *Frontier Expansion and Peasant Protest in Colombia, 1850–1936* (Albuquerque: University of New Mexico Press, 1986); Leal, *A la buena de Dios*.

26. Daniel García-Peña, interview with the author, 8 November 2019.

27. Margarita Serje, "Iron Maiden Landscapes: The Geopolitics of Colombia's Territorial Conquest," trans. Ashley Caja et al., *South Central Review* 24, no. 1 (2007): 39.

28. Jeffrey Jerome Cohen, *Monster Theory: Reading Culture* (Minneapolis: University of Minnesota Press, 1996), 4.

29. The ability to elide rigid categorizations—clearly setting apart violent chaos from peaceful Eden—is itself a quality of the monster. Cohen, 6–7.

Chapter Ten

1. Clive Gabay, *Imagining Africa: Whiteness and the Western Gaze*, 1st ed. (Cambridge: Cambridge University Press, 2018), 10, https://doi.org/10.1017/9781108652582. Throughout the

chapter, I draw on Gabay's distinction of Whiteness (capitalized) from phenotypical forms of "being white." See Gabay, 17.

2. See, e.g., Siba N. Grovogui, "Regimes of Sovereignty: International Morality and the African Condition," *European Journal of International Relations* 8, no. 3 (2002): 315–38; Oliver Jütersonke and Moncef Kartas, "The State as Urban Myth: Governance without Government in the Global South," in *The Concept of the State in International Relations*, ed. Robert Schuett and Peter M. R. Stirk (Edinburgh University Press, 2015), 108–34, https://doi.org/10.3366/edinburgh /9780748693627.003.0005.

3. Ruth Frankenberg, *White Women, Race Matters: The Social Construction of Whiteness*, Gender, Racism, Ethnicity (London: Routledge, 1993).

4. Dmitry Zhikharev, interview with the author, 8 October 2018.

5. Zhikharev interview.

6. The recording can be heard at https://dx-world.net/operations-at-1u4un/.

7. See, for example, some of the reactions on this shortwave radio operators' discussion board at https://www.eham.net/ehamforum/smf/index.php/topic,119789.0/prev_next,prev.html#new.

8. Zhikharev interview.

9. Dmitry Zhikharev, "Trademarks, Service Marks and Appellations of Origin: Bir Tawil," Federal Service of Intellectual Property 618850, Moscow, filed November 9, 2015, and issued June 5, 2017, http://www1.fips.ru/fips_servl/fips_servlet?DB=RUTM&rn=5533&DocNumber=618850&TypeFile=html.

10. Ronkainen and Zhikharev met during a visit in North Korea and formed a long friendship. They have since traveled extensively together.

11. The composition conjures Joe Rosenthal's iconic image of the flag hoisting at Iwo Jima.

12. The firm, Art.Lebedev, has some experience in rebranding murky territories. A recent commission involved a design for the Ossetian Tourist Board. The southern part of the region, which is internationally recognized as part of Georgia, has been under the de facto control of the Government of South Ossetia, a breakaway group seeking independence from Georgia and unification with the Russian-controlled North Ossetia. Explaining the depiction of both parts as a single territory, the designers proclaim, "A single identity is a bold move and a huge milestone for North and South Ossetia" (https://www.artlebedev.com/ossetia/).

13. Dmitry Zhikharev, interview with the author, 28 June 2019.

14. Zhikharev interview.

15. Dmitry Zhikharev, interview with the author, 8 October 2018.

16. Borys Kit, "Disney Picks Up Family Adventure Project 'Princess of North Sudan,'" *Hollywood Reporter*, 6 November 2014, https://www.hollywoodreporter.com/heat-vision/disney-picks -up-family-adventure-747114.

17. Jeremiah Heaton, "What Starting My Own Country Taught Me about Independence," *MEL Magazine*, 4 July 2017, https://melmagazine.com/en-us/story/what-starting-my-own-country -taught-me-about-independence.

18. "The World's First CrowdFunded Nation," Indiegogo, http://www.indiegogo.com/proj ects/1105705/fblk.

19. Mohamed Atta Abbas, "Embassy of the Sudan, Washington D.C. to Mr. Jeremiah D. Heaton," 31 August 2018.

20. Jeremiah Heaton, interview with the author, Skype, 4 July 2019.

21. "Neap Coin: Kingdom of North Sudan Digital Currency," https://www.neapcoin.com.

22. Julie Sanders, "The Politics of Escapism: Fantasies of Travel and Power in Richard

Brome's 'The Antipodes' and Ben Johnson's 'The Alchemist,'" in *Writing and Fantasy*, ed. Ceri Sullivan and Barbara White (New York: Routledge, 2014), 137–50.

23. See "Official Campaign Web Site—Jeremiah David Heaton," Library of Congress, Washington, DC, 2010, https://www.loc.gov/item/lcwaN0005688/; Mason Adams, "Democratic Contender for 9th District Drops Out," *Roanoke Times*, 2 May 2012, http://www.roanoke.com/politics /wb/308261.

24. British and Foreign State Papers, *Agreement between Her Britannic Majesty's Government and the Government of the Khedive of Egypt, Relative to the Future Administration of the Soudan*; Egyptian Minister of Interior, "Arrêté of the Minister of Interior Dated November 4, 1902, Relating to the Regions of the Nomads of Egypt and the Sudan, and Which Comprise the Tribes of Becharia and of Malikab North in the Sudan, and the Tribes of Abadia in Egypt [Done 4 November 1902]" (Revue Egyptienne de Droit International, 1958); see also Reyner, "Sudan–United Republic (Egypt) Boundary"; Daniel J. Druzek, *Parting the Red Sea: Boundaries, Offshore Resources and Transit*, ed. Clive Schofield and Shelagh Furness, Maritime Briefing 3, 2 (Durham, NC: International Borders Research Unit, 2001).

25. Heaton, "What Starting My Own Country Taught Me."

26. Merete Borch, "Rethinking the Origins of Terra Nullius," *Australian Historical Studies* 32, no. 117 (2001): 222–39; Alan Frost, "New South Wales as Terra Nullius: The British Denial of Aboriginal Land Rights," *Historical Studies* 19 (1981): 513–523; David Mercer, "Terra Nullius, Aboriginal Sovereignty and Land Rights in Australia: The Debate Continues," *Political Geography* 12, no. 4 (1993): 299–318, https://doi.org/10.1016/0962-6298(93)90043-7. For contemporary mobilization of the concept in Africa, see Charles Geisler, "New Terra Nullius Narratives and the Gentrification of Africa's 'Empty Lands,'" *Journal of World-Systems Research* 18, no. 1 (2012): 15–299, https://doi.org/10.5195/jwsr.2012.484.

27. Heaton interview.

28. During a 2019 trip to Colombia, an official permitted us to pass a military checkpoint only after he watched the entire documentary we made about the region. This was a rare exception.

29. James R. Ryan, *Photography and Exploration* (London: Reaktion Books, 2013).

30. Jacques Derrida and Anne Dufourmantelle, *Of Hospitality*, trans. Rachel Bowlby (Stanford, CA: Stanford University Press, 2000).

31. John K. Noyes, *Colonial Space: Spatiality in the Discourse of German South West Africa 1884–1915*, Studies in Anthropology and History 4 (Cham, Switzerland: Harwood Academic Publishers, 1992), 235.

32. Simon Schaffer et al., eds., *The Brokered World: Go-Betweens and Global Intelligence, 1770–1820*, Uppsala Studies in History of Science 35 (Sagamore Beach, MA: Science History Publications, 2009); Felix Driver and Lowri Jones, *Hidden Histories of Exploration* (Egham, UK: Royal Holloway, University of London, 2009).

33. Cecilia Briceno-Garmendia, "Sudan's Infrastructure: A Continental Perspective" (Rochester, NY: Social Science Research Network, 1 September 2011), https://papers.ssrn.com/abstract =1934676.

34. The country doubled kilometers of its roads between 2000 and 2008, although this has largely stalled due to international sanctions and the limited number of infrastructure firms, mostly Chinese, that are willing to work in Sudan.

35. Mohammed Amin, "Battle of the Blockades as Sudanese Protesters Plot to Choke off Military Rule," *Middle East Eye*, http://www.middleeasteye.net/news/sudan-military-rule-anti -coup-protesters-plan-choke-road-blocks. See also Mohamed Nureldin Abdallah and El Tayeb

Siddig, "Sudan Export Highway Blockaded as Protests Stoked by Trade Woes," Reuters, 10 February 2022, https://www.reuters.com/world/africa/sudan-export-highway-blockaded-protests-stoked-by-trade-woes-2022-02-10/.

36. Joe Moran, *On Roads: A Hidden History* (London: Profile Books, 2010).

37. Penny Harvey and Hannah Knox, "The Enchantments of Infrastructure," *Mobilities* 7, no. 4 (2012): 530, https://doi.org/10.1080/17450101.2012.718935.

38. In the sense that Foucault assigned to the premodern sovereign, as that which can take life and property at will but otherwise remains largely absent from the life of its subjects. See Michel Foucault, *Power/Knowledge: Selected Interviews and Other Writings, 1972–1977* (New York: Random House, 1988), 121.

39. Kathleen Stewart, "Road Registers," *Cultural Geographies* 21, no. 4 (2014): 549–63, https://doi.org/10.1177/1474474014525053.

40. Rukmini Bhaya Nair, "Postcoloniality and the Matrix of Indifference," *India International Centre Quarterly* 26, no. 2 (1999): 9.

41. Nair, 14.

42. G. W. Steevens, a journalist for the *Daily Mail* who documented the British effort to reconquer Sudan, wrote: "Halfa was the decisive point of the campaign. For in Halfa . . . was forged the deadliest weapon that Britain has ever used against Mahadiism—the Sudan Military Highway." Quoted in Mark Strage, *Cape to Cairo: Rape of a Continent* (New York: Harcourt Brace Jovanovich, 1973), 193, http://archive.org/details/capetogairo0000unse.

43. M. W. Daly, *Empire on the Nile: The Anglo-Egyptian Sudan, 1898–1934* (Cambridge: Cambridge University Press, 1986), 2–3.

44. Sandra Calkins, "How 'Clean Gold' Came to Matter: Metal Detectors, Infrastructure, and Valuation," *HAU: Journal of Ethnographic Theory* 6, no. 2 (September 2016): 182, https://doi.org/10.14318/hau6.2.013.

45. Piotr Maliński, "Searching for Nubian Desert Gold with a Metal Detector: Functioning and Organization of Dahaba Occupational Group in Sudan," in *Collectanea Sudanica*, ed. Waldemar Cisło, Jarosław Różański, and Maciej Ząbek (Pelplin, Poland: Bernardinaum, 2017), 1:132.

46. M. S. Ibrahim, "Artisanal Mining in Sudan: Opportunities, Challenges, and Impacts" (UNCTAD, 17th Africa OILGASMINE: Extractive Industries and Sustainable Job Creation, Khartoum, 2015), https://unctad.org/meetings/en/Presentation/17OILGASMINE%20Mohamed%20Sulaiman%20Ibrahim%20S4.pdf.

47. Republic of Sudan, "The Mineral Wealth and Mining (Development) Act 2015" (2015), https://kig.pl/wp-content/uploads/2018/05/Mineral-wealth-and-mining.pdf.

48. Given the ambivalent status of artisanal mining, which remains formally illegal though simultaneously deeply enmeshed in the formal economy of Sudan, the numbers remain murky. While in 2008 only a few thousand participated in gold mining, in early 2015 it was estimated to involve up to 750,000 people. By 2020, nearly 2 million people across Sudan were estimated to be involved in the gold mining industry.

49. For an excellent and highly relevant analysis of the 2007 legislation that governed mining and its drawbacks, see Enrico Ille and Sandra Calkins, "Gold Mining Concessions in Sudan's Written Laws, and Practices of Gold Extraction in the Nuba Mountains," in *Identity, Economy, Power Relations and External Interests: Old and New Challenges for Sudan and South Sudan*, ed. Grawert Elke (Addis Ababa: OSSREA, 2014), 112–26.

50. Gavin Bridge and Tomas Fredriksen, "'Order Out of Chaos': Resources, Hazards and

the Production of a Tin-Mining Economy in Northern Nigeria in the Early Twentieth Century," *Environment and History* 18, no. 3 (2012): 379.

51. According to the Bank of Russia, gold reserves in the country more than quadrupled from less than 500 tons in 2010 to more than 2,301 tons in the fourth quarter of 2021.

52. Tom Collins, "How Putin Prepared for Sanctions with Tonnes of African Gold," *The Telegraph*, 3 March 2022, https://www.telegraph.co.uk/global-health/terror-and-security/putin-prepared-sanctions-tonnes-african-gold/.

53. Theodore Murphy and Mattia Caniglia, "Khartoum's Autocratic Enabler: Russia in Sudan—European Council on Foreign Relations," *European Council on Foreign Relations* (blog), 15 December 2021, https://ecfr.eu/article/khartoums-autocratic-enabler-russia-in-sudan/.

54. Hundreds of civilians were gunned down by the RSF in June 2019 for demonstrating outside army headquarters. Bodies of the victims were dumped in the Nile River and washed up on its shores. Tim Lister, Nima Elbagir, and Sebastian Shukla, "A Russian Company's Secret Plan to Quell Protests in Sudan," *CNN*, 25 April 2019, https://www.cnn.com/2019/04/25/africa/russia-sudan-minvest-plan-to-quell-protests-intl/index.html.

55. The events here are based on interviews with several witnesses in Sudan during early March 2022. All asked to remain anonymous. It was not possible to corroborate these events with external sources I spoke to, including diplomats and officials working for some of the mining firms operating in the region.

56. Calkins, "How 'Clean Gold' Came to Matter," 181.

57. Calkins, 191.

58. Petina Gappah, *Out of Darkness, Shining Light: (Being a Faithful Account of the Final Years and Earthly Days of Doctor David Livingstone and His Last Journey from the Interior to the Coast of Africa, as Narrated by His African Companions, in Three Volumes)* (New York: Scribner, 2019), 24.

Chapter Eleven

1. Marder and Tondeur, *Chernobyl Herbarium*, 58.

2. John Masefield, *The Old Front Line* (New York: Macmillan, 1917), 70–73.

3. Archibald Frank Becke and James E. Edmonds, *Military Operations, France and Belgium, 1916* (London: Imperial War Museum; Nashville, TN: Battery Press, 1993), 375n3.

4. Cecil Lewis, *Sagittarius Rising* (London: Greenhill, 2006), 104.

5. This deep destruction was reported by the agricultural writer Henry Hitier, who remarked, "Where there has been villages one sees nothing but shellholes and trenches, everything has been disturbed and the sub-soil has been turned up to the surface." Henry Hitier, "La situation des régions libérées du Santerre," *JAP* 30 (2017): 237, qtd. in Clout, *After the Ruins*, 22.

6. William H. Scheifley, "The Depleted Forests of France," *North American Review* 212, no. 778 (1920): 378–86.

7. Quoted in Clout, *After the Ruins*, 30.

8. Nicolas Note et al., "A New Evaluation Approach of World War One's Devastated Front Zone: A Shell Hole Density Map Based on Historical Aerial Photographs and Validated by Electromagnetic Induction Field Measurements to Link the Metal Shrapnel Phenomenon," *Geoderma* 310 (15 January 2018): 257–69, https://doi.org/10.1016/j.geoderma.2017.09.029.

9. Tobias Bausinger, Eric Bonnaire, and Johannes Preuss, "Exposure Assessment of a Burning

Ground for Chemical Ammunition on the Great War Battlefields of Verdun," *Science of the Total Environment* 382 (1 October 2007): 259–71, https://doi.org/10.1016/j.scitotenv.2007.04.029.

10. Paola Filippucci, "'These Battered Hills': Landscape and Memory at Verdun (France)," in *Places of Memory: Spatialised Practices of Remembrance from Prehistory to Today*, ed. Christian Horn et al. (Oxford, UK: Archaeopress, 2020), 82–96.

11. Clout, *After the Ruins*, 3.

12. Masefield, *The Old Front Line*, 72.

13. Lord Dunsany (the pen name of Edward John Moreton Drax, eighteenth baron Dunsany), for example, writes: "You came perhaps to a wood in an agony of contortions—black, branchless, sepulchral trees, and then no more trees at all . . . there stretches for miles instead one of the world's great deserts, a thing to take its place no longer with smiling lands but with Sahara, Gobi, Kalahari, and the Karoo." Edward Dunsany, *Tales of War* (Boston: Little, Brown & Co., 1918), 30, http://archive.org/details/talesofwarbylord00dunsiala.

14. Mary Borden, *The Forbidden Zone* (Garden City, NY: Doubleday, Doran and Co., 1929), 118–19.

15. Borden, *The Forbidden Zone.*

16. Dunsany, *Tales of War*, 73–74.

17. Brantz, "Environments of Death: Trench Warfare on the Western Front, 1914–1918," 82. A more conceptual discussion of this process appears in Sloterdijk, *Terror from the Air.*

18. As George Mosse documents, the war years saw an immense surge in the idealization of nature at the exact time when natural environments were being pulverized by the war machine. The process I am concerned with here is somewhat distinct from this, and regards specifically the revival of nature in spaces from which human presence has been withdrawn. George L. Mosse, *Fallen Soldiers: Reshaping the Memory of the World Wars* (New York: Oxford University Press, 1991), ch. 6.

19. Dunsany, *Tales of War*, 62.

20. Georg Simmel, "Two Essays," *Hudson Review* 11, no. 3 (1958): 382, https://doi.org/10.2307/3848614.

21. Walter Benjamin, *Illuminations*, ed. Hannah Arendt and Harry Zohn (New York: Harcourt, 1969), 257.

22. Lisa M. Brady, "From War Zone to Biosphere Reserve: The Korean DMZ as a Scientific Landscape," *Notes and Records: The Royal Society Journal of the History of Science* 75, no. 2 (2021): 190, https://doi.org/10.1098/rsnr.2020.0023.

23. Journals of the Lewis and Clark Expedition, 29 August 1806, https://lewisandclarkjournals.unl.edu/item/lc.jrn.1806-08-29#n39082904.

24. Paul S. Martin and Christine R. Szuter, "War Zones and Game Sinks in Lewis and Clark's West," *Conservation Biology* 13, no. 1 (1999): 36–45, https://doi.org/10.1046/j.1523-1739.1999.97417.x.

25. Tasha Hubbard, "Buffalo Genocide in Nineteenth-Century North America: 'Kill, Skin, and Sell,'" in *Colonial Genocide in Indigenous North America*, ed. Alexander Laban Hinton, Andrew Woolford, and Jeff Benvenuto (Durham, NC: Duke University Press, 2014), 273–91, https://doi.org/10.1515/9780822376149.

26. Ursula K. Heise, *Sense of Place and Sense of Planet: The Environmental Imagination of the Global*, Oxford Scholarship Online. Literature Module (New York: Oxford University Press, 2008), 140.

27. Bruno Latour, *Facing Gaia: Eight Lectures on the New Climatic Regime*, trans. Catherine Porter (Cambridge, UK: Polity, 2017), 258.

28. Nor have I ever tried to. Admitting ignorance was, throughout this research, an ethical stance that allowed my interlocutors to share their knowledge and experience without the risk of being undermined or called out. Moreover, it was a position that, more than once, kept me safe. In places where asking questions from the position of knowledge and expertise can make you seem partisan, or worse, get you arrested or killed, ignorance was more easily forgiven, often generating laughter rather than suspicion.

29. Sara Reardon, "FARC and the Forest: Peace Is Destroying Colombia's Jungle—and Opening It to Science," *Nature* 558, no. 7709 (2018): 169–70, https://doi.org/10.1038/d41586-018 -05397-2.

30. Raphael Ganzenmüller, Janelle M. Sylvester, and Augusto Castro-Núñez, "What Peace Means for Deforestation: An Analysis of Local Deforestation Dynamics in Times of Conflict and Peace in Colombia," *Frontiers in Environmental Science* 10 (2022): https://www.frontiersin.org /articles/10.3389/fenvs.2022.803368.

31. The election of Gustavo Petro as Colombia's first left-wing president in 2022 marked a radical shift in government policy fossil fuels, deforestation, and environmental protection but also in the social and economic concerns of campesino communities. By the time this book was complete, it was still too soon to assess the impact of these changes, but 188 human rights defenders and social leaders were assassinated in 2023. This is virtually the same number as was registered in 2022, when 187 leaders were killed, according to data collected by Instituto de Estudios para el Desarrollo y la Paz (INDEPAZ).

32. Sigmund Freud, "Mourning and Melancholia," in *On Freud's Mourning and Melancholia*, ed. Thierry Bokanowski, Leticia Glocer Fiorini, and Sergio Lewkowicz (London: Taylor & Francis Group, 2007), 19–34.

33. Susan Sontag, *On Photography*, Penguin Modern Classics (London: Penguin Classics, 2008), 11.

34. Margarita Serje, *El revés de la nación: Territorios salvajes, fronteras y tierras de nadie* (Bogotá: Universidad de Los Andes, Facultad de Ciencias Sociales, Departamento de Antropología, CESO, 2005).

35. Nathalye Cotrino Villarreal and Juan Pappier, *Left Undefended: Killings of Rights Defenders in Colombia's Remote Communities* (New York: Human Rights Watch, 2021).

36. In December 2020, Javier Francisco Parra Cubillos, an official from regional environmental authority Cormacarena was killed while traveling through the municipality of La Macarena. A couple on a motorcycle shot him several times in broad daylight. I met with Javier several times while working on this project.

37. I discuss this history at greater length in chapter 8. See also Leal, *A la buena de Dios*; Nubia Tobar Ortiz, "En el umbral de una muerte inevitable: Los tinigua de la sierra de La Macarena," in *La recuperación de las lenguas nativas como búsqueda de identidad étnica*, symposium, VII Congreso de Antropología, CCELA (Bogotá: Universidad de los Andes, 1994).

38. Serje, "Iron Maiden Landscapes," 51.

39. There is a plethora of work around this critique. See, for a broad introduction, John Bellamy Foster, Brett Clark, and Richard York, *The Ecological Rift: Capitalism's War on the Earth* (New York: NYU Press, 2010).

40. The commercial success of Cal Flyn's *Islands of Abandonment*, which bore the subtitle,

"nature rebounding in a post-human world" speaks exactly to this point. Cal Flyn, *Islands of Abandonment: Life in the Post-Human Landscape* (London: HarperCollins Publishers, 2022).

41. Ann Laura Stoler, *Duress: Imperial Durabilities in Our Times* (Durham, NC: Duke University Press, 2016), 7, https://doi.org/10.1515/9780822373612.

42. Juanita Sundberg, "Thinking with *Duress*," *Postcolonial Studies* 21, no. 4 (2018): 539, https://doi.org/10.1080/13688790.2018.1542583.

43. There is much preoccupation with "rustalgia" and "ruin porn" these days, but I still find Brian Dillon's essay on ruins and ruination to be the most incisive introduction into the longer cultural histories of this fascination. Brian Dillon, "Fragments from a History of Ruin," *Cabinet* 20 (Winter 2005): 55–60; Kate Brown, *Dispatches from Dystopia: Histories of Places Not Yet Forgotten* (Chicago: University of Chicago Press, 2015).

44. Timothy A. Mousseau et al., "Highly Reduced Mass Loss Rates and Increased Litter Layer in Radioactively Contaminated Areas," *Oecologia* 175, no. 1 (2014): 429–37, https://doi.org/10.1007/s00442-014-2908-8.

45. Nixon, *Slow Violence and the Environmentalism of the Poor*.

46. Marder and Tondeur, *Chernobyl Herbarium*, 28.

47. Costas Constantinou, Maria Hadjimichael, and Evi Eftychiou, "Ambivalent Greenings, Collateral Conservation: Negotiating Ecology in a United Nations Buffer Zone," *Political Geography* 77 (March 2020): Art. 102096, https://doi.org/10.1016/j.polgeo.2019.102096.

48. Qtd. in Clout, *After the Ruins*, 266–67.

49. I owe this phrase to Alasdair Pinkerton who, suggested it during our first visit to the Zone Rouge in 2015.

50. "14-18 Forêts De Mémoire," *Terre Sauvage* 309 (20 November 2014): 31–53.

51. Rémi de Matos and Joseph P. Dudley, "The Conflict Landscape of Verdun, France: Conserving Cultural and Natural Heritage after WWI," in *Collateral Values: The Natural Capital Created by Landscapes of War*, ed. Todd R. Lookingbill and Peter D. Smallwood (New York: Springer, 2019), 111–32.

52. Marder and Tondeur, *Chernobyl Herbarium*, 58.

53. Vandana Shiva, *Monocultures of the Mind: Perspectives on Biodiversity and Biotechnology* (London: Zed Books; Penang, Malaysia: Third World Network, 1993).

Epilogue

1. S. Yizhar, *Stories of the Plain: Silence of the Villages* (Tel Aviv: Zmora Bitan, 1990) (in Hebrew).

2. Uri Ram, "Ways of Forgetting: Israel and the Obliterated Memory of the Palestinian Nakba," *Journal of Historical Sociology* 22, no. 3 (2009): 366–95, https://doi.org/10.1111/j.1467-6443.2009.01354.x.

3. Israeli legislation vacates land ownership and titles of Palestinians who were forced to flee their homes and made refugees. Geremy Forman and Alexander Kedar's seminal piece remains an excellent introduction: Geremy Forman and Alexander Kedar, "From Arab Land to 'Israel Lands': The Legal Dispossession of the Palestinians Displaced by Israel in the Wake of 1948," *Environment and Planning D, Society & Space* 22, no. 6 (2004): 809–30.

4. This organization was granted the land by the State of Israel after the 1967 war. One of the oldest Zionist organizations, it remains committed to exclusive Jewish ownership of land.

5. Ira Glass et al., "The Out Crowd," *This American Life*, 15 November 2019, https://www
.thisamericanlife.org/688/the-out-crowd.

6. Glass et al.

7. Scott Wilson, "Colombian President Rejects Rebel Offer," *Washington Post*, 13 January
2002, https://www.washingtonpost.com/archive/politics/2002/01/13/colombian-president-rejects
-rebel-offer/71334f07-1ce3-4db7-8a89-55bf6bd3a339/. Throughout the existence of the Clearance Zone, Pastrana was facing fierce criticism from the Colombian opposition, who saw the
abandonment of this large region at the heart of the country as a humiliating admission of the
state's inability to assert its power throughout its sovereign territory.

8. Seeking to highlight the plight of local populations in areas controlled by FARC, Íngrid
Betancourt visited the Clearance Zone on 23 February 2002 during her presidential campaign.
She was abducted by FARC forces and held for six and a half years. A French national, her case
was widely covered by the international media. An image of Betancourt during her captivity
gained iconic status and widely contributed to the extensive media coverage of her case. See
Alessandra Merlo, "La imagen cautiva: Reflexiones sobre la foto icónica de Íngrid Betancourt
durante el secuestro," *Revista Colombiana de Pensamiento Estético e Historia del Arte* 12 (2020):
158–88.

9. See chapter 3. If I were to draw an analogy to the American invasion of Iraq, I would
not choose President George W. Bush's statement that Povinelli quotes ("Amid all this violence
I know Americans ask the question: Is the sacrifice worth it? Is it worth it, and is it vital to the
future security of our country.") A more accurate sentiment was captured by Secretary of Defense Donald Rumsfeld's response to reports of looting in Iraq in the early days of the US invasion: "Stuff happens." Sean Loughlin, "Rumsfeld on Looting in Iraq: 'Stuff Happens,'" *CNN
International Edition*, 12 April 2003, https://edition.cnn.com/2003/US/04/11/sprj.irq.pentagon/.

10. A recent report by Colombia's Special Jurisdiction for Peace—known by its Spanish acronym JEP—identified more than 6,200 victims of "false positives," more than triple the previous estimates. Large parts of the former Clearance Zone were specifically noted as prominent sites of these state-sponsored massacres. See Jurisdicción Especial para la Paz (JEP), "La
JEP hace pública la estrategia de priorización dentro del Caso 03, conocido como el de falsos
positivos" (press release), https://www.jep.gov.co:443/Sala-de-Prensa/Paginas/La-JEP-hace-p%C3
%BAblica-la-estrategia-de-priorizaci%C3%B3n-dentro-del-Caso-03,-conocido-como-el-de-falsos
-positivos.aspx.

11. Correspondence with the author, 2 February 2023.

12. Ambassador Richard Mills, "Remarks at a UN Security Council Briefing on the Political
and Humanitarian Situation in Syria," *The Syrian Observer* (blog), 26 January 2023, https://syrian
observer.com/resources/81443/remarks-at-a-un-security-council-briefing-on-the-political-and
-humanitarian-situation-in-syria.html. American forces remain stationed in al-Tanf only a short
distance from Rukban, but largely refuse to provide direct aid to the camp out of fear that it
would absolve other parties from their responsibilities.

13. Neither Jordan nor Syria show any indication that they are even considering alternatives to the current reality that leaves Rukban beyond sovereign care. Neither has been willing
to make the concessions needed even to allow humanitarian aid to flow in regularly, let alone
seek a long-term resolution. For some of the policy calculations, see Jesse Marks, "Why Jordan
Won't Alleviate the Rukban Crisis," Middle East Institute, 21 April 2022, https://www.mei.edu
/publications/why-jordan-wont-alleviate-rukban-crisis.

14. Estela Schindel, "Death by 'Nature': The European Border Regime and the Spatial Production of Slow Violence," *Environment and Planning C: Politics and Space* 40, no. 2 (2022): 428–46.

15. The biblical direction to observe the Shmita comes from the book of Exodus (also see Leviticus 23:22 and 25:2–7): "And six years you shall sow your land and gather its produce; and the seventh: you shall let it lie fallow and leave it, and your people's indigent will eat, and what they leave the animal of the field will eat. You shall do this to your vineyard, to your olives" (Exodus 23:10–11).

16. David Seidenberg, "Shmita: The Purpose of Sinai," *Hazon* (blog), August 2012, https://hazon.org/wp-content/uploads/2012/08/Shmita-The-Purpose-of-Sinai.pdf.

17. Fayer Collective, "Shmita Means Total Destroy," *Jewish Currents* (Winter 2022), https://jewishcurrents.org/shmita-means-total-destroy.

18. Mbembe, *Necropolitics*, 27–29.

19. Leviticus makes clear that the abdication of this mandate will be met with violence. Informing the Israelites of the fate that will befall them if they break the covenant, God makes a ferocious promise: "And you I will scatter among the nations, and I will unsheathe the sword against you. Your land shall become a desolation and your cities a ruin. Then shall the land make up for its Sabbath years throughout the time that it is desolate and you are in the land of your enemies; then shall the land rest and make up for its Sabbath years" (Leviticus 26:33–34). The fields will lie fallow for one year every seven, or they will turn to dust and be swept away by wind and water. By flood or by fire, the land will take what it is owed.

20. Ruth Behar, *The Vulnerable Observer: Anthropology That Breaks Your Heart* (Boston: Beacon Press, 2012).

Bibliography

Abbas, Mohamed Atta. "Embassy of the Sudan, Washington D.C. to Mr. Jeremiah D. Heaton." 31 August 2018.

Abowd, Thomas. "Present and Absent." In *City of Collision: Jerusalem and the Principles of Conflict Urbanism*, edited by Philipp Misselwitz and Tim Rieniets, 328–36. Basel: Birkhauser, 2006.

Abu Zayd, Muhammad Fu'ad. *Heartbeats in Marj al-Zuhur* [*Nabaḍāt qalb fī Marj al-Zuhūr*]. Beirut: Dār al-Rashād al-Islāmīyah, 1993.

Ad-Dustour. "Al-Safadi: Jordan Will Not Allow Refugees from the Rukban Camp to Enter the Kingdom." 8 October 2017. https://shorturl.at/hBEMZ.

Agamben, Giorgio. *Homo Sacer: Sovereign Power and Bare Life*. Stanford, CA: Stanford University Press, 1998.

———. *Means without End: Notes on Politics*. Minneapolis: University of Minnesota Press, 2000.

———. *Potentialities: Collected Essays in Philosophy*. Stanford, CA: Stanford University Press, 1998.

———. *State of Exception*. Chicago: University of Chicago Press, 2005.

Aharon-Gutman, Meirav. "Art's Failure to Generate Urban Renewal: Lessons from Jerusalem." *Urban Studies* 55, no. 15 (2018): 3474–91. https://doi.org/10.1177/0042098017743682.

Alaimo, Stacy. *Exposed: Environmental Politics and Pleasures in Posthuman Times*. Minneapolis: University of Minnesota Press, 2016. https://doi.org/10.5749/j.ctt1g04zkp.

Alexander, Bevin. *Korea: The First War We Lost*. New York: Hippocrene Books, 1991.

Alexievich, Svetlana. *Voices from Chernobyl: The Oral History of a Nuclear Disaster*. Translated by Keith Gessen. New York: Picador USA, 2006.

Alimi, Eitan. *Israeli Politics and the First Palestinian Intifada: Political Opportunities, Framing Processes and Contentious Politics*. London: Routledge, 2007.

Amnesty International. "Annual Report: Colombia." 2001. https://www.refworld.org/pdfid/3b1de3734.pdf.

———. "Colombia: 'Scarred Bodies, Hidden Crimes': Sexual Violence against Women in the Armed Conflict." London, 13 October 2004. https://www.amnesty.org/download/Documents/92000/amr230402004en.pdf.

———. *Health Crisis: Syrian Government Targets the Wounded and Health Workers.* London: March 2011. https://www.amnesty.org/download/Documents/32000/mde240592011en.pdf.

———. "Syria-Jordan Border: 75,000 Refugees Trapped in 'Berm' No-Man's Land in 'Desperate' Conditions." 15 September 2016. https://www.amnesty.org.uk/press-releases/syria-jordan-bor der-75000-refugees-trapped-berm-no-mans-land-desperate-conditions.

———. "'You're Going to Your Death' Violations against Syrian Refugees Returning to Syria." 7 September 2021. https://www.amnesty.org/en/documents/mde24/4583/2021/en/.

Anderson, Benedict. *A Life beyond the Boundaries.* London: Verso, 2016.

Angelo, Anne-Marie. "'Any Name That Has Power': The Black Panthers of Israel, the United Kingdom, and the United States, 1948–1977." PhD diss., Duke University, 2013. https://duke space.lib.duke.edu/dspace/handle/10161/7264.

———. *Black Power on the Move: Migration, Internationalism, and the British and Israeli Black Panthers.* Chapel Hill: University of North Carolina Press, 2021.

Anidjar, Gil. *The Jew, the Arab: A History of the Enemy.* Stanford, CA: Stanford University Press, 2003.

Arendt, Hannah. *Eichmann in Jerusalem: A Report on the Banality of Evil.* New York: Penguin Books, 2006.

Arjona, Ana. "Civilian Resistance to Rebel Governance." In *Rebel Governance in Civil War,* edited by Ana Arjona, Nelson Kasfir, and Zachariah Mampilly, 180–202. Cambridge: Cambridge University Press, 2015.

———. *Rebelocracy: Social Order in the Colombian Civil War.* Cambridge: Cambridge University Press, 2016. https://doi.org/10.1017/9781316421925.

Azoulay, Ariella. "Citizens of Disaster." *Qui Parle* 15, no. 2 (2005): 105–37.

———. *The Civil Contract of Photography.* New York: Zone, 2008.

Azoulay, Ariella Aïsha. *Potential History: Unlearning Imperialism.* London: Verso, 2019.

Azoulay, Ariella, and Adi Ophir. *The One-State Condition: Occupation and Democracy in Israel/ Palestine.* Stanford Studies in Middle Eastern and Islamic Societies and Cultures. Stanford, CA: Stanford University Press, 2013.

Bagelman, Jennifer J. *Sanctuary City: A Suspended State.* Mobility & Politics. New York: Palgrave Macmillan, 2016.

Bagelman, Jen, and Sarah Marie Wiebe. "Intimacies of Global Toxins: Exposure & Resistance in 'Chemical Valley.'" *Political Geography* 60 (1 September 2017): 76–85. https://doi.org/10 .1016/j.polgeo.2017.04.007.

Bakshi, Anita. "A Shell of Memory: The Cyprus Conflict and Nicosia's Walled City." *Memory Studies* 5, no. 4 (2012): 479–96.

———. "Urban Form and Memory Discourses: Spatial Practices in Contested Cities." *Journal of Urban Design* 19, no. 2 (15 March 2014): 189–210. https://doi.org/10.1080/13574809.2013 .854696.

Baldwin, James. *Jimmy's Blues and Other Poems.* Boston: Beacon Press, 2014.

Balibar, Étienne. *Politics and the Other Scene.* Translated by Christine Jones, James Swenson, and Chris Turner. Radical Thinkers. London: Verso, 2011.

Balonov, Michael, Peter Jacob, Ilya Likhtarev, and Victor Minenko. "Pathways, Levels and Trends of Population Exposure after the Chernobyl Accident." In *Proceedings of the First International Conference "The Radiological Consequences of the Chernobyl Accident,"* 235–49. Brussels: European Commission, 1996. https://www.osti.gov/etdeweb/biblio/20112742.

Bausinger, Tobias, Eric Bonnaire, and Johannes Preuss. "Exposure Assessment of a Burning Ground for Chemical Ammunition on the Great War Battlefields of Verdun." *Science of the Total Environment* 382 (1 October 2007): 259–71. https://doi.org/10.1016/j.scitotenv.2007.04.029.

Beaman, Ardern Arthur Hulme. *The Squadroon*. London: John Lane, 1920. http://archive.org/details/squadroon00beam.

Becke, Archibald Frank, and James E. Edmonds. *Military Operations, France and Belgium, 1916*. London: Imperial War Museum; Nashville, TN: Battery Press, 1993.

Behar, Ruth. *The Vulnerable Observer: Anthropology That Breaks Your Heart*. Boston: Beacon Press, 2012.

Beinish, Dorit, Eliezer Rivlin, and Edmond Levi. HCJ 7337/05 Mouhammad Naif Shakir & 28 Others v. The Military Commander in Judea and Samaria (Supreme Court: High Court of Justice, 15 March 2010).

Ben-Arieh, Yehoshua, and Eliyahu Vager. "Stages in the Development of Israeli Jerusalem between the Years 1948–1967." In *Divided Jerusalem 1948–1967: Sources, Summaries, Key Issues and Aids [Yerushalayim ha-ḥatsuyah, 1948–1967]*, edited by Avi Bareli, 91–114. Idan 18. Jerusalem: Yad Izhak Ben-Zvi, 1994.

Ben Gad, Ariel. "The City Line in Jerusalem, 1948–1967" (HaKav HaIroni BeYerushalayim 1948–1967). MA thesis in history, Hebrew University of Jerusalem, 2018.

Benjamin, Andrew. "Porosity at the Edge: Working through Walter Benjamin's 'Naples.'" In *Moderne begreifen*, edited by Christine Magerski, Robert Savage, and Christiane Weller, 107–19. Wiesbaden, Germany: DUV, 2007. https://doi.org/10.1007/978-3-8350-9676-9_7.

Benjamin, Walter. "Experience and Poverty." In *Selected Writings*, vol. 2, *1927–1934*, edited by Howard Eliand, Michael W. Jennings, and Gary Smith, and translated by Rodney Livingstone, 731–35. Cambridge, MA: Belknap Press of Harvard University Press, 2003.

———. *Illuminations*. Edited by Hannah Arendt and Harry Zohn. New York: Harcourt, 1969.

———. "Naples." In *Selected Writings*, vol. 1, *1913–1926*, edited by Marcus Bullock and Michael William Jennings, 414–21. Cambridge, MA: Belknap Press of Harvard University Press, 2003.

———. "The Storyteller: Observations on the Works of Nikolai Leskov." In *Selected Writings*, vol. 3, *1935–1938*, edited by Howard Eliand and Michael W. Jennings, and translated by Edmund Jephcott, 143–49. Cambridge, MA: Belknap Press of Harvard University Press, 2003.

Benvenisti, Meron. *City of Stone: The Hidden History of Jerusalem*. Berkeley: University of California Press, 1998.

Berda, Yael. *Living Emergency: Israel's Permit Regime in the Occupied West Bank*. Stanford, CA: Stanford University Press, 2018.

Berger, Adolf. *Encyclopedic Dictionary of Roman Law*. Philadelphia: Lawbook Exchange, 1953.

Bernstein, Deborah. "Conflict and Protest in Israeli Society: The Case of the Black Panthers of Israel." *Youth and Society* 16, no. 2 (1984): 129–52.

Bey, Hakim. *T.A.Z.: The Temporary Autonomous Zone, Ontological Anarchy, Poetic Terrorism*. 2nd ed. New York: Autonomedia, 2003.

Biehl, João Guilherme. *Vita: Life in a Zone of Social Abandonment*. Berkeley: University of California Press, 2005.

Biss, Eula. *Notes from No Man's Land: American Essays*. St. Paul, MN: Graywolf Press, 2009.

Borch, Merete. "Rethinking the Origins of Terra Nullius." *Australian Historical Studies* 32, no. 117 (2001): 222–39.

Borden, Mary. *The Forbidden Zone*. Garden City, NY: Doubleday, Doran and Co., 1929.

Boswell, John. "Expositio and Oblatio: The Abandonment of Children and the Ancient and Medieval Family." *American Historical Review* 89, no. 1 (1 February 1984): 10–33. https://doi .org/10.2307/1855916.

Bourke, Joanna. *Dismembering the Male: Men's Bodies, Britain and the Great War.* Picturing History. London: Reaktion Books, 1996.

Brady, James. *The Scariest Place in the World.* New York: Thomas Dunne Books, 2005. http:// archive.org/details/scariestplaceinw00jame.

Brady, Lisa M. "From War Zone to Biosphere Reserve: The Korean DMZ as a Scientific Landscape." *Notes and Records: The Royal Society Journal of the History of Science* 75, no. 2 (2021): 189–205. https://doi.org/10.1098/rsnr.2020.0023.

Brantz, Dorothee. "Environments of Death: Trench Warfare on the Western Front, 1914–1918." In *War and the Environment: Military Destruction in the Modern Age,* edited by Charles Closmann, 68–91. College Station: Texas A&M University Press, 2009.

Briceno-Garmendia, Cecilia. "Sudan's Infrastructure: A Continental Perspective." Rochester, NY: Social Science Research Network, 1 September 2011. https://papers.ssrn.com/abstract=1934676.

Bridge, Gavin, and Tomas Fredriksen. " 'Order out of Chaos': Resources, Hazards and the Production of a Tin-Mining Economy in Northern Nigeria in the Early Twentieth Century." *Environment and History* 18, no. 3 (2012): 367–94.

British and Foreign State Papers. *Agreement between Her Britannic Majesty's Government and the Government of the Khedive of Egypt, Relative to the Future Administration of the Soudan.* London: HMSO, 1902. https://www.heinonline.org/HOL/Page?handle=hein.cow/zzsd 0003&collection=cow.

Brown, Kate. *Dispatches from Dystopia: Histories of Places Not yet Forgotten.* Chicago: University of Chicago Press, 2015.

Brown, Wendy. *Walled States, Waning Sovereignty.* New York: Zone Books, 2010.

Bryant, Rebecca, and Mete Hatay. *Sovereignty Suspended: Political Life in a So-Called State.* Philadelphia: University of Pennsylvania Press, 2020.

B'Tselem. "Facing the Abyss: The Isolation of Sheikh Sa'ad Village—Before and after the Separation Barrier." Status report, Jerusalem, February 2004. https://www.btselem.org/sites/default /files/sites/default/files2/200402_facing_the_abyss_eng.pdf.

Bucklow, Christopher. "Et in Arcadia Ego: Mishka Henner's 'No Man's Land.' " In *Deutsche Bank Prize Catalogue.* London, 2013.

Butler, Judith, and Athena Athanasiou. *Dispossession: The Performative in the Political.* Malden, MA: Polity Press, 2013.

Calkins, Sandra. "How 'Clean Gold' Came to Matter: Metal Detectors, Infrastructure, and Valuation." *HAU: Journal of Ethnographic Theory* 6, no. 2 (2016): 173–95. https://doi.org/10.14318 /hau6.2.013.

Campbell, David. "Satellite Images, Security and the Geopolitical Imagination." In *From Above,* edited by Peter Adey, Mark Whitehead, and Alison Williams, 289–98. Oxford University Press, 2014. https://doi.org/10.1093/acprof:oso/9780199334797.003.0014.

Cannon, Jack L. "Attack on Hills 673 and 749." *Leatherneck,* March 1989, 22–25.

Carman, Taylor. *Merleau-Ponty.* London: Routledge, 2008.

Carroll, James. "Angels of War." *New York Times,* 10 July 2006. https://www.nytimes.com/2006 /07/10/opinion/10iht-edcarroll.2161399.html.

Chasseaud, Peter. *Artillery's Astrologers: A History of British Survey and Mapping on the Western Front, 1914–1918.* Lewes, UK: Mapbooks, 1999.

Chernobyl Forum. "Chernobyl's Legacy: Health, Environmental and Socio-Economic Impacts." International Atomic Energy Agency, 2006. www.iaea.org/Publications/Booklets/Chernobyl /chernobyl.pdf.

Chetrit, Sami Shalom. *Intra-Jewish Conflict in Israel: White Jews, Black Jews.* London: Routledge, 2009.

Clark, Justine. "Smudges, Smears and Adventitious Marks." *Interstices* 4 (1995): 1–8.

Clark, Nigel. *Inhuman Nature: Sociable Life on a Dynamic Planet.* New York: Sage Publications, 2010.

Clout, Hugh D. *After the Ruins: Restoring the Countryside of Northern France after the Great War.* Exeter, UK: University of Exeter Press, 1996.

Cohen, Boaz. *Jewish and Roman Law: A Comparative Study.* 2 vols. New York: Jewish Theological Seminary of America, 1966.

Cohen, Jeffrey Jerome. *Monster Theory: Reading Culture.* Minneapolis: University of Minnesota Press, 1996. http://ebookcentral.proquest.com/lib/uvic/detail.action?docID=310376.

Collins, Tom. "How Putin Prepared for Sanctions with Tonnes of African Gold." *The Telegraph,* 3 March 2022. https://www.telegraph.co.uk/global-health/terror-and-security/putin-prepared -sanctions-tonnes-african-gold/.

Combined Joint Task Force, Operation Inherent Resolve. "Coalition Statement on At Tanf." Southwest Asia: US Central Command, 8 June 2017. https://www.centcom.mil/MEDIA/NEWS -ARTICLES/News-Article-View/Article/1208008/coalition-statement-on-at-tanf/.

Constantinou, Costas, Maria Hadjimichael, and Evi Eftychiou. "Ambivalent Greenings, Collateral Conservation: Negotiating Ecology in a United Nations Buffer Zone." *Political Geography* 77 (March 2020): Art. 102096. https://doi.org/10.1016/j.polgeo.2019.102096.

Coordinator of Government Activities in the Territories, Economic Branch. "Procedure for monitoring and assessing inventories in the Gaza Strip." Submitted to Gisha in the Framework of a Freedom of Information Act Petition, AP 2744/09 Gisha v. Defense Ministry, April 2009. https://www.gisha.org/UserFiles/File/HiddenMessages/FOIA_translation.pdf.

Corso, Alessandro. "Lives at the Border: Abandonment and Survival at the Frontier of Lampedusa." PhD diss., Durham University, 2019. http://etheses.dur.ac.uk/13403/.

Daly, M. W. *Empire on the Nile: The Anglo-Egyptian Sudan, 1898–1934.* Cambridge: Cambridge University Press, 1986.

Danius, Sara, and Stefan Jonsson. "An Interview with Gayatri Chakravorty Spivak." *Boundary 2* 20, no. 2 (1993): 24–50. https://doi.org/10.2307/303357.

Dawsey, Josh, and Colby Itkowitz. "Mike Pence Says Migrants Are 'Well Cared for' While Touring Border Detention Centres." *The Independent,* 13 July 2019. https://www.independent.co .uk/news/world/americas/us-politics/mike-pence-migrant-detention-centers-visit-border -camp-trump-mexico-a9003346.html.

Demetriou, Olga. "To Cross or Not to Cross? Subjectivization and the Absent State in Cyprus." *Journal of the Royal Anthropological Institute* 13, no. 4 (2007): 987–1006. https://doi.org/10 .1111/j.1467-9655.2007.00468.x.

Demetriou, Olga, and Murat Erdal Ilican. "A Peace of Bricks and Mortar: Thinking Ceasefire Landscapes with Gramsci." *International Journal of Heritage Studies* 25, no. 9 (2019): 897–913. https://doi.org/10.1080/13527258.2017.1413673.

Derrida, Jacques, and Anne Dufourmantelle. *Of Hospitality.* Translated by Rachel Bowlby. Stanford, CA: Stanford University Press, 2000.

Deutsch, James. "The Legend of What Actually Lived in the 'No Man's Land' between World

War I's Trenches." *Smithsonian Magazine*, 8 September 2014. https://www.smithsonianmag
.com/history/legends-what-actually-lived-no-mans-land-between-world-war-i-trenches
-180952513/.

Dewhurst, Patrick. "A Buffer Zone Tent Protest of Many Gripes." *Cyprus Mail*, 18 December 2011.
www.cypriot.org.uk/Documents/Haber%2011/27-Kasim.htm.

Dewitz, Bodo von. "German Snapshots from World War 1. Personal Pictures, Political Implications." In *War/Photography: Images of Armed Conflict and Its Aftermath*, edited by Anne
Tucker, Will Michels, and Natalie Zelt, 153–63. Houston, TX: Museum of Fine Arts, Houston, 2012.

Didi-Huberman, Georges. "Warburg's Haunted House." Translated by Shane Lillis. *Common
Knowledge* 18, no. 1 (2012): 50–78. https://doi.org/10.1215/0961754X-1456881.

Dillon, Brian. "Fragments from a History of Ruin." *Cabinet* 20 (Winter 2005): 55–60.

Dixon, Robert. "Spotting the Fake: C. E. W. Bean, Frank Hurley and the Making of the 1923 Photographic Record of the War." *History of Photography* 31, no. 2 (June 2007): 165–79. https://
doi.org/10.1080/03087298.2007.10443516.

Driver, Felix, and Lowri Jones. *Hidden Histories of Exploration*. Egham, UK: Royal Holloway,
University of London, 2009.

Drumsta, Emily, and Keith P. Feldman. "We Deportees: Race, Religion, and War on Palestine's
No-Man's-Land." *Social Text* 34, no. 4 (129) (2016): 87–110. https://doi.org/10.1215/01642472
-3680882.

Druzek, Daniel J. *Parting the Red Sea: Boundaries, Offshore Resources and Transit*. Edited by Clive
Schofield and Shelagh Furness. Maritime Briefing 3, 2. Durham, UK: International Borders
Research Unit, 2001.

Du Bois, W. E. B. *Souls of Black Folks*. New York: Dover, 1994.

Dunsany, Edward. *Tales of War*. Boston: Little, Brown & Co., 1918. http://archive.org/details/talesof
warbylord00dunsiala.

Editorial Team. "What Do You Know about the Al-Tanf Base?" *Horraya*, 3 January 2018. https://
horrya.net/archives/43611.

Edwards, Adrian. "Needs Soar as Number of Syrian Refugees Tops 3 Million." UNHCR, 29 August 2014. https://www.unhcr.org/news/latest/2014/8/53ff76c99/needs-soar-number-syrian
-refugees-tops-3-million.html.

Egyptian Minister of Interior. "Arrêté of the Minister of Interior Dated November 4, 1902, Relating to the Regions of the Nomads of Egypt and the Sudan, and Which Comprise the Tribes
of Becharia and of Malikab North in the Sudan, and the Tribes of Abadia in Egypt [Done
4 November 1902]." *Revue Egyptienne de Droit International*, 1958.

Espelt-Bombin, Silvia. "Makers and Keepers of Networks: Amerindian Spaces, Migrations, and
Exchanges in the Brazilian Amazon and French Guiana, 1600–1730." *Ethnohistory* 65, no. 4
(2018): 597–620. https://doi.org/10.1215/00141801-6991253.

Esposito, Roberto. *Bíos: Biopolitics and Philosophy*. Posthumanities Series 4. Minneapolis: University of Minnesota Press, 2008.

Evans, Richard J. "The European Family and the Great War." *Social History* 16, no. 3 (1991): 341–52.
https://doi.org/10.1080/03071029108567812.

Farred, Grant. "Disorderly Democracy: An Axiomatic Politics." *CR: The New Centennial Review*
8, no. 2 (2008): 43–65.

Fayer Collective. "Shmita Means Total Destroy." *Jewish Currents* (Winter 2022). https://jewish
currents.org/shmita-means-total-destroy.

Feldman, Allen. "Ground Zero Point One: On the Cinematics of History." *Social Analysis: The International Journal of Social and Cultural Practice* 46, no. 1 (1 April 2002): 110–17.

Filippucci, Paola. "'These Battered Hills': Landscape and Memory at Verdun (France)." In *Places of Memory: Spatialised Practices of Remembrance from Prehistory to Today*, edited by Christian Horn, Gustav Wollentz, Gianpiero Di Maida, and Annette Haug, 82–96. Oxford, UK: Archaeopress, 2020.

Fisher, David, Kirsten Hagon, Charlotte Lattimer, Sorcha O'Callaghan, Sophia Swithern, and Lisa Walmsley. *World Disasters Report 2018: Leaving No One Behind*. Geneva: International Federation of Red Cross and Red Crescent Societies, 2018.

Flyn, Cal. *Islands of Abandonment: Life in the Post-Human Landscape*. London: HarperCollins Publishers, 2022.

Foot, Rosemary. *A Substitute for Victory: The Politics of Peacemaking at the Korean Armistice Talks*. Cornell Studies in Security Affairs. Ithaca, NY: Cornell University Press, 1990.

Ford, Robert, and Carolyn O'Connor. "The U.S. Has Legal and Moral Responsibility to Protect Civilians at Rukban in Syria." *Just Security* (blog), 12 August 2019. https://www.justsecurity .org/65773/u-s-has-legal-and-moral-responsibility-to-protect-civilians-at-rukban-in-syria/.

Forman, Geremy, and Alexander Kedar. "From Arab Land to 'Israel Lands': The Legal Dispossession of the Palestinians Displaced by Israel in the Wake of 1948." *Environment and Planning D, Society & Space* 22, no. 6 (2004): 809–30.

Foster, John Bellamy, Brett Clark, and Richard York. *The Ecological Rift: Capitalism's War on the Earth*. New York: NYU Press, 2010.

Foucault, Michel. *Discipline and Punish: The Birth of the Prison*. New York: Pantheon Books, 1977.

———. *The History of Sexuality*. Translated by Robert Hurley. Vol. 1. New York: Pantheon, 1978.

———. "'Omnes et Singulatim': Toward a Critique of Political Reason." In *Power: Essential Works of Michel Foucault 1954–1984*, 3:298–325. New York: New Press, 2000.

———. *Power/Knowledge: Selected Interviews and Other Writings, 1972–1977*. New York: Random House, 1988.

———. *Security, Territory, Population: Lectures at the Collège de France 1977–78*. Edited by Michel Senellart. Translated by Graham Burchell. Lectures at the Collège de France. Basingstoke, UK: Palgrave Macmillan, 2009.

———. *"Society Must Be Defended": Lectures at the Collège de France, 1975–76*. Edited by Mauro Bertani and Alessandro Fontana. New York: Picador, 2003.

Franck, Thomas M. *Nation against Nation: What Happened to the UN Dream and What the US Can Do about It*. Oxford: Oxford University Press, 1985.

Frankenberg, Ruth. *White Women, Race Matters: The Social Construction of Whiteness*. Gender, Racism, Ethnicity. London: Routledge, 1993.

Freedman, Ariela. "Mary Borden's Forbidden Zone: Women's Writing from No-Man's-Land." *Modernism/Modernity* 9, no. 1 (1 January 2002): 109–24. https://doi.org/10.1353/mod.2002 .0006.

Freud, Sigmund. "Mourning and Melancholia." In *On Freud's Mourning and Melancholia*, edited by Thierry Bokanowski, Leticia Glocer Fiorini, and Sergio Lewkowicz, 19–34. London: Taylor & Francis Group, 2007.

Frost, Alan. "New South Wales as Terra Nullius: The British Denial of Aboriginal Land Rights." *Historical Studies* 19 (1981): 513–23.

Fussell, Paul. *The Great War and Modern Memory*. Oxford: Oxford University Press, 2013.

Gabay, Clive. *Imagining Africa: Whiteness and the Western Gaze*. Cambridge: Cambridge University Press, 2018. https://doi.org/10.1017/9781108652582.

Gafni, Reuven. "Life in the 'Blood Field': Jews, Arabs and Jews Again in Jerusalem's Shma'a Neighbourhood (Sha'ary Zion) 1900–1970." *Kathedra* 161 (October 2016). https://www.ybz.org.il/_Uploads/dbsArticles/Gafni.pdf.

Ganzenmüller, Raphael, Janelle M. Sylvester, and Augusto Castro-Nunez. "What Peace Means for Deforestation: An Analysis of Local Deforestation Dynamics in Times of Conflict and Peace in Colombia." *Frontiers in Environmental Science* 10 (2022). https://www.frontiersin.org/articles/10.3389/fenvs.2022.803368.

Gappah, Petina. *Out of Darkness, Shining Light: (Being a Faithful Account of the Final Years and Earthly Days of Doctor David Livingstone and His Last Journey from the Interior to the Coast of Africa, as Narrated by His African Companions, in Three Volumes)*. New York: Scribner, 2019.

Geisler, Charles. "New Terra Nullius Narratives and the Gentrification of Africa's 'Empty Lands.'" *Journal of World-Systems Research* 18, no. 1 (26 February 2012): 15–29. https://doi.org/10.5195/jwsr.2012.484.

"General Armistice Agreement between the Hashemite Jordan Kingdom and Israel." 3 April 1949. UN Doc S/1302/Rev.1. https://peacemaker.un.org/sites/peacemaker.un.org/files/IL%20JO_490403_Hashemite%20Jordan%20Kingdom-Israel%20General%20Armistice%20Agreement.pdf.

Ghanim, Hunaida. "On the Shadow and Its Shadows." In *Men In Sun*, edited by Tal Ben-Tzvi and Hana Farah. Herzliya, Israel: Herzliya Museum of Contemporary Art, 2009.

Gilligan, Carol. *In a Different Voice: Psychological Theory and Women's Development*. Cambridge, MA: Harvard University Press, 2003.

Glare, P. G. W. *Oxford Latin Dictionary*. Oxford, UK: Clarendon Press, 1968.

Glass, Ira, Aviva DeKornfeld, Molly O'Toole, and Emily Green. "The Out Crowd." *This American Life*, 15 November 2019. https://www.thisamericanlife.org/688/the-out-crowd.

Glennon, John P., Harriet D. Schwar, and Paul Claussen. "Briefing for Director of Central Intelligence Helms for a National Security Council Meeting, April 16, 1969." In *Foreign Relations of the United States, 1969–1976*, vol. 19, pt. 1, Korea, 1969–1972, doc. 11. Washington, DC: US Government Printing Office, 1983. https://history.state.gov/historicaldocuments/frus1969-76v19p1/d11.

———, eds. "The Commander in Chief, United Nations Command (Ridgway) to the Joint Chiefs of Staff, 26 July 1951." In *Foreign Relations of the United States, 1951, Korea and China*, vol. 7, pt. 1, doc. 472. Washington, DC: US Government Printing Office, 1983. https://history.state.gov/historicaldocuments/frus1951v07p1/d472.

———, eds. "The Commander in Chief, United Nations Command (Ridgway) to the Joint Chiefs of Staff, 27 July 1951." In *Foreign Relations of the United States, 1951, Korea and China*, vol. 7, pt. 1, doc. 475. Washington, DC: US Government Printing Office, 1983. https://history.state.gov/historicaldocuments/frus1951v07p1/d475.

———, eds. "The Joint Chiefs of Staff to the Commander in Chief, Far East (Ridgway), 14 November 1951." In *Foreign Relations of the United States, 1951, Korea and China*, vol. 7, pt. 1, doc. 707. Washington, DC: US Government Printing Office, 1983. https://history.state.gov/historicaldocuments/frus1951v07p1/d707.

———, eds. "The Joint Chiefs of Staff to the Commander in Chief, United Nations Command (Ridgway), 30 June 1951." In *Foreign Relations of the United States, 1951, Korea and China*,

vol. 7, pt. 1, doc. 392. Washington, DC: US Government Printing Office, 1983. https://history
.state.gov/historicaldocuments/frus1951v07p1/d475.

Golan, Arnon. "Jewish Settlement of Former Arab Towns and Their Incorporation into the Israeli Urban System (1948–50)." *Israel Affairs* 9, nos. 1–2 (2003): 149–64.

———. "Refugees, Immigrants, Abandoned Neighbourhoods: Designing the Urban System of
Jewish Jerusalem in the War of Independence and its Aftermath." In *Divided Jerusalem
1948–1967: Sources, Summaries, Key Issues and Aids* [*Yerushalayim ha-ḥatsuyah, 1948–1967*],
edited by Avi Bareli, 69–90. Idan 18. Jerusalem: Yad Izhak Ben-Zvi, 1994.

Goldstein, Daniel M. "Toward a Critical Anthropology of Security." *Current Anthropology* 51,
no. 4 (2010): 487–517. https://doi.org/10.1086/655393.

Gómez, María Mercedes. "Prejudice-Based Violence." In *Gender and Sexuality in Latin America—
Cases and Decisions*, edited by Cristina Motta and Macarena Sáez, 279–323. Ius Gentium:
Comparative Perspectives on Law and Justice. Dordrecht: Springer Netherlands, 2013. https://
doi.org/10.1007/978-94-007-6199-5_8.

Gómez Zúñiga, Sebastián. "La ecología política de las FARC-EP: Un análisis de las territorialidades, prácticas y discursos de la insurgencia frente a la naturaleza." PhD diss., Pontificia
Universidad Javeriana, Facultad de Ciencias Sociales, 2018.

Gonen, Amiram. "Widespread and Diverse Neighborhood Gentrification in Jerusalem." *Political Geography* 21, no. 5 (June 2002): 727–37. https://doi.org/10.1016/S0962-6298(02)00018-5.

Gordillo, Gastón. *Rubble: The Afterlife of Destruction*. Durham, NC: Duke University Press, 2014.

Grant, Simon. "A Terrible Beauty." *Tate Etc.*, no. 5 (Autumn 2005). http://www.tate.org.uk/con
text-comment/articles/terrible-beauty.

Green, David. "Veins of Resemblance: Photography and Eugenics." *Oxford Art Journal* 7, no. 2
(1984): 3–16.

Gregory, Derek. *The Colonial Present: Afghanistan. Palestine. Iraq*. Malden, MA: Blackwell, 2004.

———. "Divisions of Life: Journeys from No Man's Land 1914–1918." *Geographical Imaginations*
(blog), 28 April 2015. https://geographicalimaginations.com/2015/04/28/divisions-of-life/.

———. "Gabriel's Map: Cartography and Choreography in Modern War." In *Geographies of
Knowledge and Power*, edited by Peter Meusburger, Derek Gregory, and Laura Suarsana,
89–121. Dordrecht, Netherlands: Springer, 2015.

———. "The Natures of War." *Antipode* 48, no. 1 (1 January 2016): 3–56. https://doi.org/10.1111
/anti.12173.

Grovogui, Siba N. "Regimes of Sovereignty: International Morality and the African Condition."
European Journal of International Relations 8, no. 3 (2002): 315–38.

Habibi, Emile. "Mandelbaum Gate." Translated by Stacy N. Beckwith. *The Short Story Project*,
August 1999. https://shortstoryproject.com/stories/mandelbaum-gate/.

Hacohen, Dvora. *Immigrants in Turmoil: Mass Immigration to Israel and Its Repercussions in the
1950s and After*. Syracuse, NY: Syracuse University Press, 2003.

Hall, Lesley A. "Impotent Ghosts from No Man's Land, Flappers' Boyfriends, or Cryptopatriarchs? Men, Sex and Social Change in 1920s Britain." *Social History* 21, no. 1 (1996): 54–70.

Hamilton, John T. *Security: Politics, Humanity, and the Philology of Care*. Translation/Transna-
tion. Princeton, NJ: Princeton University Press, 2013.

Hamou, Ammar, and Madeline Edwards. "In Rukban, Rumors of Dead, Mistreated Returnees
Leave Displaced Residents Mulling an Uncertain Homecoming." *Syria Direct*, 15 April 2020.
https://syriadirect.org/news/in-rukban-rumors-of-dead-mistreated-returnees-leave-displaced
-residents-mulling-an-uncertain-homecoming/.

Harvey, David. *The Condition of Postmodernity: An Enquiry into the Origins of Cultural Change.* Oxford: Blackwell, 1989.

————. "The 'New' Imperialism: Accumulation by Dispossession." *Socialist Register* 40 (19 March 2009): 63–87.

Harvey, Penny, and Hannah Knox. "The Enchantments of Infrastructure." *Mobilities* 7, no. 4 (1 November 2012): 521–36. https://doi.org/10.1080/17450101.2012.718935.

Hasson, Shlomo. *Urban Social Movements in Jerusalem: The Protest of the Second Generation.* SUNY Series in Israeli Studies. Albany: State University of New York Press, 1993.

Hausmann, Raoul. "Photomontage." In *Photography in the Modern Era: European Documents and Critical Writings, 1913–1940,* edited by Christopher Phillips, 178–81. New York: Aperture, 1989.

Heaton, Jeremiah. "What Starting My Own Country Taught Me about Independence." *MEL Magazine,* 4 July 2017. https://melmagazine.com/en-us/story/what-starting-my-own-coun try-taught-me-about-independence.

Heise, Ursula K. *Sense of Place and Sense of Planet: The Environmental Imagination of the Global.* Oxford Scholarship Online, Literature Module. New York: Oxford University Press, 2008.

Held, Virginia. *The Ethics of Care: Personal, Political, and Global.* New York: Oxford University Press, 2005. https://doi.org/10.1093/0195180992.001.0001.

Heller, Sam. "What an Unfolding Humanitarian Disaster in a U.S.-Protected Enclave Tells Us about American Strategy in Syria." *War on the Rocks,* 20 November 2017. https://waronthe rocks.com/2017/11/16162/.

Herf, Jeffrey. *Reactionary Modernism: Technology, Culture and Politics in Weimar and the Third Reich.* Cambridge: Cambridge University Press, 1984.

Hermes, Walter G. *Truce Tent and Fighting Front.* Washington, DC: Office of the Chief of Military History, US Army, 1992. http://hdl.handle.net/2027/uiug.30112000735826.

Hernández Camacho, J. "Una síntesis de la historia evolutiva de la biodiversidad en Colombia." In *Nuestra diversidad biológica,* edited by Sonia Cárdenas and Darío Correa. Bogotá: CEREC and Fundación Alejandro Ángel Escobar, 1993. http://agris.fao.org/agris-search/search .do?recordID=CO1999000352.

Herța, Laura M. "Peacekeeping and (Mis)Management of Ethnic Disputes: The Cyprus Case." *Studia Universitatis Babes-Bolyai—Studia Europaea,* no. 3 (2012): 59–76.

Hesse-Honegger, Cornelia. *Heteroptera the Beautiful and the Other, or, Images of a Mutating World.* Edited by Liz Jobey. Zurich: Scalo, 2001.

Hinshaw, Arned L. *Heartbreak Ridge: Korea, 1951.* New York, 1989. http://archive.org/details/heart breakridgek00hins.

Hobbes, Thomas. *De Cive: The English Version.* Edited by Howard Warrender. Clarendon Edition of the Philosophical Works of Thomas Hobbes 2. Oxford, UK: Clarendon, 1984.

————. *Leviathan.* Online Library of Liberty. Oxford, UK: Clarendon Press, 1909.

Hochberg, Gil Z. *Visual Occupations: Violence and Visibility in a Conflict Zone.* Perverse Modernities. Durham, NC: Duke University Press, 2015.

Hubbard, Tasha. "Buffalo Genocide in Nineteenth-Century North America: 'Kill, Skin, and Sell.'" In *Colonial Genocide in Indigenous North America,* edited by Alexander Laban Hinton, Andrew Woolford, and Jeff Benvenuto, 273–91. Durham, NC: Duke University Press, 2014. https://doi.org/10.1515/9780822376149.

Human Rights Watch. "Jordan: New Satellite Images of Syrians Stranded at Border." 7 September 2016. https://www.hrw.org/news/2016/09/07/jordan-new-satellite-images-syrians-stranded -border.

————. "Jordan: Syrians Blocked, Stranded in Desert." 3 June 2015. https://www.hrw.org/news
/2015/06/03/jordan-syrians-blocked-stranded-desert.

————. "United States: Transfer 70,000 Trapped Syrians." 5 August 2015. https://www.hrw.org
/news/2016/08/05/jordan-united-states-transfer-70000-trapped-syrians.

Humanitarian Foresight Think Tank. "Jordan and the Berm: Rukban and Hadalat 2017–2018."
Institut de Relations Internationales et Stratégiques, March 2017. https://www.iris-france
.org/wp-content/uploads/2017/03/Sensitive-Jordan-and-the-Berm-1.pdf.

Hurley, Frank. *The Diaries of Frank Hurley, 1912–1941.* Edited by Robert Dixon and Christopher
Lee. London: Anthem Press, 2011.

————. "War Photography." *Australian Photo Review*, 15 February 1919.

Ibrahim, M. S. "Artisanal Mining in Sudan: Opportunities, Challenges, and Impacts." Presented
at the UNCTAD, 17th Africa OILGASMINE: Extractive Industries and Sustainable Job Creation, Khartoum, 2015. https://unctad.org/meetings/en/Presentation/17OILGASMINE%20
Mohamed%20Sulaiman%20Ibrahim%20S4.pdf.

Idan, Alon. "Tens of Pixels of Indifference." *Haaretz*, 8 May 2012. http://www.haaretz.co.il/news
/politics/1.1702532.

Ilican, Murat Erdal. "The Occupy Buffer Zone Movement: Radicalism and Sovereignty in Cyprus." *Cyprus Review* 25, no. 1 (2013): 55–80.

Ille, Enrico, and Sandra Calkins. "Gold Mining Concessions in Sudan's Written Laws, and Prac-
tices of Gold Extraction in the Nuba Mountains." In *Identity, Economy, Power Relations and
External Interests: Old and New Challenges for Sudan and South Sudan*, edited by Grawert
Elke, 112–26. Addis Ababa: OSSREA, 2014.

Ingold, Tim. *Lines: A Brief History.* London: Routledge, 2008.

Interagency Coordination Headquarters of the Russian Federation and the Syrian Arab Republic. "On the Problems Hindering the Implementation of Initiative on Refugees and Internally Displaced Persons Return to Places of Their Residence." Ministry of Defense of the
Russian Federation, 28 March 2020. https://eng.mil.ru/en/news_page/country/more.htm?id
=12284261@egNews.

————. "On the Problems of Returning Syrian Refugees and Internally Displaced Persons to
Their Homes in the Context of the Spread of Coronavirus Infection." Ministry of Defense of
the Russian Federation: Mission to Syria, 9 June 2020. http://syria.mil.ru/peacemaking_en
/info/news/more.htm?id=12296503@egNews.

————. "On the Problems of Rukban Camp Disbandment in the Context of Coronavirus Infection's Spread." Ministry of Defense of the Russian Federation, 26 June 2020. https://eng.mil
.ru/en/news_page/country/more.htm?id=12299078@egNews.

Ir Amim. "Sheikh Sa'ad and the Separation Barrier: Trends in Jerusalem." Jerusalem, 29 August
2006. https://sawahreh.wordpress.com/2009/11/12/sheikh-saad-and-the-separation-barrier
-trends-in-jerusalem/.

Isin, Engin F. "A Labour of Love (the Right to Philosophy)." *Citizenship Studies* 27, no. 3 (2023):
422–26. https://doi.org/10.1080/13621025.2023.2171256.

Jay, Martin. "Scopic Regimes of Modernity." In *Vision and Visuality*, edited by Hal Foster, 3–28.
Discussions in Contemporary Culture 2. Seattle: Bay Press, 1988.

————. "Walter Benjamin, Remembrance, and the First World War." *Estudios/Working Papers
(Centro de Estudios Avanzados en Ciencias Sociales)*, no. 87 (1996): 1.

Jean-Klein, Iris. "Nationalism and Resistance: The Two Faces of Everyday Activism in Palestine
during the Intifada." *Cultural Anthropology* 16, no. 1 (1 February 2001): 83–126.

Jefferis, Danielle C. "Institutionalizing Statelessness: The Revocation of Residency Rights of Palestinians in East Jerusalem." *International Journal of Refugee Law* 24, no. 2 (2012): 202–30. https://doi.org/10.1093/ijrl/ees026.

Jeffrey, James (US Special Representative for Syria). "The Role of the U.S. in Syria: Planning for the Future." 2019 Aspen Security Forum, Interview by Josh Rogin, *Washington Post*. Transcript, 19 July 2019. https://aspensecurityforum.org/wp-content/uploads/2019/07/The-Role -of-the-U.S.pdf.

Jeffreys, Sheila. *The Industrial Vagina: The Political Economy of the Global Sex Trade*. London: Routledge, 2008.

Johnson, Christopher D. *Memory, Metaphor, and Aby Warburg's Atlas of Images*. Signale: Modern German Letters, Cultures, and Thought. Ithaca, NY: Cornell University Press, 2012.

Jolly, Martyn. "Australian First-World-War Photography Frank Hurley and Charles Bean." *History of Photography* 23, no. 2 (1999): 141–48. https://doi.org/10.1080/03087298.1999.10443814.

Jünger, Ernst. *Der Kampf als inneres Erlebnis*. Berlin: E. S. Mittler & Sohn, 1922.

Jurisdicción Especial para la Paz (JEP). "La JEP hace pública la estrategia de priorización dentro del Caso 03, conocido como el de falsos positivos." Press release. https://www.jep.gov.co :443/Sala-de-Prensa/Paginas/La-JEP-hace-p%C3%BAblica-la-estrategia-de-priorizaci%C3%B 3n-dentro-del-Caso-03,-conocido-como-el-de-falsos-positivos.aspx.

Jütersonke, Oliver, and Moncef Kartas. "The State as Urban Myth: Governance without Government in the Global South." In *The Concept of the State in International Relations*, edited by Robert Schuett and Peter M. R. Stirk, 108–34. Edinburgh University Press, 2015. https:// doi.org/10.3366/edinburgh/9780748693627.003.0005.

Kanafani, Ghassan. *Men in the Sun & Other Palestinian Stories*. Boulder, CO: Lynne Rienner, 1999.

Kemp, Adriana. "Border Space and National Identity in Israel." In *Space, Land, Home [Merhav, Adamah, Bayit]*, edited by Yehouda A. Shenhav, 52–83. Jerusalem: Van Leer Jerusalem Institute; Tel Aviv: Hakibbutz Hameuchad Publishers, 2003.

Kemp, Martin. "Hesse-Honegger's Hand-Work." *Nature* 392, no. 6676 (1998): 555. https://doi.org /10.1038/33298.

Keshavarz, Mahmoud, and Shahram Khosravi, eds. *Seeing like a Smuggler: Borders from Below*. Anthropology, Culture and Society. London: Pluto Press, 2022.

Khamaisi, Rasim. "The Trap of Urban Planning Development in Jerusalem." *Contemporary Arab Affairs* 12, no. 2 (2019): 105–38. https://doi.org/10.1525/caa.2019.122005.

Kit, Borys. "Disney Picks Up Family Adventure Project 'Princess of North Sudan.'" *Hollywood Reporter*, 6 November 2014. https://www.hollywoodreporter.com/heat-vision/disney-picks -up-family-adventure-747114.

Klein, Naomi. *The Shock Doctrine: Rise of Disaster Capitalism*. London: Allen Lane, 2007.

Knox, Donald. *The Korean War: Uncertain Victory*. San Diego, CA: Harcourt Brace Jovanovich, 1991.

Koettl, Christoph. "Visualizing the Invisible: Stranded Syrians in the Desert." *Medium* (blog), 16 September 2016. https://medium.com/lemming-cliff/visualizing-the-invisible-stranded -syrians-in-the-desert-3feccd9707f3.

Korff, Gottfried, ed. *Kasten 117: Aby Warburg und der Aberglaube im Ersten Weltkrieg*. 1. Aufl. Untersuchungen Des Ludwig-Uhland-Instituts der Universität Tübingen, 105. Bd. Tübingen: Tübinger Vereinigung für Volkskunde, 2007.

Kristiansson, Magnus, and Johan Tralau. "Hobbes's Hidden Monster: A New Interpretation of the Frontispiece of *Leviathan*." *European Journal of Political Theory* 13, no. 3 (2014): 299–320. https://doi.org/10.1177/1474885113491954.

Kroll-Zeldin, Oren. "Institutional Separation and Sumud in Jerusalem's Periphery." *Jerusalem Quarterly* 73 (2018): 101–16.

Kutz, Christopher. *Complicity: Ethics and Law for a Collective Age*. Cambridge Studies in Philosophy and Law. Cambridge: Cambridge University Press, 2000.

Land Research Center for Arab Studies. "Demolition of Palestinian Houses Displacement Policy: Statistical Summary of Demolition of Housing in East Jerusalem during the Years 2000–2017." East Jerusalem: Arab Studies Association, 2018. http://lrcj.org/pdf/web/viewer.html?file=Jer_Demo_2000_2017_ARB_S.pdf.

Late Night Live. "The Baramki House." Australian Broadcasting Service, 27 July 2005. https://www.abc.net.au/listen/programs/latenightlive/3355344.

Latour, Bruno. *Facing Gaia: Eight Lectures on the New Climatic Regime*. Translated by Catherine Porter. Cambridge, UK: Polity, 2017.

Law-Yone, Hubert, and Rachel Kallus. "The Dynamics of Ethnic Segregation in Israel." In *The Power of Planning: Spaces of Control and Transformation*, edited by Oren Yiftachel, 171–88. Geojournal Library 67. Dordrecht, Netherlands: Kluwer Academic, 2001.

Leal, Claudia. *A la buena de Dios: Colonización en la Macarena, ríos Duda y Guayabero*. Bogotá: FESCOL and CEREC, 1995.

Leed, Eric J. *No Man's Land: Combat & Identity in World War I*. Cambridge: Cambridge University Press, 1979.

Leenders, Reinoud, and Kholoud Mansour. "Humanitarianism, State Sovereignty, and Authoritarian Regime Maintenance in the Syrian War." *Political Science Quarterly* 133, no. 2 (2018): 225–57. https://doi.org/10.1002/polq.12773.

LeGrand, Catherine C. *Frontier Expansion and Peasant Protest in Colombia, 1850–1936*. Albuquerque: University of New Mexico Press, 1986.

Leshem, Noam. *Life after Ruin: The Struggles over Israel's Depopulated Arab Spaces*. Cambridge Middle East Studies 48. Cambridge: Cambridge University Press, 2017.

———. "Spaces of Abandonment: Genealogies, Lives and Critical Horizons." *Environment and Planning D: Society and Space* 35, no. 4 (2017): 620–36. https://doi.org/10.1177/0263775816683189.

Levinson, Chaim. "Court Verdict on Israeli Cops Who Let Injured Palestinian Die Full of Errors." *Haaretz*, 2 March 2014. http://www.haaretz.com/news/national/.premium-1.577368.

———. "How Israeli Negligence Led to the Death of a Palestinian Car Thief." *Haaretz*, 17 February 2012. http://www.haaretz.co.il/news/politics/1.1643974.

Levi Strauss, David. "The Magic of the State: An Interview with Michael Taussig." *Cabinet*, Summer 2005. http://cabinetmagazine.org/issues/18/strauss_taussig.php.

Lewis, Cecil. *Sagittarius Rising*. London: Greenhill, 2006.

Lifton, Robert Jay. *The Nazi Doctors: Medical Killing and the Psychology of Genocide*. 4th ed. New York: Basic Books, 2017. http://catdir.loc.gov/catdir/enhancements/fy0831/2004695065-b.html.

Lindley, Dan. "Historical, Tactical, and Strategic Lessons from the Partition of Cyprus." *International Studies Perspectives* 8, no. 2 (2007): 224–41. https://doi.org/10.1111/j.1528-3585.2007.00282.x.

Lister, Tim, Nima Elbagir, and Sebastian Shukla. "A Russian Company's Secret Plan to Quell Protests in Sudan." *CNN*, 25 April 2019. https://www.cnn.com/2019/04/25/africa/russia-sudan-minvest-plan-to-quell-protests-intl/index.html.

Lorde, Audre. *Sister Outsider: Essays and Speeches*. New York: Potter, Ten Speed, Harmony, Rodale, 2012.

Loughlin, Sean. "Rumsfeld on Looting in Iraq: 'Stuff Happens.'" *CNN International Edition*, 12 April 2003. https://edition.cnn.com/2003/US/04/11/sprj.irq.pentagon/.

Lu, Yan, Krzysztof Koperski, Chiman Kwan, and Jiang Li. "Deep Learning for Effective Refugee Tent Extraction Near Syria-Jordan Border." *IEEE Geoscience and Remote Sensing Letters* (2020): 1–5. https://doi.org/10.1109/LGRS.2020.2999354.

Lund, Aron. "Blame Game over Syrians Stranded in the Desert." New York: Century Foundation, 18 June 2018. https://tcf.org/content/report/blame-game-syrians-stranded-desert/.

Maliński, Piotr. "Searching for Nubian Desert Gold with a Metal Detector: Functioning and Organization of Dahaba Occupational Group in Sudan." In *Collectanea Sudanica*, edited by Waldemar Cisło, Jarosław Różański, and Maciej Ząbek, 1:123–50. Pelplin, Poland: Bernardinaum, 2017.

Malkawi, Khetam, and Omar Akour. "Jordan Commander: IS Expands Hold in Border Camp for Syrians." Associated Press, 15 February 2017. https://apnews.com/6f19357cea4c4dc49631d4958373fc23.

Manning, Erin. *The Minor Gesture*. Thought in the Act. Durham, NC: Duke University Press, 2016.

Marder, Michael P., and Anaïs Tondeur. *The Chernobyl Herbarium: Fragments of an Exploded Consciousness*. Critical Climate Change. London: Open Humanities Press, 2016.

Margaroni, Maria. "Care and Abandonment: A Response to Mika Ojakangas' 'Impossible Dialogue on Bio-Power: Agamben and Foucault.'" *Foucault Studies* 2 (2005): 29–36.

Marks, Jesse. "Why Jordan Won't Alleviate the Rukban Crisis." Middle East Institute, 21 April 2022. https://www.mei.edu/publications/why-jordan-wont-alleviate-rukban-crisis.

Martin, Paul S., and Christine R. Szuter. "War Zones and Game Sinks in Lewis and Clark's West." *Conservation Biology* 13, no. 1 (1999): 36–45. https://doi.org/10.1046/j.1523-1739.1999.97417.x.

Masefield, John. *The Old Front Line*. New York: Macmillan, 1917.

Massey, Doreen. *For Space*. London: Sage, 2005.

Matos, Rémi de, and Joseph P. Dudley. "The Conflict Landscape of Verdun, France: Conserving Cultural and Natural Heritage after WWI." In *Collateral Values: The Natural Capital Created by Landscapes of War*, edited by Todd R. Lookingbill and Peter D. Smallwood, 111–32. Cham, Switzerland: Springer, 2019.

Mbembe, Achille. "Necropolitics." *Public Culture* 15, no. 1 (2003): 11–40. https://doi.org/10.1215/08992363-15-1-11.

———. *Necropolitics*. Theory in Forms. Durham, NC: Duke University Press, 2019. https://doi.org/10.1515/9781478007227.

McFarlane, Colin. *Fragments of the City: Making and Remaking Urban Worlds*. Oakland: University of California Press, 2021.

Meger, Sara. *Rape Loot Pillage: The Political Economy of Sexual Violence in Armed Conflict*. Oxford Studies in Gender and International Relations. Oxford: Oxford University Press, 2016.

Meir, Tehila, and Hamoked Centre for the Defence of the Individual. Letter to Major General Assaf Attias, IDF Civil Administration. "Restrictions on the Movement of Permanent Residents in the Sheik Sa'ad Checkpoint." 6 April 2020. http://www.hamoked.org.il/files/2020/1664210.pdf.

Mercer, David. "Terra Nullius, Aboriginal Sovereignty and Land Rights in Australia: The De-

bate Continues." *Political Geography* 12, no. 4 (1993): 299–318. https://doi.org/10.1016/0962
-6298(93)90043-7.

Merlo, Alessandra. "La imagen cautiva: Reflexiones sobre la foto icónica de Íngrid Betancourt
durante el secuestro." *Revista Colombiana de Pensamiento Estético e Historia del Arte* 12
(2020): 158–88.

Mills, Catherine. *Biopolitics*. New York: Routledge, 2017.

Mills, Richard. "Remarks at a UN Security Council Briefing on the Political and Humanitarian Situation in Syria." *Syrian Observer* (blog), 26 January 2023. https://syrianobserver.com
/resources/81443/remarks-at-a-un-security-council-briefing-on-the-political-and-humanita
rian-situation-in-syria.html.

Minca, Claudio. "Geographies of the Camp." *Political Geography* 49 (November 2015): 74–83.
https://doi.org/10.1016/j.polgeo.2014.12.005.

Ministry of Defence of the Russian Federation. "Russian and Syrian Joint Coordination Headquarters Make Another Report on Plight of the Syrians in the Rukban Camp." 12 March
2019. http://eng.mil.ru/en/news_page/country/more.htm?id=12221080@egNews.

Mitchell, W. J. T. "Method, Madness and Montage: Assemblages of Images and the Production
of Knowledge." In *Image Operations: Visual Media and Political Conflict*, edited by Jens Eder
and Charlotte Klonk, 79–85. Oxford: Oxford University Press, 2016.

Mitman, Gregg, Michelle Murphy, and Christopher Sellers. "Introduction: A Cloud over History." *Osiris* 19 (2004): 1–17.

Moeller, Susan D. *Shooting War: Photography and the American Experience of Combat*. New York:
Basic Books, 1989.

Molano, Alfredo. "Aproximación al proceso de colonización de la región del Agri-Güejar-
Guayabero." In *La Macarena: Reserva biológica de la humanidad: Territorio de conflictos*, by
Fernando Cubides, Antanas Mockus, Mario Avellaneda, Henry González, Óscar Arcila, Al-
fredo Molano, Juan Carlos Pacheco, and Ricardo Mosquera Mesa, 279–304. Bogotá: Centro
Editorial, Centro de Estudios Sociales, Facultad de Ciencias Humanas, Universidad Nacio-
nal de Colombia, 1989.

Molinares, Luis Eduardo Fernández. "Vivir bajo sospecha: Estudios de caso: Personas LGBT
víctimas del conflicto armado en Vistahermosa y San Onofre." Bogotá: Colombia Diversa,
May 2017. http://www.colombiadiversa.org/conflictoarmado-lgbt/documentos/vivir%20baja
%20sospecha.pdf.

Møller, Anders Pape, and Timothy A. Mousseau. "Biological Consequences of Chernobyl:
20 Years On." *Trends in Ecology & Evolution* 21, no. 4 (2006): 200–207. https://doi.org/10.1016
/j.tree.2006.01.008.

Mookherjee, Nayanika. *The Spectral Wound: Sexual Violence, Public Memories, and the Bangladesh War of 1971*. Durham, NC: Duke University Press, 2015.

Moran, Joe. *On Roads: A Hidden History*. London: Profile Books, 2010.

Mosse, George L. *Fallen Soldiers: Reshaping the Memory of the World Wars*. New York: Oxford
University Press, 1991.

Mould, R. F. *Chernobyl Record: The Definitive History of the Chernobyl Catastrophe*. Bristol, UK:
Institute of Physics Publishing, 2000.

Mousseau, Timothy A., Gennadi Milinevsky, Jane Kenney-Hunt, and Anders Pape Møller. "Highly
Reduced Mass Loss Rates and Increased Litter Layer in Radioactively Contaminated Areas."
Oecologia 175, no. 1 (2014): 429–37. https://doi.org/10.1007/s00442-014-2908-8.

Murav, Harriet. *As the Dust of the Earth: The Literature of Abandonment in Revolutionary Russia and Ukraine.* Bloomington: Indiana University Press, 2024.

Murchison, Roderick Impey. "Address to the Royal Geographical Society." *Proceedings of the Royal Geographical Society of London* 8, no. 5 (1864): 170–254. https://doi.org/10.2307/1799282.

Murphy, Theodore, and Mattia Caniglia. "Khartoum's Autocratic Enabler: Russia in Sudan—European Council on Foreign Relations." *European Council on Foreign Relations* (blog), 15 December 2021. https://ecfr.eu/article/khartoums-autocratic-enabler-russia-in-sudan/.

Nair, Rukmini Bhaya. "Postcoloniality and the Matrix of Indifference." *India International Centre Quarterly* 26, no. 2 (1999): 7–24.

Nancy, Jean-Luc. *The Birth to Presence.* Stanford, CA: Stanford University Press, 1993.

———. *The Inoperative Community.* Theory and History of Literature 76. Minneapolis: University of Minnesota Press, 1990.

Nash, Paul. *British Artists at the Front.* Vol. 3, *Paul Nash.* London: Country Life; George Newnes, 1918.

Ngai, Sianne. "Merely Interesting." *Critical Inquiry* 34, no. 4 (2008): 777–817. https://doi.org/10.1086/592544.

Nichols, Robert Lee. "Realizing the Social Contract: The Case of Colonialism and Indigenous Peoples." *Contemporary Political Theory* 4, no. 1 (2005): 42–62.

Nieuwenhuis, Marijn. "The Invisible Lines of Territory: An Investigation into the Make-Up of Territory." In *The Question of Space: Interrogating the Spatial Turn between Disciplines*, edited by Marjin Nieuwenhuis and David Crouch, 115–34. London: Rowman & Littlefield Publishers, 2017.

Nixon, Rob. *Slow Violence and the Environmentalism of the Poor.* Cambridge, MA: Harvard University Press, 2011.

Noam, Yoram, Karmi Mosek, and Moshe Bar-Am. Criminal Appeal 272 44-08-12 Baruch Peretz & Asaf Yekutieli v. Israel Police Internal Investigation Department (Jerusalem District Court), 24 February 2014.

Nolte, Amina. "Political Infrastructure and the Politics of Infrastructure." *City* 20, no. 3 (2016): 441–54. https://doi.org/10.1080/13604813.2016.1169778.

Note, Nicolas, Wouter Gheyle, Hanne Van den Berghe, Timothy Saey, Jean Bourgeois, Veerle Van Eetvelde, Marc Van Meirvenne, and Birger Stichelbaut. "A New Evaluation Approach of World War One's Devastated Front Zone: A Shell Hole Density Map Based on Historical Aerial Photographs and Validated by Electromagnetic Induction Field Measurements to Link the Metal Shrapnel Phenomenon." *Geoderma* 310 (15 January 2018): 257–69. https://doi.org/10.1016/j.geoderma.2017.09.029.

Noyes, John K. *Colonial Space: Spatiality in the Discourse of German South West Africa 1884–1915.* Studies in Anthropology and History 4. Chur, Switzerland: Harwood Academic Publishers, 1992.

Oberdorfer, Don. *The Two Koreas: A Contemporary History.* Rev. ed. New York: Basic Books, 2013.

Office of the Geographer, Department of State. "Sudan–Egypt (United Arab Republic) Boundary." Washington, DC: Office of the Geographer, Bureau of Intelligence and Research, US State Department, 27 July 1962.

Office of the UN High Commissioner for Human Rights. "Report of the United Nations High Commissioner for Human Rights on the Human Rights Situation in Colombia." UN Economic and Social Council, 28 February 2002. https://documents-dds-ny.un.org/doc/UNDOC/GEN/G02/111/15/PDF/G0211115.pdf?OpenElement.

Ojakangas, Mika. "Michel Foucault and the Enigmatic Origins of Bio-Politics and Govern-mentality." *History of the Human Sciences* 25, no. 1 (2012): 1–14. https://doi.org/10.1177/095 2695111426654.

Olivares, Antonio, and Theobaldo Mozo. *Reserva nacional de La Macarena*. Bogotá: Universi-dad Nacional de Colombia and Instituto Colombiano de la Reforma Agraria, 1968.

Oliver, David, and Paolo Valpolini. "The Colombian Military-Industrial Complex." *EDR Magazine*, 28 January 2018. https://www.edrmagazine.eu/the-colombian-military-industrial-complex-2.

Onishi, Yasuo, Oleg V. Voitsekovich, and Mark J. Zheleznyak, eds. *Chernobyl—What Have We Learned? The Successes and Failures to Mitigate Water Contamination over 20 Years*. Dor-drecht, Netherlands: Springer, 2007.

Ophir, Adi. *The Order of Evils: Toward an Ontology of Morals*. New York: Zone Books, 2005.

———. "The Two-State Solution: Providence and Catastrophe." *Theoretical Inquiries in Law* 8, no. 1 (2007): 117–60.

Ophir, Adi, Michal Givoni, and Sari Hanafi. *The Power of Inclusive Exclusion: Anatomy of Israeli Rule in the Occupied Palestinian Territories*. New York: Zone Books, 2009.

Oppenheim, Víctor. "Geología de la Cordillera Oriental, entre Los Llanos y el Magdalena." *Re-vista de la Academia Colombiana de Ciencias* 4, no. 14 (1941): 175–81.

Orpen, William. *An Onlooker in France, 1917–1919*. London: Williams and Norgate, 1921.

Ortiz, Nubia Tobar. "En el umbral de una muerte inevitable: Los Tinigua de la sierra de La Ma-carena." In *La recuperación de las lenguas nativas como búsqueda de identidad étnica*. Sym-posium, VII Congreso de Antropología, CCELA, Bogotá, Universidad de los Andes, 1994.

Pain, Rachel. "Everyday Terrorism: Connecting Domestic Violence and Global Terrorism." *Prog-ress in Human Geography* 38, no. 4 (2014): 531–50.

———. "Intimate War." *Political Geography* 44 (2015): 64–73.

Palacios, Marco. *Violencia pública en Colombia, 1958–2010*. Bogotá: Fondo de Cultura Económica, 2012.

Papastergiadis, Nikos. "The Invasion Complex: The Abject Other and Spaces of Violence." *Geo-grafiska Annaler: Series B, Human Geography* 88, no. 4 (2006): 429–42. https://doi.org/10.1111/j.0435-3684.2006.00231.x.

Paret, Peter. *Imagined Battles: Reflections of War in European Art*. Chapel Hill: University of North Carolina Press, 1997.

Parks, Lisa. "Digging into Google Earth: An Analysis of 'Crisis in Darfur.'" *Geoforum* 40, no. 4 (July 2009): 535–45. https://doi.org/10.1016/j.geoforum.2009.04.004.

Pease, Donald E. *The New American Exceptionalism*. Minneapolis: University of Minnesota Press, 2009.

Perlson, Inbar. *Great Joy Tonight: Arab-Jewish Music and Mizrahi Identity [Simha gdola halayla]*. Tel Aviv: Resling, 2006.

Petryna, Adriana. "Biological Citizenship: The Science and Politics of Chernobyl-Exposed Pop-ulations." *Osiris* 2, no. 19 (2004): 250–65.

———. *Life Exposed: Biological Citizens after Chernobyl*. Princeton, NJ: Princeton University Press, 2002.

Philipson, W. R., C. C. Doncaster, and J. M. Idrobo. "An Expedition to the Sierra de La Macarena, Colombia." *Geographical Journal* 117, no. 2 (June 1951): 188. https://doi.org/10.2307/1791656.

Pierre, Arnauld. *Fernand Léger, peindre la vie moderne*. Paris: Gallimard, 1997.

Povinelli, Elizabeth A. "Defining Security in Late Liberalism: A Comment on Pedersen and

Holbraad." In *Times of Security: Ethnographies of Fear, Protest, and the Future*, edited by Martin Holbraad and Morten Axel Pedersen, 28–32. Routledge Studies in Anthropology 12. London: Routledge, 2015.

———. *Economies of Abandonment: Social Belonging and Endurance in Late Liberalism*. Durham, NC: Duke University Press, 2011.

Pratt, Geraldine. "Abandoned Women and Spaces of the Exception." *Antipode* 37, no. 5 (2005): 1052–78. https://doi.org/10.1111/j.0066-4812.2005.00556.x.

Probyn-Rapsey, Fiona. "Complicity, Critique and Methodology." *ARIEL* 38, nos. 2–3 (2007): 65–82.

Puggioni, Raffaela. "Resisting Sovereign Power: Camps in-Between Exception and Dissent." In *The Politics of Protection: Sites of Insecurity and Political Agency*, edited by Jef Huysmans, Andrew Dobson, and Raia Prokhovnik, 68–83. Routledge Advances in International Relations and Global Politics 43. London: Routledge, 2006.

Pullan, Wendy, Philipp Misselwitz, Rami Nasrallah, and Haim Yacobi. "Jerusalem's Road 1." *City: Analysis of Urban Trends, Culture, Theory, Policy, Action* 11, no. 2 (2007): 176–98. https://doi.org/10.1080/13604810701395993.

Quagliati, Noemi. "Training the Eye: Production and Reception of Aerial Photography during the World Wars." *AUC Geographica* 55, no. 1 (2020): 93–111. https://doi.org/10.14712/2336 1980.2020.6.

Raffles, Hugh. *Insectopedia*. New York: Pantheon Books, 2010.

Ram, Uri. "Ways of Forgetting: Israel and the Obliterated Memory of the Palestinian Nakba." *Journal of Historical Sociology* 22, no. 3 (2009): 366–95. https://doi.org/10.1111/j.1467-6443 .2009.01354.x.

Ramírez, María Clemencia. *Between the Guerrillas and the State: The Cocalero Movement, Citizenship, and Identity in the Colombian Amazon*. Durham, NC: Duke University Press, 2011. https://doi.org/10.1215/9780822394204.

Reardon, Sara. "FARC and the Forest: Peace Is Destroying Colombia's Jungle—and Opening It to Science." *Nature* 558, no. 7709 (2018): 169–70. https://doi.org/10.1038/d41586-018-05397-2.

Regev, Motti. "Present Absentee: Arab Music in Israeli Culture." *Public Culture* 7, no. 2 (1995): 433–45. https://doi.org/10.1215/08992363-7-2-433.

Republic of Sudan. The Mineral Wealth and Mining (Development) Act 2015 (2015). https://kig .pl/wp-content/uploads/2018/05/Mineral-wealth-and-mining.pdf.

Reyner, Anthony S. "Sudan–United Republic (Egypt) Boundary: A Factual Background." *Middle East Journal; Washington* 17, no. 3 (1963): 313–16.

Rodríguez Pinzón, Erika. "Los cambios discursivos sobre el conflicto colombiano en la posguerra fría: Su impacto en la actuación de los actores locales." In *Geopolítica, guerras y resistencias*, edited by Heriberto Cairo and Jaime Pastor, 67–82. Bogotá: Trama Editorial, 2006.

Rose, Jacqueline. *States of Fantasy*. Oxford: Oxford University Press, 1998. http://www.oxford scholarship.com/view/10.1093/acprof:oso/9780198183273.001.0001/acprof-9780198183273.

Ruiz-Serna, Daniel. "Enchanted Forests, Entangled Lives: Spirits, Peasant Economies, and Violence in Northwest Amazonia." Master's thesis, McGill University, 2013.

Rusk, Dean. *As I Saw It*. Harmondsworth, UK: Penguin, 1991.

Ryan, James R. *Photography and Exploration*. London: Reaktion Books, 2013.

Said, Edward. *Orientalism*. New York: Pantheon Books, 1978.

Saint-Amour, Paul K. "Applied Modernism: Military and Civilian Uses of the Aerial Photomosaic." *Theory, Culture & Society* 28, nos. 7–8 (2011): 241–69. https://doi.org/10.1177/026 3276411423938.

——. "Modernist Reconnaissance." *Modernism/Modernity* 10, no. 2 (2003): 349–80. https://doi.org/10.1353/mod.2003.0047.

Sanders, Julie. "The Politics of Escapism: Fantasies of Travel and Power in Richard Brome's 'The Antipodes' and Ben Johnson's 'The Alchemist.'" In *Writing and Fantasy*, edited by Ceri Sullivan and Barbara White, 137–50. New York: Routledge, 2014.

Sanders, Mark. *Complicities: The Intellectual and Apartheid*. Durham, NC: Duke University Press, 2003.

Sanger, David E., and Rick Gladstone. "Defiant Bashar Al-Assad Vows to Retake 'Every Inch' of Syria." *New York Times*, 7 June 2016. https://www.nytimes.com/2016/06/08/world/middleeast/defiant-assad-vows-to-retake-every-inch-of-syria-from-his-foes.html.

Sassen, Saskia. *Expulsions: Brutality and Complexity in the Global Economy*. Cambridge, MA: Belknap Press of Harvard University Press, 2014.

Schaffer, Simon, Lissa Roberts, James Delbourgo, and Kapil Raj, eds. *The Brokered World: Go-Betweens and Global Intelligence, 1770–1820*. Uppsala Studies in History of Science 35. Sagamore Beach, MA: Science History Publications, 2009.

Scheifley, William H. "The Depleted Forests of France." *North American Review* 212, no. 778 (1920): 378–86.

Schindel, Estela. "Death by 'Nature': The European Border Regime and the Spatial Production of Slow Violence." *Environment and Planning C: Politics and Space* 40, no. 2 (2022): 428–46.

Schrader, Astrid. "Abyssal Intimacies and Temporalities of Care: How (Not) to Care about Deformed Leaf Bugs in the Aftermath of Chernobyl." *Social Studies of Science* 45, no. 5 (October 2015): 665–90. https://doi.org/10.1177/0306312715603249.

Scott, James C. *The Art of Not Being Governed: An Anarchist History of Upland Southeast Asia*. Yale Agrarian Studies Series. New Haven, CT: Yale University Press, 2009.

Segal, Gerald. *Defending China*. Oxford: Oxford University Press, 1985.

Seidenberg, David. "Shmita: The Purpose of Sinai." *Hazon* (blog), August 2012. https://hazon.org/wp-content/uploads/2012/08/Shmita-The-Purpose-of-Sinai.pdf.

Sekula, Allan. "The Body and the Archive." *October* 39 (1986): 3–64. https://doi.org/10.2307/778312.

Selmeczi, Anna. "'. . . We Are Being Left to Burn Because We Do Not Count': Biopolitics, Abandonment, and Resistance." *Global Society* 23, no. 4 (2009): 519–38. https://doi.org/10.1080/13600820903198933.

Serje, Margarita. *El revés de la nación: Territorios salvajes, fronteras y tierras de nadie*. Bogotá: Universidad de Los Andes, Facultad de Ciencias Sociales, Departamento de Antropología, and CESO, 2005.

——. "Iron Maiden Landscapes: The Geopolitics of Colombia's Territorial Conquest." Translated by Ashley Caja, Laura Rexach, Rebacca Natolini, and C. Britt Arredondo. *South Central Review* 24, no. 1 (2007): 37–55.

Shahhoud, Annsar. "Medical Génocidaires in the Syrian Civil War (2011–2019)." *Journal of Genocide Research* 25, no. 1 (2023): 89–103. https://doi.org/10.1080/14623528.2021.1979908.

Shemesh, Aharon, and Moshe Halbertal. "The Me'un (Refusal): The Complex History of Halakhic Anomaly." *Tarbitz* 82, no. 3 (2014): 377–94.

Shenhav, Yehouda. *The Arab Jews: A Postcolonial Reading of Nationalism, Religion, and Ethnicity*. Stanford, CA: Stanford University Press, 2006.

Shenhav, Yehouda, and Hannan Hever. "'Arab Jews' after Structuralism: Zionist Discourse and the (De)Formation of an Ethnic Identity." *Social Identities* 18, no. 1 (2012): 101–18. https://doi.org/10.1080/13504630.2011.629517.

Shewly, Hosna J. "Abandoned Spaces and Bare Life in the Enclaves of the India-Bangladesh Border." *Political Geography* 32 (January 2013): 23–31. https://doi.org/10.1016/j.polgeo.2012 .10.007.

Shiva, Vandana. *Monocultures of the Mind: Perspectives on Biodiversity and Biotechnology.* London: Zed Books; Penang, Malaysia: Third World Network, 1993.

Shohat, Ella. "Columbus, Palestine and Arab Jews." In *Cultural Readings of Imperialism: Edward Said and the Gravity of History*, edited by Keith Ansell-Pearson, Benita Parry, and Judith Squires, 88–105. New York: St. Martin's Press, 1997. http://archive.org/details/culturalreadings 00keit.

———. "Reflections of an Arab Jew." *Against the Current* 18 (2003): 13–14.

Shultz, James M., Ángela Milena Gómez Ceballos, Zelde Espinel, Sofia Rios Oliveros, Maria Fernanda Fonseca, and Luis Jorge Hernández Florez. "Internal Displacement in Colombia." *Disaster Health* 2, no. 1 (2014): 13–24. https://doi.org/10.4161/dish.27885.

Simmel, Georg. "The Metropolis and Mental Life." In *The Urban Sociology Reader*, 37–45. London: Routledge, 2012.

———. "Two Essays." *Hudson Review* 11, no. 3 (1958): 371–85. https://doi.org/10.2307/3848614.

Simone, AbdouMaliq. *Improvised Lives: Rhythms of Endurance in an Urban South.* After the Postcolonial. Cambridge, UK: Polity, 2019.

Sitwell, Osbert. *Laughter in the Next Room.* London: Macmillan, 1975.

slavick, elin o'Hara. "Hiroshima: After Aftermath." *Critical Asian Studies* 41, no. 2 (2009): 307–28. https://doi.org/10.1080/14672710902809443.

Sloterdijk, Peter. *Terror from the Air.* Translated by Amy Patton and Steve Corcoran. Semiotext(e) Foreign Agents Series. Los Angeles, CA: Semiotext(e), 2009.

Sontag, Susan. *On Photography.* Penguin Modern Classics. London: Penguin Classics, 2008.

———. *Regarding the Pain of Others.* London: Penguin, 2004.

Spivak, Gayatri Chakravorty. "Can the Subaltern Speak?" In *Marxism and the Interpretation of Culture*, edited by Cary Nelson and Lawrence Grossberg, 271–313. Urbana: University of Illinois Press, 1988.

Standing, Guy. *The Precariat: The New Dangerous Class.* London: Bloomsbury, 2014.

Staton, Bethan. "Syrians Trapped in Desert No Man's Land." *New Humanitarian*, 9 June 2016. https://www.thenewhumanitarian.org/special-report/2016/06/09/syrians-trapped-desert-no -man-s-land.

Stavrides, Stavros. "Open Space Appropriations and the Potentialities of a 'City of Thresholds.'" In *Terrain Vague: Interstices at the Edge of the Pale*, edited by Manuela Mariani and Patrick Barron, 48–61. New York: Routledge, 2014.

Stevenson, Lisa. *Life beside Itself: Imagining Care in the Canadian Arctic.* Berkeley: University of California Press, 2014. https://doi.org/10.1525/9780520958555.

Stewart, Kathleen. "Road Registers." *Cultural Geographies* 21, no. 4 (2014): 549–63. https://doi .org/10.1177/1474474014525053.

———. *A Space on the Side of the Road: Cultural Poetics in an "Other" America.* Princeton, NJ: Princeton University Press, 1996.

Stoler, Ann Laura. *Duress: Imperial Durabilities in Our Times.* Durham, NC: Duke University Press, 2016. https://doi.org/10.1515/9780822373612.

———. "Imperial Debris: Reflections on Ruins and Ruination." *Cultural Anthropology* 23, no. 2 (2008): 191–219.

Strage, Mark. *Cape to Cairo: Rape of a Continent*. New York: Harcourt Brace Jovanovich, 1973. http://archive.org/details/capetogairo0000unse.

Struk, Janina. *Private Pictures: Soldiers' Inside View of War*. London: I. B. Tauris, 2011.

Sundberg, Juanita. "Thinking with *Duress*." *Postcolonial Studies* 21, no. 4 (2018): 537–41. https:// doi.org/10.1080/13688790.2018.1542583.

Sweis, Rana F. "ISIS Is Said to Claim Responsibility for Attack at Jordan-Syria Border." *New York Times*, 27 June 2016. https://www.nytimes.com/2016/06/28/world/middleeast/islamic-state -jordan-suicide-attack.html.

Tamir, Yoram. *Instruction Material Guidebook: Jerusalem, a Divided City Reunited* [*Hoveret Mekorot Hadracha: Yerusalem Ir Hatzuya she-Hubra La Yahdav*]. Jerusalem: Turjeman Post Museum, 1996.

Taussig, Michael. *I Swear I Saw This: Drawings in Fieldwork Notebooks, Namely My Own*. Chicago: University of Chicago Press, 2011.

———. *The Magic of the State*. New York: Routledge, 1997.

———. *Shamanism, Colonialism, and the Wild Man: A Study in Terror and Healing*. Chicago: University of Chicago Press, 1987.

———. *Walter Benjamin's Grave*. Chicago: University of Chicago Press, 2010.

Terre Sauvage. "14–18 Forêts De Mémoire." 20 November 2014, 31–53.

Thomas, Ann. *The Great War: The Persuasive Power of Photography*. Bilingual ed. Milan: 5 Continents, 2015.

Till, Karen E. "Wounded Cities: Memory-Work and a Place-Based Ethics of Care." *Political Geography* 31, no. 1 (2012): 3–14.

Till, Karen E., Juanita Sundberg, Wendy Pullan, Charis Psaltis, Chara Makriyianni, Rana Zincir Celal, Meltem Onurkan Samani, and Lorraine Dowler. "Interventions in the Political Geographies of Walls." *Political Geography* 33 (March 2013): 52–62. https://doi.org/10.1016/j .polgeo.2012.11.005.

Tlostanova, Madina V., and Walter D. Mignolo. *Learning to Unlearn: Decolonial Reflections from Eurasia and the Americas*. Columbus: Ohio State University Press, 2012. http://muse.jhu.edu /book/24260.

Tobal, Juan Pablo. "El último tinigua." *Semana*, 20 April 2013. https://www.semana.com/especiales /articulo/el-ultimo-tinigua/340475-3.

Traverso, Enzo. *The Origins of Nazi Violence*. New York: New Press, 2003.

UN High Commissioner for Refugees. "Critical Needs for Syrian Civilians in Rukban, Solutions Urgently Needed." 15 February 2019. https://www.unhcr.org/news/briefing/2019/2/5c6699aa4 /critical-needs-syrian-civilians-rukban-solutions-urgently-needed.html.

UN Office for the Coordination of Humanitarian Affairs. "Under-Secretary-General for Humanitarian Affairs and Emergency Relief Coordinator, Mark Lowcock: Statement to the Security Council on the Humanitarian Situation in Syria, 30 October 2017." Amman, Jordan, 30 October 2017. https://www.unocha.org/sites/unocha/files/statement-and-speech/ERC _USG%20Mark%20Lowcock%20Statement%20to%20the%20SecCo%20on%20Syria%20 -%2030Oct2017%20-%20FINAL.pdf.

UN Office for the Coordination of Humanitarian Affairs and UN Resident and Humanitarian Coordinator for Syrian Arab Republic. "UN in Syria and SARC Deliver Humanitarian Assistance to 40,000 People in Rukban." Reliefweb, 6 February 2019. https://reliefweb.int/sites /reliefweb.int/files/resources/Rukban2PR_EN_PDF.pdf.

UN Population Fund. "118-Truck Convoy Delivers Urgent Aid to Stranded Residents in Rukban, Syria." 16 February 2019. https://reliefweb.int/report/syrian-arab-republic/118-truck-convoy -delivers-urgent-aid-stranded-residents-rukban-syria.

UN Security Council. "Resolution 186 (1964): The Cyprus Question." 4 March 1964. S/5575. http:// unscr.com/en/resolutions/doc/186.

Urbach, Ephraim E. "Hefker- mashehu al hamosad imekomo bametsi'ut ha-historit" ["'Hefker'— On the Place of 'Derelictio' in Historical Reality"]. *Shenaton ha-Mishpat ha-Ivri: Annual of the Institute for Research in Jewish Law* 6–7 (1979): 17–28.

Villarreal, Nathalye Cotrino, and Juan Pappier. *Left Undefended: Killings of Rights Defenders in Colombia's Remote Communities.* New York: Human Rights Watch, 2021.

Vismann, Cornelia. "Starting from Scratch: Concepts of Order in No Man's Land." In *War, Violence, and the Modern Condition*, edited by Bernd-Rüdiger Hüppauf, 46–64. Berlin: Walter de Gruyter, 1997.

Volmar, Alex. "In Storms of Steel: The Soundscape of World War I and Its Impact on Auditory Media Culture during the Weimar Period." In *Sounds of Modern History: Auditory Cultures in 19th- and 20th-Century Europe*, edited by Daniel Morat, 227–56. New York: Berghahn Books, 2014.

Watts, Michael. "Petro-Violence: Community, Extraction and Political Ecology of a Mythic Commodity." In *Violent Environments*, edited by Nancy Lee Peluso and Michael Watts, 189–212. Ithaca, NY: Cornell University Press, 2001.

Weheliye, Alexander. *Habeas Viscus: Racialising Assemblages, Biopolitics, Black Feminist Theories of the Human.* Durham, NC: Duke University Press, 2014.

Weizman, Eyal. *Forensic Architecture: Violence at the Threshold of Detectability.* New York: Zone Books, 2019.

Williams, Jill M. "From Humanitarian Exceptionalism to Contingent Care: Care and Enforcement at the Humanitarian Border." *Political Geography* 47 (2015): 11–20.

Williams, Sara Elizabeth. "World Vision Rattles Aid Groups with Solo Operation for Syrians at Jordan Border." *New Humanitarian*, 24 January 2017. https://www.thenewhumanitarian .org/investigations/2017/01/24/exclusive-world-vision-rattles-aid-groups-solo-operation -syrians-jordan.

Willis, Anne-Marie. *Picturing Australia: A History of Photography.* North Ryde, Australia: Angus & Robertson, 1988.

Wilson, Bill. "The Fight for the Ridge." Heartland Heroes: Korean War 50th Anniversary Commemoration, 2002. http://www.accesskansas.org/kskoreanwar/stories/story_wilson2.html.

Wilson, Scott. "Colombian President Rejects Rebel Offer." *Washington Post*, 13 January 2002. https://www.washingtonpost.com/archive/politics/2002/01/13/colombian-president-rejects -rebel-offer/71334f07-1ce3-4db7-8a89-55bf6bd3a339/.

World Food Programme. "Cranes Deliver Life-Saving Assistance to Syrians Stranded at Jordanian Border Areas." 5 August 2016. https://www.wfp.org/news/cranes-deliver-life-saving -assistance-to-syrians-stranded-at-jordanian-border-areas.

World Health Organization. "Integrated Food Security Phase Classification, IPC Global Initiative—Special Brief: Gaza Strip." 18 March 2024. https://ipcinfo.org/fileadmin/user_up load/ipcinfo/docs/IPC_Gaza_Strip_Acute_Food_Insecurity_Feb_July2024_Special_Brief.pdf.

Yiftachel, Oren. "The Consequences of Planning Control: Mizrahi Jews in Israel's 'Development Towns.'" In *The Power of Planning: Spaces of Control and Transformation*, edited by Oren

Yiftachel et al., 117–34. Geojournal Library 67. Dordrecht, Netherlands: Kluwer Academic Publishers, 2001.

Yiftachel, Oren. *Ethnocracy: Land and Identity Politics in Israel Palestine*. Philadelphia: University of Pennsylvania Press, 2006.

Yizhar, S. *Stories of the Plain: Silence of the Villages*. Tel Aviv: Zmora Bitan, 1990.

Zhang, Shu Guang. *Mao's Military Romanticism: China and the Korean War, 1950–1953*. Modern War Studies. Lawrence: University Press of Kansas, 1995.

Žižek, Slavoj. *The Sublime Object of Ideology*. London: Verso, 1989.

Index

Page numbers in italics refer to figures.

abandonment: abdication and, 61, 106–7; Abu Jariban and, 104–7; Arabs and, 105; Athanasiou on, 61; biblical text and, 9; Clearance Zone and, 16, 73, 133–34, 138, 143, 152, 154, 160, 192–93, 205–6; concept of, 4–8; dead zones and, 66; deportees and, 109–12; exclusion and, 59–60, 112; fantasy and, 107; Gaza and, 77–79, 104; gendered, 127–46; gestures of uncaring and, 18, 33, 63–73, 141; industry and, 104; Israel and, 59–60, 104–11; Jerusalem and, 105; Jews and, 4–5, 51, 91, 126, 144–45, 208; Jordan and, 108; Lebanon and, 59–60, 109–11; left to die, 103–12; materiality and, 106; neoliberalism and, 61, 107; Palestinians and, 103–6, 109–11; police and, 25, 104–6, 143; racial issues and, 113; refugees and, 59, 103, 109; Rukban and, 74–90, 207–8; smuggling and, 104; sovereignty and, 4–10, 19, 41, 60–63, 70–81, 92, 101, 104, 107–8, 113, 133, 136–38, 143–44, 149, 156, 206–8; violence and, 60–63, 104–7, 110, 112, 201–9; withdrawal and, 4, 6, 9–10, 59–63, 72, 77, 79–80, 89, 91–92, 96, 101, 111, 128, 196

abdication: abandonment and, 61, 106–7; Bir Tawil and, 172, 175; calculated, 9, 74, 194; of care, 3, 7–11, 18, 43, 57, 61, 65–68, 74–84, 87–88, 101, 106–7, 130, 144, 156, 174, 194, 196, 206, 208; Colombia and, 156; contours and, 43; Cyprus and, 65–66; Egypt and, 68; exposures and, 101–2; gender and, 130, 144; photographs and, 26–27, 38; of property, 91, 208; Rukban and, 74–88; sovereign, 3, 7–11, 38, 57, 65, 68, 74, 78–81, 88, 101–2, 107, 130, 156, 175, 203–6; uncaring and, 3–11, 18, 203–8; violence and, 3, 7, 9, 11, 26, 78–79, 88, 144, 156, 172, 175, 194, 196, 205, 208; World War I and, 194, 196

Abergel, Reuven, 118–19
Abu Hamad, Sudan, 171, 177–79
Abu Jariban, Omar, 104–7
Abu Tor, Jersualem, 119
Abu Zayd, Muhammad Fu'ad, 108–9, 112
aesthetics: Cyprus and, 65–66; exposures and, 98; gender and, 127; photographs and, 26–30, 33, 37–38, 190; violence and, 63; World War I and, 26–30, 33, 37–38, 190
Afghanistan, 52, 54
Agamben, Giorgio, 10, 59–60, 104, 216n15
agriculture, 5, 167, 170, 206
Ahmad, Muhammad, 177
AK-47 assault rifles, 237n15
Alimi, Eitan, 233n18
Amat, Jean-Paul, 198
Amazon: Brazil and, 154; Clearance Zone and, 155, 159; Colombia and, 12, 15, 130, 151–55, 159; Indigenous peoples and, 159
American Special Forces, 209
anarchists, 4–5, 9, 149, 159
Anderson, Benedict, 13
Aqsa Mosque, Al-, 109
Arabic, 14, 55, 125–26, 180
Arabs: abandonment and, 105; Bir Tawil and, 164, 166, 180; Black Panthers and, 122–26; contours and, 51, 55; exposures and, 51; Green Line and, 118–21; Israel and, 55, 69, 118–22, 126, 203; Palestinians and, 55, 119, 122, 125–26, 203, 235n36, 248n3; a-Sawahra area and, 69; solidarity of, 105
Arcades Project (Benjamin), 40
Arendt, Hannah, 232n11
Aristotle, 91

Arjona, Ana, 136
Around the World in 80 Days (Verne), 120
Aspen Security Forum, 74
assassination, 247n36; Colombia and, 132, 140, 172;
    community leaders and, 132, 194–96; Doumer
    on, 96, 188; FARC and, 132
asylum seekers, 204
Athanasiou, Athena, 61
Australia, 34–37, 147
Azoulay, Ariella, 77–78, 218n37
Aztecs, 14

Bakshi, Anita, 224n4
Baldwin, James, 125–26
Balkans, 67
Baq'a, Jerusalem, 119
Baramki, Andoni, 55–56
Baramki, Gabi, 56
barricades: barbed wire and, 3, 12, 16, 18, 27–28,
    33, 41, 43, 51, 55–57, 64, 66, 86, 94, 96–97, 118,
    121, 124, 203; contours and, 55–57; Cyprus and,
    64–66; dead zones and, 3; exposures and, 94,
    97; Green Line and, 119–20
barriers, 1–2, 25, 64, 170
Bashir, Omar al-, 171, 182
Bataille, Georges, 40
Battle of Bloody Ridge, 45
Battle of Heartbreak Ridge, 45–46
Baum, Shlomo, 118
Bauman, Zygmunt, 224n8
Beaman, Ardern, 147
Bean, Charles, 35
beer, 130–31, 134–35, 157, 161
Belarus, 94
Belgium, 104
Benjamin, Walter, 33–35, 40, 50
Benvenisti, Meron, 49
Betancourt, Íngrid, 249n8
Bethlehem, 1
Bible, 4, 7–10, 158, 250n15, 250n19
Bibliothek für Kulturwissenschaft, 38–39
Biehl, João, 237n11
biopolitics: abandonment and, 6, 61, 78, 84, 112,
    122, 137, 215n6, 224n7; Esposito on, 112; Gaza
    and, 78; HIV/AIDS and, 137; Palestinians and,
    122; Rukban and, 84; widening practices of, 6
Bir Murad, 179
Bir Tawil: abdication and, 172, 175; Administra-
    tive Line of 1902 and, 169; Arabs and, 164, 166,
    180; Black knowledge and, 173–74; British and,
    165, 177–79, 184; fantasy and, 162–63, 166–76,
    184–85; gold and, 16, 162, 166, 170–71, 175–84;
    Heaton and, 166–73, 184; Indigenous peoples
    and, 169, 174, 183; infrastructure of, 175–76;
    Israel and, 164, 170; mining and, 170, 177–83,
    186; neoliberalism and, 167; Nubia and, 165;

paintings and, 162, 179; police and, 169, 171, 175;
    Russia and, 162–67, 171; sovereignty and, 162,
    165–67, 175–76, 182, 184; terra nullius concept
    and, 169–70; terrorists and, 182; traveling to,
    170–72; Twenty-Second Parallel and, 68, 169;
    violence and, 162–63, 168–72, 175, 177, 183–85;
    White identity and, 162–63, 166–74, 179, 184–85;
    Zhikharev and, 163–66, 171, 174, 184; Zone 34
    and, 164
Biss, Eula, 12
Black Death, 11
Black knowledge, 173–74
Black Panthers, 122–26
Black Sea, 93
bombardment, 21–23, 45, 95, 101, 152
Bonnardeaux, Michel, 234n12
Borden, Mary, 54, 188
Brady, James, 45
Brantz, Dorothee, 22
Bridge, Gavin, 182
British: Afghanistan and, 54; Beaman and, 147; Bir
    Tawil and, 165, 177–79, 184; contours and, 49,
    54; Egypt and, 68; Gaza and, 30; Ground Sign
    Awareness and, 54; Loudon and, 65; Rukban
    and, 87; War Savings Committee, 21; World
    War I and, 30, 32, 186–87
British Artists at the Front (Gordon), 32
brothels, 135–40, 145–46
Brown, Wendy, 223n44
buffalo, 190
Buffer Zone: contours and, 52–54; Cyprus and,
    64–65, 207; Occupy Buffer Zone and, 114–17;
    Turkey and, 52–53, 64–65, 114–17
Bush, George W., 249n9

Cadete, Rodrigo, 138
Calkins, Sandra, 183–84
Campbell, David, 229n44
Carroll, James, 147–48
Central Intelligence Agency, 47
Chernobyl: Exclusion Zone, 47, 94–95, 190, 197;
    exposures and, 33, 47, 93–98, 112, 186, 190,
    196–99; Hesse-Honegger studies, 98–102, 107,
    231n19; Marder and, 93, 186, 199; radioactivity
    and, 92–101, 108, 112, 197
Chernobyl Herbarium, The (Marder), 186
Chernobyl Nuclear Plant Zone of Alienation,
    94–95
China, 44, 47, 175
Chisholm, Mairi, 28–30
Clark, Justine, 50
Clark, William, 190
Clearance Zone: abandonment and, 16, 73, 133–34,
    138, 143, 152, 154, 160, 192–93, 205–6; Amazon
    and, 155, 159; end of, 204–5; environmental
    issues and, 152, 191–96; FARC and, 73, 130, 134,

137, 143, 152, 156, 160–61, 170, 191–96, 204–6, 249n8; gender and, 130–38, 143; gestures of uncaring and, 73; La Macarena and, 12, 131, 151–52, 155–57, 192, 194, 205; melancholia of, 193; neoliberalism and, 137; scholarship on, 16; terrorists and, 155–56, 195, 206

cocaine: Colombia and, 4, 15, 130–31, 137, 139, 142, 157, 192, 196, 206; farmers and, 4; pesticides and, 206; wild years of, 130

Cohen, Jeffrey Jerome, 160

Cold War, 166

Colombia: abdication and, 156; Amazon and, 12, 15, 130, 151–55, 159; Bogotá, 15, 72, 135, 152, 155, 157, 211; Clearance Zone and, 16 (see also Clearance Zone); cocaine and, 4, 15, 130–31, 137, 139, 142, 157, 192, 196, 206; Duda River, 152, 155, 157; El Cajón, 152–56; environmental issues and, 152; fantasy and, 151–61; FARC and, 12 (see also Fuerzas Armadas Revolucionarias de Colombia [FARC]); gestures of uncaring and, 72–73; history of rebel forces in, 154–56; Indigenous peoples in, 155, 158–59, 195; La Cooperativa, 130–31, 134–35, 137, 139, 206; La Macarena, 12, 131, 151–52, 155–57, 192, 194, 205; LGBTQ+ population, 137, 141–43; Mora and, 72–73; Office of the High Commissioner for Peace, 159–60; paintings and, 152; Petro and, 247n31; police and, 73, 136; refuge zones and, 153–54; shrugging off, 72–73; sovereignty and, 74–83, 88, 156–60; Special Jurisdiction for Peace, 249n10; terrorists and, 155–56; United Nations and, 164–65; violence and, 72–73, 151–60; withdrawal and, 72–73; Yarumales, 15, 138, 145–46, 191–96, 206

Colombia Diversa, 141, 143, 239n35

Colombian National Park Service, 135

composites, 34–38, 220n26

Consuela, Doña, 131

contours: abdication and, 43; Arabs and, 51, 55; barricades and, 55–57; boundary lines and, 43–58; British and, 49, 54; Buffer Zone, 52–54; Demilitarized Zone, 44–48, 73, 190; exclusion and, 44, 47; fantasy and, 44, 48; Green Line, 55; Israel and, 48–52, 55–56; Jerusalem and, 48–52, 55–56; Jews and, 51, 55; materiality and, 46–50, 54; Military Demarcation Line, 44, 46; Musrara and, 49–51; porosity and, 50–51; smearing of, 48–52; sovereignty and, 57; technology and, 50; Thirty-Eighth Parallel, 44, 46; Turkey and, 52–53; United Nations and, 44–46, 49–53; violence and, 46–48, 52, 54–57; withdrawal and, 43–46, 57; World War I and, 54

corruption, 7, 25, 27, 176, 184, 190

Corso, Alessandro, 229n38

COVID-19 pandemic, 71, 171

Crimean War, 30

Crow tribe, 190

cruelty, 7, 9, 79, 83, 129, 204

"Cry of the Deportees, The" (Abu Zayd), 109

Cyprus, 67; abdication and, 65–66; aesthetics and, 65–66; apathy and, 65; barricades and, 64–66; Buffer Zone and, 15–16, 52–54, 64–65, 114–17, 207; conflict markers and, 64; dead zone and, 3, 64–66; explosives and, 54; ferry service and, 163; gestures of uncaring and, 64–66; looking away and, 64–66; materiality and, 64; Nicosia, 3, 15, 52–53, 64–65, 114, 170; Occupy Buffer Zone and, 114–18; peace and, 15; sovereignty and, 65; Turkey and, 53, 64–65, 116, 165; United Nations and, 52, 64–65, 116; violence and, 64–66

Czechoslovakia, 42

Dagalo, Mohammed "Hemedti" Hamdan, 182

Dayan, Moshe, 49

Dead Sea, 1

dead zones: abandonment and, 66; Buffer Zone, 15; Cyprus and, 3, 64–66; Green Line, 121; life in, 3–4; Nicosia and, 3, 64–65, 170; Occupy Buffer Zone and, 114–15, 117; United Nations and, 64–65

De Cive (On the Citizen) (Hobbes), 158–59

deforestation, 152, 154, 192, 196, 198

Demetriou, Olga, 114

Demilitarized Zone (DMZ), 44–48, 73, 190

deportees, 60, 109–12

derelictio, 91, 215n6

Der Kampf als inneres Erlebnis (The Battle as Inner Experience) (Jünger), 96

Derrida, Jacques, 99, 172

deserters, 147–48

destruction maps, 198

Deutsch, James, 147

Dewitz, Bodo von, 29

Didi-Huberman, Georges, 39–40

Dillon, Brian, 248n43

Disney, 167–68

Documents (Bataille), 40

Dodge, Richard Irving, 190

Domesday Book, 11

Doumer, Paul, 96, 188

drugs, 131, 157, 195

Drumsta, Emily, 110, 233n19

Du Bois, W. E. B., 123

Duda River, 152, 155, 157

Dunsany, Lord (Edward John Moreton Drax), 188–89, 246n13

Eagles of Marj al Zuhur, The (Ma'alawi), 110

Egypt: abdication and, 68; Bir Tawil and, 16, 67–68, 162–75, 179, 183–84, 207; British and, 68; environmental issues and, 68; gestures of uncaring and, 66–69; gold and, 16, 171, 179;

Egypt (cont.)
  Heaton and, 167; infrastructure of, 175–76;
  Nile River and, 13, 175, 177, 182, 185; Pinkerton
  and, 66–67; Red Sea and, 68; renouncing and,
  66–69; sovereignty and, 68–69; Sudan and, 16,
  67–68, 162–79, 183, 207; Twenty-Second Parallel
  and, 68; United Nations and, 67; withdrawal
  and, 68; Zone 34 and, 164
Egyptian Cultural and Educational Bureau, 67
Eichmann Trial, 232n11
Enlightenment, 46–47
environmental issues: Chernobyl and, 33, 47, 92–
  101, 108, 112, 186, 190, 196–99; Clearance Zone
  and, 152, 191–96; Colombia and, 152; deforestation, 152, 154, 192, 196, 198; destruction maps
  and, 198; Edenic utopias and, 19; Egypt and, 68;
  Exclusion Zone and, 94–95, 190, 197; Hesse-
  Honegger studies and, 98–102, 107, 231n19;
  industry and, 155 (see also industry); mining,
  170, 177–83, 186; radioactivity, 92–101, 108, 112,
  197; riverbank destruction, 154; slavick studies
  and, 100–102, 231n25; uncaring and, 208; World
  War I and, 197–200
Erfahrung (experience), 34
Erlebnis (fractured experience), 34
Espelt-Bombin, Silvia, 154
Esposito, Roberto, 112
Eurocentrism, 14
European Green Belt, 190
exclusion: abandonment and, 59–60, 112; activists
  and, 59–60; contours and, 44, 47; exposures
  and, 94–95; Green Line and, 119; management
  of, 9; Rukban and, 76, 79; zones of, 47, 95, 112
exile, 103
Exodus, book of, 250n15
expositio, 91, 215n6
"Exposure" (Owen), 108
exposures: abdication and, 101–2; aesthetics
  and, 98; Arabs and, 51; barricades and, 94, 97;
  Chernobyl and, 33, 47, 92–101, 112, 186, 190,
  196–99; clarity and, 100–102; distant, 97–100;
  environmental issues and, 96–97, 100–101;
  Exclusion Zone and, 94–95, 190, 197; flesh and,
  108–12; industry and, 96; materiality and, 100;
  paintings and, 98–99; police and, 51, 95, 102;
  radioactivity and, 92–101, 108, 112, 197; slavick
  studies and, 100–102, 231n25; sovereignty and,
  94, 101–2; state of, 104–8; technology and, 94,
  98–99; use of term, 92; violence and, 95–102;
  withdrawal and, 94–96, 101–2
Ezekiel, book of, 7

fantasy: abandonment and, 107; aesthetics and,
  27, 29; anarchists and, 4; Baldwin on, 125; Bir
  Tawil and, 162–63, 166–76, 184–85; Colombia
  and, 151–61; contours and, 44, 48; effects of,

19; of escape, 9; Fussell and, 148; Heaton and,
  166–73, 184; Hobbes and, 156–60; Leed on, 148;
  political, 148–49; of refuge, 27, 155; Rose on,
  148; Rukban and, 85; White identity, 19, 162–63,
  166–74, 179, 184–85; World War I and, 148, 189,
  193; Zhikharev and, 166–73, 184
Farred, Grant, 111
Fayer Collective, 208–9
Feldman, Allen, 37
Feldman, Keith, 110, 233n19
Fenton, Roger, 30
Fernández, Luis, 143
Filippucci, Paola, 188
First Battalion of the Irish Guards, 52
First Battle of Passchendaele, 34
Forman, Geremy, 248n3
Forty-Fifth Infantry Battalion, 33
Foucault, Michel, 7–8, 107, 218n31
Franck, Thomas, 225n7
Fredriksen, Tomas, 182
French Geographical Institute, 198
Fuerzas Armadas Revolucionarias de Colombia
  (FARC): brothels and, 135–40, 145–46; Clear-
  ance Zone and, 73, 130, 134, 137, 143, 152, 156,
  160–61, 170, 191–96, 204–6, 249n8; cocaine and,
  4, 15, 130–31, 142, 157, 192, 196, 206; deforesta-
  tion and, 192; effects of, 192, 194; FARC-EP,
  151–53; founding of, 151–52; gender and, 134–46;
  HIV/AIDS and, 137, 142; Jojoy and, 156, 205;
  La Macarena and, 12, 152, 194, 205; LGBTQ+
  population and, 137, 141–43; Mora and, 72–73,
  130, 137; negotiation with, 159–60; Pastrana
  and, 72, 160, 204–5; peace agreement with, 191;
  refuge zones and, 153–54; rules of, 132–37, 140,
  152; Russian AK-47 assault rifles, 237n15; Second Guerrilla Conference and, 152; tribunals
  and, 132
Fussell, Paul, 147–48

Gaisberg, William, 21
Galton, Francis, 220n26
Gappah, Petina, 185
García-Peña, Daniel, 159–60
Gas Shell Bombardment (record), 21–22
Gaza: abandonment and, 77–79, 104; British and,
  30; Hamas and, 227n17; Israel and, 77–79, 104,
  227n17, 227n19, 229n38; photographs and,
  30–32; Rafah, 104; Rukban and, 77–79; siege
  and, 77–80
gender: abandonment and, 127–46; abdication
  and, 130, 144; aesthetics and, 127; birdsongs
  and, 23; brothels and, 135–40, 145–46; Clearance Zone and, 130–38, 143; complicities and,
  138–44; FARC and, 134–46; Henner and, 23, 26,
  127–29, 138; HIV/AIDS and, 137, 142; Jews and,
  144–45; LGBTQ+ population, 137, 141–43; look-

ing away, 64–66, 123; masculinity, 19, 23, 101, 128, 163, 172, 236n4; paintings and, 134–35, 138, 140; patriarchies and, 125–28, 134, 144; racial issues and, 19, 92; refugees and, 128; refusals and, 144–46; sex workers and, 23, 91, 127, 135–40, 145–46; shrugging off, 72–73; sovereignty and, 130, 136–37, 143–44, 146; systems of rule and, 134–37; technology and, 138; violence and, 128, 131–46; withdrawal and, 128–30; World War I and, 128

genocide, 6–7, 18, 73, 79, 112, 120, 204

German Colony, Jerusalem, 119

gestures of uncaring: abandonment and, 18, 33, 63–73, 141; Clearance Zone and, 73; Colombia and, 72–73; Cyprus and, 64–66; Egypt and, 66–69; looking away, 64–66; Manning on, 63; Palestinians and, 69–72; photographs and, 63; renouncing, 66–69; severing, 62, 69–72

Ghanim, Hunaida, 125

Glass, Ira, 204

gold, 4; Bir Tawil and, 16, 162, 166, 170–71, 175–84; Egypt and, 16, 171, 179; expense in mining, 179–80; Mineral Wealth and Mining (Development) Act and, 181; Russia and, 183; Sudan and, 16, 170–71, 178–83, 244n48; Wagner Group and, 183–84

Gómez, Maria, 239n40

Gonzalo, Don, 130–31, 135, 139

Google Street View, 127–28

Gordon, Jan, 32

Grafton Galleries, 34

gramophones, 21

Grant, Simon, 30

Greeks, 91, 161

Green Line, 55, 118–21

Gregory, Derek, 54

Grenadier Guards, 148

Ground Sign Awareness, 54

Guayabero River, 132, 151, 153, 156

Habibi, Emile, 124–26

Hajbi, Raphael, 51

Hala'ib, 68

Hamas, 227n17

Hamilton, John, 8

Hausmann, Raoul, 28

Heartbeats in Marj al-Zuhur (Abu Zayd), 109

Heaton, Jeremiah: Bir Tawil and, 166–73, 184; Disney and, 167–68; Egypt and, 167; projects of, 167–68; terra nullius concept and, 169–70; Wild West and, 169; Zhikharev and, 166–73, 184

Hebrew, 4, 14, 126

Hebrew University, 118

Heise, Ursula, 190

Henner, Mishka, 23, 26, 127–29, 138

Hesse-Honegger, Cornelia, 98–102, 107, 231n19

Hever, Hannan, 235n36

Hezbollah, 60

Hitier, Henry, 245n5

HIV/AIDS, 137, 142

Hobbes, Thomas, 156–60, 241n21

Hochberg, Gil, 66

Homs province, Syria, 74, 207

Human Rights Watch, 76

Hüppauf, Bernd, 95

Hurley, Frank, 34–37

Ibn Taymiyya University, 110

Ilican, Murat, 114

improvised explosive devices (IEDs), 54

Indigenous peoples: Bir Tawil and, 169, 174, 183; Colombia and, 155, 158–59, 195; Native American, 190

industry: abandonment and, 104; cocaine, 139; Detroit and, 33; exposures and, 96; extractive, 155; mining, 170, 177–83, 186; Nazis and, 6; World War I and, 6, 40

Ingold, Tim, 48

interlocutors, 67, 147, 159, 179, 215n1, 247n28

Intifada, 70, 77, 233n18

Iranian Revolutionary Guards, 60

Iraq, 25–26, 103, 249n9

Iron Curtain, 190

Isin, Engin, 215n1

Israel: abandonment and, 59–60, 104–11; Arabs and, 55, 69, 118–22, 126, 203; Bir Tawil and, 164, 170; Black Panthers and, 122–26; contours and, 48–52, 55–56; and "the end of world," 1, 4; Gaza and, 77–79, 104, 227n17, 227n19, 229n38; Green Line and, 118–21; Hamas and, 227n17; Hochberg on, 66; Jordan and, 15, 48–52, 55, 77, 118–19, 124, 201–2; Lebanon and, 59–60, 109–11; Meir and, 125; Mixed Armistice Commission and, 50; occupation and, 56, 60, 69–70, 77, 106, 110, 121–22, 201–3; Palestinians and, 1–2, 55–56, 59–60, 66, 69–72, 77–79, 104, 106, 109–11, 122, 124, 126, 201–3, 225n17, 233n18, 248n3; photographs and, 33; Rukban and, 69–72; "Security Strip," 60; Supreme Court, 2, 60; Tel Aviv, 105, 201; uncaring and, 1–2, 7, 15, 201–3; West Bank and, 69, 105–6, 108, 121, 202–3

Israeli Absentee Property Law, 56

Israeli Civil Administration, 70, 78

Israel Prison Service, 105

Jabal Mukaber, Jerusalem, 69–71

Jabal Sufar, 183

Jeffrey, James, 74, 76, 226n12

Jenin Governorate, 108

Jerusalem: abandonment and, 105; Al-Aqsa Mosque, 109; Black Panthers and, 122, 124, 126; contours and, 48–52, 55–56; Green Line and,

Jerusalem (cont.)
    118–21; Hebrew University, 118; Palestinians
    and, 1, 55–56, 69–72, 109, 119, 122, 126, 201, 214,
    225n12; photographs and, 33; snipers and, 33, 51,
    118; uncaring and, 1, 15, 23, 201, 207
Jews: abandonment and, 4–5, 51, 91, 126, 144–45,
    208; Black Panthers and, 122–26; contours and,
    51, 55; destruction of temple of, 4–5; gender
    and, 144–45; Green Line and, 118–21; photo-
    graphs and, 38, 42; Rukban and, 77; Shmita
    and, 208–9; Talmud and, 91, 144–46; uncaring
    and, 4–5, 201–3, 208
Johnson, Lyndon B., 44
Jojoy, Mono, 156, 205
Jolly, Martyn, 36
Jordan: abandonment and, 108; Green Line and,
    118–21; Habibi on, 124; Israel and, 15, 48–52,
    55, 77, 118–19, 124, 201–2; Rukban and, 16–17,
    74–77, 80–81, 84–87, 207, 249n13; Syria and, 17,
    74–77, 81, 84, 86–87, 207
Jordanian Legionnaires, 118
Jünger, Ernst, 96

Kanafani, Ghassan, 103–4
Kedar, Alexander, 248n3
Kemp, Martin, 231n19
Kennedy, John F., 44
Khartoum: infrastructure of, 175–76; Nile River
    and, 13, 175, 177, 182, 185; Sudan and, 13, 16, 173,
    175–76, 179, 184
killing fields, 3, 11, 14
Kitchner, Herbert, 177
Knocker, Elsie, 28
Korea, 33, 189; Battle of Bloody Ridge, 45; Battle of
    Heartbreak Ridge, 45–46; Demilitarized Zone,
    44–48, 73, 190; Military Demarcation Line, 44,
    46; Thirty-Eighth Parallel, 44, 46; United Nations
    Command and, 44–46; Zhikharev and, 164, 166
Kristiansson, Magnus, 241n22
Kush E&P, 183
Kutz, Christopher, 140–41
Kuwait, 103, 164

Lacis, Asja, 50
La Cooperativa, Colombia, 130–31, 134–39, 206
La Macarena, Colombia: Clearance Zone and, 12,
    131, 151–52, 155–57, 192, 194, 205; FARC and, 12,
    152, 194, 205
Larsson, Torbjörn, 25–26
Latour, Bruno, 191, 196
Leal, Claudia, 155
Lebanon: abandonment and, 59–60, 109–11;
    activist expulsion to, 59–60; camp conditions
    in, 110; deportees and, 60; Israel and, 59–60,
    109–11; Palestinians and, 109–11, 159; "Security
    Strip," 60

Le Corbusier, 55
Ledra Street/Lokmaci Gate crossing, Nicosia, 114
Leed, Eric, 22, 148
Léger, Fernand, 22
Levant, 39
Leviathan (Hobbes), 156–60
Leviticus, book of, 250n19
Lewis, Cecil, 187
LGBTQ+ population, 137, 141–43
Libya, 164
Lisbon earthquake, 46–47
Livingstone, David, 185
Lone Pine, 31, 32
looking away, 64–66, 123
Lorde, Audre, 17
Loudon, Angus, 65

Ma'alawi, Sa'id, 110
Macarena National Park, 194
Magic of the State, The (Taussig), 158
Mamilla, Jerusalem, 119
"Mandelbaum Gate" (Habibi), 124
Manning, Erin, 63
Marchand, Eckart, 42
Marder, Michael, 93, 186, 199
Margaroni, Maria, 104
Marj al-Zuhur, 60, 109–12
Marks, Jesse, 77
Martig, François, 200
Marziano, Rafi, 51, 126
masculinity, 19, 23, 101, 128, 163, 172, 236n4
Masefield, John, 186, 188
Massey, Doreen, 129
"Master of No Man's Land" (Dunsany), 189
materiality: abandonment and, 106; contours and,
    46–50, 54; Cyprus and, 64; exposures and, 100;
    Occupy Buffer Zone and, 114; spatial, 32; World
    War I and, 43
Mbembe, Achille, 6, 83, 209, 216n13
mechanized warfare, 36, 95–96, 188–89
Meir, Golda, 125
Mejía, Carlos Arturo, 157–58
Men in the Sun (Kanafani), 103
Merleau-Ponty, Maurice, 112
Meroe Gold, 183
Mexico, 204
Military Demarcation Line (MDL), 44, 46
Mineral Wealth and Mining (Development) Act,
    181
mining, 170, 177–83, 186, 244n48
M-Invest, 183
Mixed Armistice Commission, 50
Mnemosyne Bilderatlas (Warburg), 40
Moeller, Susan, 30
Molano, Alfredo, 154–55
montage, 38–41

Mookherjee, Nayanika, 136
Mora, Enrique, 72–73, 130, 137
Morocco, 118, 164
Mosse, George, 246n18
Mukhayyam al-ʿAwda (Camp of Return), 60
Murchison, Roderick Impey, 12–13
murder, 7, 88, 155–56, 160, 195
Muslala art collective, 235n34
Muslim Brotherhood, 108
Musrara, Jerusalem, 49–51, 118–22
Mustafa, Mouaz, 82
mustard gas, 21

Nair, Rukmini Bhaya, 177
Nakba, 103
Nancy, Jean-Luc, 111, 217n29
Nash, Paul, 32
National Geographic, 44
Native Americans, 190
NATO, 167
Navarro-Yashin, Yael, 224n4
Nazar, 173–74, 174, 176, 179
Nazis, 6, 216n15, 232n11
Neap Coin, 168
neoliberalism: abandonment and, 61, 107; Bir
    Tawil and, 167; Clearance Zone and, 137; Green
    Line and, 120; Occupy Buffer Zone and, 114;
    Povinelli on, 5–6; Rukban and, 80; uncaring
    and, 5–7
New York Times, 147
Nichols, Robert, 159
Nicosia: Airport, 53, 53, 65; barriers and, 64, 170;
    Buffer Zone and, 15; Cyprus and, 3, 15, 52–53,
    64–65, 114, 170; dead zones and, 3, 64–65, 170;
    Occupy Buffer Zone and, 114; United Nations
    and, 52–53
Nile River, 13, 175, 177, 182, 185
Nixon, Rob, 197
Noam, Yoram, 106
No Man's Land (Chisholm), 28
No Man's Land (Henner), 23, 26, 127–29, 138
No Man's Land Common, England, 12
Notes from No Man's Land (Biss), 12
Noyes, John, 173
Nuclear Engineering Laboratory, 98

Occupied Palestinian Territories, 70, 77, 201
Occupy Buffer Zone (OBZ): Buffer Zone and,
    114–17; Cyprus and, 114–18; dead zones and,
    114–15, 117; materiality and, 114; neoliberalism
    and, 114; Nicosia and, 114; police and, 115, 117;
    sovereignty and, 116–17; terrorists and, 117;
    Turkey and, 114–17; United Nations and, 115–16;
    violence and, 114, 117
Office National des Forêts, 199
Ojeda, Diana, 134, 211

Ophir, Adi, 77–78
Orpen, William, 26
Out of Darkness, Shining Light (Gappah), 185
Owen, Wilfred, 108–9
Oxford English Dictionary, 11

Pain, Rachel, 238n19
paintings: Arcadian landscapes and, 127; Bir Tawil
    and, 162, 179; Colombia and, 152; exposures and,
    98–99; gender and, 134–35, 138, 140; Nash and,
    32; Rukban and, 88; Somme and, 26; visual
    disorientation and, 22; World War I and, 26, 191
Palacios, Marco, 156
Palestinian Authority, 70–71
Palestinians: abandonment and, 103–6, 109–11;
    activist expulsion of, 59–60; Agamben and,
    59–60; Arabs and, 55, 119, 122, 125–26, 203,
    235n36, 248n3; Baramki, 55–56; Black Panthers
    and, 122, 124–26; Green Line and, 119; Hezbol-
    lah and, 60; Hochberg on, 66; Intifada and, 70,
    77, 233n18; Iranian Revolutionary Guards and,
    60; Iraq and, 26; Israel and, 1–2, 55–56, 59–60,
    66, 69–72, 77–79, 104, 106, 109–11, 122, 124, 126,
    201–3, 225n17, 233n18, 248n3; Jabal Mukaber,
    69; Jerusalem and, 1, 55–56, 69–72, 109, 119,
    122, 126, 201, 214, 225n12; Lebanon and, 109–11,
    159; Nakba and, 103; Occupied Palestinian Ter-
    ritories, 70, 77, 201; refugees and, 25–26; ruined
    land and, 77–79; severing and, 69–72; Sheikh
    Saʿad and, 1–2, 4, 69–72, 215n2; sovereignty and,
    70–72; Syria and, 3, 74, 77; al-Tanf and, 25–26,
    76, 83; uncaring and, 69–72, 201–3; violence
    and, 71
Palma, Hernando, 155, 156
Paret, Peter, 31–32
Parks, Lisa, 229n44
Parra Cubillos, Javier Francisco, 247n36
Pastrana, Andrés, 72–73, 160, 204–5
patriarchies, 125–28, 134, 144
Pawnee tribe, 190
Pease, Donald, 148
Pence, Mike, 218n32
Petro, Gustavo, 247n31
Petryna, Adriana, 95
photographs: abdication and, 26–27, 38; actuality
    recordings and, 21; aerial, 40; aesthetics and,
    25–34, 37–38, 190; cameras and, 15, 24, 26–36,
    110, 127, 174, 176; Chisholm and, 28–30; com-
    posites and, 34–38, 220n26; documentation by,
    25–42; Fenton and, 30; Gaza and, 30–32; ges-
    tures of uncaring and, 63; Henner and, 23, 26,
    127–29, 138; hidden truths and, 27–28; Hurley
    and, 34–37; image afterlife and, 41–42; images
    from chaos, 28–34; Jerusalem and, 33; Jews and,
    38, 42; Knocker and, 28; Larsson and, 25–26;
    montage and, 38–41; refugees and, 25;

photographs (*cont.*)
  Rosenthal and, 242n11; Sontag on, 193; sovereignty and, 38, 41; Syria and, 25–26; technology and, 15, 24–41, 110, 127–28, 174, 176; Turkey and, 39; unlearning and, 32; violence and, 25–30, 33, 37–41; Warburg and, 38–42; World War I and, 21–23, 26–29, 34–35, 38, 40, 65–66, 85, 95, 154
Pinkerton, Alasdair, 66–68, 171–73, 211
poetry, 110; Abu Zayd, 109; Baldwin, 125–26; Borden, 54; fantasy and, 149; Masefield, 186; Owen, 108; refugees and, 109–10; Zachs, 118
Poland, 42
policing: abandonment and, 25, 104–6, 143; Bir Tawil and, 169, 171, 175; Black Panthers and, 124, 126; Colombia and, 73, 136; exposures and, 51, 95, 102; Occupy Buffer Zone and, 115, 117; Rukban and, 82–83; uncaring and, 2–3, 8, 194
Politics (Aristotle), 91
porosity, 50–51, 112
Povinelli, Elizabeth, 5–6, 61
Pratt, Geraldine, 237n5
Prigozhin, Yevgeny, 183
Princess of North Sudan, The (Disney), 167
Probyn-Rapsey, Fiona, 140
Prussia, 166

Qur'an, 110

race: abandonment and, 113; Black knowledge and, 173–74; Black Panthers and, 121–26; gender and, 19, 92; Green Line and, 120–21; White identity, 162–63, 166–74, 179, 184–85
radioactivity: Chernobyl and, 92–101, 108, 112, 197; Hesse-Honegger studies and, 98–102, 107, 231n19; slavick studies and, 100–102, 231n25
Rafah, 104
Rapid Support Forces (RSF), 182–83, 245n54
recordings, 15, 21–23, 73
Red Sea, 68
Red Zone, 198–200
Reeves, Sergeant, 52–54
refugees: abandonment and, 59, 103, 109; asylum seekers and, 204; gender and, 128; Palestinians and, 25–26; photographs and, 25; poetry and, 109–10; Rukban and, 16–17, 74–77, 83, 85; al-Tanf and, 25–26, 76, 83; uncaring and, 4, 203
refuge zones, 153–54
Rehavya, Jerusalem, 120
Rehovot, Israel, 105
renouncing, 19, 66–69, 169, 208
Ridgway, Matthew B., 45
Rivera, Doris, 170
Rodríguez, Fernando Palma, 14
Rogin, Josh, 74
Romans, 91, 215n6
Ronkainen, Mikhail, 164, 173

Rosenthal, Joe, 242n11
Royal Geographical Society, 12
Ruin, The (Simmel), 189
Rukban: abandonment and, 74–90, 207–8; abdication and, 74–88; American Special Forces base near, 209, 249n12; Aspen Security Forum and, 74; British and, 87; caring at a distance and, 84–87; conditions of, 74–77, 80–84; exclusion and, 76, 79; fantasy and, 85; Gaza and, 77–79; Israel and, 69–72; Jews and, 77; Jordan and, 16–17, 74–77, 80–81, 84–87, 207, 249n13; neoliberalism and, 80; paintings and, 88; police and, 82–83; refugees and, 16–17, 74–77, 83, 85; remoteness of, 207–8; Russia and, 76–77, 82, 87; siege and, 77–80; smuggling and, 74–75, 80–84, 88, 207, 229n37; sovereignty and, 249n13; Syria and, 16–17, 26, 74–77, 80–87, 208, 228n27, 249n13; technology and, 84–85; terrorists and, 75, 84, 87; United Nations and, 75, 77, 80–81, 84–85; violence and, 74–80, 83, 88; withdrawal and, 77, 79–82, 89
Rusk, Dean, 44
Russia: AK-47 rifles, 237n15; Bir Tawil and, 162–67, 171; Chernobyl and, 33, 47, 93–98, 112, 186, 190, 196–99; Cold War and, 166; exposures and, 94; gold and, 183; Rukban and, 76–77, 82, 87; Soviet, 44, 47, 94, 97, 100, 121; Syria and, 76–77, 82, 87; Wagner Group and, 183–84; Zhikharev and, 163–66, 170–74, 184
Russian Defense Ministry, 82, 87

Sa'ad Said, Jerusalem, 55
Sanders, Mark, 141
Sassen, Willem, 232n11
Saudi Arabia, 164, 166
Saving, Alberto, 51
Schindel, Estella, 208
Schrader, Astrid, 99
Scott, James, 153
Security, Territory, Population (Foucault), 7
"Security Strip," Israeli occupied zone in southern Lebanon, 60
Seidenberg, David, 208
Selmeczi, Anna, 223n6
Serje, Margarita, 160, 195
severing, 62, 69–72
sex workers: ancient Rome and, 91; brothels and, 135–40, 145–46; Europe and, 23, 127; Henner and, 23
Sheba Medical Center, 105
Sheikh Sa'ad, 1–2, 4, 69–72, 215n2
shelling, 21–22
Shell Petroleum Company, 154–55
Shemesh, Kochavi, 122
Shenhav, Yehouda, 235n36
Shewly, Hosna, 237n5

Shmita, 208–9, 250n15
Shohat, Ella, 235n36
shrugging off, 72–73
silence, 21–22, 73, 133, 136, 138, 186
Simmel, Georg, 64–65, 189
Simone, AbdouMaliq, 54
Sioux tribe, 190
Sitwell, Osbert, 148
slavick, elin o'Hara, 100–102, 231n25
smuggling: abandonment and, 104; growing
    network of, 74; Rukban and, 74–75, 80–84, 88,
    207, 229n37
snipers, 33, 50–51, 55, 118
Somme, 26, 147, 186–88
sonic awareness, 22–23
Sontag, Susan, 193
sovereignty: abandonment and, 4–10, 19, 41,
    60–63, 70–81, 92, 101, 104, 107–8, 113, 133, 136–38,
    143–44, 149, 156, 206–8; abdication and, 3, 7–11,
    38, 57, 65, 68, 74, 78–81, 88, 101–2, 107, 130, 156,
    175, 203–6; Agamben on, 59; Bir Tawil and, 162,
    165–67, 175–76, 182, 184; Black Panthers and,
    123, 125; Colombia and, 74–83, 88, 156–60; con-
    tours and, 57; Cyprus and, 65; Egypt and, 68–
    69; exposures and, 94, 101–2; gender and, 130,
    136–37, 143–44, 146; Occupy Buffer Zone and,
    116–17; Palestinians and, 70–72; photographs
    and, 38, 41; Rukban and, 249n13; uncaring and,
    3–19, 24, 202–8
Soviets, 44, 47, 94, 97, 100, 121
Spivak, Gayatri, 218n37
Squadroon, The (Beaman), 147
State of Exception (Agamben), 59
Statist, The (magazine), 187
Stavrides, Stavros, 64
Stevenson, Lisa, 107
Stewart, Kathleen, 176, 237n13
Stoler, Ann, 197
"Storyteller, The" (Benjamin), 34
Sudan: al-Bashir and, 171, 182; Bir Tawil and, 16,
    67–68, 162–75, 179, 183–84, 207; British and, 68,
    164, 177–79, 184; Egypt and, 16, 67–68, 162–79,
    183, 207; gold and, 16, 170–71, 178–83, 244n48;
    Heaton and, 167; infrastructure of, 175–76;
    Khartoum, 13, 16, 173, 175–76, 179, 184; Kitchner
    and, 177; Mineral Wealth and Mining (Devel-
    opment) Act and, 181; mining and, 170, 180–83;
    Rapid Support Forces and, 182–83, 245n54;
    Zone 34 and, 164
Sundberg, Juanita, 197
Swiss Federal Institute for Technology, 98
Syria: civil war, 163; Iraq and, 25–26; Jordan and, 17,
    74–77, 81, 84, 86–87, 207; Palestinians and, 3, 74,
    77; photographs and, 25–26; Rukban and, 16–17,
    26, 74–77, 80–87, 208, 228n27, 249n13; Russia
    and, 76–77, 82, 87; smuggling routes and, 207

Syrian Emergency Task Force (SETF), 82
Syrian Red Crescent, 84

Talbiyah, Jerusalem, 119, 120
Talmud, 91, 144–46
Tanf, al-, 25–26, 76, 83
Taussig, Michael, 154, 158
technology: contours and, 50; divine ordination
    and, 180; documentation, 21; of evasion, 203;
    exposures and, 94, 98–99; gender and, 138;
    governmental, 6–9; industrial logic and, 200;
    integration and, 175; mechanized warfare and,
    36, 95–96, 188–89; photographs and, 15, 24–41,
    110, 127–28, 174, 176; radioactivity and, 92–101,
    108, 112, 197; Rukban and, 84–85; shortwave
    radio, 164–65
Tel Aviv, 105, 201
Tell, Abdullah al-, 49
terrorists: Bir Tawil and, 182; Clearance Zone and,
    155–56, 195, 206; Colombia and, 155–56; Occupy
    Buffer Zone and, 117; Rukban and, 75, 84, 87;
    war on terror and, 195
Thirty-Eighth Parallel, 44, 46
This American Life (radio show), 204
Till, Karen, 88
Touma, Juliette, 75–76
Tralau, Johan, 241n22
trash, 69, 127, 248n43
Tropical Oil Company, 155
Truth and Reconciliation Commission, 141
Turkey: beauty of, 39; Buffer Zone and, 52–53,
    64–65, 114–17; contours and, 52–53; Cyprus and,
    15–16, 52–54, 64–65, 114–17, 165, 207; Occupy
    Buffer Zone and, 114–17; photographs and, 39
Turkish Republic of Northern Cyprus, 115–16, 165
Twenty-Second Parallel, 68, 169

Ukraine, 94–95, 99–100, 182
uncaring: abdication and, 3–11, 18, 203–8; Arabs
    and, 203; concept of, 4–8; disinterest and, 9;
    environmental issues and, 208; gestures of,
    18, 33, 63–73, 141; Israel and, 1–2, 7, 15, 201–3;
    Jerusalem and, 1, 15, 23, 201, 207; Jews and, 4–5,
    201–3, 208; neoliberalism and, 5–7; Palestinians
    and, 69–72, 201–3; photographs and, 25–42;
    police and, 2–3, 8, 194; refugees and, 4, 203;
    sovereignty and, 3–19, 24, 202–8; violence and,
    3–11, 17–19, 22, 24; withdrawal and, 4–10, 15,
    18–19, 91–92, 205
UNHCR, 226n2
UNICEF, 75, 80
United Nations: Colombia and, 164–65; contours
    and, 44–46, 49–53; Cyprus and, 64–65; dead
    zones and, 64–65; Egypt and, 67; Franck and,
    225n7; Mandelbaum Gate and, 124; Nicosia
    and, 52–53; Occupy Buffer Zone and, 115–16;

United Nations (*cont.*)
  peacekeepers of, 65, 67, 225n6, 234n12; Rukban and, 75, 77, 80–81, 84–85; World Food Programme, 81
United Nations Command (UNC), 44–46
University of Khartoum, 184
unlearning: no man's land connotations and, 11–17, 23–24; photographs and, 32; World War I and, 11
UNOSAT, 85
USAID, 167
US Army, 33

Valéry, Paul, 39
Valley of the Shadow of Death, The (Fenton), 30
Van Fleet, James, 45
Verdun, 32
Verne, Jules, 120
Vietnam, 104
violence: abandonment and, 60–63, 104–7, 110, 112, 201–9; abdication and, 3, 7, 9, 11, 26, 78–79, 88, 144, 156, 172, 175, 194, 196, 205, 208; aesthetics and, 63; assassination and, 96, 132, 140, 172, 188, 194–96, 247n36; Bir Tawil and, 162–63, 168–72, 175, 177, 183–85; Black Panthers and, 123–26; Colombia and, 72–73, 151–60; colonial, 3; conflict spaces and, 4; contours and, 46–48, 52, 54–57; Cyprus and, 64–66; exposures and, 95–102; gender and, 128, 131–46; genocidal, 6–7, 18, 73, 79, 112, 120, 204; Green Line and, 119–20; labor and, 4, 6, 66, 91, 114, 153, 158; medical, 216n15; Occupy Buffer Zone and, 114, 117; Palestinians and, 71; photographs and, 25–30, 33, 37–41; Rukban and, 74–80, 83, 88; uncaring and, 3–11, 17–19, 22, 24; World War I and, 28, 30, 40, 54, 95, 128, 197

Wadi Halfa, Sudan, 171, 177–78
Wadi Nar, 1
Wagner Group, 183–84
Walled City, Nicosia, 114
Warburg, Aby, 38–42
Warburg Institute, 38
"War Photography" (Hurley), 36
War Savings Committee, 21
Washington Post, 74
Watts, Michael, 155
Weheliye, Alexander, 112
Weizman, Eyal, 237n13
West Bank, 202–3; Abu Jariban and, 105–6; Jenin, 108; Jerusalem and, 121; Sheikh Sa'ad and, 69

White identity: Bir Tawil and, 162–63, 166–74, 179, 184–85; fantasy and, 19, 162–63, 168, 171–74, 184–85; masculine conquest and, 163; privilege and, 163, 168, 172
Wilson, Bill, 46
withdrawal: abandonment and, 4, 6, 9–10, 59–63, 72, 77, 79–80, 89, 91–92, 96, 101, 111, 128, 196; Black Panthers and, 125; Colombia and, 72–73; contours and, 43–46, 57; Egypt and, 68; exposures and, 94–96, 101–2; gender and, 128–30; Green Line and, 120; Rukban and, 77, 79–82, 89; uncaring and, 4–10, 15, 18–19, 91–92, 205; World War I and, 189, 196, 198
World War I: aesthetics and, 26–30, 33, 37–38; Australia and, 34–37, 147; British and, 30, 32, 186–87; contours and, 54; deserters and, 147–48; destruction of, 197–99; environmental issues and, 197–200; Eurocentrism and, 14; fantasy and, 148, 189, 193; gender and, 128; as Great War, 21, 30, 38, 97, 128, 236n4; industry and, 40; killing fields and, 3; legends of, 147; materiality and, 43; mechanized warfare and, 36, 95–96, 188–89; mine detonation and, 186–87; paintings and, 26, 191; photographs and, 21–23, 26–29, 34–35, 38, 40, 65–66, 85, 95, 154; poetry and, 108; soldiers going "over the top" and, 186; Somme and, 26, 147, 186–88; sounds of, 21–23; unlearning and, 11; violence and, 8, 30, 40, 54, 95, 128, 197; Western Front, 11, 21, 26, 28, 29, 38, 86, 96, 109, 112, 151, 188, 217n28; withdrawal and, 189, 198
World War II, 14, 44, 85

Yarumales, 15; brothels and, 138, 145–46; Clearance Zone and, 138, 145–46, 191–96, 206
Yemen, 164
Yizhar, S., 203
Ypres Salient, 28

Zachs, Arieh, 118
Zhikharev, Dmitry: Bir Tawil and, 163–66, 171, 174, 184; Heaton and, 166–73, 184; Ronkainen and, 164, 173; as royalty, 163–66; Russia and, 163–66, 170–74, 184; shortwave radio and, 164–65
Zionists, 248n4
Žižek, Slavoj, 116
Zone Rouge, 198–200
Zone 34, 164
Zonnebeke Railway Station, 34